PRAISE FOR *SOCCERNOMICS*

"*Soccernomics* is the most intelligent book ever written about soccer."
—*San Francisco Chronicle*

"Many explanations [of England's poor form] can be found in the book *Soccernomics* in a segment entitled 'Why England Loses.' (This is well worth a read for any English football fan; essentially, you overvalue your football heritage and undervalue the benefits of innovation.)"
—Stephen J. Dubner, co-author of *Freakonomics*

"Fascinating." —*VanityFair.com*

"The authors take what 'everybody' knows about success and failure in soccer and subject it to rigorous empirical analysis embedded in good stories that carry the narrative along. . . . Highly recommended. All readers."
—*Choice*

"It's a really good book. If more people read it, they'd understand some of the reasons why England [doesn't] win. Everyone can have an opinion, but they back it up with stats." —**Jamie Carragher, Liverpool F.C.**

"*Soccernomics* [is] a sharply written and provocative examination of the world's game seen through the prism of economics and statistical data. It demolishes almost everything that most soccer fans believe about the game and how professional soccer teams should operate."
—***Globe and Mail*** **(Canada)**

"Oh, Rooney's the best. [My son] Ben thinks that England might be in the top four, but that's it. He knows the starting lineup of every European team. We're reading this very interesting book about [soccer] together."
—**Lorrie Moore, author of *A Gate at the Stairs and Birds of America***

"With *Soccernomics*, the *Financial Times'* indispensable Simon Kuper and top-flight sports economist Stefan Szymanski bring scrupulous economic analysis and statistical rigor to a sport long dependent on hoary—and, it seems, unfounded—assumptions. . . . Gripping and essential."
—Slate.com, Best Books of 2009

"[The book] is a sporting tale in the *Freakonomics* mode of inquiry, using statistics to come up with fascinating conclusions."
—*Independent* (UK), Best Books of 2009

"[Szymanski and Kuper] entertainingly demolish soccer shibboleths. . . . Well argued and clear headed." **—*Financial Times*, Best Books of 2009**

"Using data analysis, history and psychology, [*Soccernomics*] punctures dozens of clichés about what it takes to win, and who makes money in soccer—and in sports in general." ***—Associated Press***

"There just aren't that many interesting, intelligent, analytical books about the world's most popular game, but this *is* one." *—Blogcritics*

"A must read for any fan of the business of soccer. . . ."
—Footiebusiness.com

"*Soccernomics* . . . tackles the soccer world's most probing questions with a dispassionate analysis based on economic formulas, which separate fact from accepted-as-fact myths perpetuated by legions of fans."
—Forbes.com

"It's quite a book. . . . *Soccernomics* explains how the lessons of *Moneyball* (sports teams are not completely rational) apply to the world's favorite sport." **—Huffington Post**

"[Kuper and Szymanski] do for soccer what *Moneyball* did for baseball. It puts the game under an analytical microscope using statistics, economics, psychology and intuition to try to transform a dogmatic sport."
—New York Times

"It's a fascinating book with the potential to effect genuine change in the sport." ***—Booklist* (starred)**

"Small book, big wallop! . . . Enthusiastically recommended to all soccer fans, general and specialized, as well as those thinking of becoming one."
—*Library Journal*

"[Kuper and Szymanski] have created a blend of *Freakonomics* and *Fever Pitch*, bringing surprising economic analysis to bear on the world's most popular sport. . . . This mix of economic analysis and anecdote makes for a thought-provoking, often amusing read. Here, at last, is a British answer to Michael Lewis's baseball-meets-cash bestseller *Moneyball.*"
—*Bloomberg News*

"[Kuper and Szymanski] combine their skills to entertaining and mostly convincing effect." —*Economist*

"If you're a football fan, I'll save you some time: read this book . . . compulsive reading . . . thoroughly convincing." —*Daily Telegraph (UK)*

"Szymanski has recently published the best introduction to sports economics . . . while Kuper is probably the smartest of the new generation of super-smart sportswriters . . . fascinating stories." —*Observer* (UK)

"[Kuper and Szymanski] basically trash every cliché about football you ever held to be true. It's bravura stuff . . . the study of managers buying players and building a club is one you'll feel like photocopying and sending to your team's chairman. . . ." —*Metro* (UK)

"More thoughtful than most of its rivals and, by football standards, positively intellectual. . . . Kuper, a brilliantly contrary columnist, and Szymanski, an economics professor . . . find plenty of fertile territory in their commendable determination to overturn the lazy preconceptions rife in football." —*The Times* (UK)

"Kuper and Szymanski are . . . a highly effective and scrupulously rational team, combining the former's detailed and nuanced understanding of European football with the latter's sophisticated econometric analysis. With a remarkable lightness of touch, they demonstrate the limits of conventional thinking in football, as well as the real patterns of behaviour that shape sporting outcomes." —*Prospect* (UK)

"Books about sport are a bit like players—some are pretty dreadful, most are about the same standard and so don't really stand out, and occasionally one comes along that excels to the point that they change the way you watch and think about the game. *Soccernomics* by Simon Kuper and Stefan Szymanski is such a book. . . . Any fan of the Socceroos who reads *Soccernomics* or indeed any sports fan ready to take on board new ways of thinking might, like me, never look at a penalty kick or a league table and certainly not follow a major international tournament quite the same way again." **—Peter Newlinds, *ABC News* (Australia)**

"Should still be compulsory reading for all poor suffering England fans."
—Jim O'Neill, Former Chairman of Goldman Sachs Asset Management

SOCCERNOMICS

ALSO BY SIMON KUPER

Retourtjes Nederland (Atlas, 2006)

Soccer Against the Enemy (Nation Books, 2006)

Soccer Men: Profiles of the Rogues, Geniuses, and Neurotics Who Dominate the World's Most Popular Sport (Nation Books, 2011)

Ajax, the Dutch, the War: The Strange Tale of Soccer During Europe's Darkest Hour (Nation Books, 2012)

ALSO BY STEFAN SZYMANSKI

Fans of the World, Unite! A Capitalist Manifesto for Sports Consumers (with Stephen F. Ross; Stanford University Press, 2008)

Il business del calcio
(with Umberto Lago and Alessandro Baroncelli; Egea, 2004)

National Pastime: How Americans Play Baseball and the Rest of the World Plays Soccer
(with Andrew Zimbalist; Brookings Institution, 2005)

Playbooks and Checkbooks: An Introduction to the Economics of Modern Sports (Princeton University Press, 2009)

Winners and Losers: The Business Strategy of Football
(with Tim Kuypers; Viking Books, 1999; Penguin Books, 2000)

BOOKS EDITED:

Handbook on the Economics of Sport
(with Wladimir Andreff; Edward Elgar, 2006)

Transatlantic Sports: The Comparative Economics of North American and European Sports
(with Carlos Barros and Murad Ibrahim; Edward Elgar, 2002)

SOCCERNOMICS

Why England Loses, Why Spain, Germany, and Brazil Win, and Why the US, Japan, Australia—and Even Iraq—Are Destined to Become the Kings of the World's Most Popular Sport

Simon Kuper and Stefan Szymanski

Published by Nation Books, A Member of the Perseus Books Group
116 East 16th Street, 8th Floor
New York, NY 10003

Nation Books is a co-publishing venture of the Nation Institute and the Perseus Books Group.

Library of Congress Cataloging-in-Publication Data

Kuper, Simon.
Soccernomics : why England loses, why Germany and Brazil win, and why the U.S., Japan, Australia, Turkey and even India are destined to become the kings of the world's most popular sport / Simon Kuper and Stefan Szymanski.—Third editon.
p. cm.
Includes bibliographical references and index.
ISBN 978-1-56858-481-2 (pbk. : alk. paper)—ISBN 978-1-56858-480-5 (e-book)
1. Soccer—Social aspects. I. Szymanski, Stefan. II. Title.

GV943.9.S64K88 2014
796.334—dc23

2014005100

10 9 8 7 6 5 4 3 2 1

From Simon:

To Pamela

(who doesn't know about soccer,

but knows about writing) for her astonishing tolerance.

And to

Leila, Leo, and Joey,

for all the smiles.

From Stefan:

To my father.

We never saw eye to eye,

but he taught me to question everything.

CONTENTS

1

DRIVING WITH A DASHBOARD

In Search of New Truths About Soccer

A few years ago, the data department at Manchester City carried out a study of corner kicks. City hadn't been scoring much from corners, and the analysts wanted to find out the best way to take them. They watched more than four hundred corners, from different leagues, over several seasons, and concluded: the most dangerous corner was the inswinger to the near post.

The beauty of the inswinger was that it sent the ball straight into the danger zone. Sometimes an attacker would get a head or foot to it and divert it in from point-blank range. Sometimes the keeper or a defender stopped the inswinger on the line, whereupon someone bashed it in. And occasionally the ball just swung straight in from the corner. All in all, the analysts found, inswingers produced more goals than outswingers.

They took their findings to the club's then manager, Roberto Mancini, who like almost all managers is an ex-player. He heard them out politely. Then he said, more or less: "I was a player for many years, and I just *know* that the outswinger is more effective." He was wrong, but we can understand why he made the mistake: outswingers tend to create beautiful goals (ball swings out, player meets it with powerful header, ball crashes into net) and beautiful goals stick in the memory. The messy goals generally produced by inswingers don't.

It's a story that captures where soccer is today. On the one hand, the March of the Geeks has advanced fast since we first published *Soccernomics* in 2009. Soccer is becoming more intelligent. The analysts who now crunch "match data" at almost all big European clubs (and at many smaller ones) are just one symptom of the shift.

Today's plugged-in clubs know stats like "pass completion rates in the final third of the field," kilometers run in each phase of the game, and pace of sprints for all their players. These numbers increasingly inform decisions on which players to buy and sell. Sigi Schmid, coach of the Seattle Sounders, says that before Seattle's expansion draft in 2008, the club's executives headed down to the Match Analysis company in Emeryville in Northern California to study players' statistics. Match Analysis's numbers helped guide the club's choices. Schmid thinks that is why Seattle's expansion draft was more successful than Portland's or Vancouver's.

On the other hand, as Mancini's certainty about corner kicks shows, there is still widespread suspicion of numbers in soccer. John Coulson of the data provider Opta told us, "There are still maybe a lot of teams that view data as a threat rather than as a tool." Baseball has had its "Moneyball" revolution, but in soccer, the transformation has only just begun. This new, updated, expanded edition of *Soccernomics—Soccernomics 3.0*, as we think of it—uses data to clarify thinking on topics ranging from tackles through transfers to the rise of Spain.

Soccernomics began in the Hilton in Istanbul one winter's day in 2007. From the outside the hotel is squat and brutalist, but once the security men have checked your car for bombs and waved you through, the place is so soothing you never want to go home again. Having escaped the 14 million–person city, the only stress is over what to do next: a Turkish bath, a game of tennis, or yet more overeating while the sun sets over the Bosporus? For aficionados, there was also a perfect view of the Besiktas soccer stadium right next door. And the staff were so friendly, they were even friendlier than ordinary Turkish people.

The two authors of this book, Stefan Szymanski (a sports economist) and Simon Kuper (a journalist), met here. Fenerbahce soccer club was marking its centenary by staging the "100th Year Sports and Science Congress" and had flown us both in to give talks.

Over beers in the Hilton bar we found that we thought much the same way about soccer. Stefan as an economist is trained to torture the data until they confess, while Simon as a journalist tends to go around interviewing people, but those are just surface differences. We both think that much in soccer can be explained, even predicted, by studying data—especially data found outside soccer.

Until very recently, soccer had escaped the Enlightenment. Soccer clubs are still run mostly by people who do what they do because they have always done it that way. These people used to "know" that black players "lacked bottle," and they therefore overpaid mediocre white players. Today they discriminate against black managers, buy the wrong players, and then let those players take corners and penalties the wrong way. (We can, incidentally, explain why Manchester United won the penalty shoot-out in the Champions League final in 2008. It's a story involving a secret note, a Basque economist, and Edwin van der Sar's powers of detection.)

Entrepreneurs who dip into soccer also keep making the same mistakes. They buy clubs promising to run them "like a business" and disappear a few seasons later amid the same public derision as the previous owners. "I screwed up," Tony Fernandes, chairman of Queens Park Rangers, told us. Fans and journalists aren't blameless, either. Many newspaper headlines rest on false premises: "Sunderland Lands World Cup Star" or "World Cup Will Be Economic Bonanza." The game is full of unexamined clichés: "Soccer is becoming boring because the big clubs always win," "Soccer is big business," and perhaps the greatest myth in the English game, "The England team should do better." None of these shibboleths has been tested against the data.

Most male team sports have long been pervaded by the same overreliance on traditional beliefs. Baseball, too, was until quite recently an old game stuffed with old lore. Since time immemorial, players had stolen bases, hit sacrifice bunts, and been judged on their batting averages. Everyone in baseball just *knew* that all this was right.

But that was before Bill James. Like Dorothy in *The Wizard of Oz*, James came from rural Kansas. He hadn't done much in life beyond keeping the stats in the local Little League and watching the furnaces in a pork-and-beans factory. However, in his spare time he had begun to study baseball statistics with a fresh eye and discovered that "a great portion of the sport's traditional knowledge is ridiculous hokum." James wrote that he wanted to approach the subject of baseball "with the same kind of intellectual rigor and discipline that is routinely applied, by scientists great and poor, to trying to unravel the mysteries of the universe, of society, of the human mind, or of the price of burlap in Des Moines."

In self-published mimeographs masquerading as books, the first of which sold seventy-five copies, James began demolishing the game's myths. He found, for instance, that the most important statistic in batting was the rarely mentioned "on-base percentage"—how often a player manages to get on base. James and his followers (statisticians of baseball who came to be known as sabermetricians) showed that good old sacrifice bunts and base stealing were terrible strategies.

His annual *Baseball Abstracts* turned into real books; eventually they reached the best-seller lists. One year the cover picture showed an ape, posed as Rodin's *Thinker*, studying a baseball. As James wrote in one *Abstract*, "This is *outside* baseball. This is a book about what baseball looks like if you step back from it and study it intensely and minutely, but from a distance."

Some Jamesians started to penetrate professional baseball. One of them, Billy Beane, general manager of the little Oakland A's, is the hero of Michael Lewis's earth-moving book *Moneyball* and the film starring Brad Pitt. In recent years Beane, like so many Americans, has become a soccer nut. He spends a lot of time thinking about how his insights into baseball might apply to the very different sport played on the other side of the world. (We'll say more later about Beane's brilliant gaming of baseball's transfer market and its lessons for soccer.)

For several seasons Beane's Oakland A's did so well using Jamesian ideas that eventually even people inside baseball began to get curious about James. In 2002 the Boston Red Sox appointed James "senior baseball operations adviser." That same year the Red Sox hired one of his followers, the twenty-eight-year-old Theo Epstein, as the youngest general manager in the history of the major leagues. (Beane had said yes and then no to the job.) The "cursed" club quickly won two World Series. Today large statistical departments are the norm at Major League Baseball clubs.

Now soccer is embarking on its own Jamesian revolution.

A NUMBERS GAME

It's strange that soccer always used to be so averse to studying data, because one thing that attracts many fans to the game is precisely a love of numbers.

The man to ask about that is Alex Bellos. He wrote the magnificent *Futebol: The Brazilian Way of Life,* but his book about math, *Here's Looking at Euclid,* appeared in 2010. "Numbers are incredibly satisfying," Bellos tells us. "The world has no order, and math is a way of seeing it in an order. League tables have an order. And the calculations you need to do for them are so simple: it's nothing more than your three-times table."

Though most fans would probably deny it, a love of soccer is often intertwined with a love of numbers. There are the match results, the famous dates, and the special joy of sitting in a café with the newspaper on a Sunday morning "reading" the league table. Fantasy soccer leagues are, at bottom, numbers games.

In this book we want to introduce new numbers and new ideas to soccer: numbers on suicides, on wage spending, on countries' populations, on passes and sprints, on anything that helps to reveal new truths about the game. Though Stefan is a sports economist, this is not a book about money. The point of soccer clubs is not to turn a profit (which is fortunate, as almost none of them do), nor are we particularly interested in any profits they happen to make. Rather, we want to use an economist's skills (plus a little geography, psychology, and sociology) to understand the game on the field, and the fans off it.

Some people may not want their emotional relationship with soccer sullied by our rational calculations. On the other hand, the next time their team loses a penalty shoot-out in a World Cup quarterfinal these same people will probably be throwing their beer glasses at the TV, when instead they could be tempering their disappointment with some reflections on the nature of binomial probability theory.

We think it's a good time to be rewriting this book. The world has entered the era of "big data." The phrase describes the unprecedented mountain of information that is now collected every day. This information comes mostly from the Internet (from innumerable search terms, Facebook pages, and e-mails) and from sensors that are attached to ever more physical objects—among them, soccer players during training sessions. By one estimate, the daily amount of data generated worldwide doubles approximately every forty months.

Big data has reached soccer too. For the first time in the sport's history, there are a lot of numbers to mine. Traditionally the only data that existed in the game were goals and league tables. (Newspapers published attendance figures, but these were unreliable.) Now clubs are ceasing to rely on gut alone. Increasingly they work with data companies such as Prozone and Opta to analyze games and players. Every day, data analysts collect ever more information about every player's every move on the pitch or the training ground.

Academics are pitching in as well. At the end of the 1980s, when Stefan went into sports economics, only about twenty or thirty academic articles on sports had ever been published. Now countless academics work on soccer. Many of the new truths they have found have not yet reached most fans.

Another new source of knowledge is the bulging library of soccer books. When Pete Davies published *All Played Out: The Full Story of Italia '90,* there were probably only about twenty or thirty good soccer books in existence. Now—thanks partly to Davies, who has been described as John the Baptist to Nick Hornby's Jesus—there are thousands. Many of these books (including Bellos's *Futebol*) contain truths about the game that we try to present here.

So unstoppable has the stream of data become that even people inside the game are finally starting to sift it. Michael Lewis, author of *Moneyball,* wrote in 2009, "The virus that infected professional baseball in the 1990s, the use of statistics to find new and better ways to value players and strategies, has found its way into every major sport. Not just basketball and football, but also soccer and cricket and rugby and, for all I know, snooker and darts—each one now supports a subculture of smart people who view it not just as a game to be played but as a problem to be solved."

This statistical virus has even spread from baseball to more serious activities. Before the US elections of 2004, the Republican campaign manager Ken Mehlman told his staff to read *Moneyball.* Michael Turk, who worked at the Republican National Committee, recalled for the *New York*

Times years later: "I was like, 'What does a baseball book have to do with politics?' Once I actually took the time to digest it, I realized what he was trying to do—which was exactly the kind of thing that the Obama team just did [in the 2012 elections]: understanding that not every election is about home runs but instead getting a whole bunch of singles together that eventually add up to a win."

Or look at the career of Nate Silver. In childhood he was an obsessive fan of the Detroit Tigers. Soon after leaving college, he developed a statistical method to forecast performance and career development for baseball players. He also dabbled in soccer: during the World Cup of 2010, he correctly predicted the outcomes of thirteen of the sixteen games in the knockout stages. But the onetime sabermetrician is best known as a political analyst. In the US presidential elections in 2008, Silver correctly called the winner in forty-nine states. In 2012 he got all fifty plus the District of Columbia. In other words: Nate Silver won the US election. Afterward he returned to sports, joining ESPN as an all-purpose guru. Silver stands for the March of the Geeks. Smart people like him are on the rise inside sports and beyond.

In soccer, these smart men (it's part of the game's own "ridiculous hokum" that they have to be men) have even begun gaining key roles at some of Europe's biggest clubs. English soccer, professional on the field since the late nineteenth century, is finally creaking into professionalism off the field, too. Given the global obsession with the game, there could come a time when some of the best and brightest young people are working in the front offices of soccer clubs. Already the rising generation of club executives understands that in soccer today, you need data to get ahead. If you study figures, you will see more and win more.

Yet another harbinger of the Jamesian takeover of soccer is the Milan Lab. Early on, AC Milan's in-house medical outfit found that just by studying a player's jump, it could predict with 70 percent accuracy whether he would get injured soon. Later it began testing, almost day by day, each player's muscle weaknesses, the movement of his eyes, the rise and fall of his heart rate, his breathing, and many other obvious and less obvious indicators. Jean-Pierre Meersseman, the lab's cigarette-puffing director, was given a power of veto over the club's prospective signings. "The last signature on the contract before the big boss signs is mine," he told us in 2008. By 2013 the lab had performed 1.2 million physical tests on Milan's players, collected millions of pieces of data on computers, logged even the slightest injury to every player, and in the process had stumbled upon the secret of eternal youth. (It's still a secret: no other club has a Milan Lab, and the lab hasn't divulged its findings, which is why players at most other clubs are generally finished by their early thirties.)

Most of Milan's starting eleven who beat Liverpool in the Champions League final of 2007 were thirty-one or older: Paolo Maldini, the captain, was thirty-eight, and Filippo Inzaghi, scorer of both of Milan's goals, was thirty-three. (After the final whistle, Inzaghi still had enough juice to kick a ball around on the field for fun.) In large part, that trophy was won by the Milan Lab and its database. It is another version of the March of the Geeks story. In recent years, cash-strapped AC Milan has reduced the lab's funding and power. However, other big clubs all over Europe are now crunching data to find out how to reduce injuries, and how to predict which twelve-year-old will grow into the next Xavi. Meersseman says the lab's data-driven scientists seem to be better than experienced youth coaches at making those predictions. He told us: "In soccer, they say, 'You know about soccer or you don't.' And when you go and test the ones who 'know,' it's surprising how little they know. It's based on the emotion of the moment."

As Stefan and Simon talked more and began to think harder about soccer and data for this book, we buzzed around all sorts of questions. Could we find figures to show which country loved soccer the most? Might the game somehow deter people from killing themselves? And perhaps we could have a shot at predicting which clubs and countries—the United States most likely, perhaps even Iraq—would dominate the soccer of the future. When we began writing, Stefan lived in London and Simon in Paris, so we spent a year firing figures, arguments, and anecdotes back and forth across the English Channel.

What started as a book turned into a long-term collaboration. Together with Ben Lyttleton we founded the Soccernomics consultancy. On its website, Soccernomics-agency.com, we began publishing an occasional blog with our thoughts on soccer. And we kept rewriting and updating this book, through about twenty different foreign editions and three American versions so far.

For this latest edition, our contact was transatlantic: Stefan is now at the University of Michigan in Ann Arbor. The new edition comes with a new chapter on how UEFA's "financial fair play" rules might change the game, and an afterword arguing that soccer has never had it so good. We have also expanded our thoughts on some mystifying questions, such as: How do clubs use data to judge, buy, and sell players? And we've watched fans and media shift to our point of view on certain issues: most people now recognize that hosting World Cups doesn't make you rich, and that England shouldn't expect to win trophies. (Sadly, we cannot claim responsibility for shifting global opinion.) In every chapter in the book we found stories and analyses to update, and new thoughts to add.

All the while, we have continued to distrust every bit of ancient soccer lore, and tested it against the numbers. As Meersseman says, "You can drive a car without a dashboard, without any information, and that's what's happening in soccer. There are excellent drivers, excellent cars, but if you have your dashboard, it makes it just a little bit easier. I wonder why people don't want more information." We do.

PART I
The Clubs

Racism, Stupidity, Bad Transfers, Capital Cities, the Mirage of the NFL, and What Actually Happened in That Penalty Shoot-Out in Moscow

2

GENTLEMEN PREFER BLONDS

How to Avoid Silly Mistakes in the Transfer Market

In 1983 AC Milan spotted a talented young black forward playing for Watford just outside London. The word is that the player the Italians liked was John Barnes and that they then confused him with his black teammate Luther Blissett. Whatever the truth, Milan ended up paying Watford a "transfer fee" of $1.4 million for Blissett.*

As a player Blissett became such a joke in Italy that the name "Luther Blissett" is now used as a pseudonym by groups of anarchist writers. He spent one unhappy year in Milan, before the club sold him back to Watford for just over half the sum it had paid for him. At least that year gave soccer one of its best quotes: "No matter how much money you have here," Blissett lamented, "you can't seem to get Rice Krispies." More on Rice Krispies later.

Transfers in soccer are very different from trades in American sports. In soccer, when a good player moves, his new club usually pays a "transfer fee" to his old club. Moreover, the player's old contract is torn up, and he negotiates a new deal with his new club. In 2013 European clubs paid each other a total of about $2.3 billion in transfer fees. That year Real

*A note about currencies: almost always in this book, we have cited sums of money in dollars. When converting from pounds or other currencies, we have used the dollar equivalent at the time the sum was spent. (A British pound bought more dollars in 1980 than in 2013, for instance.)

FIGURE 2.1. Premier League and Championship teams: 2003–2012

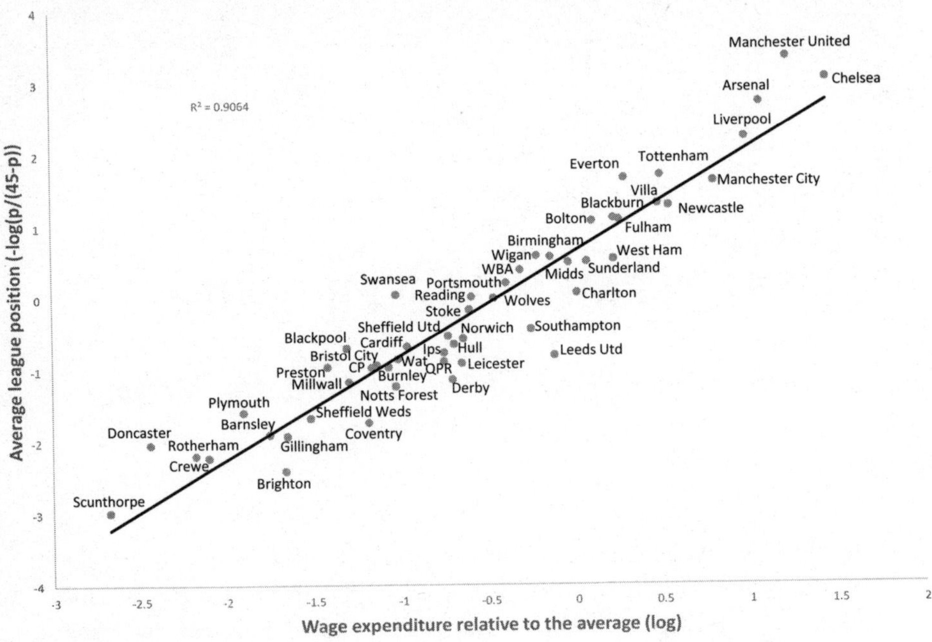

Madrid broke the world record for a transfer fee (a record it already held) by paying Tottenham Hotspur a reported $132 million for Gareth Bale.

Unfortunately, much of the money thrown around in the transfer market is wasted. In fact, the net amount that almost any club spends on transfer fees bears little relation to where it finishes in the league. We studied the spending of forty English clubs between 1978 and 1997, and found that their net outlay on transfers (i.e., each club's transfer fees paid minus transfer fees received) explained only 16 percent of their total variation in league position. In other words, taken over many years, the mere fact of being a "buying club" in the transfer market didn't help a team perform significantly better than a "selling club."

By contrast, clubs' spending on salaries was extremely telling. The size of their wage bills explained a massive 92 percent of variation in their league positions, if you took each club's average for the entire period. That correlation shows little sign of going away. We show the same result using data for the Premier League and the Championship (the second tier of English soccer) for the decade through 2012 (see Figures 2.1 and

FIGURE 2.2. The more you pay your players, the higher you finish: 2003–2012

club	Wage Spending relative to the average	Average league position	club	Wage Spending relative to the average	Average league position
Manchester United	3.37	2	Blackpool	0.27	29
Chelsea	4.23	2	Cardiff City	0.38	30
Arsenal	2.89	3	Ipswich Town	0.47	30
Liverpool	2.65	5	Leicester City	0.52	31
Tottenham Hotspur	1.63	8	Queens Park Rangers	0.47	31
Everton	1.33	8	Watford	0.36	31
Manchester City	2.21	9	Crystal Palace	0.34	31
Aston Villa	1.61	10	Preston North End	0.24	31
Newcastle United	1.71	11	Burnley	0.32	32
Fulham	1.29	12	Bristol City	0.31	32
Blackburn Rovers	1.25	12	Derby County	0.49	33
Bolton Wanderers	1.10	12	Millwall	0.27	33
Wigan Athletic	0.80	16	Nottingham Forest	0.36	33
Birmingham City	0.87	17	Plymouth Argyle	0.15	36
West Ham United	1.25	17	Sheffield Wednesday	0.22	37
Sunderland	1.07	17	Colchester United	0.15	37
Middlesbrough	0.96	18	Coventry City	0.31	37
West Bromwich Albion	0.73	19	Doncaster Rovers	0.09	38
Charlton Athletic	1.01	20	Gillingham	0.19	38
Portsmouth	0.67	20	Rotherham United	0.11	39
Swansea City	0.36	22	Barnsley	0.17	39
Reading	0.55	23	Brighton & Hove Albion	0.19	39
Wolverhampton Wanderers	0.63	23	Walsall	0.19	40
Stoke City	0.54	24	Crewe Alexandra	0.12	40
Southampton	0.77	25	Bradford City	0.12	41
Sheffield United	0.48	27	Peterborough United	0.06	41
Norwich City	0.53	27	Southend United	0.14	42
Hull City	0.50	28	Scunthorpe United	0.07	42
Leeds United	0.89	28	Grimsby Town	0.14	44

2.2). In that period, wage spending still explained more than 90 percent of the variation in league position. It seems that over the long term, high wages help a club much more than do spectacular transfers.

Obviously we don't believe that if you took a random bunch of players, and doubled their salaries, they would suddenly play twice as well. It's not that high pay *causes* good performance. Rather, we think that high pay *attracts* good performers. Manchester United can afford to pay Wayne Rooney's wages, whereas Norwich City cannot. And if you have Rooney and other good players, you will win lots of matches. Rich clubs pay high salaries to get good players to win trophies.

It must be said that for any one given season, the correlation between salaries and league position is weaker. That's because in such a short period, luck plays a big role in performance. Injuries, dodgy referees, poor form, and any host of other factors cause big swings in performance from year to year. For any one season, clubs' wage spending explains only about 70 percent of the variation in league position.

But true luck (i.e., statistical randomness) tends to even out over the years. So if you track each club's performance over a longer period—fifteen or twenty years, say—then salaries explain about 90 percent of the variation in league position.

In short, the more you pay your players in wages, the higher you will finish, but what you pay *for* them in transfer fees doesn't seem to make much difference.

While the market for players' wages is pretty efficient—the better a player, the more he earns—the transfer market is inefficient. Much of the time, clubs buy the wrong players. Even now that they have brigades of international scouts, they still waste fortunes on flops like Blissett. (The transfer market is also of dubious legality—do clubs really have a right to "buy" and "sell" employees?—but that's another matter.)

As a case study of bad transfer policy, let's take Liverpool from 1998 through 2010. The club's managers in this period, Gérard Houllier and Rafael Benitez, kept splashing out on big transfer fees, yet Liverpool hardly ever even threatened to win the league. Jamie Carragher, who played for Liverpool throughout these years, provides a dolefully comic commentary on some of the club's misguided signings in his excellent autobiography, *Carra*:

- "Sean Dundee was not a Liverpool footballer."
- "The signing I didn't rate was Sander Westerveld. . . . I thought he was an average goalkeeper who seemed to think he was Gordon Banks."
- "What about Josemi? He struggled to find a teammate six yards away. Djimi Traore had the same weakness."
- "To be blunt, [Christian] Ziege couldn't defend."
- "The names El-Hadji Diouf and Salif Diao now make the legs of the toughest Liverpudlians shudder in fear. . . . The first concern I had with Diouf is his pace. He didn't have any. . . . Do you remember being at school and picking sides for a game of football? We do

this at Liverpool for the five-a-sides. Diouf was 'last pick' within a few weeks."

"'You paid ten million for him and no one wants him in their team,' I shouted to Gérard."

- "If Diouf was a disappointment, Diao was a catastrophe. . . . But even he wasn't the worst arrival of this hideous summer [of 2002]. Houllier also signed Bruno Cheyrou."
- On Djibril Cissé, who cost Liverpool $26 million: "He was supposed to be a strong, physical target man who scored goals. He was neither one nor the other."
- "The greatest disappointment was Fernando Morientes. . . . He was a yard off the pace."

When Benitez replaced Houllier in 2004, writes Carragher, the Spaniard encountered "a host of poor, overpaid players and expectations as great as ever." But the new man didn't do much better than his predecessor. Carragher's book is gentler with Benitez than with Houllier, presumably because the Spaniard was still his boss when he wrote it, but the waste of the Benitez years is remarkable. Most strikingly, perhaps, in 2008 Benitez handed Tottenham Hotspur £20 million (then about $40 million) for the twenty-eight-year-old forward Robbie Keane. The much-touted fact that Keane was a lifelong Liverpool fan turned out not to help much. Six months after buying the player, Benitez decided that Keane wasn't the thing after all and shipped him back to Tottenham (which itself would soon regret buying him) at a loss of £8 million ($12 million). Virgin Trains took out newspaper advertisements that said, "A Liverpool to London return faster than Robbie Keane."

For all the spending, most of Liverpool's best performers during the Houllier-Benitez years were homegrown players who had cost the club nothing: Steven Gerrard, Michael Owen, and Carragher himself. Another stalwart for a decade, centerback Sami Hyppiä, had come for only $4.1 million from little Willem II in the Netherlands. In short, there didn't seem to be much correlation between transfer spending and quality.

In October 2009, after Benitez's sixth and last summer masterminding Liverpool's transfers, Britain's *Sunday Times* newspaper calculated the damage. It found that in those six years at Anfield, Benitez had spent

£122 million (about $220 million) more than he had received in transfer fees. Alex Ferguson's net spend at Manchester United in the same period was only £27 million ($49 million), yet in those years United had won three titles to Liverpool's none. Arsène Wenger at Arsenal had actually received £27 million ($49 million) more in transfer fees than he had spent during the period, the newspaper estimated. From 2005 through 2009, Benitez had even outspent Chelsea on transfers. Yet at the end of this period he had the nerve to complain, "It is always difficult to compete in the Premier League with clubs who have more money." Ferguson later commented that he hadn't been able to see any "strategy" in Benitez's buying. "It amazed me that he used to walk into press conferences and say he had no money to spend," Ferguson wrote in his 2013 autobiography. "He was given plenty. It was the quality of his buys that let him down. If you set aside Torres and Reina, few of his acquisitions were of true Liverpool standard. There were serviceable players—Mascherano and Kuyt, hard-working players—but not real Liverpool quality."

Benitez's failure at Liverpool was partially disguised by one night in Istanbul: the victory in the Champions League final of 2005, after having been 3–0 down to Milan at the end of the first half. However, as we'll discuss later in the book, a large chunk of luck is involved in winning knockout competitions—even leaving aside the fact that Benitez got his tactics wrong going into the game and had to turn his team upside down at halftime. The most reliable gauge of a team's quality is its performance in the league, and here Houllier and Benitez failed. Their expensive transfers didn't bring commensurate results. If you add in agents' fees, taxes on transfers, and the constant disruption to the team, all this wheeling and dealing helps explain how Liverpool got left behind by Manchester United. To quote Carragher, "As I know to my cost at Anfield, having money is no guarantee of success. The skill is spending it on the right players."

The question, then, is what clubs can do to improve their status. If you are Liverpool now, run by a man like John Henry who understands statistics, and you have this knowledge of the relative importance of wages and unimportance of transfers, how can you win more matches? The obvious answer is to spend less of your income on transfers and more of it on wages. In general, it may be better to raise the pay of your leading players than to risk losing a couple of them and have to go out and buy replacements. Benitez had a net transfer spend of minus $220 million in six years. If he had merely balanced his transfer budget in that period, let alone made a profit as Wenger did, he could have raised his team's salaries by $36 million a year. In the 2008–2009 season, that boost would have given Liverpool a slightly larger wage bill than United. United won the title that year.

Soccer clubs need to make fewer transfers. They buy too many Dioufs. But they will keep buying players, and the transfer market is probably the area in which clubs can most easily improve their performance. They need to learn from the few clubs and managers who have worked out some of the secrets of the transfer market.

Any inefficient market is an opportunity for somebody. If most clubs are wasting most of their transfer money, then a club that spends wisely is going to outperform. Indeed, a handful of wise buyers have consistently outperformed the transfer market: Brian Clough and his assistant–cum–soul mate Peter Taylor in their years at Nottingham Forest, Wenger during his first decade at Arsenal, and, most mysteriously of all, Olympique Lyon, which rose from obscure provincial club to a period of dictatorial rule over French soccer. From 2002 through 2008, Lyon won the French league seven times running. That era is now over, and the club has made mistakes since, as it has tried and failed to compete with clubs with much higher revenues, like Real Madrid or Manchester United. Lyon got tempted into paying big transfer fees for supposed "stars"—for instance, gambling $28 million on the slow French playmaker Yoann Gourcuff in 2010. Nonetheless, its seven-year reign remains an extraordinary feat. The usual way to win things in soccer is to pay high salaries. These clubs found a different route: they worked out the secrets of the transfer market.

There is a fourth master of the transfer market who is worth a look, even if he works in a different sport across an ocean: Billy Beane, general manager of the Oakland A's baseball team. In his book *Moneyball*, Michael Lewis explains how for a few years Beane turned one of the poorest teams in baseball into one of the best by the simple method of rejecting what everyone in the sport had always "known" to be true about trading for players. Lewis writes, "Understanding that he would never have a Yankee-sized checkbook, Beane had set about looking for inefficiencies in the game." It's odd how many of the same inefficiencies exist in soccer, too.

MARKET INCOMPETENCE

If we study these masters of transfers, it will help us uncover the secrets of the market that all the other clubs are missing. First of all, though, we present a few of the most obvious inefficiencies in the market. Although it doesn't take a Clough or a Beane to identify these, they continue to exist.

A New Manager Wastes Money

Typically the new manager wants to put his mark on his new team. So he buys his own players. He then has to "clear out" some of his predecessor's purchases, usually at a discount.

Strangely, it's Tottenham during its years under a famously tightfisted chairman, Alan Sugar, that provides the worst example. In May 2000 the club's manager, George Graham, paid Dynamo Kiev $16.5 million—nearly twice Spurs's previous record fee—for the Ukrainian striker Sergei Rebrov. Clearly Rebrov was meant to be a long-term investment.

But nine months later, Sugar sold his stake in Tottenham, whereupon the new owners sacked Graham and replaced him with Glenn Hoddle. Hoddle didn't appreciate Rebrov. The record signing ended up on the bench, was sent on loan to a Turkish team, and in 2004 moved to West Ham on a free transfer.

This form of waste is common across soccer: a new manager is allowed to buy and sell on the pretense that he is reshaping the club for many years to come, even though in practice he almost always leaves pretty rapidly. A terrible recent example was Paolo di Canio at Sunderland in 2013: in the six months and thirteen games that he managed the club, he spent about $30 million on transfers, brought in fourteen players and let fifteen leave. When he was sacked, he left his successor, Gus Poyet, a team in last place in the Premier League. Tony Fernandes, the Queens Park Rangers chairman who spent a net $65 million on transfer fees while getting relegated from the Premier League in 2012–2013, told us mournfully: "Sunderland's going through, in some ways, what we went through. The manager comes in, he changes everyone, and Gus Poyet is already saying, 'I want to control the transfer budget.' If you change a manager, I don't care who they are, they're going to have a different opinion, right? Mark Hughes liked a certain player, Harry [Redknapp] doesn't like a certain player."

But why couldn't a chairman just say no to a shopaholic new manager? "You yourself see the results," replied Fernandes, "and you think, 'God, we need some change.'"

A manager typically doesn't care how much his wheeler-dealing costs: he doesn't get a bonus if the club makes a profit. Billy Beane told us, "When you think of the structure of most sports teams, there is no benefit to a head coach in the NFL or a soccer manager to think years ahead. The person who has access to the greatest expenditure in the business has no risk in the decision-making." He added that the exception to this rule was Wenger. Beane said, "When I think of Arsène Wenger, I think of Warren Buffett. Wenger runs his football club like he is going to own the club for one hundred years."

Stars of Recent World Cups, or European Championships Are Overvalued

The worst time to buy a player is in the summer when he's just done well at a big tournament. Everyone in the transfer market has seen how good the player is, but he is exhausted and quite likely sated with success. As Ferguson admitted after retiring from United: "I was always wary of buying players on the back of good tournament performances. I did it at the 1996 European Championship, which prompted me to move for Jordi Cruyff and Karel Poborský. Both had excellent runs in that tournament, but I didn't receive the kind of value their countries did that summer. They weren't bad buys, but sometimes players get themselves motivated and prepared for World Cups and European Championships and after that there can be a leveling off."

Moreover, if you buy a player because of a good tournament, you are judging him on a very small sample of games. Take, for instance,

Arsenal's purchase of the Danish midfielder John Jensen in July 1992. The previous month, Jensen had scored a cracking long-range goal in the European Championship final against Germany. Arsenal's then manager, George Graham, told the British media that Jensen was a goal-scoring midfielder.

But he wasn't. The goal against Germany had been a one-off. Jensen would go years without scoring for Arsenal. Over time this failing actually turned him into a cult hero: whenever he got the ball, even in his own penalty area, the crowd at Highbury would joyously shout, "Shoot!" By the time Jensen left Arsenal in 1996, he had scored one goal in four years. (Arsenal fans printed T-shirts saying, "I was there when John Jensen scored.") Graham's mistake had been to extrapolate from that single famous goal against Germany. This is an example of the so-called availability heuristic: the more available a piece of information is to the memory, the more likely it is to influence your decision, even when the information is irrelevant.

Signing these shooting stars fits what *Moneyball* calls "a tendency to be overly influenced by a guy's most recent performance: what he did last was not necessarily what he would do next."

Real Madrid is of course the supreme consumer of shooting stars. This is largely because the club's fans demand it. Madrid (or Spurs, or Marseille in France) probably isn't even trying to be rational in the transfer market. The club's aim is not to buy the best results for as little money as possible. When it handed over a combined total of $226 million for Cristiano Ronaldo and Kaká in 2009, it probably suspected it was paying more for the duo than the benefit it was likely to get in results or higher revenues. But big signings of this type (like Newcastle buying fragile Michael Owen from Madrid for $30 million) are best understood as marketing gifts to a club's fans, its sponsors, and the local media. (It's hugely in the interest of *Marca,* the Spanish sports newspaper, for Real always to be buying players, or else hardly anyone would bother reading the paper over the three-month summer break.) As Ferguson explained Real's purchase of Ronaldo: "Madrid paid £80 million in cash for him, and do you know why? It was a way for Florentino Pérez, their president, to say to the world, 'We are Real Madrid, we are the biggest of the lot.'" In 2013, Madrid's purchase of Bale made the same statement. Probably nobody at

Madrid believed that the Welshman was twice as good a player as Mesut Özil—sold to Arsenal for half Bale's transfer fee—but he was deliciously new. His record fee only enhanced his glamour. The $132 million is unlikely to bring commensurate reward, but Real probably doesn't care very much. The club is not a business. It's a populist democracy. Few soccer clubs pursue bean-counting quests for return on investment.

Buying a big name makes every person in the club feel bigger. Christoph Biermann, in his pioneering German book on soccer and data, *Die Fussball-Matrix,* cites the president of a Bundesliga club who said his coach got very excited whenever the club paid a large transfer fee. Biermann explains, "For this coach it was a status symbol to be allowed to buy players who cost many millions of euros. My car, my house, my star signing!"

Buying names also gives supporters the thrill of expectation, a sense that their club is going somewhere, which may be as much fun as actually winning things. Buying big names is how these clubs keep their customers satisfied during the summer shutdown. (And some managers buy players to make themselves some illicit cash on the side, as George Graham did when he signed Jensen, but that's another story.)

Certain Nationalities Are Overvalued

Clubs will pay more for a player from a "fashionable" soccer country. American goalkeeper Kasey Keller says that in the transfer market, it's good to be Dutch. "Giovanni van Bronckhorst is the best example," Keller told Christoph Biermann. "He went from Rangers to Arsenal, failed there, and then where did he go? To Barcelona! You have to be a Dutchman to do that. An American would have been sent straight back to DC United."

More recently Belgian players have come into fashion. But the most enduringly fashionable nationality in the transfer market is Brazilian. As Alex Bellos writes in *Futebol: The Brazilian Way of Life,* "The phrase 'Brazilian soccer player' is like the phrases 'French chef' or 'Tibetan monk.' The nationality expresses an authority, an innate vocation for the job—whatever the natural ability." A Brazilian agent who had exported very humble Brazilian players to the Faeroe Islands and Iceland told Bellos,

"It's sad to say, but it is much easier selling, for example, a crap Brazilian than a brilliant Mexican. The Brazilian gets across the image of happiness, party, carnival. Irrespective of talent, it is very seductive to have a Brazilian in your team."

A wise club will buy unfashionable nationalities—Bolivians, say, or Belorussians—at discounts.

Gentlemen Prefer Blonds

One big English club noticed that its scouts who watched youth matches often came back recommending blond players. The likely reason: when you are scanning a field of twenty-two similar-looking players, none of whom yet has a giant reputation, the blonds tend to stand out (except, presumably, in Scandinavia). The color catches the eye. So the scout notices the blond boy without understanding why. The club in question began to take this distortion into account when judging scouting reports. We suspect the bias toward blonds disappears when scouts are assessing adult players who already have established reputations. Then the player's reputation—"World Cup hero," say, or simply "Brazilian"—guides the scout's judgment.

Similarly, Beane at the Oakland A's noticed that baseball scouts had all sorts of "sight-based prejudices." They were suspicious of fat guys or skinny little guys or "short right-handed pitchers," and they overvalued handsome, strapping athletes of the type that Beane himself had been at age seventeen. Scouts look for players who look the part. Perhaps in soccer, blonds are thought to look more like superstars.

This taste for blonds is another instance of the "availability heuristic": the piece of information is available, so it influences your decision. Blonds stick in the memory.

| |

The inefficiencies we have cited so far are so-called systemic failures: more than just individual mistakes, they are deviations from rationality. All this is what you might call Transfer Market 101. To learn more about how to play the market, we need to study the masters.

DRUNKS, GAMBLERS, AND BARGAINS: CLOUGH AND TAYLOR AT FOREST

"Cloughie likes a bung," Alan Sugar told the High Court of England and Wales in 1993. Sugar's former manager at Spurs, Terry Venables, had told him so.

A "bung" is British slang for an illegal under-the-table payment to sweeten a deal. The court heard that when Clough bought or sold a player for Nottingham Forest, he expected to get a bung. In a perfect world, he liked it to be handed over at a highway rest stop. Clough denied everything—"A bung? Isn't that something you get from a plumber to stop up the bath?"—and was never prosecuted. Yet what seems likely is this: "Old Big Head" (as Clough called himself) was so good at transfers, making profits even while turning a little provincial club into European champions, that he felt he deserved the odd bonus. More than anyone else in his day, Clough and his right-hand man, Peter Taylor, had succeeded in gaming the transfer market.

Clough and Taylor met while playing in a "Probables versus Possibles" reserve game at Middlesbrough in 1955. They seem to have fallen in love at first sight. Pretty soon they were using their free time to travel around the North of England watching soccer and coaching children together. Taylor never became more than a journeyman keeper, but Clough scored the fastest two hundred goals ever notched in English soccer until, at the age of twenty-seven, he wrecked his right knee skidding on a frozen field on Boxing Day in 1962. Three years later he phoned Taylor and said, "I've been offered the managership of Hartlepools and I don't fancy it. But if you'll come, I'll consider it." He then immediately hung up. Taylor took the bait, though to get in he had to double as Hartlepool's medical department, running onto the field with the sponge on match days. It was the prelude to their legendary years together at Derby and Nottingham Forest.

David Peace's novel *The Damned United*—and Tom Hooper's film of it—is in large part the love story of Clough and Taylor. The men's wives have only walk-on parts. As in all good couples, each partner has an assigned role. As Peace's fictional Clough tells himself, "Peter has the eyes and the ears, but you have the stomach and the balls." Taylor found the players, and Clough led them to glory.

The relationship ended in "divorce" in 1982, with Taylor's resignation from Forest. It seems that the rift had opened two years before, when Taylor published his excellent but now forgotten memoir, *With Clough by Taylor*. More of this in a moment, because it is the closest thing we have to a handbook to the transfer market.

But clearly the couple had other problems besides literature. Perhaps Clough resented his partner because he needed him so badly—not the sort of relationship Clough liked. Indeed, the film *The Damned United* depicts him failing at Leeds partly because Taylor is not there to scout players, and finally driving down to Brighton with his young sons to beg his partner's forgiveness. He finds Taylor doing the gardening. At Taylor's insistence, he gets down on his knees in the driveway and recites, "I'm nothing without you. Please, please, baby, take me back." And Taylor takes him back, and buys him the cut-price Forest team that wins two European Cups. Whatever their precise relationship, the duo certainly knew how to sign players. Here are a few of their coups:

- Buying Gary Birtles from the nonleague club Long Eaton for $3,500 in 1976 and selling him to Manchester United four years later for $2.9 million. A measure of what a good deal this was for Forest: United forked out about $500,000 more for Birtles than it would pay to sign Eric Cantona from Leeds twelve years later, in 1992. Birtles ended up costing United about $175,000 a goal, and after two years was sold back to Forest for a quarter of the initial fee.
- Buying Roy Keane from an Irish club called Cobh Ramblers for $80,000 in 1990 and selling him to Manchester United three years later for $5.6 million, then a British record fee.
- Buying Kenny Burns from Birmingham City for $250,000 in 1977. Taylor writes in *With Clough by Taylor* that Burns was then regarded as "a fighting, hard-drinking gambler . . . a stone [fourteen pounds] overweight." In 1978, English soccer writers voted Burns the league's player of the year.
- Twice buying Archie Gemmill cheaply. In 1970, when Gemmill was playing for Preston, Clough drove to his house and asked him

> to come to Derby. Gemmill refused. Clough said that in that case he would sleep outside in his car. Gemmill's wife invited him to sleep in the house instead. The next morning at breakfast Clough persuaded Gemmill to sign. The fee was $145,000, and Gemmill quickly won two league titles at Derby. In 1977 Clough paid Derby $35,000 and the now forgotten goalkeeper John Middleton to bring Gemmill to his new club Forest, where the player won another league title.

If there was one club where almost every penny spent on transfers bought results, it was Forest under Clough. In the 1970s the correlation must have been off the charts: Forest won two European Cups with a team assembled largely for peanuts. Sadly, there are no good financial data for that period, but we do know that even from 1982 to 1992, in Clough's declining years, after Taylor had left him, Forest performed as well on the field as clubs that were spending twice as much on wages. Clough had broken the usually iron link between salaries and league position.

Clough himself seemed to think that what explained Forest's success was his and Taylor's eye for players, rather than, say, any motivational gift or tactical genius. Phil Soar, the club's chairman and chief executive for four years at the end of the 1990s, e-mailed us: "In hours of musings with Clough (I had to try to defend him from the bung charges) I obviously asked him what made this almost absurdly irrelevant little provincial club (my home town of course) into a shooting star. And he always used to say, 'We had some pretty good players you know.'"

It's hard to identify all of Clough and Taylor's transfer secrets, and if their rivals at the time had understood what they were up to, everyone would have simply imitated them. Taylor's book makes it clear that he spent a lot of time trying to identify players (like Burns) whom others had wrongly undervalued due to surface characteristics, but then everyone tries to do that. Sometimes Forest did splurge on a player who was rated by everybody, like Trevor Francis, soccer's first "million-pound man," or Peter Shilton, whom it made the most expensive goalkeeper in British history.

Yet thanks to *With Clough by Taylor* we can identify three of the duo's rules. First, be as eager to sell good players as to buy them. "It's as important in soccer as in the stock market to sell at the right time," wrote Taylor. "A manager should always be looking for signs of disintegration in a winning side and then sell the players responsible before their deterioration is noticed by possible buyers." (Or in Billy Beane's words: "You have to always be upgrading. Otherwise you're fucked.")

The moment when a player reaches the top of his particular hill is like the moment when the stock market peaks. Clough and Taylor were always trying to gauge that moment, and sell. Each time they signed a player, they would give him a set speech, which Taylor records in his book: "Son, the first time we can replace you with a better player, we'll do it without blinking an eyelid. That's what we're paid to do—to produce the best side and to win as many things as we can. If we see a better player than you but don't sign him then we're frauds. But we're not frauds." In 1981, just after Kenny Burns had won everything with Forest, the club offloaded him to Leeds for $800,000.

Second, older players are overrated. "I've noticed over the years how often Liverpool sell players as they near or pass their thirtieth birthday," notes Taylor in his book. "Bob Paisley [Liverpool's then manager] believes the average first division footballer is beginning to burn out at thirty." Taylor added, rather snottily, that that was true of a "running side like Liverpool," but less so of a passing one like Forest. Nonetheless, he agreed with the principle of selling older players.

The master of that trade for many years was Wenger. Arsenal's manager is one of the few people in soccer who can view the game from the outside. In part, this is because he has a degree in economic sciences from the University of Strasbourg in France. As a trained economist, he is inclined to trust data rather than the game's received wisdom. Wenger sees that in the transfer market, clubs tend to overvalue a player's past performance. That prompts them to pay fortunes—in transfer fees and salaries—for players who have passed their prime. FIFA TMS (the department of FIFA that oversees international transfers) analyzed the pay of players who moved internationally to Brazil, Argentina, England, Germany, Italy, and Portugal in 2012, and found, remarkably, that the average man earned his peak fixed salary at the ripe old age of thirty-two.

All players are melting blocks of ice. The job of the club is to gauge how fast they are melting, and to get rid of them before they turn into expensive puddles of water. Wenger often lets defenders carry on until their mid-thirties, but he usually gets rid of his midfielders and forwards much younger. He got rid of Patrick Vieira for $25 million at age twenty-nine, Thierry Henry for $30 million at age twenty-nine, Emmanuel Petit for $10.5 million at age twenty-nine, and Marc Overmars for $37 million at age twenty-seven, and none of them ever did as well again after leaving Arsenal. (Wenger's uncharacteristic decision at the very end of August 2011 to sign twenty-eight-year-old Andre Santos, twenty-nine-year-old Mikel Arteta, and thirty-one-year-old Yossi Benayoun shows his pressing need at that moment for quick success. In any case, he had built up the cashbox to afford it. It didn't work out well.)

Curiously, precisely the same overvaluation of older players exists in baseball, too. The conventional wisdom in the game had always been that players peak in their early thirties. Then along came Bill James from his small town in Kansas. In his mimeographs, the father of sabermetrics showed that the average player peaked not in his early thirties, but at just twenty-seven. Beane told us, "Nothing strangulates a sports club more than having older players on long contracts, because once they stop performing, they become immoveable. And as they become older, the risk of injury becomes exponential. It's less costly to bring a young player. If it doesn't work, you can go and find the next guy, and the next guy. The downside risk is lower, and the upside much higher."

Finally, Clough and Taylor's third rule: buy players with personal problems (like Burns, or the gambler Stan Bowles) at a discount. Then help them deal with their problems.

Clough, a drinker, and Taylor, a gambler, empathized with troubled players. While negotiating with a new player they would ask him a stock question, "to which we usually know the answer," wrote Taylor. It was: "Let's hear your vice before you sign. Is it women, booze, drugs, or gambling?"

Clough and Taylor believed that once they knew the vice, they could help the player manage it. Clough was so confident of his psychological skills that he even thought he could handle Manchester United's alcoholic womanizing genius George Best. "I'd sort George out in a week," he boasted. "I'd hide the key to the drinks cabinet and I'd make sure he was tucked up with nothing stronger than cocoa for the first six months.

Women? I'd let him home to see his mum and his sisters. No one else in a skirt is getting within a million miles of him."

Taylor says he told Bowles, who joined Forest in 1979 (and, as it happens, failed there), "Any problem in your private life must be brought to us; you may not like that but we'll prove to you that our way of management is good for all of us." After a player confided a problem, wrote Taylor, "if we couldn't find an answer, we would turn to experts: we have sought advice for our players from clergymen, doctors and local councilors." Taking much the same approach, Wenger helped Tony Adams and Paul Merson combat their addictions.

All this might sound obvious, but the usual attitude in soccer is, "We paid a lot of money for you, now get on with it," as if mental illness, addiction, or homesickness should not exist above a certain level of income.

RELOCATION, RELOCATION, RELOCATION: THE RICE KRISPIES PROBLEM

Clough and Taylor understood that many transfers fail because of a player's problems off the field. In a surprising number of cases, these problems are the product of the transfer itself.

Moving to a job in another city is always stressful; moving to another country is even more so. The challenge of moving from Rio de Janeiro to Manchester involves cultural adjustments that just don't compare with moving from Springfield, Missouri, to Springfield, Ohio. An uprooted soccer player has to find a home and a new life for his family, and gain some grasp of the social rules of his new country. Yet European clubs that pay millions of dollars for foreign players are often unwilling to spend a few thousand more to help the players settle in their new homes. Instead the clubs typically tell them, "Here's a plane ticket, come over, and play brilliantly from day one." The player fails to adjust to the new country, underperforms, and his transfer fee is wasted. "Relocation," as the industry of relocation consultants calls it, has long been one of the biggest inefficiencies in the transfer market.

All the inefficiencies surrounding relocation could be assuaged. Most big businesses know how difficult relocation is and do their best to smooth the passage. When a senior Microsoft executive moves between countries, a relocation consultant helps his or her family find schools and a house and learn the social rules of the new country. If Luther Blissett had been working for Microsoft, a relocation consultant could have found him Rice Krispies. An expensive relocation might cost $25,000, or 0.1 percent of a large transfer fee. But in soccer, possibly the most globalized industry of all, spending anything at all on relocation was until very recently regarded as a waste of money.

Boudewijn Zenden, who played in four countries, for clubs including Liverpool and Barcelona, told us during his stint in Marseille in 2009:

> It's the weirdest thing ever that you can actually buy a player for 20 mil, and you don't do anything to make him feel at home. I think the first thing you should do is get him a mobile phone and a house. Get him a school for the kids, get something for his missus, get a teacher in for both of them straightaway, because obviously everything goes with the language. Do they need anything for other family members, do they need a driving license, do they need a visa, do they need a new passport? Sometimes even at the biggest clubs it's really badly organized.
>
> Milan: best club ever. AC Milan is organized in a way you can't believe. Anything is done for you: you arrive, you get your house, it's fully furnished, you get five cars to choose from, you know the sky's the limit. They really say: we'll take care of everything else; you make sure you play really well. Whereas unfortunately in a lot of clubs, you have to get after it yourself. . . . Sometimes you get to a club, and you've got people actually at the club who take profit from players.
>
> For any foreign player, or even a player who comes in new, they could get one man who's actually there to take care of everything. But then again, sometimes players are a bit—I don't want to say abusive, but they might take profit of the situation. They might call in the middle of the night, just to say there's no milk in the fridge. You know how they are sometimes.

In soccer, bad relocations have traditionally been the norm. In 1961, two fifteen-year-olds from Belfast took the boat across the Irish Sea to become apprentices with Manchester United. George Best and Eric

McMordie had never left home before. When they landed at Liverpool docks, they couldn't find anyone from the club to meet them. So they worked out for themselves how to get a train to Manchester, eventually found the stadium, and wound up so lonely and confused that on their second day they told the club: "We want to go back on the next boat." And they did, recounts Duncan Hamilton in his biography of Best, *Immortal.* In the end, Best decided to give Manchester one last try. McMordie refused. He became a plasterer in Belfast after leaving school, though he did later make a respectable soccer career with Middlesbrough. Just imagine how the botched welcome of Best might have changed United's history.

Yet bad relocations remained the norm for decades, like Chelsea signing Dutch cosmopolitan Ruud Gullit in 1996 and sticking him in a hotel in the ugly London dormitory town of Slough, or Ian Rush coming back to England from a bad year in Italy marveling, "It was like another country." Many players down the decades would have understood that phrase. But perhaps the great failed relocation, one that a Spanish relocation consultant still cites in her presentations, was Nicolas Anelka's to Real Madrid in 1999.

A half hour of conversation with Anelka is enough to confirm that he is self-absorbed, scared of other people, and not someone who makes contact easily. Nor does he appear to be good at languages, because after well over a decade in England he still speaks very mediocre English. Anelka is the sort of expatriate who really needs a relocation consultant.

Real had spent $35 million buying him from Arsenal. The club then spent nothing on helping him adjust. On day one the shy, awkward twenty-year-old reported to work and found that there was nobody to show him around. He hadn't even been assigned a locker in the dressing room. Several times that first morning, he would take a locker that seemed to be unused, only for another player to walk in and claim it.

Anelka doesn't seem to have talked about his problems to anyone at Madrid. Nor did anyone at the club ask him. Instead he talked to *France Football,* a magazine that he treated as his newspaper of record, like a 1950s British prime minister talking to *The Times.* "I am alone against the rest of the team," he revealed midway through the season. He claimed to possess a video showing his teammates looking gloomy after he had scored his first goal for Real after six months at the club. He had tried to give this video to the coach, but the coach hadn't wanted to see it. Also, the other black Francophone players had told Anelka that the other players wouldn't pass to him. Madrid ended up giving him a forty-five-day ban, essentially for being maladjusted.

Paranoid though Anelka may have been, he had a point. The other players really didn't like him. And they never got to know him, because nobody at the club seems ever to have bothered to introduce him to anyone. As he said later, all that Madrid had told him was, "Look after yourself." The club seems to have taken the strangely materialistic view that Anelka's salary should determine his behavior. But even in materialistic terms, that was foolish. If you pay $35 million for an immature young employee, it is bad management to make him look after himself. Wenger at Arsenal knew that, and he had Anelka on the field scoring goals.

Even a player with a normal personality can find emigration tricky. Tyrone Mears, an English defender who spent a year at Marseille, where his best relocation consultant was his teammate Zenden, said, "Sometimes it's not a problem of the player adapting. A lot of the times it's the family adapting." Perhaps the player's girlfriend is unhappy because she can't find a job in the new town. Or perhaps she's pregnant and doesn't know how to negotiate the local hospital, or perhaps she can't find Rice Krispies ("or beans on toast," added Zenden, when told about the Blissett drama). The club doesn't care. It is paying her boyfriend well. He simply has to perform.

Soccer clubs never used to bother with anything like an HR department. As late as about 2005, there were only a few relocation consultants in soccer, and most weren't called that, and were not hired by clubs. Instead they worked either for players' agents or for sportswear companies. If Nike or Adidas is paying a player to wear its shoes, it needs him to succeed. If the player moves to a foreign club, the sportswear company—knowing that the club might not bother—sometimes sends a minder to live in that town and look after him.

The minder gives the player occasional presents, acts as his secretary, friend, and shrink, and remembers his wife's birthday. The minder of a young midfielder who was struggling in his first weeks at Milan said that his main task, when the player came home from training frustrated, lonely, and confused by Italy, was to take him out to dinner. At dinner the player would grumble and say, "Tomorrow I'm going to tell the coach what I really think of him," and the minder would say, "That might not be such a brilliant idea. Here, have some more *linguine alle vongole.*" To most players, this sort of thing comes as a bonus in a stressful life. To a few, it is essential.

Years after international transfers became standard, most clubs still did nothing about relocation. Didier Drogba in his autobiography recounts joining Chelsea from Olympique Marseille in 2004 for $44 million. He writes, "I plunged into problems linked to my situation as an expatriate. Chelsea didn't necessarily help me." Nobody at the club could help him find a school for his children. All Chelsea did to get him a house was put him in touch with a real estate agent who tried to sell him one for $18 million. For "weeks of irritation" the Drogba family lived in a hotel while Drogba, who at that point barely spoke English, went house hunting after practice.

All Chelsea's expensive foreign signings had much the same experience, Drogba writes. "We sometimes laughed about it with Gallas, Makelele, Kezman, Geremi. 'You too, you're still living in a hotel?' After all these worries, I didn't feel like integrating [at Chelsea] or multiplying my efforts."

Chelsea was no worse than other clubs. The same summer Drogba arrived in London, Wayne Rooney moved thirty-five miles up the motorway from Everton to Manchester United and had an almost equally disorienting experience. United had paid $49 million for him but then stuck its eighteen-year-old star asset in a hotel room. "Living in such a place I found horrible," reports Rooney in his *My Story So Far.* The nearest thing to a relocation consultant he found at United seems to have been a teammate: "Gary Neville tried to persuade me to buy one of his houses. I don't know how many he has, or whether he was boasting or winding me up, but he kept telling me about these properties he had."

At a conference in Rome in 2008, relocation consultants literally lined up to tell their horror stories about soccer. Lots of them had tried to get into the sport and been rebuffed. A Danish relocator had been told by FC Copenhagen that her services weren't required because the players' wives always helped one another settle. Many clubs had never even heard of relocation. Moreover, they had never hired relocation consultants before, so given the logic of soccer, not hiring relocation consultants must be the right thing to do. One Swedish relocator surmised, "I guess it comes down to the fact that they see the players as merchandise."

The only relocation consultants who had penetrated soccer happened to have a friend inside a club or, in the case of one Greek woman, had married a club owner. She had told her husband, "All these guys would be happier if you find out what their needs are, and address their needs."

Another relocator had entered a German club as a language teacher and worked her way up. She said, "I was their mother, their nurse, their real estate agent, their cleaning lady, their everything. They didn't have a car; they didn't speak the language." Did her work help them play better? "Absolutely." The club was happy for her to work as an amateur, but as soon as she founded a relocation company, it didn't want her anymore. She had become threatening.

And so countless new signings continued to flop abroad. Clubs often anticipated this by avoiding players who seemed particularly ill-equipped to adjust. For instance, on average Brazilians are the world's best players. Yet historically, English clubs rarely bought them, because Brazilians don't speak English, don't like cold weather, and don't tend to understand the core traditions of English soccer, like drinking twenty pints of beer in a night. Few Brazilians adjust easily to English soccer.

Instead of Brazilians, English clubs traditionally bought Scandinavians. On average, Scandinavians are worse soccer players than Brazilians, but they are very familiar with English, cold weather, and twenty pints of beer. Scandinavians adapted to England, and so the clubs bought them. But the clubs were missing a great opportunity. Anyone who bought a great Brazilian player and hired a good relocation consultant to help him adjust would be onto a winner. Yet few clubs did. Years used to go by without any English club buying a Brazilian.

In 2008 Manchester City took a gamble on Robinho. As a Brazilian forward who had had his moments in the World Cup of 2006, he was bound to be overvalued, and was also very likely to relocate badly. So it's little wonder that City paid a British record transfer fee of $55 million for him, or that eighteen months later it gave up on him and sent him home to Santos on loan. Robinho never returned to English soccer. The experience obviously taught City a lesson, because for the next two years the club switched to a policy of buying only players who had already established themselves in England. It also finally began to take relocation seriously.

Bit by bit in recent years, the soccer business has started to become smarter. Way back in the mid-1990s, Liverpool had become one of the first clubs to hire some sort of employee to help new players settle. Ajax Amsterdam was another pioneer. The woman who first handled relocations at Ajax found that some of the problems of new players were absurdly easy to solve. When Steven Pienaar and another young South African player came to Amsterdam, they were teenagers, had never lived on their own before, and suddenly found themselves sharing an apartment in a cold country at the other end of the earth. Inevitably, they put their music speakers on the bare floor and cranked up the volume. Inevitably, the neighbors complained. The South Africans had a miserable time in their building, until the woman from Ajax came around to see what was wrong and suggested they put their speakers on a table instead. They did. The noise diminished, their lives got easier, and that might just have made them better able to perform for Ajax.

Most clubs in the Premier League now have "player liaison officers"—soccer code for relocation consultants. Some of these officers are full-timers, others not. Some do a serious job. Manchester City in particular learned from Robinho's failure. When we visited the club's training ground in 2012, on a wall just behind reception we saw a map of Manchester's surroundings, designed to catch the eyes of passing players. The map highlighted eight recommended wealthy towns and suburbs for them to live; not on the list was Manchester's city center with its vibrant nightlife.

These recommendations are just the start. City's "player-care department" aims to take care of almost every need a new immigrant might have, whether it's a nanny or a "discreet car service." Even before a new player signs, the club has already researched his off-duty habits and his girlfriend's taste in restaurants. When he arrives for preseason training, the club might say to him, "Well, you're going to be busy for a couple of weeks, but here's a little restaurant your girlfriend might like." It's not true that behind every successful soccer player there is a happy wife, but it probably does help. Any Latin players needing additional help could consult City's Argentine fullback Pablo Zabaleta, who after four Mancunian years was considered practically English by his teammates.

In 2011 City signed Zabaleta's compatriot Sergio Agüero. Nobody doubted the young striker's talent. However, many doubted whether he would adapt to English football and rainy provincial life. His transfer fee of $61 million seemed a gamble, even for Manchester City. But Agüero scored twice on debut. He finished his first English season with thirty goals, including the last-second strike in the last game of the season against Queens Park Rangers that won City their first league title since 1968. In part, Agüero succeeded thanks to City's excellence at relocation. Gavin Fleig, the club's head of performance analysis, told us: "The normal transition time for a foreign player is considered in the industry to be about a year. Normally those players are in a hotel for the first three months. We were able to get from agreeing a fee to Sergio living in his house within two weeks, with a Spanish sat-nav [GPS] system in his car, linked to the Spanish community in Manchester. We had our prize asset ready to go from day one."

Still, a few clubs continue to neglect relocation. One player liaison officer in the Premier League told us, "Some very well-known managers have said to me they can't understand why you can possibly need it. They have said, 'Well, when I moved to a foreign country as a player I had to do it myself.' Well, yes, but that doesn't mean it's right. You probably had to clean boots, too, but nobody does that now."

THE NICEST TOWN IN EUROPE: HOW OLYMPIQUE LYON BOUGHT AND SOLD THEIR WAY TO THE TOP

If you had to locate the middle-class European dream anywhere, it would be in Lyon. It's a town the size of Oakland, about two-thirds of the way down France, nestled between rivers just west of the Alps. On a warm January afternoon, drinking coffee outside in the eighteenth-century Place Bellecour where the buildings are as pretty as the women, you think: nice. Here's a wealthy town where you can have a good job, nice weather, and a big house near the mountains.

Lyon also has some of the best restaurants in Europe, known locally as *bouchons,* or "corks." Even at the town's soccer stadium you can have a wonderful three-course pregame meal consisting largely of intestines or head cheese, unless you prefer to eat at local boy Paul Bocuse's brasserie across the road and totter into the grounds just before kickoff. And then, for a remarkable decade or so, you could watch some very decent soccer, too.

Until about 2000 Lyon was known as the birthplace of cinema and nouvelle cuisine, but not as a soccer town. It was just too bourgeois. If for some reason you wanted soccer, you drove thirty-five miles down the highway to gritty proletarian Saint-Étienne. In 1987 Olympique Lyon, or OL, or *les Gones* (the Kids), was playing in France's second division on an annual budget of about $3 million. It was any old backwater provincial club in Europe. From 2002 through 2008 Lyon ruled French soccer. The club's ascent was in large part a story of the international transfer market. Better than any other club in Europe, for a while Lyon worked out how to play the market.

In 1987 Jean-Michel Aulas, a local software entrepreneur with the stark, grooved features of a Roman emperor, became club president. Aulas had played fairly good handball as a young man and had a season ticket at OL.

"I didn't know the world of soccer well," he admitted to us in 2007 over a bottle of OL mineral water in his office beside the stadium (which he was aiming to tear down and replace with a bigger one). Had he expected the transformation that he wrought? "No."

Aulas set out to improve the club step by step. "We tried to abstract the factor 'time,'" he explained. "Each year we fix as an aim to have sporting progress, and progress of our financial resources. It's like a cyclist riding: you can overtake the people in front of you." Others in France preferred to liken Aulas to "*un bulldozer*."

In 1987 even the local Lyonnais didn't care much about *les Gones*. You could live in Lyon without knowing that soccer existed. The club barely had a personality, whereas Saint-Étienne was the "miners' club" that had suffered tragic defeats on great European nights in the 1970s. Saint-Étienne's president at the time said that when it came to soccer, Lyon was a suburb of Saint-Étienne, a remark that still rankles. At one derby after Lyon's domination began, *les Gones'* fans unfurled a banner that told the Saint-Étienne supporters, "We invented cinema when your fathers were dying in the mines."

Aulas appointed local boy Raymond Domenech as his first coach. In Domenech's first season, OL finished at the top of the second division without losing a game. Right after that it qualified for Europe. Aulas recalled, "At a stroke the credibility was total. The project was en route."

It turned out that the second city in France, even if it was a bit bourgeois, was just hungry enough for a decent soccer club. The Lyonnais were willing to buy match tickets if things went well, but if things went badly, they weren't immediately waving white handkerchiefs in the stands and demanding that the president or manager or half the team be gotten rid of. Nor did the French media track the club's doings hour by hour. It's much easier to build for the long term in a place like that than in a "soccer city" like Marseille or Newcastle. Moreover, players were happy to move to a town that is hardly a hardship posting. Almost nothing they got into in Lyon made it into the gossip press. Another of Lyon's advantages: the locals had money. "It allowed us to have not just a 'popular clientele,' but also a 'business clientele,'" said Aulas.

Talking about money is something of a taboo in France. It is considered a grubby and private topic. Socially, you're never supposed to ask anyone a question that might reveal how much somebody has. Soccer, to most French fans, is not supposed to be about money. They find the notion of a well-run soccer club humorless, practically American.

It therefore irritated them that Aulas talked about it so unabashedly. He might have invented the word *moneyball.* Aulas's theme was that over time, the more money a club makes, the more matches it will win, and the more matches it wins, the more money it will make. In the short term you can lose a match, but in the long term there is a rationality even to soccer. (And to baseball. As *Moneyball* describes it, Beane believes that winning "is simply a matter of figuring out the odds, and exploiting the laws of probability. . . . To get worked up over plays, or even games, is as unproductive as a casino manager worrying over the outcomes of individual pulls of the slot machines.")

In Aulas's view, rationality in soccer works more or less like this: if you buy good players for less than they are worth, you will win more games. You will then have more money to buy better players for less than they are worth. The better players will win you more matches, and that will attract more fans (and thus more money), because Aulas spotted early that most soccer fans everywhere are much more like shoppers than like religious believers: if they can get a better experience somewhere new, they will go there. He told us in 2007, "We sold 110,000 replica shirts last season. This season we are already at 200,000. I think Olympique Lyon has become by far the most beloved club in France."

Polls suggested he was right: in Sport+Markt's survey of European supporters in 2008, Lyon emerged as the country's most popular club just ahead of Olympique Marseille. This popularity was a new phenomenon. In 2002, when Lyon first became champions of France, the overriding French emotion toward the club had still been, "Whatever." The editor of *France Football* magazine complained around that time that when Lyon won the title, his magazine didn't sell. But as the club won the title every year from 2002 through 2008—the longest period of domination by any club in any of Europe's five biggest national leagues ever—many French fans began to care about them.

With more fans, Lyon made more money. On match days you could get a haircut at an official OL salon, drink an OL Beaujolais at an OL café, book your holiday at an OL travel agency, and take an OL taxi to the game—and many people did. Lyon used that money to buy better players.

But for all Aulas's OL mineral water, what made the club's rise possible was the transfer market. On that warm winter's afternoon in Lyon, Aulas told us, "We will invest better than Chelsea, Arsenal, or Real Madrid. We will make different strategic choices. For instance, we won't try to have the best team on paper in terms of brand. We will have the best team relative to our investment." Here are Lyon's rules of the transfer market:

Use the wisdom of crowds. When Lyon was thinking of signing a player, a group of men would sit down to debate the transfer. Aulas would be there, and Bernard Lacombe, once a bull-like center forward for Lyon and France, and for most of the past twenty-five years the club's technical director. Lacombe is known for having the best pair of eyes in French soccer. He coached Lyon from 1997 to 2000, but Aulas clearly figured out that if you have someone with his knack for spotting the right transfer, you want to keep him at the club forever rather than make his job contingent on four lost matches. The same went for Peter Taylor at Forest.

Whoever happened to be Lyon's head coach at the moment would sit in on the meeting, too, and so would four or five other coaches. "We have a group that gives its advice," Aulas explained. "In England the manager often does it alone. In France it's often the technical director." Lacombe told us that the house rule was that after the group had made the decision, everyone present would then publicly get behind the transfer.

Like Lyon, the Oakland A's sidelined their manager, too. Like Lyon, the A's understood that he was merely "a middle manager" obsessed with the very short term. The A's let him watch baseball's annual draft. They didn't let him say a word about it.

Lyon's method for choosing players is so obvious and smart that it's surprising all clubs don't use it. The theory of the "wisdom of crowds" says that if you aggregate many different opinions from a diverse group of people, you are much more likely to arrive at the best opinion than if you just listen to one specialist. For instance, if you ask a diverse crowd to guess the weight of an ox, the average of their guesses will be very nearly right. If you ask a diverse set of gamblers to bet on, say, the outcome of a presidential election, the average of their bets is likely to be right, too. (Gambling markets have proved excellent predictors of all sorts of outcomes.) The wisdom of crowds fails when the components of the crowd are not diverse enough. This is often the case in American sports. But in European soccer, opinions tend to come from many different countries, and that helps ensure diversity.

Clough and Taylor at least were a crowd of two. However, the typical decision-making model in English soccer is not "wisdom of crowds," but short-term dictatorship. At most clubs the manager is treated as a sort of divinely inspired monarch who gets to decide everything until he is sacked. Then the next manager clears out his predecessor's signings at a discount. Lyon, noted a rival French club president with envy, never had expensive signings rotting on the bench. It never had revolutions at all. It understood that the coach was only a temp. OL won its seven consecutive titles with four different coaches—Jacques Santini, Paul Le Guen, Gérard Houllier, and Alain Perrin—none of whom, judging by their subsequent records, was exactly a Hegelian world-historical individual. When a coach left Lyon, not much changed. No matter who happened to be sitting on the bench, the team always played much the same brand of attacking soccer (by French standards).

Emmanuel Hembert grew up in Lyon supporting OL when it was still in the second division. Later, as head of the sports practice of the management consultancy A. T. Kearney in London, he was always citing the club as an example to his clients in soccer. "A big secret of a successful club is stability," Hembert explained over coffee in Paris a few years ago. "In Lyon, the stability is not with the coach, but with the sports director, Lacombe."

Another Lyon rule: *the best time to buy a player is when he is in his early twenties.* Aulas said, "We buy young players with potential who are considered the best in their country, between twenty and twenty-two years old." It's almost as if he has read *Moneyball.* The book keeps banging away about a truth discovered by Bill James, who wrote, "College players are a better investment than high school players by a huge, huge, laughably huge margin."

Baseball clubs traditionally preferred to draft high school players. But how good you are at seventeen or eighteen is a poor predictor of how good you will become as an adult. By definition, when a player is that young there is still too little information to judge him. Beane himself had been probably the hottest baseball prospect in the United States at seventeen, but he was already declining in his senior year at high school, and he then failed in the major leagues. Watching the 2002 draft as the A's general manager, he "punches his fist in the air" each time rival teams draft schoolboys.

It's the same in soccer, where brilliant teenagers tend to disappear soon afterward. Here are a few winners of the Golden Ball for best player at the under-seventeen World Cup: Philip Osundo of Nigeria, William de Oliveira of Brazil, Nii Lamptey of Ghana, Scottish goalkeeper James Will, and Mohammed al-Kathiri of Oman. Once upon a time they must have all been brilliant, but none of them made it as adults. (Will ended up a policeman in the Scottish Highlands playing for his village team.) The most famous case of a teenager who flamed out is American Freddy Adu, who at fourteen was the next Pelé and Maradona.

Only a handful of world-class players in each generation, most of them creators—Pelé, Maradona, Wayne Rooney, Lionel Messi, Cesc

Fabregas—reach the top by the age of eighteen. Most players get there considerably later. Almost all defenders and goalkeepers do. You can be confident of their potential only when they are more mature.

Beane knows that by the time baseball players are in college—which tends to put them in Lyon's magical age range of twenty to twenty-two—you have a pretty good idea of what they will become. There is a lot of information about them. They have grown up a bit. They are old enough to be nearly fully formed, but too young to be expensive stars. FIFA TMS analyzed international transfers to England in 2013 and found that players moving at ages twenty to twenty-two were 18 percent cheaper than players ages twenty-five to twenty-seven. Better yet, the younger players tended to have lower salaries, and higher future resale values.

Lyon always tried to avoid paying a premium for a star player's "name." Here, again, it was lucky to be a club from a quiet town. Its placid supporters and local media didn't demand stars. By contrast, the former chairman of a club in a much more raucous French city recalls, "I ran [the club] with the mission to create a spectacle. It wasn't to build a project for twenty years to come." A team from a big city tends to need big stars.

Soccer being barely distinguishable from baseball, the same split between big and small towns operates in that sport, too. "Big-market teams," like the Boston Red Sox and the New York Yankees, hunt players with names. Their media and fans demand it. In *Moneyball,* Lewis calls this the pathology of "many foolish teams that thought all their questions could be answered by a single player." (It's a pathology that may sound strangely familiar to European soccer fans.) By contrast, the Oakland A's, as a small-market team, were free to forgo stars. As Lewis writes, "Billy may not care for the Oakland press but it is really very tame next to the Boston press, and it certainly has no effect on his behavior, other than to infuriate him once a week or so. Oakland A's fans, too, were apathetic compared to the maniacs in Fenway Park or Yankee Stadium." But as Beane told us, English soccer is "even more emotional" than baseball. "It's the biggest sport in the world," he said. "And that's the biggest league in the world, and then you put in sixty million people and a four-hour drive from north to south, and that's what you have."

That's why most English soccer clubs are always being pushed by their fans to buy stars. Happy is the club that has no need of heroes. Lyon was free to buy young unknowns like Michael Essien, Florent Malouda, or Mahamadou Diarra just because they were good. And unknowns accept modest salaries. According to the French sports newspaper *L'Equipe,* in the 2007–2008 season Lyon spent only 31 percent of its budget on players' pay. The average in the English Premier League was about double that. Like Clough's Forest, Lyon for many years performed the magic trick of winning things without paying silly salaries.

Here are a few more of Lyon's secrets. First, try not to buy center forwards. Center forward is the most overpriced position in the transfer market. (Goalkeeper is the most underpriced, even though keepers have longer careers than outfield players; in baseball the most overpriced position pre-*Moneyball* was pitcher.) Admittedly Lyon "announced" itself to soccer by buying the Brazilian center forward Sonny Anderson for $19 million in 1999, but the club mostly scrimped on the position afterward. Houllier left OL in 2007 grumbling that even after the club sold Malouda and Eric Abidal for a combined total of $45 million, Aulas still wouldn't buy him a center forward.

Second, help your foreign signings relocate. All sorts of great Brazilians have passed through Lyon: Sonny Anderson; the longtime club captain, Cris; the future internationals Juninho and Fred; and the world champion Edmilson. Most were barely known when they joined the club. Aulas explained the secret: "We sent one of our old players, Marcelo, to Brazil. He was an extraordinary man, because he was both an engineer and a professional soccer player. He was captain of Lyon for five years. Then he became an agent, but he works quasi-exclusively for OL. He indicates all market opportunities to us." As a judge of players, Marcelo was clearly in the Lacombe or Peter Taylor class.

Marcelo said he scouted only "serious boys." Or as the former president of a rival French club puts it, "They don't select players just for their quality but for their ability to adapt. I can't see Lyon recruiting an Anelka or a Ronaldinho."

After Lyon signed the serious boys, it made sure they settled. Drogba noted enviously, "At Lyon, a translator takes care of the Brazilians, helps them to find a house, get their bearings, tries to reduce as much as possible the negative effects of moving. . . . Even at a place of the calibre of Chelsea, that didn't exist."

Lyon's "translator," who worked full-time for the club, sorted out the players' homesickness, bank accounts, nouvelle cuisine, and whatever else. Other people at the club taught the newcomers Lyon's culture: no stars or showoffs. By concentrating on Brazilians, the club could offer them a tailor-made relocation service. Almost all the other foreign players Lyon bought spoke French.

Finally, sell any player if another club offers more than he is worth. This is what Aulas meant when he said, "Buying and selling players is not an activity for improving the soccer performance. It's a trading activity, in which we produce gross margin. If an offer for a player is greatly superior to his market value, you must not keep him." The ghost of Peter Taylor would approve.

Like Clough and Taylor, and like Billy Beane, Lyon never got sentimental about players. In the club's annual accounts, it booked each player for a certain transfer value. (Beane says, "Know exactly what every player in baseball is worth to you. You can put a dollar figure on it.") Lyon knew that sooner or later its best players would attract somebody else's attention. Because the club expected to sell them, it replaced them even before they went. Ferguson at United also pursued a strategy of early replacement: "I did feel sentimental about great players leaving us. At the same time, my eye would always be on a player who was coming to an end. An internal voice would always ask, 'When's he going to leave, how long will he last?' Experience taught me to stockpile young players in important positions."

Bringing in replacements before they are needed avoids a transition period or a panic purchase after the player's departure. Aulas explained, "We will replace the player in the squad six months or a year before. So when Michael Essien goes [to Chelsea for $43 million], we already have a certain number of players who are ready to replace him. Then, when the opportunity to buy Tiago arises, for 25 percent of the price of Essien, you take him."

Before Essien's transfer in 2005, Aulas spent weeks proclaiming that the Ghanaian was "untransferable." He always said that when he was about to transfer a player, because it drove up the price. In his words, "Every international at Lyon is untransferable. Until the offer surpasses by far the amount we had expected."

ABSTINENCE: JUST SAY NO TO TRANSFERS

There's one other kind of mastery of the transfer market to discuss: abstinence. Some clubs—notably Barcelona for most of this century—understand the inefficiencies of the transfer market and therefore avoid buying players wherever possible. These clubs try to just say no.

One Saturday lunchtime in July 2009 we caught up with Joan Oliver in his office at the Nou Camp. Barcelona's then CEO had escaped there for a rare bit of peace and quiet, away from the madness of the summer transfer market.

Barça's aim, Oliver told us, was "to have one of the best, perhaps the best, team in the world, without having to spend X million on players. The image of that is the final in Rome this year [against Manchester United], with a team of seven players from our academy. The total acquisition cost of our team has been—I don't remember, but something below 70 million euros." (In 2011 Barça again won the Champions League final, having started the game with seven homegrown players.)

It may seem odd that a big-city club like Barcelona can mostly abstain from the market—buying one great player for a large fee every year or so rather than constantly overhauling its team. After all, we have seen that other big clubs with a frenzied local fan base and media are practically forced to keep buying "stars." Barcelona for decades did the same thing. But then, under President Joan Laporta from 2003, the club began to make greater use of its peculiar profile. Barça presents itself as "the unarmed army of Catalonia." That image means a lot to the club's fans. It means they are as happy to see local boys like Sergio Busquets (son of a Barça goalkeeper) or Gerard Piqué (grandson of a Barça director) break into the team as they are to see a foreign star brandishing his new shirt at the flashbulbs of the local newspapers. And so Barcelona discovered that it could please its fans by avoiding transfers and bringing in kids instead. The club's most successful coach, Josep Guardiola, was praised for his willingness to throw teenagers into the first team, but he could do it because the crowd supported the policy. Oliver said of the reliance on the club's academy, the Masia, "It's not only an economic strategy. It's part of the identity of the club." Growing its own players boosts Barcelona's brand, and the brand makes the club money.

There's another advantage to shunning the transfer market, Oliver added. He called it the "one-second rule." The success of a move on the pitch is decided in less than a second. If a player needs a few extra fractions of a second to work out where his teammate is going, because he doesn't know the other guy's game well, the move will usually break down. You can therefore lose a match in under a second. A corollary of that, thought Oliver, is that a new signing is likely to underperform in his first season. The new man is still working out what his role in the team is, and what everyone else is trying to do. That means that if you do buy a player, it's only worth it if you keep him around for the longer term.

All this sounds worthy, and easy to say when things are going well. However, Barcelona in recent years has largely stuck to these principles even in bad times. After the failed 2007–2008 season, when another club might have loaded up on stars, Barcelona did buy Dani Alves for $50 million, but it also sold two of its biggest names, Ronaldinho and Deco. When the club does buy, it rightly tends to focus on "top ten" players: men who are arguably among the ten best footballers on earth, such as Zlatan Ibrahimovic, David Villa, Fabregas, or Neymar. Those players cost a lot, but the risk of their failing is small (unless you buy them when they are getting old, like Thierry Henry). Part of being one of the ten best players on earth is that you perform almost whatever the circumstances.

Oliver and Laporta have since been ousted, but Barcelona still tries to field an unchanging homegrown core supplemented only by rare (and usually expensive) transfers. Abstinence works for Barça. Other big clubs like Manchester United and Chelsea have also recently tried to keep the cores of their teams together for years at a time. This may be a new trend in soccer. Nonetheless, many other clubs are still with Saint Augustine: "Give me chastity and continence, Lord, but not yet."

"The problem with the football business," said Oliver, "is that usually it is managed with very, very short-term goals. After a bad year, it's very difficult not to fall in the temptation of buying a lot of people. Clubs spend irrationally and compulsively on players. And that's very difficult to restrain. You have always the temptation of thinking that if you buy two or three players, perhaps you will reverse the situation. That was perhaps the case of Chelsea in the past, and the case of Manchester City or, I think, of Real Madrid now."

If clubs feel bound to continue to buy players, we can at least offer them a free service. Here are the twelve main secrets of the transfer market in full:

A new manager wastes money on transfers; don't let him.
Use the wisdom of crowds.
Stars of recent World Cups or European championships are overvalued; ignore them.
Certain nationalities are overvalued.
Older players are overvalued.
Center forwards are overvalued; goalkeepers are undervalued.
Gentlemen prefer blonds: identify and abandon "sight-based prejudices."
The best time to buy a player is when he is in his early twenties.
Sell any player when another club offers more than he is worth.
Replace your best players even before you sell them.
Buy players with personal problems, and then help them deal with their problems.
Help your players relocate.

Alternatively, clubs could just stick with the conventional wisdom.

3

THE WORST BUSINESS IN THE WORLD

Why Soccer Clubs Don't (and Shouldn't) Make Money

A man we know once tried to do business with a revered institution of English soccer. "I can do business with stupid people," he said afterward, "and I can do business with crooks. But I can't do business with stupid people who want to be crooks."

It was a decent summary of the soccer business, if you can call soccer a business. People often do. William McGregor, the Scottish draper who founded the English Football League in 1888, was probably the first person to describe soccer as "big business," but the phrase has since become one of the game's great clichés. In fact, McGregor was wrong. Soccer is neither big business nor good business. It arguably isn't even business at all.

"BIG BUSINESS"

Few people have heard of United Natural Foods. The company was formed out of a merger of two food distributors in 1996. Today it distributes natural, organic, and specialty foods, and it has done well out of the rise of foodies in North America. Still, it hasn't quite made its way onto the list of the five hundred big publicly traded American companies that make up the S&P 500. Its annual revenues for the year to August 2013 were $6.06 billion, for net income of $108 million. United Natural Foods, whose headquarters are on Iron Horse Way in Providence, Rhode Island, is not big business. For comparison: in 2012–2013 the biggest company in the S&P 500, Wal-Mart Stores, had revenues that were more than seventy-five times bigger.

But United Natural Foods is a much larger business than any soccer club on earth. In September 2013 Real Madrid reported record revenues of €520.9 million (or $688 million) for the fiscal year 2012–2013. That's a tidy sum, more than any other club in any sport has ever achieved. However, it's just one-eighth of United Natural Foods' revenues, and barely 0.2 percent the size of Wal-Mart's. To put it very starkly: the Finnish financial analyst Matias Möttölä calculates that in terms of revenue, Real Madrid would still only be the 120th largest company in Finland (a country with a population of just 5.4 million people, or about the same as Minnesota).

It's worth noting, too, that Deloitte's "Football Money League" ranks clubs based on how much they sell. When business analysts judge normal companies, they usually focus on profits, or the company's value if it were sold on the market. However, neither of those methods works with soccer clubs. Because hardly any clubs are quoted on the stock market anymore, for extremely good reasons, it is hard to work out their value. We can certainly say that not even Real Madrid or Barcelona—Deloitte's top two in 2013—would get anywhere near the S&P 500.

And if Deloitte ranked clubs by their profits, the results would be embarrassing. Not only do most clubs make losses and fail to pay any dividends to their shareholders, but many of the "bigger" clubs would rank near the bottom of the list. Chasing prizes, they spend themselves into the red.

Whichever way you measure it, no soccer club is a big business. Even Madrid, Barcelona, and Manchester United are dwarfed by United Natural Foods. As for all the rest, the author Alex Fynn noted in the 1990s that the average English Premier League club had about the same revenue as a British supermarket—not a chain of supermarkets, but one single large Tesco store. True, soccer clubs have grown since then: by 2012 the average club in the Premier League had a turnover of nearly $190 million. However, Tesco has around twenty superstores that each generate more revenue than this. Remember also that Premier League clubs are the giants of global soccer. UEFA's most recent annual club licensing report found that the average revenue of the 235 clubs that play in UEFA competitions was a mere €33 million ($44 million).

A good way to visualize the size of the soccer industry is to visit the headquarters of UEFA, the European soccer association, in the Swiss town of Nyon. The building has a lovely view of Lake Geneva, but it looks like the offices of a small insurance company. Soccer is small business.

This feels like a contradiction. We all know that soccer is huge. Some of the most famous people on earth are soccer players, and the most watched television program in history is generally the most recent World Cup final. Nonetheless, soccer clubs are puny businesses. This is partly a problem of what economists call appropriability: soccer clubs can't make money out of (can't appropriate) more than a tiny share of our love of soccer.

It may be that season tickets are expensive and replica shirts overpriced, but buying these things once a year represents the extravagant extreme of soccer fanaticism. Most soccer is watched not from $1,500 seats in the stadium but on TV—sometimes at the price of a subscription, often at the price of watching a few commercials, or for the price of a couple of beers in a bar. Compare the cost of watching a game in a bar with the cost of eating out or watching a movie, let alone going on vacation.

Worse still, soccer generates little income from reruns of matches or transfers to DVD. And watching soccer (even on TV) is only a tiny part of the fan's engagement with the game. There are newspaper reports to be read, Internet sites to be trawled, and a growing array of computer games to keep up with. Then there is the soccer banter that passes time at the dinner table, work, or the bus stop. All this entertainment is made possible by soccer clubs, but they usually cannot appropriate a penny of the value we attach to it. Chelsea cannot charge us for talking or reading or thinking about Chelsea. As the Dutch international Demy de Zeeuw says, "There are complaints that we [players] earn too much, but the whole world earns money from your success as a player: newspapers, television, companies." In fact, the world earns more from soccer than the soccer industry itself does.

BAD BUSINESS

Soccer is not merely a small business. It's also a bad one. Until very recently, and to some degree still today, anyone who spent any time inside soccer soon discovered that just as oil was part of the oil business, stupidity was part of the soccer businchs.

This became obvious when people in soccer encountered people in other industries. Generally the soccer people got exploited because people in other industries understood business better. In 1997 Peter Kenyon, then chief executive of the sportswear company Umbro, invited a few guests to watch a European game at Chelsea, the club he would end up running a few years later. After the game, Kenyon took his guests out for dinner. Over curry he reminisced about how the sportswear industry used to treat soccer clubs. Before the 1980s, he said, big English clubs used to *pay* companies like Umbro to supply their clothing. It was obviously great advertising for the gear makers to have some of England's best players running around in their clothes, but the clubs had not yet figured that out. And so sportswear companies used to get paid to advertise themselves.

In fact, when England hosted the World Cup in 1966, it hoped merely that its usual supplier would give it a discount on shoes and shirts, "particularly in the opening ceremony . . . with the Queen present," writes Mihir Bose in *The Spirit of the Game.* As it happened, the English did even better: Umbro offered to supply the team for free. The company must have been pleased when England became world champion.

Ricky George saw the ignorance of soccer in those days from point-blank range. In 1972, when George scored the famous goal for little semiprofessional Hereford that knocked Newcastle out of the FA Cup, he was working for Adidas as a "soccer PR." His job was to represent Adidas to England players, former world champions like Bobby Moore, Bobby Charlton, and Gordon Banks. There was little need to persuade them to choose Adidas. Most of them wore the three stripes for free anyway. George says, "It is quite a fascinating thing if you compare it with today. There were no great sponsorship deals going on. All that happened is that you would give the players boots. But even then, at the beginning of every season the clubs would go to their local sports retailer and just buy twenty, thirty pairs of boots and hand them out. For a company like Adidas, it was the cheapest type of PR you could imagine."

Only on special occasions did George have to pay players. "When it came to a big international, and the game was going to be televised, my job was to go to the team hotel, hang around there, make myself known, and a couple of hours before the game I would go into the players' rooms and paint the white stripes on their boots with luminous paint so it was more visible. My bosses used to be keenly watching the television to make sure the stripes were visible, and if they weren't I would be in for bollocking."

For this service, an England player would receive seventy-five pounds per match, which was then about two hundred dollars—not a princely sum even in 1972. George recalls, "Bobby [Moore], the most charming of people, didn't take the money on the day of the game. He just used to say to me, 'Let it build up for a few games, and I'll ring you when I need it.' And that's what he did." Then the most famous defender of the era would pocket a cumulative few hundred dollars for having advertised an international brand to a cumulative audience of tens of millions.

Only in the late 1980s did English soccer clubs discover that people were willing to buy replicas of their team shirts. That made it plain even to them that their gear must have some value. They had already stopped paying sportswear companies for the stuff; now they started to charge them.

Gradually over time, soccer clubs have found new ways of making money. However, the ideas almost never came from the clubs themselves. Whether it was branded clothing, or the gambling pools, or television, it was usually people in other industries who first saw there might be profits to be made. It was Rupert Murdoch who went to English clubs and suggested putting them on satellite TV; the clubs would never have thought of going to him. In fact, the clubs often fought against new moneymaking schemes. Until 1982 they refused to allow any league games to be shown live on TV, fearing that it might deter fans from coming to the stadium. They couldn't grasp that games on television meant both free money and free advertising. There is now a good deal of research into the question of how many fans are lost when a game is shown on TV. Almost all the evidence shows that the number is tiny, and that the gate revenue that would be lost is usually well below the amount that would be made from selling extra matches for television coverage.

It took clubs a long time to realize just how much soccer was worth to television. When Greg Dyke was chairman of the UK's ITV Sport in the 1980s, he offered five big clubs £1 million each for the TV rights for English soccer. Dyke, who today is chairman of England's Football Association, fondly recalls: "It's funny now, when you look at the money that's involved: these chairmen had eyes bulging. They couldn't believe it." In total, Dyke bought the entire TV rights for English professional soccer for £12 million a year—a bit under $20 million at the time. Soon afterward, he went up to Nottingham to try to talk Brian Clough, Forest's then manager, into coming back on TV as a pundit. When Dyke arrived at the club, Clough came up to him and said: "Thank you. I want to shake your hand, Mr. Dyke, because you're the first person that's given football what it's due: twelve million quid."

In 1992 Rupert Murdoch began paying about $100 million a season for the television rights to the new Premier League. Now the league gets nearly thirty times as much a season from worldwide TV. "I've been screwed by television," admitted Sir John Hall, then the Newcastle chairman, one rowdy night at Trinity College Dublin in 1995. "But I'll tell you one thing: I won't be screwed again."

Or take the renovation of English stadiums in the early 1990s. It was an obvious business idea. Supermarkets don't receive customers in sheds built in the Victorian era and gone to seed since. They are forever renovating their stores. Yet soccer clubs never seem to have thought of spending money on their grounds until the Taylor Report of 1990 forced them to. They did up their stadiums, and bingo: more customers came.

All this proves how much like consumers soccer fans are. It's not that they come running when a team does well. Rather, it seems that soccer can quickly become popular across a whole country. All teams then benefit, but particularly those that build nice new stadiums where spectators feel comfortable and safe. That would explain why the three English clubs whose crowds grew fastest over the 1990s were Manchester United, Sunderland, and Newcastle. Later, when Arsenal moved from Highbury to the much larger Emirates, the new stadium filled up despite the fact that the club stopped winning prizes. In other leagues, clubs such as Juventus, Ajax, and Celtic have also drawn big new crowds to their new grounds. There is such a close link between building a nice stadium and drawing more spectators that the traditional fans' chant of "Where were you when you were shit?" should be revised to "Where were you when your stadium was shit?"

Yet like almost all good business ideas in soccer, the Taylor Report was imposed on the game from outside. Soccer clubs are classic late adopters of new ideas. Several years after the Internet emerged, Liverpool, a club with millions of fans around the world, still did not have a website. It's no wonder that from 1992 through May 2008, even before the financial crisis struck, forty of England's ninety-two professional clubs had been involved in insolvency proceedings, some of them more than once. The proportions have been even higher in Spanish soccer in recent years.

HOW THE TRIBE CHOOSES ITS CHIEFS

Rather than stack up endless examples of the dimness of soccer clubs, let's take one contemporary case study: how clubs hire the person they believe to be their key employee, the manager. English fans are still asking themselves how Steve McClaren ever got to be appointed England manager in 2006, but in fact it is unfair to single him out. The profusion of fantasy soccer leagues, in which office workers masquerade as coaches, indicates the widely held suspicion that any fool could do as well as the people who actually get the jobs. The incompetence of soccer managers may have something to do with the nonsensical and illegal methods by which they are typically recruited.

Soccer "is a sad business," says Bjørn Johansson, who runs a headhunting firm in Zurich. Like his colleagues in headhunting, Johansson is never consulted by clubs seeking managers. Instead a club typically chooses its man based on the following factors.

The New Manager Is Hired in a Mad Rush

In a panel at the International Football Arena conference in Zurich in 2006, Johansson said that in "normal" business, "an average search process takes four to five months." In soccer, a club usually finds a coach within a couple of days of sacking his predecessor. "Hesitation is regarded as weak leadership," explained another panelist in Zurich, Ilja Kaenzig, then general manager of the German club Hannover 96. Brian Barwick, the English Football Association's former chief executive, has noted that McClaren's recruitment "took from beginning to end nine weeks," yet the media accused the FA of being "sluggish." If only it had been more sluggish.

A rare slow hire in soccer became perhaps the most inspired choice of the past two decades: Arsenal's appointment of Arsène Wenger in 1996. Wenger, working in Japan, was not free immediately. Arsenal waited for him, operating under caretaker managers for weeks, and was inevitably accused of being sluggish. Similarly, in 1990 Manchester United's chairman, Martin Edwards, was derided as sluggish when he refused to sack his losing manager, Alex Ferguson. Edwards thought that in the long term, Ferguson might improve.

The New Manager Is Interviewed Only Very Cursorily

In "normal" business, a wannabe chief executive writes a business plan, gives a presentation, and undergoes several interviews. In soccer, a club calls an agent's cell phone and offers the job.

The New Manager Is Always a Man

The entire industry discriminates illegally against women. The new manager is also almost always white, with a conservative haircut, aged between thirty-five and sixty, and a former professional player. Clubs know that if they choose someone with that profile, then even if the appointment turns out to be terrible they won't be blamed too much, because at least they will have failed in the traditional way. As the old business saying went, "Nobody ever got fired for buying IBM."

The idea is that there is something mystical about managing a team, something that only former players can truly understand. Naturally, former players like this idea. Once in the 1980s, when Kenny Dalglish was in his first spell managing Liverpool, a journalist at a press conference questioned one of his tactical decisions. Dalglish deadpanned, in his almost impenetrable Scots accent, "Who did you play for, then?" The whole room laughed. Dalglish had come up with the killer retort: if you didn't play, you couldn't know.

A former chairman of a Premier League club told us that the managers he employed would often make that argument. The chairman (a rich businessman who hadn't played) never knew how to respond. He hadn't played, so if there really was some kind of mystical knowledge you gained from playing, he wouldn't know. Usually he would back down.

"Who did you play for, then?" is best understood as a job protection scheme. Ex-players have used it to corner the market in managerial jobs.

But in truth, their argument never made sense. There is no evidence that having been a good player (or being white and of conservative appearance) is an advantage for a soccer manager. Way back in 1995 Stefan Szymanski did a study of 209 managers in English football from 1974 to 1994, looking at which ones consistently finished higher in the league than their teams' wage bills predicted. He reported:

> I looked at each manager's football career, first as a player (including number of games played, goals scored, position on the field, international appearances, number of clubs played for) and then as a manager (years of experience, number of clubs played for, and age while in management). Playing history provides almost no guide, except that defenders and goalkeepers in particular do not do well (most managers were midfielders, forwards are slightly more successful than average).

Dalglish finished at the top of Stefan's sample of 209 managers, just ahead of John Duncan, Bob Paisley, George Curtis, Ken Furphy, and Bill Shankly. (Clough wasn't in the sample because no good financial data existed for his clubs, Derby County and Nottingham Forest, or else he'd have surely won. Stefan recently updated his study, and we'll say more about his new findings in Chapter 6.)

Dalglish was a great player and an overperforming manager. However, Bobby Moore, another great player, was 193rd on the managers' list. Taken overall, a good career as a player predicted neither success nor failure as a manager. The two jobs just didn't seem to have much to do with each other. As Arrigo Sacchi, a terrible player turned great manager of Milan, phrased it, "You don't need to have been a horse to be a jockey."

A horse's knowledge doesn't help a jockey. Here is one player-turned-manager testifying anonymously in *Football Management,* an insightful book by Sue Bridgewater of Warwick Business School:

> I got the job and on the first day I showed up and the secretary let me into my office, the manager's office with a phone in and I didn't know where I was supposed to start. I knew about football, I could do the on-pitch things, but I had never worked in an office and I just sat there and I waited for something to happen but no one came in so after a while I picked up the phone and rang my Mum.

Even this man's claim that "I knew about football, I could do the on-pitch things" is dubious. Does Diego Maradona know more about the game than Jose Mourinho? Did Roy Keane's knack for geeing up teammates on the field translate once he had become a jockey?

Playing and coaching are different skill sets. Mourinho, who barely ever kicked a ball for money, is match for match among the most successful coaches in soccer's history. When Milan's then coach Carlo Ancelotti noted his almost nonexistent record as a player, the Portuguese replied, "I don't see the connection. My dentist is the best in the world, and yet he's never had a particularly bad toothache." Asked why failed players often become good coaches, Mourinho said, "More time to study."

The problem with ex-pros may be precisely their experience. Having been steeped in the game for decades, they just know what to do: how to train, who to buy, how to talk to their players. They don't need to investigate whether these inherited prejudices are in fact correct. Rare is the ex-pro who realizes, like Billy Beane at the Oakland A's, that he needs to jettison what he learned along the way. Michael Lewis writes in *Moneyball,* "Billy had played pro ball, and regarded it as an experience he needed to overcome if he wanted to do his job well. 'A reformed alcoholic,' is how he described himself." Even Ancelotti seems to have changed his mind about the usefulness of a playing career. Once a canny midfielder with Milan, and now coach of Real Madrid, he told us in 2013: "Experience as a player can help you just in one situation: I can understand what the players are thinking. But the job is different. You have to study to be a manager."

There are some recent signs that ex-players are losing their monopoly on managerial jobs. By early 2014, three men who never played professionally were managing Premier League clubs: Mourinho at Chelsea, Brendan Rodgers at Liverpool, and Rene Meulensteen at Fulham. The Premier League's historical average is just one nonplaying manager out of twenty. Moreover, Roy Hodgson—whose career peaked in Crystal Palace's youth team—was the England manager. Meanwhile, former great players like Roy Keane, Ruud Gullit, Marco van Basten, Paul Ince, Tony Adams, and Diego Maradona no longer seem to be in demand as managers of serious clubs. This looks like another indication that soccer is slowly becoming less stupid.

Managers Don't Need Professional Qualifications

Only in 2003 did UEFA insist that new managers in the Premier League pass the Pro Licence course. In England's lower divisions this remains unnecessary. Yet Sue Bridgewater showed that managers with the Pro Licence won significantly more matches than managers without it. She also showed that experienced managers outperformed novices. That qualifications and experience are useful is understood in every industry except soccer, where a manager is expected to work the magic he acquired as a superhero player.

The New Manager Is Often Underqualified Even If He Has Qualifications

Chris Brady, a business school professor, has taught finance and accounting in the Pro Licence course. He told us his entire module took half a day. No wonder some English managers mismanage money: they don't understand it. Clubs are ceasing to entrust their finances to managers, giving them instead to more qualified executives like Kaenzig, who guarantee stability by staying longer than the club manager's average two-year tenure. That at least is the theory: the week after that conference in Zurich, Hannover released Kaenzig.

Immediate Availability

The new manager is appointed either because he is able to start work immediately (often as a result of having just been sacked), or because he has achieved good results over his career, or, failing that, because he achieved good results in the weeks preceding the appointment. McClaren became England manager only because his team, Middlesbrough, reached the UEFA Cup final in 2006 and avoided relegation just as the English Football Association was deciding who to pick. By the time Middlesbrough was waxed 4–0 by Sevilla in the final, McClaren already had the job.

His period under review was so short as to be a random walk. The same went for the main candidates to manage England in 1996: Bryan Robson, Frank Clark, Gerry Francis, and the eventual choice, Glenn Hoddle. Today none of them works as a manager, none had his last job in the Premier League, and none will probably work that high again. They were in the frame in 1996 because they had had good results recently, had been good players, and were English—another illegal consideration in hiring.

Star Power

The new manager is generally chosen not for his alleged managerial skills but because his name, appearance, and skills at public relations are expected to impress the club's fans, its players, and the media. That is why no club hires a woman—stupid fans and players would object—and why it was so brave of Milan to appoint the unknown Sacchi, and Arsenal the unknown Wenger. Tony Adams, Arsenal's then captain, doubted the obscure foreigner on first sight. In his autobiography, *Addicted*, the player recalls thinking, "What does this Frenchman know about soccer? He wears glasses and looks more like a schoolteacher. He's not going to be as good as George. Does he even speak English properly?"

A manager must above all look like a manager. Clubs would rather use traditional methods to appoint incompetents than risk doing anything that looks odd.

BAD STAFF

The most obvious reason soccer is such an incompetent business is that soccer clubs have historically tended to hire incompetent staff. The manager is only the start of it. Years ago one of us requested an interview with the chairman of an English club quoted on the stock market. The press officer asked me to send a fax (a 1980s technology revered by soccer clubs). I sent it. She said she never got it. On request I sent three more faxes to different officials. She said none arrived. This is quite a common experience for soccer journalists. Because soccer clubs are the only businesses that get daily publicity without trying to, they treat journalists as humble supplicants instead of as unpaid marketers of the clubs' brands. The media often retaliate by being mean. This is not very clever of the clubs, because almost all their fans follow them through the media rather than by going to the stadiums.

A month after all the faxes, I was granted permission to send my request by e-mail. When I arrived at the club for the interview, I met the press officer. She was beautiful. Of course she was. Traditionally, soccer clubs recruit the women on their office staff for their looks, and the men because they played professional soccer or are somebody's friend.

If soccer clubs wanted to, they could recruit excellent executives. Professors at business schools report that many of their MBA students, who pay on average about $40,000 a year in tuition fees, dream of working in soccer for a pitiful salary. Often the students beg clubs to let them work for free as summer interns. The clubs seldom want them (though here again, as the soccer business gradually gets smarter, more MBAs are creeping in). If you work for a soccer club, your goal is generally to keep working there, not to be shown up by some overeducated young thing who has actually learned something about business.

In part this is because much of the traditionally working-class soccer industry distrusts education. In part, says Emmanuel Hembert of A. T. Kearney, it is because many clubs are dominated by a vain owner-manager: "Lots of them invested for ego reasons, which is never a good thing in business. They prefer not to have strong people around them, except the coach. They really pay low salaries." If you work for a soccer club as anything but a player or manager, you get paid in stardust.

Historically, only Manchester United recruited respected executives from normal industries (such as Peter Kenyon from Umbro), though now a few other big clubs like Barcelona have started to do so, too.

Baseball for a long time was just as incompetent. In *Moneyball* Lewis asked why, among baseball executives and scouts, "there really is no level of incompetence that won't be tolerated." He thought the main reason was "that baseball has structured itself less as a business than as a social club. . . . There are many ways to embarrass the Club, but being bad at your job isn't one of them. The greatest offense a Club member can commit is not ineptitude but disloyalty." Club members—and this applies in soccer as much as in baseball—are selected for clubbability. Clever outsiders are not clubbable, because they talk funny, and go around pointing out the things that people inside the Club are doing wrong. "It wasn't as simple as the unease of jocks in the presence of nerds," wrote Lewis—but that unease does have a lot to do with it.

The staff of soccer clubs tends not merely to be incompetent. They are also often novices. This is because staff turnover is rapid. Whenever a new owner arrives, he generally brings in his cronies. The departing staff rarely joins a new club, because that is considered disloyal (Kenyon, an exception, was persecuted for moving from United to Chelsea), even though players change clubs all the time. So soccer executives are always having to reinvent the wheel.

Worse, the media and fans often make it impossible for clubs to take sensible decisions. They are always hassling the club to do something immediately. If the team loses three games, fans start chanting for the club to sack the coach or buy a new player, in short tear up the plans it might have made a month ago. Tony Fernandes, the Malaysian businessman who had run a tight ship at his airline AirAsia, couldn't do the same after taking over QPR in 2011. "Two things are different from AirAsia," he told us in 2013. "One is I can control almost everything in AirAsia. You can do whatever you want in football, but it's up to the eleven guys on the pitch at the end of the day, right? The second thing is, you have a very vocal bunch of shareholders—called fans. Everyone has an opinion. The plans get thrown out of the window when you start losing. The excitement you get when you win a football game is unbelievable. The downside is that when you lose you want to kill yourself."

"Consumer activism in this industry is extreme," agreed A. T. Kearney in its report *Playing for Profits.* Hembert says, "The business plan—as soon as you sign a player for £10 million, you blow up your business plan. Commercial employees have to fight for £100,000 of spending here or there, but then suddenly the club spends £10 million."

Or more. Sven Goran Eriksson once flew into Zurich to tell the International Football Arena a "good story" about his time managing Lazio. "The chairman I had was very good," Eriksson recalled for an audience of mostly Swiss businessmen. "If I wanted a player, he would try to get that player. One day I phoned him up and I said: 'Vieri.'"

Christian Vieri was then playing for Atletico Madrid. Eriksson and Lazio's chairman, Sergio Cragnotti, flew to Spain to bid for him. Atletico told them Vieri would cost 50 billion Italian lire. At the time, in 1998, that was nearly $29 million. Eriksson reminisced, "That was the biggest sum in the world. No player had been involved for that." He said the talks then went more or less as follows:

CRAGNOTTI: That's a lot of money.
ERIKSSON: I know.

At this point Atletico mentioned that it might accept some Lazio players in partial payment for Vieri.

CRAGNOTTI: Can we do that?
ERIKSSON: No, we can't give away these players.
CRAGNOTTI: What shall we do then?
ERIKSSON: Buy him.
CRAGNOTTI: Okay.

Eriksson recalled in Zurich: "He didn't even try to pay 49. He just paid 50."

Nine months after Vieri joined Lazio, Inter Milan wanted to buy him. Once again, Eriksson reported the conversation:

CRAGNOTTI: What shall I ask for him?
ERIKSSON: Ask for double. Ask 100.
CRAGNOTTI: I can't do that.

Eriksson recalled: "So he asked 90. And he got 90. That's good business." (Or the ultimate example of the greater-fool principle.)

Someone in the audience in Zurich asked Eriksson whether such behavior was healthy. After all, Lazio ran out of money in 2002 when Cragnotti's food company, Cirio, went belly-up. Cragnotti later spent time in prison, which even by the standards of Italian soccer is going a bit far.

Eriksson replied, "It's not healthy. And if you see Lazio, it was not healthy. But we won the league. And we won the Cupwinners Cup. We won everything."

The point is that soccer clubs, prompted by media and fans, are always making financially irrational decisions in an instant. They would like to think long term, but because they are in the news every day they end up fixating on the short term. As the British writer Arthur Hopcraft wrote in his book *The Football Man* in 1968, "It is the first characteristic of football that it is always urgent." An executive with an American entertainment corporation tells a story about his long-arranged business meeting with Real Madrid. His company was hoping to build a relationship with the club. But on the day of the meeting, Madrid ritually sacked its manager. The usual chaos ensued. Two of the club officials scheduled to attend the meeting with the American executive did not show up. That's soccer.

NOT BUSINESSES AT ALL

When businesspeople look at soccer, they are often astonished at how unbusinesslike the clubs are. Every now and then one of them takes over a club and promises to run it "like a business." Alan Sugar, who made his money in computers, became chairman of Tottenham Hotspur in 1991. His brilliant wheeze was to make Spurs live within its means. Never would he fork out 50 billion lire for a Vieri. After Newcastle bought Alan Shearer for $23 million in 1996, Sugar remarked, "I've slapped myself around the face a couple of times, but I still can't believe it."

He more or less kept his word. In the ten years that he ran Spurs, the team lived within its means. But most of the fans hated it. The only thing Spurs won in that decade was a solitary League Cup. It spent most of its

FIGURE 3.1. Pretax profit/loss of Premier League clubs by league position: 1993–2012

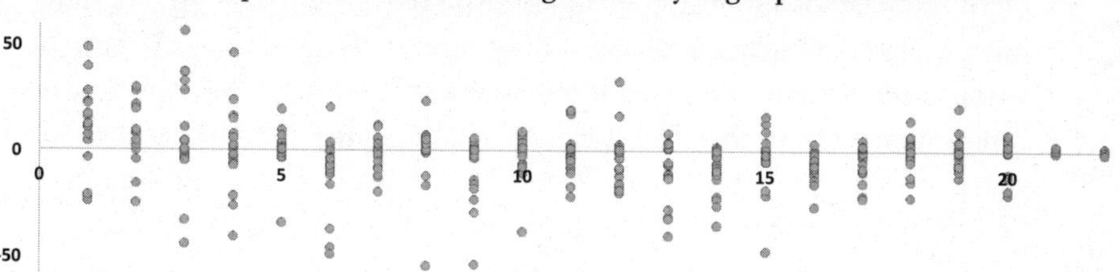

time in midtable of the Premier League, falling far behind its neighbor Arsenal. Nor did it even make much money: about $3 million a year in profits in Sugar's first six years, which was much less than Arsenal and not very good for a company its size. Sugar's Spurs disappointed both on and off the field, and its experience also illustrated a paradox: when businesspeople try to run a soccer club as a business, then not only does the soccer suffer, but so does the business.

Other businessmen pursue a different strategy than Sugar's. They assume that if they can get their clubs to win prizes, profits will inevitably follow. But they too are wrong. Even the best teams seldom generate profits. We plotted the league positions and profits of all the clubs that have played in the Premier League from its inaugural season of 1992–1993 until the 2011–2012 season in Figure 3.1.

The figure shows how spectacularly unprofitable the soccer business is. Each point on the chart represents the combination of profit and position for a club in a particular year. One obvious point to note is that most of the dots fall below zero on the profit axis: these clubs were making losses. But the figure also shows that there was barely any connection between finishing high and making money. Although there is some suggestion that a few clubs at the top of the table make more money than other clubs, the chart also shows that other clubs in these positions can make huge losses. Manchester United's profitability is clearly the exception. In thc thirty years before being taken over by the Glazer family in 2005, the club generated more than £250 million (about $400 million) in pretax profits while also winning eight league titles. Indeed, other American owners might never have bothered buying into English soccer without United's example. But no other club could replicate its success.

For most English clubs, our graph shows that there is not even a connection between changing league position and changing profits. In 45 percent of all cases, when a club changed its league position, its profits moved in the opposite direction: higher position, lower profits or lower position, higher profits. Only 55 percent of the time did profits and position move in the same direction. Had there been no correlation at all between winning and making profits, that figure would have been much the same, namely, 50 percent. Clearly, winning games is not the route to making money. As Francisco Pérez Cutiño notes in an unpublished MBA thesis at Judge Business School in Cambridge, it's not that winning matches can help a club make profits. Rather, the effect works the other way around: if a club finds new revenues, that can help it win matches.

It has in fact proved almost impossible to run a soccer club like a solid, profit-making business. This is because there are always rival owners—the Cragnottis, the Abramoviches, or the Gadhafis, who owned a chunk of Juventus—who don't care about profits and will spend whatever it takes in the hope of winning prizes. All other club owners are forced to keep up with them. If one owner won't pay large transfer fees and salaries, somebody else will, and that somebody else will get the best players and win prizes. The consequence is that the biggest slice of money that soccer makes gets handed over to the best players. As A. T. Kearney says, you could even argue that soccer clubs are nothing more than vessels for transporting soccer's income to players. "The players are completely free to move," explains Hembert. "They are a key factor in winning, and also in the ego, in pleasing the fans. And they all have pretty savvy agents who are able to maximize their bargaining power."

It means that even the cautious Sugar type cannot make decent profits in soccer. In fact, because his team will win fewer matches than its free-spending rivals, some fans will desert him. That will eat further into his profits. From 1991 to 1998 average attendance in the Premier League rose 29 percent, but Tottenham's crowds fell 5 percent.

"I thought we could make it [QPR] profitable, definitely," Fernandes admitted to us. "I haven't yet," he added, laughing. Even in the 2011–2012 season, when the club survived in the Premier League, it lost £22.6 million. The next season, when it kept buying players but got relegated regardless, it lost a lot more. "On the pitch it was just a disaster," said Fernandes. He mused: "Football has survived on benefactors. Shareholders coming in and pumping money in, and then the next sucker comes in and pumps money in." Did he consider himself a sucker, a benefactor, or a businessman in soccer? "Now I would define myself as a sucker," he replied. "And benefactor. And I hope I will become a benefactor-stroke-businessman."

Good luck to him. So far in soccer's history, running a club as a profit-making business has looked like a lost cause. Stefan and the Spanish economist Pedro Garcia del Barrio (of the Universidad Internacional de Cataluña) were curious to know whether anyone even aspired to do it. They studied the behavior of Spanish and English clubs between 1993 and 2005 to see whether the clubs were chiefly pursuing profits off the field or victories on it.

If a club wanted to make profits, clearly it would have to spend less than it earned. That would mean limiting its players' wages. Any club that paid players less would suffer on the field, because as we have seen, paying high wages wins soccer matches. It's a trade-off: if you want glory, you have to forget maximizing profits. If you want maximum profits, give up hope of glory. Stefan and Pedro estimated, for instance, that if Barcelona wanted to maximize profits, it would have to aim to finish fifteenth in the league, because it would need to slash its wages. A profit-driven Real Madrid should expect to finish a mere seventeenth, just above the relegation spots. Most other teams—such as Atletico Madrid, Athletic Bilbao, Sevilla, or Villareal—would maximize their profit potential by playing in the second division. There they could save a lot of money on players' wages.

On the other hand, if a club's main aim was to win matches, it would have to spend every cent it earned (and borrow more besides). So what were clubs chasing, profits or wins?

Stefan and Pedro estimated how each club in the top two Spanish divisions would have behaved on average in the 1994–2005 period if it were pursuing profits, and how it would have behaved if it wanted wins. Then they looked at how clubs behaved in real life. Their unambiguous finding: clubs didn't care about profits. They were spending what it took to win games. "On average," Stefan and Pedro concluded, looking at ten years of league tables, "the Spanish teams were twelve places above their profit-maximizing position over the sample period, but less than half a place below their win-maximizing position." In short, club presidents were spending way more than they would have done if they were hardheaded businessmen out to make profits. Though many of the presidents were in fact hardheaded businessmen in real life, they weren't treating their soccer clubs as businesses. Nor was there any sign that any other actors—lending banks, say—were pressuring them to make profits.

Building magnates like Florentino Pérez and Jesús Gil y Gil seemed especially prone to blowing what looked like absurd sums of money on players. Possibly they were pursuing a business logic after all: they may have reasoned that making a name in local soccer would help them befriend bankers and get planning permission from local government for their construction projects. That would have boosted their non-soccer businesses. Fred Wilpon, the real estate developer who took over the New York Mets, discovered that a similar effect operated in baseball. Jeffrey Toobin wrote in a profile of Wilpon in the *New Yorker* magazine:

> He didn't anticipate that owning the Mets would boost his seemingly unrelated business interests. "No one had heard of us before we bought the Mets, and afterward the change was dramatic," Wilpon told me. "I don't think someone has not returned one of my telephone calls in thirty years. It's a small club, owning a baseball team, and people want to be near it."

Owning a soccer team might help the owner's other businesses. But all Spanish soccer clubs tended to pursue wins rather than profits. In a sense, they had to. If your rivals are spending whatever it takes to win, then you must as well. Any team that pursued the highest possible profits would probably end up being relegated, because it wouldn't be spending enough to hire good players. And if the club got relegated, it would lose much of its revenues. So soccer becomes an arms race: every club overspends for fear of the neighbors.

No matter how much money Spanish clubs got their hands on, they spent it. In the decade that Stefan and Pedro studied, the average revenues of a club in the Spanish first division (Primera División) rose nearly fourteenfold, from €4.3 million in 1994 to €59 million in 2004. (By 2011 the figure was €85 million.) Yet the share of revenue that clubs spent on player wages didn't drop much throughout the period: in that decade, first-division clubs paid over an average of 62 percent of their revenues to their players. In other words, the clubs weren't able to save all the additional money or do much else with it, such as build new stadiums or cut ticket prices. Most of the money that came in just went straight out again into players' bank accounts. In the second division, a whopping 93 percent of clubs' revenues went to the players. These clubs really were just vessels for transporting money to players.

The clubs weren't content with giving the players what money they had. They also gave them money they didn't have. According to the Spanish economists Angel Barajas Alonso and Plácido Rodriguez Guerrero, in the 2007–2008 season clubs including Real Murcia, Real Zaragoza, Real Betis, Valencia, La Coruña, and Atletico Madrid were spending more than their entire annual operating revenues on players. The consequences of this sort of arms race, pursued over many years, are predictable. Professor José Maria Gay de Liébana of the University of Barcelona compiled this authoritative list of the debts of clubs in the Primera División at the end of the 2009–2010 season:

Club	*Total Debt in Millions of Euros*
FC Barcelona	548.6
Real Madrid	659.9
Valencia	470.6
Sevilla FC	112.3
RCD Mallorca	85.2
Getafe	51.9
Villareal	267.4
Athletic Bilbao	51.2
Atletico Madrid	452.0
Deportivo La Coruña	107.0
Espanyol	173.7
Osasuna	59.2
Almería	27.3
Real Zaragoza	142.2
Sporting Gijón	28.8
Racing CS	74.8
Málaga	37.5
Real Valladolid	48.5
Tenerife	31.0
Xerez CD	0.0

All this added up to a total debt of €3.43 billion, or about $4.7 billion. It must be said that this figure includes a lot of unpaid interclub debt, which therefore inflates the data. Still, it's an astonishing figure. Clearly Atletico Madrid and Valencia, in particular, are never going to repay their creditors. In effect, banks and local governments and therefore the poor Spanish treasury (and possibly European taxpayers too) are subsidizing these clubs. Ordinary citizens are paying for the center forward's Ferrari.

By the standards of a normal business, this sort of debt spending is nuts. But for soccer clubs, it makes sense: the only way to win matches is to overspend. Nobody runs a soccer club to turn a tidy annual profit.

Nor, it might be argued, should anyone attempt it. Most of a club's customers (its fans) and employees (its players and coaches) and even usually its owners would say that the club exists to play good soccer and win things, not to turn a profit. That's why a 1974 report by the British Commission on Industrial Relations quoted an anonymous club chairman as saying, "Any club management which allows the club to make a profit is behaving foolishly." Traditionally soccer clubs have behaved more like charitable trusts than like businesses. In the not-so-distant past the English Football Association used to forbid club owners from profiting from their investment. Directors couldn't get paid, and dividends were capped. The aim was to ensure that clubs were run by "the right class of men who love football for its own sake." These rules were abolished in the early 1980s. If they still existed, they might have stopped the businessmen Tom Hicks and George Gillett at Liverpool and the Glazer family at Manchester United from burdening these clubs with a combined $1.5 billion in debt simply to finance their takeovers.

Making profits deprives a club of money that it could spend on the team. The business of soccer is soccer. Almost all soccer clubs that are not Manchester United should ditch the fantasy of making a profit. But that doesn't mean they should continue to be badly run. The weight of money that now washes through soccer demands a more businesslike approach to managing cash. Bungs might have been no big deal when transfer fees were measured in the hundreds of thousands of dollars, but they become a problem when they run into the tens of millions.

Soccer clubs need to know what they are. They shouldn't kid themselves that they are United Natural Foods. Rather, they are like museums: public-spirited organizations that aim to serve the community while remaining reasonably solvent. It sounds like a modest goal, but few of them achieve even that.

4

SAFER THAN THE BANK OF ENGLAND

Why Soccer Clubs Almost Never Disappear

On September 15, 2008, the investment bank Lehman Brothers collapsed, followed almost immediately by the world's stock markets.

Any soccer club on earth was a midget next to Lehman. In the fiscal year ending in September 2007, the bank had income of $59 billion (148 times Manchester United's at the time) and profits of $6 billion (fifty times Manchester United's), and was valued by the stock market at $34 billion. If United's shares had been traded on the market at the time, they probably would have been worth less than 5 percent of Lehman's. Yet Lehman no longer exists, while United very much does.

In the years before the global economic crisis, people worried a lot more about the survival of soccer clubs than that of banks. Yet it was many of the world's largest banks that disappeared. Then, after the recession began, worries about soccer clubs increased again. Many people pointed out that when Chelsea met Manchester United in the final of the Champions League in 2008, the two clubs had a combined debt of about $3 billion. Michel Platini, president of UEFA, warned in 2009 that half of Europe's professional clubs had financial troubles of some kind. "If this situation goes on," he added, "it will not be long before even some major clubs face going out of business."

Yet the notion that soccer clubs are inherently unstable businesses is wrong. They virtually never go bust. Despite being incompetently run, they are some of the most stable businesses on earth. Not only do the soccer authorities worry far too much about clubs going out of business, but they worry about the wrong clubs.

First, some facts. In 1923 the English Football League consisted of eighty-eight teams spread over four divisions. In the 2011–2012 season, eighty-five of these clubs still existed (97 percent),* and eighty remained in the top four divisions (91 percent). Forty were in the same division as they had been in 1923. And only six teams still in the top four divisions were two or more divisions away from where they had been in 1923. (No team that was in the First Division in 1923 was placed lower than the third tier in 2012.) It is a history of remarkable stability.

You would have expected the Great Depression of the 1930s, in particular, to pose the clubs something of a threat. After all, the Depression bit deepest in the North of England, where most of the country's professional clubs were based, and all romantic rhetoric aside, you would think that when people cannot afford to buy bread they would stop going to soccer matches.

Crowds in the Football League did indeed fall 12 percent between 1929 and 1931. However, by 1932 they were growing again, even though the British economy was not. And clubs helped one another through the hard times. When Orient in east London hit trouble in 1931, Arsenal wrote its tiny neighbor a check for £3,450 to tide it over. Clubs know they cannot operate without opponents, and so unlike in most businesses, the collapse of a rival is not cause for celebration.

The Depression culled only a couple of clubs. Merthyr Town, after failing to be reelected to the league in 1930, folded a few years later, the victim of economic hardship in the Welsh valleys (as well as competition from far more popular rugby). Wigan Borough went bankrupt a few games into the 1931–1932 season. It left the league, and its remaining fixtures were never played. Aldershot was elected to replace it, and sixty

* The three lost clubs are Aberdare (disbanded 1928), New Brighton (which folded in 1983, was reborn, then folded again in 2012), and South Shields (taken over by Gateshead in 1930). Several other clubs have folded and been reborn, such as Accrington Stanley, Bradford Park Avenue, Durham City, Halifax Town, Merthyr Town, Nelson, and Newport County.

years later, in another recession, it became only the second English club in history to withdraw from the league with fixtures unplayed.

Almost equally hard as the Depression for English clubs was the "Thatcher recession" of the early 1980s. Again many working-class fans lost their factory jobs. The league's attendance dropped from 24.6 million to 16.5 million between 1980 and 1986. Soccer seemed to be in terminal decline. As Ken Friar, then managing director of Arsenal, put it, "Football is the oddest of industries. It sells one product and has ninety-two outlets for it. In any other business, if not all ninety-two outlets were doing well, there would be some talk of closing some of them down. But in football, all ninety-two outlets claim an equal right to survive."

Many clubs in the early 1980s seemed to be dicing with death. Looking at one of the diciest, Bristol City, will help us understand just how soccer clubs almost always survive.

Bristol City is one of two professional teams that share the midsize town of Bristol in western England. City got into trouble in the same way a lot of clubs do. In 1976 it had been promoted to the old first division, then the highest tier in English soccer, a status the club had last enjoyed before World War I. The fans were excited: attendance jumped from 14,000 per game in 1974–1975 to 24,500 in 1976–1977. The average ticket then cost less than £1, but the higher ticket sales still boosted the club's income from around £250,000 per year to £665,000. City survived three seasons in the top flight. As we've already seen, that took money. The club paid handsomely in the transfer market, and its wage bill doubled: all City's extra income was channeled straight to players.

Sadly, the money didn't do the trick. In the 1979–1980 season, the club was relegated just as Britain, in the first year of the new Thatcher government, was entering recession. First-division attendances dropped 5 percent that season, but Bristol City's gates fell 15 percent while its wage costs rose 20 percent.

Clearly the club needed to lose some of its expensive players. Unfortunately, the manager, Alan Dicks, who had just overseen the most successful period in Bristol City's modern history, had signed many of them on extraordinarily lengthy contracts—some as long as eleven years. Soon after relegation, Dicks was sacked. But by the end of the next season, 1980–1981, City's average attendance had collapsed to 9,700 per game (half the level of the previous season) and the club was relegated to the third division. Income was tumbling, yet most of the squad was still drawing first-division wages. When City's accounts were published on October 15, 1981, it was apparent that the club was in deep trouble, but the best the club's new chairman could say in his report was that "so much of this depends on success on the playing field."

It is doubtful that promotion back to the second division would have improved the club's financial position materially in 1981–1982, but that's a purely academic question, since by the end of 1981 Bristol City was heading for the fourth division. By then only 6,500 fans were showing up each week, about a quarter the number from four years earlier. An independent financial report produced that December showed that the club owed far more (over £1 million) than it could realistically repay in the foreseeable future. Early in 1982 Bristol City Football Club PLC—the limited company that owned the stadium at Ashton Gate, the players' contracts, and a share in the Football League—was on the verge of appointing a trustee to liquidate the company. That would have meant the end. In a liquidation all the players' contracts would have been void, the share in the league would have been returned to the league, and the stadium would have been sold, probably to a property developer, with any proceeds used to pay creditors. Like so many British companies at the time, Bristol City seemed headed for extinction.

But soccer clubs command more love than widget makers. Just before Bristol City could fold, Deryn Coller and some other local businessmen who were also fans offered to take over the club. It was at this point that the "phoenixing" plan emerged.

Coller and his associates created a new company, BCFC (1982) PLC, which was to be a new Bristol City: a phoenix from the ashes of the old club. The Coller group aimed to sell shares in the new company to fans. With the money, the group would buy Ashton Gate from the trustee. The group also asked the Football League to acquire the old club's share in the league. Then the new Bristol City could "replace" the old one in the fourth division. In short, the new company would take over almost everything of the old club—except, crucially, its debts and unaffordable players. Coller's group intended to ask City's most expensive players, left over from the club's first-division days, to tear up their contracts. You can see the appeal of the plan, as long as you were not one of those players.

The Football League said the plan was fine as long as Gordon Taylor, head of the Professional Football Association (PFA), would agree to the deal on the players. Taylor was by no means sure that things were as bad at Bristol City as the directors said (after all, directors are always complaining about wages), but eventually he was convinced that the deal was the only way to save the club. No union wants to see an employer go bust, especially not an ancient employer loved by thousands of people.

The final decision was down to the players. Naturally they were reluctant martyrs. But the pressure on them was intense, including some threats from fans. In the end, after a few sweeteners were thrown in, the players agreed. Peter Aitken, Chris Garland, Jimmy Mann, Julian Marshall, Geoff Merrick, David Rodgers, Gerry Sweeney, and Trevor Tainton are not the biggest names in soccer's history, but few players can claim to have given more for their clubs. On February 3, 1982, the "Ashton Gate Eight" agreed to tear up contracts worth £290,000 (the better part of $1.5 million in today's money) and accept redundancy to save their employer. By the standards of the time, they were on very good pay. Most of them, nearing the end of their careers, would never earn as much again. They got a miserly payoff of two weeks' wages, and afterward they retired from soccer, moved abroad, or joined lower-division clubs. The eight really deserve statues outside Ashton Gate. They gave Bristol City a future.

The phoenix rose from the ashes: the club was transferred as an entity from the ownership of Bristol City PLC, a company heading for liquidation, to BCFC (1982) PLC. The directors of the new business still faced the formidable task of finding the money to buy Ashton Gate. They had negotiated a price with the trustee of just over £590,000. They raised £330,000 by selling shares in the new club to fans and well-wishers. They might have raised more, but they felt obliged to close the share offer early when rumors emerged that an unknown bidder was considering buying a majority of the shares on offer, possibly with the aim of selling off the ground to property developers. (Ashton Gate is handily located close to downtown.) The rest of the cash was raised from short-term loans.

Today Bristol City still plays at Ashton Gate, in League One, the third tier of the English game. (And Ashton Gate is now much more than a mere soccer stadium. "Ashton Gate Stadium, Bristol's premier conference and events venue, features a wide range of function rooms available for both corporate and private hire," proclaims its website, Ashtongatestadium.co.uk.) The "phoenixing" of Bristol City was the first of its kind in English soccer and established a template that, like the club itself, survives to this day.

Other clubs quickly cottoned onto the joy of phoenixing. Between 1982 and 1984 Hereford, Hull, Wolves, Derby, Bradford, and Charlton went through much the same experience as Bristol City. All these troubled clubs survived either by creating a new "phoenix" company (Wolves, Bradford, and Charlton) or by getting creditors to agree to suspend their claims (a moratorium), under the threat that a phoenix might be the alternative. In all cases, the bankrupt company was ditched, but the immortal club inside it salvaged.

Phoenixing—the creation of a new company—turned out to be a brilliant wheeze to escape creditors. Clearly there is something suspect about the method. Phoenixing allowed disastrous directors to escape the consequences of their decisions. Their clubs survived, but at the expense of creditors (often players, banks, and the taxman), who never saw their money again.

Still, this was just what hapless soccer clubs needed. Many of them struggled during the Thatcher recession, and several survived only thanks to a "sub"—financial support—from the PFA. Charlton and Bristol City's neighbor Bristol Rovers had to move grounds because they could not pay the rent. However, nobody resigned from the league.

Soon after that recession, a new law made it even easier for British clubs to survive. The UK's traditional method of liquidation—the bankrupt company's assets were sold, the debts repaid as far as possible, and the company liquidated—had become discredited. Critics said it gave stricken companies little chance to recover. They praised the American approach, which treated failure as a frequently necessary precursor to eventual success. In 1979 the US had introduced the now famous Chapter 11 provisions. These protect a firm from its creditors, while it tries to work out a solution that saves the business. Britain—where insolvencies hit an all-time high during the Thatcher recession—wanted some of that.

The British Insolvency Act of 1986 introduced a new procedure called "administration." Now when a company went into administration, an independent insolvency practitioner was called in, and charged with finding a way to keep the business running while repaying as much money as possible to the creditors. After the new law came in, stricken soccer clubs typically entered administration, struck deals with creditors, and then swiftly emerged from administration. That's what Tranmere and Rotherham did in spring 1987, for instance. For most clubs, financial collapse was becoming something of a breeze.

True, Aldershot FC was liquidated in 1992, but supporters simply started a new club almost identical to the old one. The "new" Aldershot Town AFC has a badge that shows a phoenix rising from the ashes. Aldershot reentered the Football League in 2008. Other tiny British clubs that folded—Maidstone United, Newport County, Accrington Stanley—also were eventually resuscitated and now stumble on somewhere in the semiprofessional or professional game. Accrington Stanley's rebirth was surely the most drawn-out: it resigned from the Football League in 1962 with debts of £63,000, got liquidated in 1966, was newly created by fans in 1968, and returned to the Football League in 2006, its brand still very much alive, probably even enhanced by the drama. "Above the turnstiles now, the welcoming sign is, 'The Club that Wouldn't Die,'" Accrington's then chairman, Ilyas Khan, told us proudly in 2012.

The new British law was so kind to insolvent companies that ever more companies decided to enter insolvency. Some did it just to wipe off their debts. The method became more popular even as the economy improved. Company insolvencies in the recession of the early 1980s had run at an average of around 10,000 per year. In the boom period between 1994 and 2001 they ran at 16,000 per year. Soccer clubs, too, loved the new law: more of them went insolvent in the 1990s boom than in the early 1980s bust. They rarely even needed to bother to create a new "phoenix" company anymore. Clubs would run up unpayable debts, go insolvent, and hey presto, months later would be fine and signing expensive players again. Better-run rivals complained that insolvency and phoenixing were giving the culprits an unfair advantage. In 2004 this argument prompted the league to introduce a ten-point penalty for clubs that went into administration. Still, it hasn't proved a huge deterrent.

There's something else to note about these near-death experiences: they almost always happen only to small clubs. There was a great kerfuffle in England in early 2010 when Portsmouth FC of the mighty Premier League entered administration. The club had been on much the same journey as Bristol City thirty years earlier, just with larger sums. It had overspent on good players, won an FA Cup, and ended up in trouble.

On the one hand, Portsmouth's story was all too familiar: soccer club goes bust and after many premature reports of its demise is reborn. The shared fan angst about their club disappearing has a useful psychological function: it's a communal ritual that gives supporters a chance to join together to affirm their love of the club. As we write, Portsmouth is bumping along in League Two, the bottom tier of English soccer. It has had a miserable few years, but like every other professional club in England, it's still around.

Yet in another way, Portsmouth's story was exceptional. No club in the Premier League had ever gone into administration before. The other sixty-six cases of insolvency in English soccer from 1982 through 2010 involved teams in the lower divisions. That is something that doomsayers like Platini should note. They often complain about the debts of rich clubs: the hundreds of millions of dollars owed by the likes of Real Madrid, Barcelona, and Manchester United. They ask how Chelsea would survive if Roman Abramovich falls under a bus.

In fact, though, big clubs are not the problem. Across Europe, lower-tier teams live on the edge of insolvency, while the top-tier teams, even though they too mostly lose money, seldom become insolvent. The highest risk of all is for recently relegated teams. We have been able to identify about a dozen European clubs that have disappeared since the start of the economic crisis in 2008: UD Salamanca, Lorca, and CD Badajoz in Spain; Haarlem, Veendam, AGOVV, and RBC Roosendaal in Holland; Beerschot in Belgium; Gretna in Scotland; Arsenal Kyiv in Ukraine; and Unirea Urziceni in Romania. There is not a single big name among them. Admittedly Unirea played in the Champions League in 2009–2010, but historically it was a tiny club from a small town. It owed its brief rise to a passing sugar daddy. When he lost interest, Unirea expired.

None of these clubs got into trouble by gambling tens of millions to compete with the big boys. Rather, they were tiny outfits (Badajoz in its 107 years of existence never once made it to Spain's top division) who had soldiered on gamely through the years. When the crisis hit, their relatively puny debts overwhelmed them. Haarlem, for instance, owed a fairly manageable $2.5 million. It's just that hardly anybody was interested enough to fight for the club's life. Anyway, several of the defunct clubs were immediately refounded in a slightly different form. Gretna 2008 now plays amateur soccer in Scotland, as do RBC and AGOVV in Holland. Salamanca actually has three successor clubs, each claiming the mantle.

Perhaps because English professional clubs are older established brands than most continental teams, even the littlest among them survived the crisis. But if Platini is determined to worry about clubs going bust, it's the Salamancas he should worry about, not the Real Madrids. And he probably shouldn't worry too much about the issue at all. If European soccer clubs really did collapse beneath their debts, there would now be virtually no European soccer clubs left. "We must be sustainable," clubs say nowadays, parroting the latest business cliché. In fact, they are fantastically sustainable. They survive even when they go bust. You can't get more sustainable than that. Match-fixing, say, is a much bigger problem for European soccer than bankruptcy. The near immortality of soccer clubs makes you wonder exactly what problem UEFA's rules on "financial fair play" are meant to solve.

Platini worries about clubs' debts. But it's precisely because clubs are practically immortal that they have such large debts. They know from experience that they can take on whatever debt they like, and survive. If things go wrong, they simply don't repay their debt, the old directors walk away, and new ones come in promising to sweep up the mess (while also buying shiny new Brazilian center forwards). A club like Bayern Munich, which shuns debt, is in fact missing a trick. Bayern could easily borrow a few hundred million dollars to make itself invincible against human opposition on the long term. Even if it flushed the money down the toilet and then said "Nanananana" to the lenders, the club would survive. Right now Bayern is a marvelous self-sustaining debt-free business, whereas most English clubs aren't. But the point of a soccer club isn't to have nice accounts—after all, the clubs with horrible accounts survive, too. The point of a soccer club is to win trophies. Bayern won the Champions League in 2013, but in the previous thirty-six years it had won the trophy only once. That's a meager return for the biggest club of Western Europe's biggest country.

Once again, the comparison between soccer clubs and "real" businesses breaks down. When clubs get into trouble, they generally "do a Leeds," a maneuver named in honor of the spectacularly badly run Leeds United of the early 2000s. "Doing a Leeds" means cutting your wages, getting relegated, and competing at a lower level. Imagine if other businesses could do this. Suppose that Ford could sack skilled workers and hire unskilled ones to produce worse cars, or that American Airlines could replace all its pilots with people who weren't as well qualified to fly planes. The government would stop it, and in any case, consumers would not put up with terrible products. (President Ronald Reagan did sack striking air-traffic controllers in 1981 and replaced them with new hires, but that was something of a one-off.)

Soccer clubs have it easy. Recall that almost every English professional club has survived the Great Depression, the Second World War, recessions, corrupt chairmen, appalling managers, and the current economic crisis. By contrast, economic historian Les Hannah made a list of the top one hundred global companies in 1912, and researched what had become of them by 1995. Nearly half the companies—forty-nine—had ceased to exist. Five of these had gone bankrupt, six were nationalized, and thirty-eight were taken over by other firms. Even among the businesses that survived, many had gone into new sectors or moved to new locations.

What made these non-soccer businesses so unstable was, above all, competition. There is such a thing as brand loyalty, but when a better product turns up, most people will switch sooner or later. So normal businesses keep having to innovate or die. They face endless pitfalls: competitors pull ahead, consumers' tastes change, new technologies make entire industries obsolete, cheap goods arrive from abroad, the government interferes, recessions hit, companies overinvest and go bust or simply get unlucky.

By contrast, soccer clubs are immune from almost all these effects: a club that fails to keep up with the competition might get relegated, but it can always survive at a lower level. Some fans lose interest, but clubs have geographical roots. A bad team might find its catchment area shrinking, but not disappearing completely. The "technology" of soccer can never become obsolete, because the technology is the game itself. At worst soccer might become less popular.

Foreign rivals cannot enter the market and supply soccer at a lower price. The rules of soccer protect domestic clubs by forbidding foreign competitors from joining their league. English clubs as a whole could fall behind foreign competitors and lose their best players, but foreign clubs have financial problems and incompetent management of their own.

The government is not about to nationalize soccer.

Clubs often overinvest, but this almost never destroys the club, only the wealth of the investor. At worst, the club gets relegated.

A club's revenues might decline in a recession, but it can always live with lower revenues.

In most industries a bad business goes bankrupt, but soccer clubs almost never do. No matter how much money they waste, someone will always bail them out. This is what is known in finance as "moral hazard": when you know you will be saved no matter how much money you lose, you are free to lose money.

There is a strange parallel here between professional soccer and communism. When we ask, "Why do soccer clubs almost always survive?" we are echoing the great question asked about communism by one of our favorite economists, the Hungarian János Kornai. He grew up in Hungary, briefly worked for a communist newspaper despite knowing that the system was all nonsense, and after making his way to the West tried to answer the question: Why *exactly* did communism not work?

Kornai's answer could be summed up in four words: "the soft-budget constraint." Imagine that you are a tractor factory in communist Hungary. Each year the state gives you a budget. But if at the end of the year you've overspent the budget and haven't made any profits, the state just gives you a bit more money to make up the difference. In communism, bad companies were propped up forever. In other words, the "budget constraint" on communist firms was soft. If they wanted to overspend their budgets, they could. The obvious consequence: unprofitable overspending became rife.

As scholars such as Wladimir Andreff and Rasmus Storm have noted, Kornai's "soft-budget constraint" applies beautifully to soccer clubs. Like tractor factories in communism, clubs lose money because they can. They have no need to be competent. The professional investors who briefly bought club shares in the 1990s got out as soon as they discovered this.

Luckily, as we've seen, society can keep unprofitable soccer clubs going fairly cheaply. The total revenues of European professional clubs for the 2011–2012 season were $24.6 billion, according to Deloitte. That's just one-fifth of the revenues of McKesson, the US pharmaceutical supply-chain company. The two-bit losses of soccer clubs hardly matter when set beside the enormous love they command. These tiny businesses are great enduring brands. Creditors dare not push them under. No bank manager or tax collector wants to say, "The century-old local club is closing. I'm turning off the lights." Society swallows the losses and lets even a Bristol City soldier on. In a sense, these clubs are too small to fail.

Unlike most businesses, soccer clubs survive crises because some of their customers stick with them no matter how lousy the product. Calling this brand loyalty is not quite respectful enough of the sentiment involved. To quote Rogan Taylor, a Liverpool fan and Liverpool University professor, "Soccer is more than just a business. No one has their ashes scattered down the aisle at Tesco."

5

IN PRAISE OF SUGAR DADDIES

Why "Financial Fair Play" Is Bad for Soccer

When the Russian oligarch Roman Abramovich decided to buy a soccer club, he had a look around in Spain and Italy. But ownership there seemed complicated. In Italy, many of the families who owned clubs had been doing business with each other for generations. In Spain, horror of horrors, the fans themselves owned the biggest clubs. As for the Bundesliga, Abramovich never seems to have considered it.

And so in April 2002 he flew to Manchester to watch United. After the game, write Dominic Midgley and Chris Hutchins in their biography *Abramovich*, Rio Ferdinand drove him to Manchester airport, and the Russian charmed the player by joining in a sing-along with a fellow passenger, Ferdinand's four-year-old half-brother.

Not long after that, the story goes, Abramovich was flying in a helicopter over London when he spotted a soccer stadium handily located near his house in west London. "What's that?" he reportedly asked. It was Chelsea. He bought the club, sealing the deal with the departing owner, Ken Bates, over a bottle of Evian water in London's Dorchester Hotel. The Russian was then still happy to talk to journalists. When the *Financial Times* rang to ask about his purchase, he revealed that his favorite player was Thierry Henry (then at Arsenal), and explained why he had bought Chelsea: "I'm looking at it as something to have fun with rather than having to realise a return. I don't look at this as a financial investment." He has barely spoken another word in public since, but two things have become clear: (1) Buying a soccer club made this unknown billionaire world-famous. (2) As he predicted, the purchase hasn't been a "financial investment." In his first eight years as owner, Chelsea lost a total of about $1 billion.

Despite the losses, Abramovich seems to have inspired the era of billionaire sugar daddies in global soccer. Men like him have taken over Manchester City, Paris Saint-Germain, Monaco, and most big Russian clubs. Sugar daddies in soccer aren't like investors in normal businesses. They are willing to lose money just to be part of the game. They have helped drive up wages and salaries for the best players to unprecedented levels. Now UEFA is trying to end that. In 2010 the European soccer association introduced rules on "financial fair play" that aim, above all, to stop clubs spending more than they earn. If a club's annual revenues are $400 million, say, it won't be able to spend $500 million even if an Abramovich wants to give it the money. Any offending club can be banned from European competition.

UEFA seems to have come up with FFP largely out of a sense that soccer's debt had gotten out of hand, and that what was needed was a dose of austerity. In that sense, FFP mirrors the "austerity" policies imposed by European governments at about the same time. The "FFP rules" are full of loopholes, and take full effect only in 2018, but they do seem aimed at the sugar daddies. The idea seems to be, if not to drive the Abramoviches out of soccer, at least to curb their spending. That would allow rival clubs to spend less, and let them make profits at last. Arsenal's Arsène Wenger, for one, has welcomed the new rules. "Financial fair play will make a big difference," he says, "because you cannot imagine the world will go on just splashing money out without any return." Many fans, too, seem to regard "FFP" as soccer's long-needed dose of sanity. We disagree. We don't think financial fair play will be fully implemented, but if it is, we think it will be bad for soccer. And we don't think clubs should make profits. On balance, we think the Abramoviches are good for the game.

| |

FFP itself has two dimensions, one of which is uncontroversial: that every club must be solvent. Solvency means the capacity to pay your debts—that is, the reasonable expectation that your future income will be enough to pay what you owe. In most European countries, solvency is a basic requirement for doing business. If the directors of a company know it is insolvent, then legally they should stop doing business until either solvency is restored or the company is shut down. Solvency can be restored if the creditors agree to write off some of their debts. If the creditors won't do that, then the business can be closed, the assets sold, and the creditors paid off to the greatest extent possible.

Insolvency is a very common business problem. There are thousands of cases across Europe every year. Generally the problem affects small businesses, and so these events go unnoticed by most of us. Occasionally, though, very large companies go insolvent, and it becomes headline news. But as we've already shown, soccer clubs almost never close down. They are practically always bailed out. This appears to be one reason European clubs seem forever to be in financial trouble: they overspend because they can. In the past many clubs have restored their finances by refusing to pay small creditors, banks, and the taxman—daring any of them to take on the label of the creditor that destroyed a soccer club. Very few creditors have chosen to tread this path. And perhaps in the days when there was almost no money in soccer it didn't matter. Local banks can usually write off a debt that might be no more than a few tens of thousands of dollars (a lot to an individual perhaps, but not much for a modestly sized bank).

Now, though, the income generated by European soccer is starting to add up to something. These days, when a club can't pay, a lot of creditors get hurt. Often the victims are small local businesses, or even charities—notably St. John's Ambulance, which provides emergency medical aid to fans in British soccer grounds. Clearly it's wrong for a club to pay its players millions and then try to get out of paying its creditors. So we applaud FFP for demanding solvency. The solvency rule mostly affects smaller clubs—which, as we have seen, are the ones that tend to become insolvent. In the big countries smaller clubs tend to play in the lower divisions, which means UEFA's rules are irrelevant to them anyway. Financial fair play applies only to teams entering UEFA competitions. The requirement for solvency would therefore mostly impact clubs qualifying for European competitions from smaller or poorer countries: Finland, Romania, and the like. It shouldn't affect the Chelseas and Real Madrids.

The second, controversial element of FFP is the breakeven rule. This requires that, averaged over a three-year period, a club's "relevant income" must match its "relevant expenses." In other words, clubs can spend only what they earn. This rule will exclusively impact big clubs. That is because the breakeven rules allow a financial loss of €5 million (nearly $7 million). According to UEFA, in 2011 only 77 out of 726 top-division clubs in Europe had annual income over €50 million, and were therefore likely to make losses of over €5 million. Hardly any club outside the elite will notice the effect of breakeven.

The chief target of breakeven seems to be the sugar daddies. This is because UEFA's definition of "relevant income" includes gate money, broadcast income, and income from sponsorship and merchandising, but excludes the owner's own money. Breakeven is not a solvency issue—it's not as if Chelsea faces any real risk that Abramovich will be unwilling or unable to cover losses as long as he owns the club. Indeed, in 2009 he converted the hundreds of millions of dollars that Chelsea theoretically owed him into shares in the club. That means that if he walks away tomorrow, he can't ask Chelsea for his money back.

UEFA presumably isn't worried about Chelsea's solvency. Rather, it seems to think that money from an owner somehow gives a club an unfair competitive advantage. The FFP rules allow a club owner to put money into the stadium or youth academy, but not into buying stars for the first team.

The breakeven rules shouldn't hurt the old "aristocrats" of soccer, the likes of Manchester United, Arsenal, and Bayern Munich. These clubs generate plenty of income from "relevant" sources—chiefly fans, sponsors, and TV companies. No wonder, then, that the aristocrats support financial fair play. FFP would tend to weaken their rivals, who can compete with the aristocrats only by borrowing fortunes (something banned under the insolvency rule) or by getting fortunes from a sugar daddy (something banned under the breakeven rule). If FFP works, the aristocrats will celebrate.

Let's compare the breakeven rule to the salary cap, widely used in American major-league sports. A salary cap generally restricts teams' spending on players to a fixed percentage of average club income (55 percent, say). UEFA's breakeven rule restricts player spending to the level of club income defined as "relevant." The key difference is that the US cap is the same for all clubs, whereas breakeven caps each club at the level of its own resources—a lot for the larger clubs, not so much for the smaller clubs. So while the American salary cap encourages competitive balance between clubs (it stops the Dallas Cowboys from spending infinitely more than the Jacksonville Jaguars), UEFA's breakeven rule cements inequality by making it harder for smaller clubs to compete with the aristocrats. This hardly seems fair, unless by "fair" you mean the idea that big clubs should be protected from competition from upstarts.

Jean-Louis Dupont, a lawyer who helped bring about the Bosman ruling in 1995, decided in 2013 to challenge the FFP rules under European competition law. His main argument was not that FFP is unfair to smaller clubs. Rather, he said it was unfair on players and their agents. FFP will surely put downward pressure on players' salaries, since it aims to stop at least some clubs (such as Chelsea and Manchester City) from spending as much as they want. Stefan and the Flemish economist Thomas Peeters developed a model to estimate the effect the breakeven rule will have. Note that the rule puts indirect as well as direct downward pressure on wages. The direct pressure would work like this: Manchester City complies with breakeven by spending less on players' salaries. But on top of that comes the indirect effect: by spending less, City becomes less of a competitive threat to other clubs. The cost of winning for these other clubs falls, and so they need to spend less on wages to achieve success.

If the FFP rules have enough bite, clubs will be able to choose their strategy. Either they can continue to spend the same proportion of their "relevant income," even though they need to spend less now to win, or they can aim for the same level of on-field performance as before FFP, and pocket the surplus as profits. Either way, Stefan and Peeters predicted a very large fall in spending on players as a result of FFP. Using 2010 as a benchmark, and using data from the top divisions of England, France, Italy, and Spain (financial data for individual German clubs is not available), the model suggests that player spending would have been between €400 million and €800 million lower in those four leagues had the FFP rules applied. That would represent a fall in wage spending of up to 15 percent. The higher spending the league, the larger the fall in wages—so FFP would be worst news of all for players trying to earn a crust in the Premier League.

Some people might think lower players' wages would be justification enough for FFP. But remember two things: First, FFP makes soccer at the top less competitive. Imagine if FFP had been in force since 2003, and Abramovich at Chelsea and Sheikh Mansour at Manchester City hadn't been allowed to spend their fortunes to buy English titles. What would have happened instead? Quite likely, Manchester United would have won the Premier League ten years running. With FFP, as Gabriele Marcotti warned in the *Wall Street Journal,* "instead of soccer having a 1 percent lording it over everyone else, it could become a 0.1 percent."

Second, if FFP does cut players' wages, there is no promise that the money saved will go back into soccer. More probably, the money will go into the pockets of billionaire owners.

We should say at this point that FFP might not actually take force as planned. More likely, clubs and UEFA will both give a bit. UEFA's main concern will be to stop penniless clubs risking insolvency, and so it will enforce the solvency rule hard. Any Bulgarian club that has lost over €5 million in three years will find itself chucked out of European competition. By contrast, big clubs with sugar daddies may be cut more slack if they fail to break even. In any case, some of these clubs are already finding ways around FFP. Manchester City, for instance, has signed a ten-year deal believed to be worth a flabbergasting $550 million with Etihad Airways for stadium naming rights and shirt sponsorship. Skeptics note that Etihad, like City's owners, comes from Abu Dhabi. They hint that the deal is a trick to allow City to inject outside money while evading the FFP rules.

However, UEFA might struggle to prove in court that the $550 million was excessive, or that Etihad's owners had anything to do with City's owners (beyond both sets of people coming from the elite of the same tiny emirate). The sugar-daddy clubs will hire expensive lawyers to defend them, and will dare UEFA to ban teams full of great players from the Champions League. That will give UEFA pause. It doesn't want to stage a Champions League without Paris's Zlatan Ibrahimovic or Manchester City's Sergio Agüero. It must also worry that any excluded clubs might try to start their own rival competition. UEFA president Michel Platini sounded cautious when telling the *London Evening Standard* in 2013, "Sanctions will be decided upon. Do not think we are going to take five to ten clubs out of the European competition. Definitely that would be the very, very last straw. If we have repeat offenders, okay, yes, they will have to be punished severely—possibly. We are not out to kill the clubs."

Presumably, then, deals like City's with Etihad will be left to stand. FFP may not transform soccer. Ivan Gazidis, chief executive of Arsenal, told us, "Are there loopholes in the way FFP works? Quite possibly. FFP is not part of our strategy."

Still, our question is: What if FFP actually happens, and works? If UEFA does manage to force clubs to spend only what they earn, then sugar daddies would drift out of the game. After all, there wouldn't be much point in buying Chelsea if you couldn't spend any money to win trophies. You might still want to buy a huge club like Manchester United that can challenge for trophies without your cash, but there aren't many clubs like that. If FFP triumphs, the Abramovich era ends. We think that would be bad news for soccer.

Sugar daddies are often depicted as a curse on the game. It's easy to see why a Manchester United fan, or an Arsenal fan, would dislike Manchester City or Chelsea. Setting aside local rivalry, it's the age-old disdain of the aristocracy for the nouveaux riches. City and Chelsea are upstarts who have used wallets full of foreign currency to barge their way onto the top table. When City won the Premier League in 2012, it did so with several players bought from Arsenal, and at the expense of United. Of course United fans oppose sugar daddies.

What's less clear is why fans of smaller clubs should care. It's not as if the sugar daddy clubs are taking *their* places. Smaller clubs never win anything anymore anyway. In twenty-plus years of the Premier League, only the sugar-daddy clubs Manchester City, Chelsea, and Blackburn (when funded by Jack Walker in 1995) have wrested titles from the vise-like grip of Manchester United and Arsenal. Sugar daddies threaten the strong, but they hardly threaten the already weak.

In most other walks of life we welcome the outsider who comes in and shakes up the existing order. Taking the aristocrats down a notch is the plot of endless feel-good movies. Why should it be different for soccer? It certainly seems that when fans of a particular club learn that a sugar daddy is in the offing, they perk up. Soon after Abramovich bought Chelsea and began buying expensive players, the club's fans came up with a song in his honor (more or less):

He's got Veron in his pocket
We got Johnson from West Ham
If you want the best
Then don't ask questions
Cos Roman, he's our man
Where it all comes from is a mystery
Is it guns? Is it drugs?

The sentiment of the song is clear: finding a sugar daddy is like winning the lottery. For most clubs, it's their only hope of competing with the aristocrats.

Some argue that the "excessive" spending of sugar daddies drives smaller clubs into bankruptcy. In fact, if anything, the opposite is true. Sugar daddies buy players in the transfer market and then pay them very high wages. The usual argument is that this forces other clubs to pay their players higher salaries to stay. However, (a) this will apply only to a small number of players, and (b) no club can be forced to pay more than it can afford. Certainly if clubs without a sugar daddy try to match the ambitions of the sugar daddies, that will end in tears, but then that must also be the case for clubs that try to compete with aristocrats. Whether you want to be a Manchester United or an Abramovich-funded Chelsea, if you have no sugar daddy, you will fail. The problem for small clubs is that they just don't have the resources to compete with the dominant clubs, and have not had them for half a century or more. This has very little to do with sugar daddies.

But sugar daddies are good for the soccer economy for one big reason: the cash they inject supports other clubs. In Sheikh Mansour's first five years of owning Manchester City, from 2008 through 2013, the club spent £505 million *net* on acquiring players (around $800 million). This money was pumped into a European market where top-division clubs in 2011 alone lost a cumulative €1.6 billion (over $2 billion). Some of the sheikh's money ended up with agents, but by far the biggest chunk of transfer fees went to clubs. Deloitte calculates that the Premier League benefited from a total of £2 billion ($3.2 billion) of additional finance coming from wealthy owners from 2006 through 2013. And of course the new transfer spending didn't all go to other Premier League clubs. Some of it went to clubs playing in lower divisions in England, or in leagues abroad. Some of that money was spent on players, and some on improving training facilities or building better stadiums.

We lament the seizing of so much of the world's wealth by a small number of billionaires—many of them heirs, criminals, or tax dodgers—but it has been good news for soccer. After someone becomes a billionaire, he tends to want to convert some of that money into excitement and prestige. Perhaps the best way to do that is by buying a soccer club. If Abramovich ever wanted to sell Chelsea, sugar daddies would probably be lining up trying to buy it from him. Ehud Olmert, the former Israeli prime minister who has supported Manchester United since the Munich air crash of 1958, told us a story about the "eastern investor" who sent him to visit the Glazer family with an offer to buy United. For the many people wanting to buy United, an early obstacle is the difficulty of actually meeting the Glazers. They don't get out much. But they are great friends of Israel, and were delighted to meet Olmert. At their country club in Palm Beach, he handed them a check for about $1.6 billion to take over United. The Glazers said no straight away. "This is the strongest brand name in the sports world," they explained. Still, if they ever decide to sell, we think that a few of the 1,426 billionaires on *Forbes* magazine's list for 2013 might be interested.

To understand how sugar daddies help soccer, it's instructive to study the Glazers, because they are the opposite of sugar daddies. Most United fans blame them for sucking cash out of the club. It has been estimated that the net cost of the Glazers to the club since their takeover in 2005 is more than £500 million (over $800 million). So if sucking money out of clubs is a bad thing, then putting money into them is surely a good thing.

If FFP succeeds, sugar daddies might fade out of soccer. If that happens, there must be a real danger that investment in European clubs will dry up. If so, more clubs will probably go insolvent. In the nightmare scenario, the sugar daddies' money might be channeled into emerging leagues elsewhere (the United States, China, the Gulf?). That could undermine Europe's dominance. It's hard to think of any other activity in which organizations actively seek to stop wealthy people from investing. Not many universities, art galleries, opera houses, or aid agencies say no to sugar daddies.

HORROR OF HORRORS: MIGHT BIG SOCCER CLUBS BECOME PROFITABLE?

We've shown in the previous chapters that soccer clubs almost never make profits. However, in part because of FFP, that may soon change, at least for some of the biggest clubs.

Losses were always a fact of life in soccer, and as more money came into the game, the losses just kept growing. Every year, UEFA's "club licensing benchmark report" summarizes financial information for around 650 clubs playing in the top divisions of Europe's national leagues. Between the financial year 2008 and 2012, revenues grew 15 percent (pretty impressive in an economic crisis), yet the number of clubs declaring an operating loss rose from 54 percent to 63 percent.

Then something changed. Late in 2013, UEFA trailed some figures from its as yet unpublished report for the financial year 2012 (to appear early in 2014). The message: losses were down by 36 percent. Various factors probably contributed to that decline. FFP may already be starting to curb clubs' spending. The jump in global broadcast income for Bundesliga and Premier League clubs presumably helped too. And with the widespread panic about clubs' losses, the Spanish government in particular has cracked down on clubs' spending.

All this may sound like good news. The opposite of a loss is a profit, so if losses are bad, then profits must be good, right? But that takes us back to the Glazers: they make sure United makes a very large profit. Yet that profit represents money that the owners can then take out of the business. That's precisely why most United fans resent the Glazers. United's profits would have been more welcome had they been reinvested in buying players, or building a bigger stadium, or even funding a cut in ticket prices—but then of course they would have ceased to be profits.

We expect more owners of European clubs to follow the Glazers' lead. Six of the twenty Premier League clubs are now owned by Americans.

These people come from a country where many sports franchises actually make money. Most of these people didn't buy into soccer because they love the game, but as a business proposition. They think soccer has the power to capture foreign markets in a way that American sports don't. They see the ceaseless rise in the Premier League's broadcast income. They believe FFP will stop sugar daddies from driving up wages and transfer fees. No doubt encouraged by the American owners, the Premier League has backed FFP, and is even considering introducing its own version of FFP in England. FFP could turn into a blunt instrument to make soccer more capitalist. In the end, these profit-driven owners hope to take money out of the game.

To imagine what the future might look like, think of Arsenal. Wenger, the club's manager, doesn't like spending money. His austerity won zero trophies from 2006 to 2013, but it probably pleased Arsenal's American majority owner, Stan Kroenke. From 2002 through early 2013, Arsenal's share price jumped nearly 1,200 percent, compared with a rise of just 60 percent for British shares in general.

Arsenal hasn't been a great soccer club lately, but it has been a good business. This is what a soccer club run as a business looks like: high ticket prices, little desire to win trophies, and respectable profits. If FFP takes force, and other big clubs end up being run like Arsenal rather than like Abramovich's Chelsea, then we predict:

- A fall in players' wages
- A fall in transfer fees, which would mean less money trickling down from big clubs to the rest
- A rise in club profits, which would mean more money being taken out of the game by people like the Glazers

It's often said, in current jargon, that a profitable soccer club is "sustainable." We disagree. Fans shouldn't want their clubs to make profits. If soccer becomes a hard-nosed profit-making industry, supporters may end up pining for the days when it was the worst business in the world.

6

NEED NOT APPLY

Does English Soccer Discriminate Against Black People?

In 1991 Ron Noades, chairman of Crystal Palace, popped up on British TV talking about blacks. "The problem with black players," explained Noades, whose heavily black team had just finished third in England, "is they've great pace, great athletes, love to play with the ball in front of them. . . . When it's behind them it's chaos. I don't think too many of them can read the game. When you're getting into the midwinter you need a few of the hard white men to carry the athletic black players through."

Noades's interview was one of the last flourishes of unashamed racism in British soccer. Through the 1980s racism had been more or less taken for granted in the game. Fans threw bananas at black players. Pundits like Emlyn Hughes explained the curious absence of black players at Liverpool and Everton by saying, "They haven't got the bottle." The writer Dave Hill summed up the stereotypes: "'No bottle' is a particular favorite, lack of concentration another. 'You don't want too many of them in your defense,' one backroom bod told me, 'they cave in under pressure.' Then there is the curious conviction that blacks are susceptible to the cold and won't go out when it rains."

It's clear that English soccer in those days was shot through with racism: prejudice based on skin color. But what we want to know is whether that racism translated into discrimination: unfair *treatment* of people. People like Noades may have been prejudiced against black players, but did they make it harder for these players to get jobs in soccer? The '80s black striker Garth Crooks thought they did: "I always felt I had to be 15 percent better than the white person to get the same chance," he said.

Yet the notion of discrimination against blacks clashes with something we think we know about soccer: that on the field at least, the game is ruthlessly fair. In soccer good players of whatever color perform better than bad ones. Fans and chairmen and managers may walk around with Noadesian fantasies in their heads, but when a black player plays well, everyone can see it. Nick Hornby writes in *Fever Pitch,* in his famous riff on Gus Caesar, "One of the great things about sport is its cruel clarity; there is no such thing, for example, as a bad one-hundred-metre runner, or a hopeless center-half who got lucky; in sport, you get found out. Nor is there such a thing as an unknown genius striker starving in a garret somewhere."

In short, it would seem that in soccer there is no room for ideologies. You have to be right, and results on the field will tell you very quickly whether you are. So would clubs really discriminate against blacks at the cost of winning matches? After all, even Ron Noades employed black players. (He seems to have known something about soccer, too: after leaving Palace he bought Brentford, appointed himself manager, won promotion, and was voted manager of the year in the second division.) In fact, the very success of blacks on the field might be taken as evidence that the opportunities were there.

It's also often hard to prove objectively that discrimination exists. How can you show that you failed to get the job because of prejudice rather than just because you weren't good enough? Liverpool and Everton might argue that they employed white players in the 1980s simply because the whites were better.

Luckily, there is no need to get into a "he said, she said" argument. We have data to prove that English soccer discriminated against black players. We can show when this particular kind of discrimination ended. And we can predict that the new forms of discrimination that pervade English soccer today will be harder to shift.

||

The first black person to set foot in the British Isles was probably a soldier in Julius Caesar's invading army, in 55 BC. The "indigenous" English themselves arrived only about four hundred years later, during the collapse of the Roman Empire.

Much later, under Victoria, Britain's own empire ruled a large share of the world's black people. A few of the better-educated or entrepreneurial ones made their way from the British Raj in India, the Caribbean, or Africa to Britain. Arthur Wharton, born in 1865 in the Gold Coast (now Ghana), became the world's first black professional soccer player. As well as keeping goal for Preston, he set the world record of ten seconds for the one hundred–yard sprint.

But until the 1950s most Britons had probably never seen a black person. Unlike Americans, they never developed any kind of relationship with blacks, whether positive or negative. Then, after the Second World War, hundreds of thousands of colonial immigrants began arriving. The influx was small enough—less than 5 percent of Britain's total population, spread over a quarter of a century—to pose little threat to the concepts of Englishness, Scottishness, or Welshness. Nonetheless, the signs went up in the windows of boardinghouses:

NO COLOUREDS

One of the authors of this book, Stefan Szymanski, is the son of an immigrant from Poland who had escaped to London in 1940 and joined the British army to fight the Nazis. Stefan remembers his father telling him about looking for lodging in London in the early 1950s and finding signs in the windows saying

ROOMS TO LET—NO POLES, NO HUNGARIANS

Not only was this kind of discrimination legal, but Stefan's father accepted it. In his mind, he was the immigrant, and it was his job to fit in. Luckily for him (and for Stefan), he was an educated man, able to find a reasonable job and make a reasonable living. He was also a racist. This might sound harsh, but by today's standards most British adults seemed to be racist in the 1970s, when Stefan was growing up. In the popular comedy series of the time, *Till Death Us Do Part,* the hero, Alf Garnett, was a ludicrously prejudiced Londoner who favored labels like "coon," "nig-nog," "darky," "Paki," and "the Jews up at Spurs" (Garnett supported West Ham). Not only were these words used on the BBC, but they were accompanied by canned laughter. Admittedly the joke of the series was ultimately on Garnett, who was regularly exposed to the falsity of his own prejudices. But Stefan used to argue that these labels were offensive. His father took this as evidence of a lack of a sense of humor.

It was against this 1970s background of instinctive racism that black players began arriving in English soccer. Most were the British-born children of immigrants. That didn't stop them from being treated to monkey noises and bananas. (As Hornby notes in *Fever Pitch,* "There may well be attractive, articulate and elegant racists, but they certainly never come to soccer matches.") For a while, neo-Nazi parties even imagined that they could lead a revolution from the soccer terraces.

Given the abuse the early black players received, it would have been easy for them to give up on soccer. It was thinkable that they would be driven out of the game. Instead they stayed, played, and triumphed. In 1978, when Viv Anderson became the first black man to play for England, it became apparent that children of Caribbean immigrants might have something of a role to play in English soccer. Still, even after the black winger John Barnes scored his solo goal to beat Brazil in Rio in 1984, the Football Association's chairman was harangued by England fans on the flight back home: "You fucking wanker, you prefer sambos to us."

As late as 1993 you could still witness the following scene: a crowd of people in a pub in London's business district, the "City," is watching England-Holland on TV. Every time Barnes gets the ball, one man—in shirtsleeves and a tie, just out of his City office—makes monkey noises. Every time, his coworkers laugh. If anyone had complained, let alone gone off to find a policeman and asked him to arrest the man, the response would have been: "Where's your sense of humor?" (Hornby's line on this sort of problem: "I wish I were enormous and of a violent disposition, so that I could deal with any problem that arises near me in a fashion commensurate with the anger I feel.")

Whenever people reminisce about the good old days, when ordinary working people could afford to go to soccer matches, it's worth scanning the photographs of the cloth-capped masses standing on the terraces for the faces you don't see: blacks, Asians, women. It's true that today's all-seaters in the Premier League exclude poor people. However, the terraces before the 1990s probably excluded rather more varieties of people. In the 1970s and 1980s, when soccer grew scary, the violence forced out even many older white men.

| |

In the late 1980s Stefan began thinking about the economics of soccer. He was then working for the Centre for Business Strategy at London Business School. Everyone in the center was an economist, and therefore tempted to think that markets more or less "worked." The theory was that any businessperson who came up with a brilliant innovation—inventing the telephone, say—would not keep his advantage for long, because others would imitate him and compete.

But the economists were interested in the few companies that stayed successful despite competition. Clearly there must be something to learn from them. Stefan suggested looking for these paragons in soccer. It was obviously a highly competitive industry, yet some clubs succeeded in dominating for years on end. How did they manage to stay ahead for so long?

Stefan enlisted the support of Ron Smith, who had taught him when he was writing his PhD. Smith, as well as being an expert on Marxist economics and the economics of defense, is a well-known econometrician. Econometrics is essentially the art of finding statistical methods to extract information from data—or, as a lawyer friend of Stefan's likes to put it, taking the data down into the basement and torturing them until they confess. Studying the accounts of soccer clubs, Stefan and Ron could see how much each club spent on salaries. The two discovered that this spending alone explained almost all the variation in positions in the English Football League. When Stefan analyzed the accounts of forty clubs for 1978 through 1997, he found that their wage spending accounted for 92 percent of the variation in their league positions.

Clearly the market in players' pay was highly efficient: the better a player, the more he earned. And this made sense, because soccer is one of the few markets that indisputably meets the conditions in which competition can work efficiently: there are large numbers of buyers and sellers, all of whom have plenty of information about the quality of the players being bought and sold. If a player got paid less than he was worth, he could move to another club. If he got paid more, he would soon find himself being sold off again.

But what about the variation in league position that remained unexplained after adjusting for players' pay? If buying talent was generally enough to win titles—as rich club chairmen like Jack Walker at Blackburn Rovers and Roman Abramovich at Chelsea would soon demonstrate—what else accounted for a team's success? If it was something that was easy to copy—a new tactic, for instance—then other teams would copy it, and the advantage would disappear. That got Stefan thinking about discrimination. What if owners were simply not willing to copy the secret of others' success, because they didn't want to hire the kinds of players who brought that success? He began to search for discrimination against black players.

In most industries, there is a way to demonstrate that discrimination exists. Suppose you could construct a sample of all applicants for a job, and also of all their relevant qualifications. If you then found that a much larger proportion of relevantly qualified white applicants received job offers than relevantly qualified black applicants, you could reasonably infer the presence of discrimination. For example, if 50 percent of whites with doctorates in philosophy got job offers from university philosophy departments but only 10 percent of their black equivalents did, then you should suspect discrimination.

This is essentially how economists have tried to identify job discrimination. The method also works for wage discrimination. If equivalently qualified blacks (or women, or left-handers, or whoever) get lower wages for equivalent jobs, then there is probably discrimination going on. Researchers have put together databases of thousands of workers, each identified by dozens of relevant qualifications, to test whether discrimination exists. When it comes to ethnic minorities and women, the evidence usually shows that it does.

The problem is that there are few measurable qualifications that make someone a great soccer player. When a company is accused of racism, it often says that while the black (or purple, or female) candidates may possess some of the relevant characteristics, there are other, less quantifiable characteristics that they don't have. Intellectually, this point is hard to overturn. Hundreds of cases of racial discrimination have been fought in American courts, and evidence based on the kinds of studies we have mentioned has often run into trouble.

Happily, there is another way to test for discrimination in soccer. Once again, it relies on evidence from the market. As a general rule, the best way to find out what people are up to is to see how they behave when faced with a price. Don't know whether you prefer Coke to Pepsi? Well, let's see what you choose when they both cost the same. (Most people choose Coke.) Do managers prefer white players to blacks? Well, let's see how they spend their clubs' money.

If clubs discriminate, then they will prefer to hire a white player to an equivalently talented black player. If they do that, then blacks will find it harder to get jobs as professional soccer players. The blacks will then be willing to accept lower wages than equivalently talented whites. After all, when demand for what we sell is lower, we tend to lower our asking price. So black players become cheaper than white players. If there is discrimination, we would expect to find black players earning less than equally talented whites.

If black players are being discriminated against, that creates an economic opportunity for unprejudiced clubs. By hiring black players they can do just as well in the league as an equivalently talented (but more expensive) team of whites. That means that a simple experiment will reveal whether discrimination exists: *if teams with more black players achieve higher average league positions for a given sum of wage spending, then the teams with fewer black players must have been discriminating.* Otherwise, the whiter teams would have seen that black players were good value for the money and would have tried to hire them. Then black players' wages would have risen due to increased competition for their services, and the relative advantage of hiring black players would have disappeared.

Note that the argument is not that some teams hire more black players than others. That could happen for many reasons. Rather, we can infer discrimination if (a) some teams have more black players than others and (b) those same teams consistently outperform their competitors for a given level of wage spending.

After Stefan figured this out, he had the luck of running into just the right person. Around that time he was also researching the relationship between the pay of senior executives in the biggest British companies and the performance of their companies. (Very unlike soccer players' wages, there turned out to be almost no correlation between the pay of senior executives and the performance of a company's share price, until share options became common in the 1990s.) Stefan was interviewed for a BBC program by the political journalist Michael Crick. Over time he and Crick got to talking about soccer.

Crick is a famously thorough researcher. Book reviewers delight in finding errors, no matter how trivial, but they never succeed with Crick's political biographies. And as it happens, Crick supports Manchester United. In 1989 he wrote a fascinating history of the club with David Smith, describing how United packaged its legend for commercial gain. About this time Crick became interested in whether soccer clubs discriminated in their hiring. Everyone knew of the suspicious cases of the day, chiefly Liverpool and Everton.

Crick began collecting data from the 1970s onward to see which clubs had hired black players. This was no easy task. How do you decide who is "black"? Crick took a commonsense approach. He started with the old Rothmans Football Yearbooks, which published a photograph of every English league team. From this he made a judgment as to which players "looked black." He then followed up by asking clubs and supporters' clubs to fill in any gaps. It took him months to come up with a list of players who, to most fans, would have appeared to be black. This sounds arbitrary, but it is precisely what was required. Prejudice is based on appearance. For example, several years after Crick did his research, it emerged that Ryan Giggs's father was black. Giggs even spoke publicly about his pride in his Caribbean ancestry. However, until that point, most people would not have considered Giggs a black player. He didn't *look* black, and for that reason he would have been unlikely to face discrimination. So Crick was right not to count Giggs as black.

When Crick told Stefan about his list of black players, it was a cinch to create a test for discrimination. All that was necessary was to count how many times each black player had played for his club in a given season. It would then be clear which teams employed a larger proportion of black players.

Stefan then matched these data with figures on each team's league position and its spending on wages. If there were no discrimination in the market, then wages alone would almost entirely explain league performance. Everything else would just be random noise—"luck." But if black players were systematically being paid less than equally talented white players, then logically the teams that hired an above-average proportion of black players would do systematically better than their wage bill alone would predict.

Back in the 1970s, there were very few black players in English soccer. Combining our data on wages with Crick's database had given us a sample of thirty-nine out of the ninety-two professional league teams. In the 1973–1974 season only two of these clubs had fielded any black players at all. By 1983–1984 there were still twenty teams in our sample that did not field a black player all season. However, at this point there seems to have been a major breakthrough. By 1989 every team in the sample had fielded at least one black player at some point. By 1992, when the Premier League was founded, only five teams in the sample did not field a black player that season. This implied that about 90 percent of clubs were putting blacks in the first team. Attitudes were changing. Bananas left the game. When Noades voiced his theories on black players in 1991, he was widely mocked.

It is interesting to look at the characteristics of the black players in the English game in these years. For purposes of comparison, Stefan constructed a random sample of an equal number of white players with similar age profiles. Almost all the black players (89 percent) were born in Britain, not very different from the white players (95 percent). Most of the black players were strikers (58 percent), compared with only 33 percent of white players. There were no black goalkeepers at the time. Noades would have noted the fact that black players seemed underrepresented in defense. But then strikers always carry a premium to defenders in the market: it takes more talent to score than to stop other people from scoring.

Certain facts about the sample stood out: the careers of the black players averaged more than six years, compared to less than four for the whites. And 36 percent of the blacks had played for their countries, compared with only 23 percent of the whites. On this evidence, it looked suspiciously as if the black players were better than the whites.

The proof came when Stefan deployed the economist's favorite tool, regression analysis. He used it to isolate the distinct effects of wages and the share of black players on each club's league performance. What he found was discrimination. The data showed that clubs with more black players really did have a better record in the league than clubs with fewer blacks, after allowing for wage spending. If two teams had identical annual wage budgets, the team with more blacks would finish higher in the league. The test implied that black players were systematically better value for money than whites. Certain teams of the 1980s like Arsenal, Noades's Palace, and Ron Atkinson's West Bromwich Albion (this was years before Atkinson called Marcel Desailly "a fucking lazy thick nigger" on air) benefited from fielding blacks.

The clubs with fewer blacks were not suffering from a lack of information. Anyone who knew soccer could judge fairly easily how good most players were just by watching them play. So the only credible reason clubs would deny themselves the opportunity to hire these players was prejudice. Clubs didn't like the look of black players, or they thought their fans wouldn't, either simply because of skin hue or because they perceived weaknesses that just were not there. By testing the behavior of managers against the market, it proved possible to uncover evidence of discrimination.

In soccer you can judge someone's performance only against other competitors. This means that I lose nothing by being inefficient if my competitors are inefficient in the same way as I am. I can go on hiring mediocre players as long as other clubs do, too. As long as all clubs refused to hire talented black players, the cost of discriminating was low. What the data showed was that by the beginning of the 1980s, so many teams were hiring talented blacks that the cost of discriminating had become quite high. Teams that refused to field black players were overpaying for white players and losing more matches as a consequence. Yet some level of discrimination persisted. Even by the end of the 1980s, an all-white team like Everton would cost around 5 percent more than an equally good team that fielded merely an average proportion of black players. As Dave Hill wrote in the fanzine *When Saturday Comes* in 1989, "Half a century after Jesse Owens, a quarter of a century after Martin Luther King, and 21 years after two American sprinters gave the Black Power salute from the Olympic medal rostrum, some of these dickheads don't even know what a black person is." But by the time Hill wrote that, precisely because soccer is so competitive, more and more clubs had begun to hire black players. In 1995 even Everton signed the Nigerian Daniel Amokachi. The economic forces of competition drove white men to ditch their prejudices.

Quite soon, enough clubs were hiring blacks that black players came to be statistically overrepresented in English soccer. Only about 1.6 percent of people in the 1991 British census described themselves as black. Yet in the early 1990s about 10 percent of all players in English professional soccer were black. By the end of the decade, after the influx of foreign players, the share was nearer 20 percent.

So did clubs learn to overcome their prejudices? A few years after Stefan ran his first test for discrimination, he badgered some students who were looking for undergraduate projects into compiling a list of black players for another six seasons. That took the data set up to the 1998–1999 season. Once again Stefan merged the data with figures on wages and league performances. Now he could run the regression to the end of the 1990s. For these six additional years, there was no evidence that the share of black players in a team had any effect on team performance, after allowing for the team's wage bill. In other words, by then black players were on average paid what they were worth to a team.

Perhaps the best witness to the acceptance of blacks in soccer is Lilian Thuram. A black man born on the Caribbean island of Guadeloupe and raised in a town just outside Paris, Thuram played professionally from 1991 to 2008 and became France's most capped player. He won the World Cup of 1998 with that famous multicolored French team. He is also a French intellectual, possibly the only soccer player ever to have spoken the words, "There's an interesting young ethnographer at the Musée de l'Homme . . . "

Thuram is acutely sensitive to racism. He now runs an antiracism foundation. Nonetheless, in 2008, in the final months of his long playing career, he insisted to us that soccer was innocent of the sin. Over late-night pasta in an Italian restaurant in Barcelona, he explained, "In soccer it's harder to have discrimination, because we are judged on very specific performances. There are not really subjective criteria. Sincerely, I've never met a racist person in soccer. Maybe they were there, but I didn't see it." In fact, he added, "In sport, prejudices favor the blacks. In the popular imagination, the black is in his place in sport. For example, recently in Barcelona, the fitness coach said about Abidal [the black French defender], 'He's an athlete of the black race.' It's not because he stays behind after training to run. No, it's because he's black."

So by the 1990s discrimination against black players had disappeared. Gradually they came to feel at home in the industry. Here is a scene from inside the marble halls of the old Arsenal stadium, after a game in 1995: Arsenal's black Dutch winger Glenn Helder is introducing his black teammate Ian Wright (one of Ron Noades's former players) to some Dutch people. Then Helder says, "Ian, show these guys what I taught you." A look of intense concentration appears on Wright's face, and he begins jumping up and down and shouting in Dutch, "Buzz off! Dirty ape! Dirty ape!" He and Helder then collapse laughing. There was still racism in soccer, but by then blacks could mock it from the inner sanctums of the game's establishment.

The story of racism in American sports followed much the same arc. Right through the Second World War, baseball and basketball had segregated blacks into Negro Leagues. In 1947 Branch Rickey of the Brooklyn Dodgers broke an unspoken rule among baseball owners and hired black infielder Jackie Robinson to play for his team. Robinson eventually became an American hero. However, the costar of his story was economics. The Dodgers had less money than their crosstown rivals, the New York Yankees. If Rickey wanted a winning team, he had to tap talent that the other owners overlooked. Racism gave him an opportunity.

Of course, discrimination against black players persisted in American sports long after Robinson. Lawrence Kahn, an economist at Cornell University, surveyed the data and found little evidence that before the 1990s baseball teams were withholding jobs or pay from blacks. But he did think they were giving black players unduly short careers, and using them only in certain positions. In basketball, Kahn did find wage discrimination. When he repeated his study in 2000, he discovered, like Stefan the second time around, that discrimination was fading. British and American sports were becoming fair to black athletes.

We suspect that discrimination still exists in some other soccer leagues. In Russia in 2012 for instance, fans from Zenit St. Petersburg's largest supporters' group, Landscrona, wrote to their club demanding that black and gay players be excluded from the team. They said that black players were "forced down Zenit's throat," while gay players were "unworthy of our great city." These views are pretty common in Russian soccer, and in eastern Europe more generally. In that kind of atmosphere, a club brave enough not to practice racial discrimination can still expect to pick up good players cheaply.

We had thought that in western Europe at least, this kind of discrimination had died out. But there is a strange postscript to our story. In April 2011, the French website Mediapart leaked the minutes of a secret meeting at France's soccer federation.

The meeting, held in November 2010, had begun fairly innocuously. At first the officials had mused about admitting fewer youngsters of double nationality (often French plus African) into the federation's academies. It bothered the officials that some of these youngsters eventually chose to play for Algeria, say, rather than for France. However, the discussion quickly spread to scarier territory: complaints about black players per se.

France's coach, Laurent "*Le Président*" Blanc (a French hero who had played alongside Thuram in the black-white-Arab French team of '98), was quoted as telling the meeting, "You have the feeling that we are producing really only one prototype of player: big, strong, fast . . . and who are the big, strong, fast players? The blacks. That's the way it is. That's the way things are today."

According to the leaked minutes, Blanc continued, "I think we need to refocus, above all for boys of thirteen-fourteen, twelve-thirteen—introduce other parameters, adjusted to our own culture. . . . The Spanish say to me: 'We don't have this problem. We don't have any blacks.'" Blanc did add that he was talking about soccer qualities, not color. He wouldn't mind if the whole French team was black, he said, as long as there was a balance of size and skill.

Even so, it's difficult to know where to start with a critique of his position. Most obviously, Blanc seemed to be conflating the dull uncreative physical French style of recent years with the presence of black players. Second, the issue of double nationality scarcely mattered: a player of African origin good enough to play for France, like the Senegalese-born Patrick Vieira, will choose France. It's generally only French-raised players rejected by France, such as Marouane Chamakh (Morocco) or Benoit Assou-Ekotto (Cameroon), who will represent another country.

Yet some inside the French federation seemed to want to let fewer boys of African origin into the academies. Blocking the pipeline to professional soccer would mean job discrimination against blacks. It would be a return to the practices of English soccer of the 1980s. Nobody—we had previously thought—was barred from top-class soccer in western Europe anymore because of his skin color. Whereas ordinary Arabs and blacks in France struggled to find jobs, we had imagined that Arab and black soccer players in France did not.

But even before the federation's secret meeting, many French soccer fans had started to call for discrimination. There had long been popular grumbling about the number of nonwhite players in the national team. Every year France's National Consultative Commission on Human Rights publishes a big survey on racist attitudes. In 1999 a new question was inserted into the survey: Were there "too many players of foreign origin in the French soccer team?" You would not have imagined anyone thought so. The players of foreign origin had just made *les Bleus* world champions. Yet in 1999, 31 percent of respondents either totally or mostly agreed with this statement. In 2000, 36 percent agreed. More than a third of French people did not want this team even when it was the best on earth. Jean-Marie Le Pen, then leader of France's racist Front National party, knew exactly what he was doing when he led the grumbles about France's black players.

As the team began playing worse after 2000 and became blacker, public disquiet only grew. The philosopher Alain Finkielkraut (and in France, philosophers are heard) voiced the thoughts of many French people when he complained that the "black-black-black" team had become an international joke.

In 2010 France's then coach, Raymond Domenech, omitted three gifted young men of north African origin from his squad for the World Cup: Samir Nasri, Karim Benzema, and Hatem Ben Arfa. We are sure that Domenech made his choices without any racist intention. There were soccer-based arguments against each of the trio. Nevertheless, says the French sociologist Stéphane Beaud, author of *Traîtres à la Nation?* ("Traitors of the Nation?"), a book on *les Bleus* and ethnicity, Domenech seemed unable to deal with a new, more assertive generation of north African youth.

The *Bleus* of 2010 were different from those of 1998, explains Beaud. The '98 team had come mostly from stable, fairly comfortably off working-class families not all that far from the French mainstream. Thuram, for instance, had grown up playing for an ethnically Portuguese team in the far-from-deprived Parisian suburb of Fontainebleu. But the 2010 team reflected the later wave of immigration to France: many players were from poorer and broken immigrant families who lived in the ghettos outside France's big cities. These men had grown up at a distance from the French mainstream. And whereas most of the heroes of '98 had spent many years earning relatively modest salaries in the French league, getting married, and raising children, the new lot tended to have moved abroad very young, had spent their whole careers playing for top-level teams amid huge stress, and often had chaotic private lives, says Beaud.

The new generation can be harder to deal with for an older white Frenchman like Domenech (himself of Spanish descent). He was furious when Benzema (of Tunisian descent) said he didn't want to come on as a sub in a game against Romania. In the minds of many white Frenchmen, the image of *les Bleus* became that of spoiled young globalized multimillionaires slouched on the team bus wearing massive headphones, ignoring fans who had waited hours to see them. And of course, these *Bleus* weren't white.

Popular anger erupted one Sunday night during the World Cup of 2010. French TV showed live how the players, angry with Domenech at their training ground in the South African tourist town of Knysna, reached for an authentically French remedy: they went on strike. They got onto their bus refusing to train. Nicolas Anelka swore at Domenech. The phrase "the bus of shame" entered the French language. Knysna was "a national affair, a political affair," says Beaud. These mostly black and brown players were perceived as rejecting France. Worse than losing to Mexico and South Africa, they had (briefly) refused to sweat the blue shirt. France's national anger against the young black players echoed the national anger of 2005 against the young black rioters in the ethnic ghettos. "Scum," then interior minister Nicolas Sarkozy had called the rioters. In 2010 President Sarkozy instituted an inquiry into the football team.

A few months later came the federation's meeting in Paris. In a horrible way it made sense that officials of a national federation should be tempted by discrimination. Clubs are all about winning. National teams, however, have an additional function: to incarnate the nation. Many white French people—and of course the federation's officials were overwhelmingly white—seemed to feel that their nation could not be incarnated by a nonwhite team. If the officials had complained about black players publicly rather than in secret, a lot of French people would have been delighted.

After Mediapart leaked the minutes of the meeting, Thuram broke the unwritten social code of soccer to attack his old teammate Blanc. Three years earlier Thuram had told us that discrimination in soccer was impossible. Now he argued that Blanc had been guilty at least of "unconscious racism" and promoting "racial stereotypes." If you say that blacks are stronger and faster than whites, Thuram argued, you open the door to saying that whites are more intelligent than blacks. Vieira, another black hero of 1998, complained, too. "I know Laurent Blanc and I don't think he is racist," he said. "But I don't understand how any of the officials present at that meeting can stay in their job."

In the end, Blanc and the others did stay in their jobs, cleared by a government inquiry, to the joy of most French fans.

The secret meeting, and the scandal that followed it, had changed nothing. Even the black players stayed on the team. They were the best, and that is still (almost always) what matters in soccer.

7

DO COACHES MATTER?

The Cult of the White Manager

Trevor Phillips points a finger at his own shaven black head: "Excuse me, here I am: bull's-eye!" The son of an early Caribbean immigrant to Britain, Phillips was raised in London and has supported Chelsea for over fifty years. But in the 1970s, when throwing darts was the favorite sport of Chelsea's Shed Stand, he didn't go to matches. His head felt like an obvious target. Hardly any black people went to Chelsea then. "Now I can take my daughters," he marvels.

Yet the longtime head of Britain's Equality and Human Rights Commission (he held the post until 2012) doesn't think soccer has slain discrimination yet. Over breakfast one snowy morning a few years ago, Phillips identified an enduring type of discrimination in British soccer: "Loads of black players on the field and none in the dugout."

You might think this form of discrimination would eventually disappear, that just as competition pushed clubs into buying black players, it will push them into hiring black managers. But in fact, the prejudice against black managers has proved harder to shift. As soon as you get to thinking about what it will take to get more black people into coaching jobs, you are brought face to face with the great question about the soccer coach: Does he really matter? It turns out that coaches or managers (call them what you like) simply don't make that much difference. Consequently, the market in soccer managers is much less efficient than the market in soccer players. That means blacks will continue to have a hard time finding coaching jobs.

Like discrimination against black players, discrimination against black managers first became visible in American sports. As early as 1969 Jackie Robinson, who had become quite rebellious as he grew older, refused to attend Old Timers' Day at Yankee Stadium, in protest of baseball's shunning of black coaches and managers.

The issue hit Britain only when the first generation of black players began to retire (it being a long-standing article of faith in soccer that only ex-players had what it took to become managers). The former England international Luther Blissett, who as a player had made that ill-fated transfer to Milan, applied for twenty-two jobs as a manager in the 1990s. He did not get a single interview. Stella Orakwue, who recounts his story in her 1998 book, *Pitch Invaders,* concludes, "I feel a British black managing a Premiership team could be a very long way off." Indeed, only in 2008, ten years after she wrote this, did Blackburn give Paul Ince a chance. After Ince's appointment, John Barnes, who himself had struggled to get work as a manager in Britain, still maintained, "I believe the situation for black managers is like it was for black players back in the 1970s." Ince lasted less than six months at Blackburn. He hasn't had a chance in the Premier League since.

Not even good results with Newcastle could save the black manager Chris Hughton in 2010: he had won the club promotion to the Premier League the season before, but four months into the new season, with Newcastle safely in eleventh place in the top division, he was sacked. "Regrettably the board now feels that an individual with more managerial experience is needed to take the club forward," the club explained. Newcastle finished the season in twelfth place.

True, the black managers Ruud Gullit and Jean Tigana did get longer stints in the Premier League. But as Orakwue notes, the crucial point is that they were foreigners. They were perceived in Britain first of all as Dutch or French, and only secondarily as black. Gullit was cast as a typical sophisticated Dutch manager, not as an untried "black" one.

At the time of writing, in early 2014, Hughton at Norwich is the only black manager in the Premier League. The "Rooney Rule" in the NFL—which requires teams to interview at least one minority candidate when recruiting a head coach or other senior officials—has no equivalent in European soccer. That's a shame, as the rule has made quite a difference in the NFL.

You would think that given this discrimination, unprejudiced soccer clubs could clean up by hiring the best black (or female) managers at low salaries. A small club like Tranmere Rovers, say, could probably take its pick of the world's black managers. It could get the best female manager in history. Yet it probably won't. That's because the market in soccer managers is so different from the market in players. Markets tend to work when they are transparent—when you can see who is doing what and place a value on it. That is preeminently true of soccer players, who do their work in public. When you can't see what people do, it's very hard to assign a value to their work. Efficient markets punish discrimination in plain view of everyone, and so discrimination tends to get rooted out. Inefficient markets can maintain discrimination almost indefinitely.

Black soccer players became accepted because the market in players is transparent. It is pretty obvious who can play and who can't, who's "got bottle" and who hasn't. The market in players' salaries, as we have seen, is so efficient that it explains about 90 percent of the variation in clubs' league positions in the long run. Typically the club with the best-paid players finishes at the top, and the one with the worst-paid finishes in the cellar. However, the market in managers doesn't work nearly as well. If players' salaries determine results almost by themselves, then it follows that the vast majority of managers are not very relevant.

Still, there is an important caveat: players' wages don't explain everything—merely almost everything at most clubs. That leaves some room for a few good managers to make a difference. The question then is: Which elite managers finish consistently higher with their teams than their wage bills would predict? In other words, to borrow a phrase from José Mourinho: Who are the special ones? Stefan has tried to answer that question.

First he got ahold of the financial accounts of English clubs in all four divisions from 1973–1974 through 2009–2010. This is not as hard as it sounds. All clubs except one were limited companies during this period, and therefore obliged by law to file annual accounts with Companies House. You can obtain copies online for a small fee (if you want to buy your club's accounts for last year, it will cost you all of $1.50). Going back thirty-seven years is a bit more complicated. Five percent of accounts were missing, while 15 percent of clubs had filed abbreviated accounts that didn't reveal wage spending. That left Stefan with wage data for 80 percent of clubs for the thirty-seven-year period.

Stefan began by identifying all managers who had been with a club for at least a full season. There were 699 of them in the database. However, it's unfair to judge a manager on just a couple of seasons, because in such a short period, luck plays a big role. So Stefan ranked only managers who had worked in the game for five or more full seasons: 251 men. It must be said that few of the other 448 managers, the ones who worked fewer than five seasons, looked like overachievers. Indeed, most of them had drifted out of the game early because of their poor records. Some of the worst performers exited the profession fastest.

Stefan then examined how our 251 survivors had performed relative to their players' wage bills. The telling stat is the size of a club's wages relative to those of its rivals. There are twenty clubs in the Premier League, which means that the average club spends 5 percent of the league's total wages. Roughly speaking, if a club spending 5 percent finished in the top half of the table, the manager appeared to have been overachieving. If it finished in the bottom half, he appeared to be underachieving. One season of overachievement doesn't make a star. That could be due to any number of things, above all luck. What counted was the manager's record measured over five years or more.

Only a very few of these 251 managers were underachievers: men who consistently finished lower with their teams than the players' wage bill would have predicted. Malcolm Allison (a fêted assistant manager with Manchester City in the late 1960s, but a failure as a go-it-alone manager afterward) made our list of shame, as did Alan Mullery, Harry Gregg, and a few lesser-known names it would be kindest not to mention. However, even this handful of failures didn't seem to be terrible managers. Their underachievement was not what statisticians call "statistically significant." In simple English: it could have been due simply to chance.

Stefan didn't treat all divisions equally. There are ninety-two professional teams in England, spread over the four divisions. A manager in the bottom tier, League Two, who has the ninetieth budget in England but manages to finish eightieth in the country is doing well. However, a manager with the third-highest budget in England who succeeds in winning the Premier League is probably doing even better. At the top of soccer, competition is fiercer, the amount of money typically required to jump a place is much higher, and so Stefan's model gave more credit to overachieving managers in the Premier League than to overachievers lower down. Still, his model does allow some lower-division managers to make it to the top of our rankings.

All in all, he estimated that somewhere between forty and seventy of the managers in our sample seemed to make a positive difference: that is, they usually overachieved with their teams. Note that that's at most 28 percent of the 251 survivors in our database—and these survivors would themselves tend to be the elite, because underachieving managers rarely survive five years in the game. In other words, at best 10 percent of the 699 managers we have observed since 1973 look like overachievers. These managers tend to have stayed in their posts relatively long, which makes sense.

We ended up with two lists of overachievers. For our first list, we put all English clubs together and ranked each club's wage spending relative to the other ninety-one. The second list separated the clubs into four divisions, and measured each club's spending relative to the other clubs in its division. We mention this because each method produced a slightly different list of overachieving managers. (Please see Figure 7.1 on page 116.)

It should be noted that the great Brian Clough, who appears on one of our lists, undoubtedly would have ranked somewhere in the top on both if only we'd had financial data for his glory years with Nottingham Forest in the 1970s. Uniquely within the (then) Football League, Forest was not a limited company at the time. It was a members' club, and therefore didn't lodge annual accounts at Companies House. Our list shows that even in his declining alcoholic years from 1982 onward, Clough was among the elite.

Our final ranking of managers who made both lists can be found on page 117.

This list of nineteen names must stand as our best stab at identifying the best managers in England in these years. Paisley, for those who are new to soccer, won six league titles and three European Cups with Liverpool from 1974 to 1983.

FIGURE 7.1. Overachieving managers in England, 1974–2010

"Total wage" method		*"Divisional wage" method*	
Rank	Manager	Rank	Manager
1	Bob Paisley	1	Bob Paisley
2	Alex Ferguson	2	Bobby Robson
3	Kenny Dalglish	3	Alex Ferguson
4	Arsène Wenger	4	Arsène Wenger
5	Rafael Benitez	5	David Moyes
6	Bobby Robson	6	Kenny Dalglish
7	Gérard Houllier	7	John Beck
8	Steve Parkin	8	Dave Mackay
9	Dave Mackay	9	Howard Kendall
10	Roy Evans	10	Steve Tilson
11	Howard Kendall	11	Rafael Benitez
12	Steve Tilson	12	Ronnie Moore
13	George Graham	13	Lou Macari
14	Martin Allen	14	Paul Sturrock
15	Martin Ling	15	Steve Coppell
16	Paul Simpson	16	George Graham
17	Ronnie Moore	17	Martin Allen
18	David Hodgson	18	Ray Mathias
19	Steve Wignal	19	Dave Stringer
20	Ian Atkins	20	Sam Allardyce
21	John Beck	21	Martin O'Neill
22	Sean O'Driscoll	22	Mel Machin
23	Leroy Rosenior	23	Jimmy Sirrel
24	Brian Clough	24	Keith Peacock
25	David Moyes	25	Tony Pulis
26	Russell Slade	26	Dave Smith
27	Steve Cotterill	27	Jack Charlton
28	Gary Peters	28	Paul Simpson
29	Micky Adams	29	Bobby Gould
30	Brian Laws	30	Gary Megson
31	Kevin Keegan	31	Terry Venables
32	Ron Atkinson	32	Danny Wilson
33	Dave Stringer	33	David O'Leary
34	David O'Leary	34	Trevor Francis
35	Paul Sturrock	35	Joe Kinnear
36	Keith Alexander	36	Graham Taylor
37	Gary Johnson	37	John Neal
38	Terry Neill	38	Steve Parkin
39	Barry Fry	39	Mike Buxton
40	Roy McFarland	40	Dave Bassett

FIGURE 7.2. The special ones

Name	*Rank* ("divisional wage" method)	*Rank* ("total wage" method)
Bob Paisley	1	1
Alex Ferguson	3	2
Bobby Robson	2	6
Arsène Wenger	4	4
Kenny Dalglish	6	3
Rafael Benitez	11	5
Dave Mackay	8	9
Howard Kendall	9	11
Steve Tilson	10	12
John Beck	7	21
Ronnie Moore	12	17
George Graham	16	13
David Moyes	5	25
Martin Allen	17	14
Paul Simpson	28	16
Steve Parkin	38	8
Paul Sturrock	14	35
Dave Stringer	19	33
David O'Leary	33	34

Of course, there are all sorts of caveats to attach. First, our valuations are by no means precise. Wenger ranks a touch higher than Dalglish in our table, but please don't read that as saying that Wenger is the better manager. Our list cannot be that exact. Working at Arsenal in the 1990s and 2000s was a different experience from working at Liverpool, Blackburn, and Newcastle in the 1980s and 1990s. Many other factors besides the manager might have caused each club's overachievement. It's notable that Paisley and Benitez also overachieved with Liverpool relative to wages, and George Graham with Arsenal. Perhaps it's easier to overachieve at Arsenal and Liverpool than at other clubs because these two have produced many excellent youth players, allowing managers to do well without spending a fortune on wages. Perhaps Liverpool's famous "boot room" of the 1970s and 1980s—the gang of old-time coaches and scouts who would sit around drinking whiskey and scheming for games together—gave Paisley and Dalglish the wisdom of crowds. Quite likely

Paisley, Dalglish, Wenger, and Graham landed in helpful settings. Yet they do seem to have been good managers, too.

There's another caveat to make. Our table measures only spending on wages, not on transfers. We saw in Chapter 2 that Wenger and Ferguson had relatively low net spending on transfers, which makes their high rankings in our list even more impressive. But we also saw that Benitez (likewise high on our list) blew fortunes on transfers at Liverpool. So even though he economized on wages, he didn't get his league positions cheaply.

In fact, every manager in this table requires closer analysis. Just as you cannot sign a player simply on the basis of his match data, you cannot simply hire a manager from our list and sit back and wait for the trophies to roll in (although it would certainly be a much better method than hiring a guy because he was a good player). Some managers on our list succeeded in circumstances that might not be repeatable elsewhere. For instance, we suspect Bobby Robson did so well for Ipswich in the 1970s because he was one of the few managers of the time to strive for passing soccer and to scout on the Continent. Today he'd have had to find new tricks.

Critics will ask why such a high proportion of our highest-ranked managers work for giant clubs. Well, for a start, the best managers tend to end up at the best clubs. Arsenal hired Wenger after he'd excelled at Monaco; Manchester United signed Ferguson after he'd broken the Celtic-Rangers duopoly with Aberdeen in Scotland. In fact, Ferguson might have ranked even higher in our table had we been able to include his brilliant Aberdeen years. Unfortunately, we had to omit Scottish clubs because the financial data wasn't detailed enough.

A second reason that managers of giant clubs dominate our list: by definition, more overachieving clubs will end up at the top of the league than at the bottom. And third, as we've said, the top of soccer is more competitive than the bottom, and so we have given extra credit to managers who overachieve at the summit.

Some may wonder whether a manager of Manchester United and Arsenal can overachieve by much. After all, United has the highest revenues in English soccer, and Arsenal isn't far behind. Surely clubs that rich ought to be winning league titles? (Indeed, we must admit that we used to think so ourselves. Simon now blushes with shame to think that he once wrote that if he managed United, with all its money, he would probably do about as well as Ferguson did.)

Certainly, even if United's squad were to operate as an anarchist workers' collective without a manager, it would probably do very well. But Ferguson and Wenger do seem to have added value. Once you look at the numbers, it turns out that for many years Ferguson's United and Wenger's Arsenal spent little or no more on wages than did some of their frustrated rivals. Both clubs habitually live within their means. Manchester United almost always makes operating profits, used to pay dividends to shareholders, and now forks out large sums each year to repay the debts of its owners, the Glazer family. That didn't leave Ferguson fortunes to spend on players' wages. He didn't seem to need it.

We've seen that the average club in the Premier League spends 5 percent of the division's total wage bill. Of course Manchester United is always above that 5 percent line, but especially in the 1990s it wasn't above it by very much. In 1995–1996, for instance, the club spent just 5.8 percent of the Premier League's total wages yet won the title. From 1991 through 2000, United's average league position was 1.8 (i.e., somewhere between first and second place) and yet in that decade the club spent only 6.8 percent of the Premier League's average on wages. Ferguson was getting immense bang for his buck. In part, he owed this to the Beckham generation. Beckham, the Neville brothers, Paul Scholes, Nicky Butt, and Ryan Giggs were excellent players who performed with great maturity almost as soon as they entered the first team, but given their youth they would then have been earning less than established stars. Furthermore, because Ferguson was at Old Trafford from 1986 until 2013, he had chosen every player at the club himself. He wasn't paying the unwanted signings of his predecessors large sums to rot in the stands. That helped keep United's wages down.

Ferguson continued to overachieve in the 2000s, even after the Beckham generation had become big names earning top dollar. Admittedly his overperformance was less striking than in the 1990s. From 2001 through 2010 United's average league position was again 1.8, but in this decade he spent nearly 9 percent of the Premier League's total on wages. Another way of putting it: in the 1990s he spent only 35 percent more than the division average, whereas in the 2000s he spent 80 percent more than the average to achieve the same result. No wonder, because life had become ever more competitive at the top, with Chelsea and Manchester City getting shots of oil money and Arsenal and Liverpool receiving ever more income from the Champions League. None of that had happened in the 1990s.

The amount of money Ferguson required to dominate seemed to keep rising. In 2010, the last year in our database, United's share of the Premier League's wage spending peaked at just over 10 percent. Yet even that wasn't outsize. Manchester City that year spent about the same proportion, and Chelsea accounted for 14 percent of the Premier League's total outlay on wages from 2004 through 2010—the largest share for any top-division club in the thirty-seven years of our database. Other clubs, too, have exceeded 10 percent of the division's total spending in the past, notably Leeds United, which was at nearly 12 percent when Clough spent his infamous forty-four days there in 1974. In short, Ferguson was a phenomenon for most of his time at Old Trafford. From 2003 through 2013 he consistently had to compete against clubs with higher wages. Mostly he won. Even so, it's hard to work out exactly what he was doing right. If it were obvious, other managers would simply have copied him.

Wenger's record is almost as awesome. In his first seven seasons at Arsenal, from 1996–1997 onward, the Frenchman achieved an average league position of 1.6 while accounting for 7.5 percent of the Premier League's wages. That was a bigger share than Ferguson was spending then, but hardly plutocratic. Admittedly Wenger's performance has declined slightly in recent years. In the six seasons to 2009–2010, Arsenal had an average league position of 3.3 while spending 8.8 percent of the Premier League's wages. That's still overachievement, but less striking than before.

We can explain why he might have declined. When Wenger arrived in insular England in 1996, there were still knowledge gaps to exploit. He brought knowledge that nobody else in the country possessed at that point. He was one of the only managers already using statistics to analyze players' performance; he knew what food soccer players should eat; and above all, he knew foreign transfer markets. He seems to have been the only manager in England to realize that Milan's reserve Patrick Vieira and Juventus's reserve Thierry Henry were great players. Spotting that didn't require mystical insight—Vieira convinced the Highbury crowd of the same fact inside forty-five minutes on his debut against Sheffield Wednesday—but none of Wenger's British rivals appeared to have even watched Vieira before. And so Wenger overachieved magnificently.

His problem was that he was too successful for his own good. Other managers began to study what he was doing. They copied his innovations in diet, scouting, and statistics. Meanwhile, like many brilliant pioneers, Wenger seems to have fallen into the trap of becoming more like himself—less willing to learn new tricks or listen to intelligent criticism—as he got older.

Eventually, when everyone had more or less the same knowledge, Arsenal was overtaken by clubs with bigger wage bills. That is what happens to knowledge gaps inside a league: they close fast. This would explain why Wenger's Arsenal won nothing from 2005 through 2013.

Yet during his worst moments, especially after the 8–2 defeat at Old Trafford in August 2011, his critics were much too harsh on him. Given that he was up against several richer clubs, and against another great overachieving manager in Ferguson, it would have been astonishing had Arsenal continued to win titles. It was particularly unfair to castigate Wenger for fielding teams that kept getting outmuscled by Chelsea. There is a common belief that Wenger actively doesn't want players who are both brilliant and strong, such as Didier Drogba, Cristiano Ronaldo, and Vieira himself. In fact, Wenger built his first Arsenal team around Vieira, and privately regrets that he never managed to sign Drogba and Ronaldo when he could afford them. It's just that he knows that nowadays Arsenal cannot afford players who have it all. The club has to economize on one quality or another, and forced to choose, Wenger has tended to prefer players who are gifted and fast but not strong. Chelsea hasn't had to make that choice.

Arsenal's board cannot very well tell the fans, "Forget it. We probably can't compete with United, Chelsea, and City over a whole season." But the board knows that this is true. It doesn't expect Wenger to win titles anymore. That's why, even in the darkest moments of 2011, the board never even considered sacking him.

As we've seen, since Abramovich took over Chelsea in 2003, he has thrown money at the problem. In the 1970s Chelsea was still spending a touch less than the average in the top division. Only from the mid-1990s did the club's spending start to rise, and at the end of the 1990s it hit 8 percent of the Premier League's total. By about 2000 the Italian manager Gianluca Vialli was spending more than 10 percent of the Premier League's wage bill, yet Ferguson repeatedly won the league on less.

When Abramovich bought Chelsea, he gave his manager Claudio Ranieri a mammoth 16 percent of the Premier League's wage spending for 2003–2004. Of course, Ranieri ought to have won the league that season. However, we shouldn't be too harsh on him. Even with the highest wage bill, it's tricky to finish on top, because you are competing against both bad luck and the well-funded overachievers Wenger and Ferguson. Though José Mourinho's Chelsea outspent its rivals, he deserves credit for winning two straight titles. But Mourinho spent only three full seasons in England before his return in 2013, and therefore doesn't figure in our rankings.

Chelsea was the country's biggest-spending club for six or seven years until the rise of Manchester City, and Abramovich's money bought him three league titles. By 2013, City almost certainly had the highest wage bill in England. Yet Ferguson kept his neighbor from a title, confounding the odds one last time.

So far we've discussed only overperforming managers of giant clubs. However, several of our best managers of the past thirty-seven years—men such as Paul Sturrock, Steve Parkin, Ronnie Moore, and John Beck—have spent their careers in the lower reaches of the game. As we write, in early 2014, Moore is managing Tranmere in League One, England's third tier, Parkin is assistant manager of Bradford in the same division, while Sturrock and Beck don't have clubs at all. (Beck left semi-professional Kettering Town in 2012, escorted from the stadium just before a game, and Sturrock was sacked by Southend in 2013.) These men are titans of the lower divisions, but hardly anybody higher up pays any attention to titans of the lower divisions. It seems that the market in managers does not work very efficiently: many of the best do not seem to get rewarded, while hundreds of managers who add no value continue to muddle on and get jobs, often good ones.

Admittedly some of our lower-division titans have succeeded by playing a long-ball game that might not work higher up. "I think my style of play has been successful in the lower leagues," Sturrock told us cautiously in his bare little office at Southend one winter's night. Yet most good managers could surely adjust their methods to better players. We suspect these men are being undervalued because they don't physically look the part, or lack charisma, or have had their reputations unfairly tarnished somewhere along the way. Sturrock thinks this happened to him during his only, brief stint in the Premier League: his thirteen matches with Southampton in 2004. He complains, "Everybody to this day thinks that I was fired. I walked out of the football club. It was an agreement between me and the chairman. It was the best for both of us. So maybe people tagged me that I'd failed in that environment. But if you look at my games ratio to any of the other managers that were round about me at that time, I probably had the most successful thirteen games any manager's had there." Indeed, Sturrock won five of those games—pretty good at a small club—but fell out with Southampton's chairman, Rupert Lowe. He never got a chance at the top level again. In his Southend office, he reflects, "'I've been to the show,' as the Americans would say. The one thing I'll say is that I enjoyed every minute of it."

We're not telling Manchester City or Newcastle to go and hire Sturrock or one of the other lower-league titans on our list tomorrow morning. But it couldn't hurt to take a look.

We've focused here on overachieving managers. However, the key point is that they are the exceptions. The vast bulk of managers appear to have almost no impact on their teams' performance and do not last very long in the job. They seem to add so little value that it is tempting to think that they could be replaced by their secretaries, or their chairmen, or by stuffed teddy bears, without the club's league position changing. In typical soccer talk, the importance of managers is vastly overestimated. As Sturrock says, "Money talks and money decides where you finish up in the leagues." All in all, Jamie Carragher gets the significance of managers about right in his autobiography:

> The bottom line is this: if you assemble a squad of players with talent and the right attitude and character, you'll win more football matches

> than you lose, no matter how inventive your training sessions, what system you play or what team-talks you give. But anything that can give you the extra 10 per cent, whether that's through diet, your general fitness or the correct word in your ear, also has merit.

Tony Fernandes of QPR insists: "I think managers do play a big part." But he adds: "Ultimately, if you have rubbish players, there's nothing a manager can do." Perhaps the main service a manager can perform for his club is to avoid spending much money on transfers. After all, transfers usually fail, and they waste funds that could have been spent on boosting the all-determining players' wages. Wenger is a better manager than Benitez in part because he blows less of his budget on transfer fees. But there isn't much else most club managers can do to push their teams up the table. After all, players matter much more. As Johan Cruijff said when he was coaching Barcelona, "If your players are better than your opponents, 90 percent of the time you will win."

There cannot be many businesses where a manager would make such an extravagant claim. The chairman of General Motors does not say that the art of good management is simply hiring the best designers or the best production managers. Instead he talks about organization, motivation, or building a team. We typically think of businesses as complex organisms. Yet when it comes to soccer, someone as insightful as Cruijff describes management as little more than assembling the best players. Seldom has a prescription for successful management been so simple.

As we'll argue later in the book, we think that managers of national teams have a better chance of making a difference. A manager can outperform when he brings his team foreign knowledge that it didn't previously have. Fabio Capello arguably did that for England, and Guus Hiddink for the foreign countries he managed until his decline after 2008. These men passed on to their players some of the latest western European soccer know-how. However, it's very rare for such knowledge gaps to exist in a league like England's. All serious English clubs are now stuffed with people from all over the world and have access to current best practice. The Premier League is like a market with almost perfect information. Consequently, very few club managers can make much difference.

The counterargument to ours would be that the clubs that pay their players the most also tend to pay their managers the most. So the clubs with the best players would also be the clubs with the best managers.

We believe this argument is false in most cases. First, if some managers are good and others are bad, why does the performance of managers over time vary so much more than the performance of players? Wayne Rooney and Frank Lampard are always good players. They will have the odd bad match, but over the years nobody ever thinks they are terrible and in need of sacking. The history of management, by contrast, is littered with blokes appointed as the Messiah and sacked as a loser a few months later. Most managers' careers seem to follow a random walk: some good seasons, some bad ones. And anyway, how can managers make much difference when most of them last so briefly in each job? In 1992 the average manager's tenure in English soccer was 3.5 years. By the summer of 2013, it was little over a year, and of the ninety-two managers of English league clubs, only Wenger had held his job for more than seven years.

Chris Anderson and David Sally take on our argument about managers in their book *The Numbers Game.* They say that managers matter rather more than we say, and they point to studies of chief executives making a difference in other industries. However, soccer isn't like most other industries. For a start, CEOs in other industries tend to stay in their jobs for much longer. In 2011, the average tenure of chief executives of companies ranked in the S&P 500 (the stock-market index of five hundred big American companies) was 8.4 years. These people have more time to make a difference than a manager of a soccer club. Secondly, although CEOs in all industries like to make speeches about "the talent of our people," individual talent probably matters more in soccer than it does at, say, Wal-Mart. For a big retailer, having the right processes and technology is probably what matters most. But if you want to beat Chelsea, you need eleven excellent soccer players. That might help explain the difference in wages between soccer players and workers in other industries.

Furthermore, the individual soccer manager has probably become even less important in recent years. Managers at big clubs now tend to work with dozens of staffers, ranging from physical trainers to defensive coaches to data analysts. Often these staffers have been appointed by the club chairman or the technical director, and will stay in their jobs long after the manager leaves. The manager still appears at the post-match press conference, and gets public credit for victory and blame for defeat. Day to day, though, his staffers may have a bigger impact on results. Fernandes says coaching staff are "underrated. . . . I think coaching staff make a big difference."

Most media love to focus on great men, but today it probably makes more sense to talk of management teams rather than individual managers. Indeed, you could argue that the main point of the "top job" now is as a focus of competition for the other staffers, who can aspire to become manager one day. Brendan Rodgers, André Villas-Boas, and Steve Clarke, for instance, all made it from Mourinho's staff at Chelsea to managing big clubs of their own.

It's doubtful anyway whether many clubs or countries choose a manager chiefly because they think he will maximize performance. Often the manager is chosen more for his suitability as a symbolic figurehead than for his perceived competence. In other words, he's more of a king, or head of public relations, than an executive.

When a club or country appoints as manager a former iconic player like Maradona or Bryan Robson, it is not simply betting that he will garner more points than some unknown bloke like Avram Grant or Villas-Boas. Performance is only one of the three main criteria used for hiring a manager. That's because a club or country exists only partly to win matches. Its other job is to incarnate the club or country's eternal spirit. So a national team has to be the nation made flesh. Nobody could incarnate Argentina better than Maradona, and so he was made manager. Winning soccer matches had little to do with it. Whereas players are almost always employed because the club thinks they help win matches, that doesn't go for managers. Popular ex-players often get the job because they are easily accepted by fans, media, players, and sponsors. They are hired as much for who they were as for what they can do.

The third criterion in hiring a manager is typically his gift for PR. A manager might not affect his team's result, but after the game he's the person who explains the result at the press conference. He is the club's face and voice. That means he has to look good—which is why so many of them have glossy, wavy hair—and say the right things in public. This aspect has become ever more important as soccer has received ever more media coverage. The late Helenio Herrera, Inter Milan's legendary manager in the 1960s, once told us that before his time, managers were unpaid men of low status. "In those days it was the players who ran the teams," he said. "You had the team of Di Stefano, the team of Mazzola, the team of Sivori, and the trainer was the man who carried the bags," and he mimicked an overburdened porter.

Televised press conferences have probably done more than anything else to create the modern myth of the omnipotent manager. No wonder that the thing Tony Blair seemed to like best about soccer (according to his former right-hand man, Alastair Campbell) was the post-match press conference. When Blair was British prime minister, he'd often spend time on weekends slumped on the sofa watching soccer on TV. He took a mild interest in Burnley, the club Campbell supported. But Campbell tells us that Blair grew fascinated with the then Burnley manager Stan Ternent, a character with a thick northeastern accent and a gift for exuding gloom. After games Blair, a born actor, liked to put on his best Burnley accent and ring Campbell: "Reet, Ally, 'ow did Burnley get on today, then?"

The forte of most managers is not winning matches—something over which they have little control—but keeping all the interest groups in and around the club (players, board, fans, media, sponsors) united behind them. That's why so many managers are charismatic. Their charisma may not help their teams win matches, but it does help the managers keep support.

The general obsession with managers is a version of the Great Man Theory of History, the idea that prominent individuals—Genghis Khan, or Napoleon, or even Stan Ternent—cause historical change. Academic historians, incidentally, binned this theory decades ago.

The myth of managerial omnipotence has been both good and bad for managers. When the manager became the face of the club, his salary and fame rose. On the other hand, he also became more vulnerable. If the team was losing matches, the obvious thing to do was to get rid of its symbolic figurehead.

Sacking the manager has become a ritual, soccer's version of the Aztecan human sacrifice. English clubs spent an estimated $157 million sacrificing their managers in the 2010–2011 season, if you add up the cost of compensation, legal fees, and "double contracts" (paying the old and new manager at the same time), according to the League Managers Association. All this money could have been more usefully spent on players' wage bills or on improving stadiums.

As it happens, after the manager is sacrificed, a team's performance does tend to improve briefly. Sue Bridgewater, professor at Warwick Business School in the UK, analyzed sackings in the Premier League from 1992 to 2008 and found that "there is a boost for a short honeymoon period." For instance, after Manchester City sacked Mark Hughes at Christmas 2009, it won its first four games under Roberto Mancini. However, that's not because Mancini or any other new manager can work magic. The short honeymoon is easy to explain. Typically the average club earns 1.3 points a match. Typically, Bridgewater found, a club sacks its manager when it averages only 1 point a match—that is, at a low point in the cycle. Any statistician can predict what should happen after a low point: whether or not the club sacks its manager, or changes its brand of teacakes, its performance will probably regress to the mean. Simply put, from a low point you are always likely to improve. The club may have hit the low due to bad luck, or injuries, or a tough run of fixtures, or—as perhaps in Manchester City's case—the time it takes for a largely new team to gel.

Whatever the reason for hitting a low, things will almost inevitably improve afterward. The new manager rarely causes the pendulum to swing. He's just the beneficiary of the swing. Perhaps some players do briefly work harder to impress him, though on that logic clubs should sack managers even more often.

Eventually results regress to the mean. Bridgewater found that three months after a sacking, the typical club averaged the standard 1.3 points a game. Sheikh Mansour, City's billionaire owner, should probably have just stuck with Hughes and waited for results to rebound, but in business doing nothing is often the hardest thing. (And not just in business. Harold Macmillan, British prime minister during the Cuban missile crisis, mused then "on the frightful desire to *do* something, with the knowledge that *not* to do anything . . . was prob. the right answer.")

Inevitably Mancini was credited with City's short honeymoon. "Mancini really is magic," proclaimed *The Sun* newspaper, and people began to whisper that the Italian might win that season's Premier League. No wonder, because the wavy-glossy-haired Italian looks like a manager and boasts a glittering résumé as a player. Those facts reassure fans, media, players, and sponsors, even if they don't help City win matches. Mancini's salary—like any manager's—therefore reflected his iconic status and his gift for PR as much as his expected contribution to performance. So it will not be the case that the best-paid managers are the best performers.

It's different for players. They are judged almost solely on results. Very occasionally a player does get bought because he is an icon, or good at PR. However, those qualities in themselves won't sustain him in the team. Any player who doesn't play well will be out the door swiftly, no matter how wavy his hair or how white his skin. As we've just shown, being a player is all about performance. Being a manager isn't. Although clubs pay players only for their contribution to performance, that's not true of how they pay managers.

Perhaps one day clubs will dispense with managers altogether and let a large sample of their fans pick the team instead. In 2007 the English semiprofessional side Ebbsfleet United gave its 30,000 fan-owners—who had each paid £35 for the privilege—a vote in player selection. Coincidence or not (and the money the fan-owners put in probably made the biggest difference), Ebbsfleet almost immediately experienced its greatest triumph, victory in the FA Trophy Final at Wembley in May 2008. Afterward the club's performance declined, as many of the fans stopped paying, and most of the players had to be let go. Still, it was interesting to see a club select its team using the wisdom of crowds. It would be even more interesting to see what happened if more clubs did this—if they stopped hiring managers and allowed an online survey of registered fans to pick the team. We suspect the club would perform decently, perhaps even better than most of its rivals, because it would be harnessing the wisdom of crowds. And it could use the money it saved on managers to up those crucial players' wages.

None of this is good news for black managers. Because it is so hard to measure a manager's performance without complex grinding of stats over many seasons, it will probably never become painfully obvious that clubs are undervaluing black managers. That means clubs can continue to choose their managers based on appearance. Any club appointing someone who is not a white male ex-player with a conservative haircut must worry about looking foolish if its choice fails. Hiring a black manager feels risky, because as Barnes says, "Black guys haven't proved themselves as managers." White guys have—or at least some of them appear to have.

Soccer players get more or less the jobs they deserve. If only other professions were as fair.

8

THE ECONOMIST'S FEAR OF THE PENALTY KICK

Are Penalties Cosmically Unfair, or Only If You Are Nicolas Anelka?

A famous soccer manager stands up from the table. He's going to pretend he is Chelsea's captain, John Terry, about to take the crucial penalty against Manchester United in the Champions League final in Moscow in 2008.

The manager performs the part with schadenfreude; he is no friend of Chelsea. He adjusts his face into a mask of tension. He tells us what Terry is thinking: "If I score, we win the Champions League." And then, terrifyingly, "But first I have to score."

The manager begins pulling at the arm of his suit jacket: he is mimicking Terry pulling at his captain's armband. Terry is telling himself (the manager explains), "I am captain, I am strong, I will score."

Still pulling rhythmically at his suit, the manager looks up. He is eyeing an imaginary, grotesquely large Edwin van der Sar, who is guarding a goal a very long twelve yards away. Terry intends to hit the ball to Van der Sar's left. We now know that a Basque economist told Chelsea that the Dutch keeper tended to dive right against right-footed kickers. Terry runs up—and here the manager, cackling, falls on his backside.

Van der Sar did indeed dive right, as the Basque economist had foreseen, but Terry slipped on the wet grass, and his shot into the left-hand corner missed by inches.

"This really is football," the manager concludes. A player hits the post, the ball goes out, and Chelsea's coach, Avram Grant, is sacked even though he is exactly the same manager as if the ball had gone in. All in all, Terry's penalty may have been the most expensive miskick in the history of soccer.

The penalty is probably the single thing in soccer about which economists have most to say. The penalty feels cosmically unfair; economists say otherwise. Penalties are often dismissed as a lottery; economists tell both kicker and goalkeeper exactly what to do. (Indeed, if only Nicolas Anelka had followed the economist's advice, Chelsea would have won the final.) And best of all, penalties may be the best way in the known world of understanding game theory.

DIABOLICAL: ARE PENALTIES REALLY UNFAIR?

At first sight, the penalty looks like the most unfair device in all of sports. First of all, it may be impossible for a referee to judge most penalty appeals correctly, given the pace of modern soccer, the tangle of legs and ball, and the levels of deception by players. When the Canadian writer Adam Gopnik watched the World Cup of 1998 on TV for the *New Yorker,* he as an outsider to soccer immediately focused on this problem. The "more customary method of getting a penalty," he wrote, " . . . is to walk into the 'area' with the ball, get breathed on hard, and then immediately collapse . . . arms and legs splayed out, while you twist in agony and beg for morphine, and your teammates smite their foreheads at the tragic waste of a young life. The referee buys this more often than you might think. Afterward the postgame did-he-fall-or-was-he-pushed argument can go on for hours." Or decades. The fan at home is often unsure whether it really should have been a penalty even after watching several replays.

And the referee's misjudgments matter, because the penalty probably has more impact than any other refereeing decision in sports. Umpires in baseball and tennis often fluff calls, but there are fifty-four outs in a baseball game, and countless points in a tennis match, and so no individual decision tends to make all that much difference. Referees in rugby and football blunder, too, but because these games are higher scoring than soccer, individual calls rarely change outcomes here, either. In any case, officials in all these sports can now consult instant replays.

But soccer referees cannot. And since important soccer matches usually hinge on one goal, the penalty usually decides the match. As Gopnik says, the penalty "creates an enormous disproportion between the foul and the reward."

No wonder the penalty drives managers crazy. As Arsène Wenger lamented at the end of the 2007–2008 season, "Every big game I've seen this year has been decided, offside or not offside, penalty or not penalty." Indeed, it's now a standard tactic for managers in England, after their teams have lost, to devote the post-match press conference to a penalty given or not given. It's a ritual song of lament, which goes like this: *The penalty completely changed the outcome of the game. We were clearly winning/tying but lost because of the (diabolical, unjust) penalty.*

The manager knows that most media prefer covering personality clashes to tactics, and so the "match" reports will be devoted to the press conference rather than his team's losing performance. Meanwhile, the winning manager, when asked about the penalty, recites, *It made no difference whatever to the outcome of the game. We were clearly winning and would inevitably have done so without the (entirely just) penalty.*

These two ritual managerial chants amount to two different hypotheses about how penalties affect soccer matches. The first manager is claiming that randomly awarded penalties distort results. The second manager is saying penalties make no difference. On occasion, either manager might be right. But over the long term, one of them must be more right than the other. So which is it—do penalties change results, or don't they? We have the data to answer this question.

Our guru is Dr. Tunde Buraimo. One of the growing band of sports econometricians—the British equivalent of baseball's sabermetricians—Tunde works, appropriately, in the ancient heartland of professional soccer at the University of Central Lancashire in Preston. As the saying goes, the plural of "anecdote" is "data," and Tunde prefers to work with tens of thousands of pieces of evidence rather than a few random recollections.

To help us with our book, he examined 1,520 Premier League games played over four years, from the 2002–2003 season until 2005–2006. For each game he knew the pattern of scoring and, crucially, which team was expected to win given the prematch betting odds.

Our test of the two rival hypotheses about penalties is simple. We asked Tunde to divide the games into two groups:

1. Games in which penalties were awarded
2. Games in which they were not

We then asked him to compare how often the home team won when there was a penalty, and how often when there wasn't. Figure 8.1 shows what he found.

Look at the last column first. Taking all games in the database, 47.30 percent ended in home wins, 27.37 percent in away wins, and 25.33 percent in ties. These frequencies reflect the intrinsic advantage of home teams. Now imagine that the first manager is right: penalties change the outcome of the game. How will they do that? It might be that penalties always favor home teams (because referees are cowards), in which case we would expect the percentage of home wins to be greater when penalties are given. Alternatively, it might be that penalties favor away teams (perhaps enabling a team that has its back against the wall to make an escape). If so, the proportion of away wins (or ties) would rise with penalties.

FIGURE 8.1. Comparison of home team and penalties

	Penalty awarded in match?		
Result	No	Yes	Total
Home win	577 46.76%	142 49.65%	719 47.30%
Away win	336 27.23%	80 27.97%	416 27.37%
Tie	321 26.01%	64 22.38%	385 25.33%
Total	1,234 100%	286 100%	1,520 100%

But in fact, as the first two columns show, the percentages for all results barely change whether a penalty is given or not. The percentage of home wins is about three points higher when there is a penalty (up from 46.76 percent to 49.65 percent), and the percentage of ties is commensurately lower (down to 22.38 percent from 26.01 percent). The percentage of away wins remains almost identical (27.97 percent against 27.23 percent) with or without penalties. So in games with penalties, there are slightly more home wins and slightly fewer ties.

It's tempting to read significance into this: to think that the rise in home wins when there is a penalty big enough to show that penalties favor the home team. However, statisticians warn against this kind of intuitive analysis. The absolute number of home wins when there were penalties in the game was 142. Had the frequency of home wins been the same as in games when there was no penalty, the number of home wins would have been 134. The difference (eight extra home wins) is too small to be considered statistically significant and the difference is likely due to chance. It would have been a different matter had the number of home wins when there was a penalty exceeded 150 (or 52 percent of the games concerned). Then the increase would have met the standard generally used by statisticians for confidence that there was a statistically reliable difference in outcomes depending on the award of a penalty. As it is, though, the data suggest that awarding a penalty does not affect home wins, away wins, or ties.

FIGURE 8.2. **Penalty effects on match results**

	Penalty awarded in match?		
Result	No	Yes	Total
Favorite win	633 51.30%	147 51.40%	780 51.32%
Underdog win	254 20.58%	67 23.43%	321 21.12%
Tie	347 28.12%	72 25.17%	419 27.57%
Total	1,234 100%	286 100%	1,520 100%[a]

[a]The totals should add up to 100%, but there are rounding errors.

But perhaps penalties have a different effect on match results. Perhaps they help favorites (if refs favor the big team). Or do they help underdogs (if penalties truly are given randomly, they should help the worse team more than the better one)? Tunde tested these hypotheses, too.

It's obvious even to the naked eye that penalties have no impact at all on whether the favorite wins: favorites win 51.3 percent of games without a penalty, and 51.4 percent with a penalty. It's true that underdogs win nearly 3 percent more often when there is a penalty than when there is not, but once again the tests demonstrate that this fact has no statistical significance. We can put the increase down to chance. Match results appear to be the same with or without penalties. Penalties do not matter.

Now, this is a statistical statement that requires a very precise interpretation. Penalties do matter in that they often change the outcome of individual games. Clearly a team that scores from a penalty is more likely to win, and so, whatever a manager says, a converted penalty will affect the evolution of almost any game.

However, *on average,* taken over a large sample of games, a penalty does not make it any more likely that home teams or away teams or favorites or underdogs win. If penalties were abolished tomorrow, the pattern of soccer results would be exactly the same.

This sounds counterintuitive. After all, we argued that penalties look like the most unfair device in sport. They are often wrongly awarded, they cause a lot of goals, and many of these goals decide matches. So surely penalties should make results less fair?

To explain why penalties don't change the pattern of match results, we need to consult Graham Taylor. The retired manager is now remembered as the "turnip" whose long-ball game cost England qualification for the World Cup of 1994. However, the long-ball game had previously served Taylor very well at his clubs Watford and Aston Villa. No wonder, because it rested on one crucial insight into soccer: you will score goals only if you get possession in the opposition's final third of the field.

Much the same insight applies to penalties: in practice you will get them only if you have possession (or at least a decent chance of winning possession) in the opponent's penalty area. A penalty is often wrongly given. But it is almost always a reward for deep territorial penetration. That makes it, on average, a marker of the balance of power in the game.

That's why good teams get proportionately more penalties than bad teams, and why home teams get more than away teams. On average, a penalty is given with the grain of a game.

RIGHT, LEFT, OR LET VAN DER SAR DECIDE FOR YOU? GAME THEORY IN BERLIN AND MOSCOW

The next question is how to take them. Economists may have no idea when housing prices will crash, but they do know something about this one.

A surprising number of economists have thought hard about the humble penalty kick. Even Steve Levitt, author of *Freakonomics* and winner of perhaps the most important prize in economics (the Clark Medal, which some insiders think outranks the Nobel), once cowrote a little-known paper on penalties. Probably only a trio of economists would have watched videos of 459 penalties taken in the French and Italian leagues. "Testing Mixed-Strategy Equilibria When Players Are Heterogeneous: The Case of Penalty Kicks in Soccer" is one of those you might have missed, but it always won Levitt handshakes from European economists. Here's an American who gets it, they must have thought. Levitt, P.-A. Chiappori, and T. Groseclose explain that they wrote the paper because "testing game theory in the real world may provide unique insights." Economists revere the penalty as a real-life example of game theory.

Game theory was developed in the 1940s by the likes of John von Neumann, a brilliant mathematician who also helped create the architecture of the modern computer. It is the study of what happens when people find themselves in situations exactly like a penalty-taker facing a goalkeeper: when what I should do depends on what you do, and what you should do depends on what I do.

The American government used game theory extensively during the cold war to plan its interactions with the Soviet Union and to try to predict Soviet moves. (It is said that game-theoretic advice was given during the Cuban missile crisis to consider questions like, "If we bomb Cuba, then the Russians will seize West Berlin, and then we'll have to attack Russian troops, and then they'll use nuclear bombs, and then . . .") Today economists use game theory all the time, particularly to plan government policies or analyze business strategy. Game theory even plays a big role in research on biology.

The key to game theory is the analysis of how the strategies of different actors interact. In a penalty kick, for instance, the kicker and the keeper must each choose a strategy: where to kick the ball and where to dive. But each person's strategy depends on what he thinks the other person will do.

Sometimes in game theory, what's best for the actors is if they both do the same thing—going to the same restaurant to meet for dinner, for instance. These kinds of situations are known as coordination or cooperative games. But the penalty kick is a noncooperative game: the actors succeed by achieving their objectives independently of others. In fact, the penalty is a "zero-sum game": any gain for one player is exactly offset by the loss to the other side (plus one goal for me is minus one goal for you).

The issue of game theory behind the penalty was best put in "The Longest Penalty Ever," a short story by the Argentine writer Osvaldo Soriano. A match in the Argentine provinces has to be abandoned seconds before time when a bent referee, who has just awarded a penalty, is knocked out by an irate player. The league court decides that the last twenty seconds of the game—the penalty kick, in effect—will be played the next Sunday. That gives everyone a week to prepare for the penalty.

At dinner a few nights before the penalty, "Gato Díaz," the keeper who has to stop it, muses about the kicker:

> "Constante kicks to the right."
>
> "Always," said the president of the club.
>
> "But he knows that I know."
>
> "Then we're fucked."
>
> "Yeah, but I know that he knows," said el Gato.
>
> "Then dive to the left and be ready," said someone at the table.
>
> "No. He knows that I know that he knows," said Gato Díaz, and he got up to go to bed.

Game theorists try to work out strategies for players in different types of games, and try to predict which strategy each player will pursue. Sometimes the prediction is easy. Consider the game in which each player has only two choices: either "develop a nuclear bomb" or "don't develop a nuclear bomb." To make a prediction, you have to know what the payoff is to each player depending on the game's outcome. Imagine the players are India and Pakistan (but it could be Israel and Iran, or any other pair of hostile nations). Initially Pakistan does not know if India will or won't develop a bomb, so it figures:

if India has no bomb, then
(a) We don't get a bomb: we can live alongside each other, but there will always be incidents.
(b) We get a bomb: India will have to treat us with respect.

if India has a bomb
(c) We don't get a bomb: we can't resist anything India does.
(d) We get a bomb: India will have to treat us with respect.

Plainly, if you are Pakistan, you will end up developing the bomb, whether India has the bomb or not. Likewise, India will choose the same strategy, and will develop the bomb whether Pakistan does or doesn't. So the equilibrium of this game is for both nations to acquire a bomb. This is the gloomy logic of an arms race. The logic of soccer is much the same, and there are many examples of arms races in the sport, from inflation of players' wages to illegal doping.

PIECES OF PAPER IN STUTTGART, MUNICH, BERLIN, AND MOSCOW

The problem for experienced penalty-takers and goalkeepers is that over time, they build up track records. People come to spot any habits they might have—always shooting left, or always diving right, for instance. Levitt and his colleagues observed "one goalie in the sample who jumps left on all eight kicks that he faces (only two of eight kicks against him go to the left, suggesting that his proclivity for jumping left is not lost on the kickers)."

There have probably always been people in the game tracking the past behavior of kickers and keepers. Back in the 1970s, a Dutch manager named Jan Reker began to build up an archive of index cards on thousands of players. One thing he noted was where the player hit his penalties—or at least the penalties that Reker happened to know about. The Dutch keeper Hans van Breukelen would often call Reker before an international match for a briefing.

Nobody paid much attention to this relationship until 1988. That May, Van Breukelen's PSV reached the European Cup final against Benfica. Before the match in Stuttgart, the keeper phoned Reker. Inevitably the game went to a penalty shoot-out. At first Reker's index cards didn't seem to be helping much—Benfica's first five penalties all went in—but Van Breukelen saved the sixth kick from Veloso, and PSV was the European champion. A month later, so was Holland. They were leading the USSR 2–0 in the final in Munich when a silly charge by Van Breukelen conceded a penalty. But using Reker's database, he saved Igor Belanov's weak kick.

In Berlin in 2006, the World Cup quarterfinal between Germany and Argentina also went to penalties. Jens Lehmann, the German keeper, emerged with a crib sheet tucked into his sock. On a little page of hotel notepaper ("Schlosshotel, Grunewald," it said), the German keeper's trainer, Andreas Köpke, had jotted down the proclivities of some potential Argentine penalty-takers:

1. Riquelme	left
2. Crespo	long run-up/right short run-up/left
3. Heinze	6 [His shirt number, presumably given for fear that Lehmann would not recognize him] left low
4. Ayala	2 [shirt number] waits long time, long run-up right
5. Messi	left
6. Aimar	16, wait a long time, left
7. Rodriguez	18, left

Apparently the Germans had a database of 13,000 kicks. The crib sheet might just have tipped the balance. Of the seven Argentines on the list, only Ayala and Maxi Rodríguez actually took penalties. However,

Ayala stuck exactly to Lehmann's plan: he took a long run-up, the keeper waited a long time, and when Ayala dutifully shot to Lehmann's right, the keeper saved. Rodríguez also did his best to oblige. He put the ball in Lehmann's left-hand corner as predicted, but hit it so well that the keeper couldn't reach.

By the time of Argentina's fourth penalty, Germany was leading 4–2. If Lehmann could save Esteban Cambiasso's kick, the Germans would maintain their record of never losing a penalty shoot-out in a World Cup. Lehmann consulted his crib sheet. Sönke Wortmann, the German film director, who was following the German team for a fly-on-the-wall documentary, reports what happened next: "Lehmann could find no indication on his note of how Cambiasso would shoot. And yet the piece of paper did its job, because Lehmann stood looking at it for a long time. Köpke had written it in pencil, the note was crumpled and the writing almost illegible."

Wortmann says that as Cambiasso prepared to take his kick, he must have been thinking, "What do they know?" The Germans knew nothing. But Cambiasso was psyched out nonetheless. Lehmann saved his shot, and afterward there was a massive brawl on the field.

Both Van Breukelen's and Lehmann's stories have been told before. What is not publicly known is that Chelsea received an excellent crib sheet before the Champions League final in Moscow in 2008.

In 1995 the Basque economist Ignacio Palacios-Huerta, who was then a graduate student at the University of Chicago, began recording the way penalties were taken. His paper, "Professionals Play Minimax," was published in 2003.

One friend of Ignacio's who knew about his research was a professor of economics and mathematics at an Israeli university. It so happened that this man was also a friend of Avram Grant. When Grant's Chelsea reached the final in Moscow in 2008, the professor realized that Ignacio's research might help Grant. He put the two men in touch. Ignacio then sent Grant a report that made four points about Manchester United and penalties:

1. Van der Sar tended to dive to the kicker's "natural side" more often than most keepers did. This meant that when facing a right-footed kicker, Van der Sar would usually dive to his own right, and

when facing a left-footed kicker, to his own left. So Chelsea right-footed penalty-takers would have a better chance if they shot to their "unnatural side," Van der Sar's left.

2. Ignacio emphasized in his report that "the vast majority of the penalties that Van der Sar stops are those kicked to a mid-height (say, between 1 and 1.5 meters), and hence that penalties against him should be kicked just on the ground or high up."
3. Cristiano Ronaldo was another special case. Ignacio wrote in the report, "Ronaldo often stops in the run up to the ball. If he stops, he is likely (85%) to kick to the right-hand side of the goalkeeper." Ignacio added that Ronaldo seemed able to change his mind about where to put the ball at the very last instant. That meant it was crucial for the opposing keeper not to move early. When a keeper moved early, Ronaldo always scored.
4. The team that wins the toss before the shoot-out gets to choose whether to go first. But this is a no-brainer: it should always go first. Teams going first win 60 percent of the time, presumably because there is too much pressure on the team going second, which is always having to score to save the game.

Few seem to know this initial advantage exists. TV commentators rarely even mention the toss. Bookmakers don't shift their odds immediately after the toss is done—a mistake from which gamblers could benefit. A month after Chelsea–Manchester United in Moscow, Italy's captain, Gianluigi Buffon, may have decided the outcome of Euro 2008 when he won the toss for a shoot-out against Spain but let the Spaniards shoot first. They won—not necessarily gladdening the heart of the Basque Ignacio—and then won the tournament.

Ignacio doesn't know how his research was used by Chelsea in Moscow, but watching the shoot-out on TV, he was certain it was being used. Indeed, once you know the content of Ignacio's note, it's fascinating to study the shoot-out on YouTube. The Chelsea players seem to have followed his advice almost to the letter—except for poor Anelka.

United's captain, Rio Ferdinand, won the toss, and turned to the bench to ask what to do. Terry tried to influence him by offering to go first. Unsurprisingly, Ferdinand ignored him. United went first, meaning that they were now likely to win. Carlos Tevez scored from the first kick.

Michael Ballack hit Chelsea's first penalty high into the net to Van der Sar's left. Juliano Belletti scored low to Van der Sar's left. Ignacio had recommended that Chelsea's right-footed kickers choose that side. But at this early stage, he still couldn't be sure that Chelsea was being guided by his report. He told us later, "Interestingly, my wife had been quite skeptical about the whole thing as I was preparing the report for Coach Grant, not even interested in looking at it. But then the game went into extra time, and then into a penalty shoot-out. Well, still skeptical."

At this point Cristiano Ronaldo stepped up to take his kick for United. Watching on TV, Ignacio told his wife the precise advice he had given Chelsea in his report: Chelsea's keeper shouldn't move early, and if Cristiano paused in his run-up, he would most probably hit the ball to the keeper's right. Cristiano did indeed pause in his run-up.

To Ignacio's delight, Chelsea's keeper, Petr Cech, stayed motionless—"not even blinking," in the Spanish football phrase. Then, when Cristiano duly shot to Cech's right as predicted, the keeper saved. Ignacio recalled later, "After that, I started to believe that they were following the advice quite closely." As for his wife, "I think she was a bit shocked."

What's astonishing—though it seems to have passed unnoticed at the time—is what happened after that. Chelsea's next four penalty-takers, Frank Lampard, Ashley Cole, John Terry, and Salomon Kalou, all hit the ball to Van der Sar's left, just as Ballack and Belletti had done. In other words, the first six Chelsea kicks went to the same corner.

Ashley Cole was the only one of the six who partly disregarded Ignacio's advice. Cole was left-footed, so when he hit the ball to Van der Sar's left, he was shooting to his own "natural side"—the side that Ignacio had said Van der Sar tended to choose. Indeed, the Dutchman chose correctly on Cole's kick, and very nearly saved the shot, but it was well struck, low (as Ignacio had recommended), and just wriggled out of the keeper's grip. But all Chelsea's right-footed penalty-takers had obeyed Ignacio to the letter and kicked the ball to their "unnatural side," Van der Sar's left.

So far, Ignacio's advice had worked very well. Much as the economist had predicted, Van der Sar had dived to his natural side four times out of six. He hadn't saved a single penalty. Five of Chelsea's six kicks had gone in, while Terry's, as the whole world knows, flew out off the post with Van der Sar in the wrong corner.

It was Anelka's turn to kick. On United's bench, Alex Ferguson was growing frustrated with his keeper. "As Anelka jogged to the penalty spot," Ferguson later recalled, "I was thinking, 'Dive to your left.' Edwin kept diving to the right."

But after six kicks, Van der Sar, or someone else at Manchester United, had figured out that Chelsea was pursuing a strategy. The Dutchman had noticed that the team was putting all its kicks to his left.

As Anelka prepared to take Chelsea's seventh penalty, the gangling keeper, standing on the goal line, extended his arms to either side of him. Then, in what must have been a chilling moment for Anelka, the Dutchman pointed with his left hand to the left corner. "That's where you're all putting it, isn't it?" he seemed to be saying. (This is where books fall short as a medium. We urge you to watch the shoot-out on YouTube.)

Now Anelka had a terrible dilemma. This was game theory in its rawest form. United had come pretty close to divining Chelsea's strategy: Ignacio had indeed advised right-footed kickers like Anelka to put the ball to Van der Sar's left side.

So Anelka knew that Van der Sar knew that Anelka knew that Van der Sar tended to dive right against right-footers. What was Anelka to do? He decided to avoid the left corner, where he had presumably planned to put the ball. Instead he kicked to Van der Sar's right. That might have been fine, except that he hit the ball at mid-height—exactly the level that Ignacio had warned against. Watching the kick on TV, Ignacio was "very upset." Perhaps Anelka was at sea because Van der Sar had pressured him to change his plans at the last moment. Van der Sar saved the shot. Ferguson said afterward, "That wasn't an accident, his penalty save. We knew exactly where certain players were putting the ball." Anelka's decision to ignore Ignacio's advice probably cost Chelsea the Champions League.

RANDOMIZATION: FRANCK RIBÉRY CRACKS GAME THEORY

Crib sheets like Lehmann's might just work on penalty shoot-outs. Many of the players who take kicks in a shoot-out aren't regular penalty-takers. (After Gareth Southgate missed England's crucial kick at Euro '96, his mother said that the last time he'd taken a penalty was three years before, and he'd missed that one, too.) These inferior penalty-takers are not skilled or steady-headed enough to be able to vary their strategy. Quite likely, they will just aim for their favorite corner, hoping that their lack of a track record means the other side won't know their preference.

However, that is not how a good penalty-taker—his team's regular man—thinks.

Suppose the good kicker always chose the same corner for his penalty (game theorists call this a "pure strategy"). It would be easy to oppose: if the kicker always kicks left, then the goalkeeper knows what to do. Pure strategies don't work for penalty-taking. As Levitt and company found, "There are no kickers in our sample with at least four kicks who always kick in one direction." Take that, Jens Lehmann. According to the goalkeeper's crib sheet, Messi's penalties tended to go left. In fact, the mini-Argentine randomizes his spot kicks almost perfectly. "He can also change his mind at the very last instant," adds Ignacio. Sometimes Messi waits for the keeper to shift his weight very slightly to one side, then shoots to the other corner.

Even a more complicated pure strategy than always choosing the same corner does not work. For example, suppose the kicker always shoots in the opposite corner to the one he chose last time. (Diego Forlán tended to do this.) Then a future opponent studying this player might discover the sequence—left, right, left, right, left, right—and with a bit of thought guess what comes next. The essence of good penalty-taking is unpredictability: a good penalty-taker will be one whose next penalty cannot be predicted with confidence from his history of penalty-taking.

This is a particular kind of unpredictability. It does not mean that the kicker should go left half of the time and right half of the time. After all, most kickers have a natural side, and favoring that side gives them a higher chance of scoring. But even if you naturally shoot to the keeper's right, as most right-footed kickers do, sometimes you have to shoot to his left, just to keep him honest. In fact, if a kicker knows his chances of scoring for either corner of the net (depending also on which way the goalkeeper dives), he can choose the proportion of kicks to his natural side that maximizes the probability of scoring. A right-footed kicker won't put 100 percent of his kicks to his natural right side, because that would give the goalkeeper certainty. Even a small change, like kicking right only 99 percent of the time, would raise the chances of scoring considerably by creating uncertainty in the goalkeeper's mind.

Kicking to the left 50 percent of the time would leave the keeper very uncertain. However, it would also entail the kicker hitting many poor shots to his unnatural side. So the kicker does best by hitting somewhere over half his kicks to his natural right side.

Likewise, we can calculate the proportion of times a goalkeeper should dive left or right. (Note that we are assuming the goalkeeper cannot know which way the ball is going before he decides which way to dive.) Kickers and keepers who mix it up like this are pursuing what game theorists call "mixed strategies."

Mixed strategies are peculiar because they require the actor to incorporate randomness into decision-making. Should I go to the pub or the cinema? A mixed strategy requires me to toss a coin, which sounds odd, since one might expect that I prefer one to the other. With a mixed strategy, you let the coin make the decision for you.

Game theorists have wondered for years whether people in the real world follow mixed strategies. They have found in tests that people tend not to use mixed strategies even when it is profitable for them to do so. In fact, our behavior seems to fall short of mixed play in a very specific way: in most cases our sequence of choices is predictable, because people tend to do the opposite of what they have done in the past. For instance, they choose first left, then right, then left, then right, left, right, left, right, confusing change with randomness. These guinea pigs would not make good penalty-takers.

Eventually game theorists began to test mixed strategies in the natural laboratory of penalty-taking. Years before Ignacio Palacios-Huerta advised Chelsea, he collected a database of 1,417 penalties taken between 1995 and 2000. First he calculated the proportion of successful kicks based on whether the kicker went to his natural side (left or right). The success rate was 95 percent if the kicker went to his natural side and the goalkeeper went to the opposite side (the remaining 5 percent of kicks missed the goal). The success rate was 92 percent if the kicker went to his "unnatural" side and the goalkeeper went to his own natural side. Obviously the kicker's success rates were lower if the keeper chose correctly: a scoring rate of 70 percent if both keeper and kicker went to the kicker's natural side, and 58 percent if both went to the other side.

Using these figures, Ignacio calculated the optimal mixed-strategy choices for each player. To maximize the chance of scoring, an imaginary penalty-taker would have to hit 61.5 percent of his kicks to his natural side and 38.5 percent to the other side. In reality, the penalty-takers Ignacio observed got pretty close to this: they hit 60 percent to their natural side and 40 percent the other way.

A keeper's best strategy (if he insists on diving rather than standing still) is to dive to the kicker's natural side 58 percent of the time and to the other side 42 percent of the time. The actual figures, Ignacio found, were scarily close: 57.7 percent and 42.3 percent. Levitt's team, using a different database of penalties, found that keepers went to the right 57 percent of the time. So, it looks as if keepers as well as penalty-takers really do follow mixed strategies.

But what we most want to know are the choices of individual kickers and goalkeepers, not the overall averages. Ignacio studied twenty-two kickers and twenty goalkeepers, each of whom was involved in more than thirty penalties in his database. Again, Ignacio calculated the success rates depending on the side the kicker and goalkeeper chose, and calculated the frequencies in each direction that would maximize the chances of success for kickers and keepers.

In real life, the actual frequencies the players observed were indistinguishable from the best mixed-strategy choices in more than 95 percent of cases. We can say with a high degree of confidence that penalty-takers and goalkeepers really do use mixed strategies. Levitt's paper found the same thing: except for the bizarre keeper who always dived left, almost all the other kickers and keepers played mixed strategies.

Finally Ignacio tested the most important question of all: Are soccer players capable of constructing a truly random sequence in their penalty-taking decisions, as the mixed-strategy theory requires? Careful statistical testing showed that indeed they are. In other words, it is impossible to predict which way a regular penalty-taker will kick based on his history of kicks. Each time he chooses his corner without any reference to what he did the last time.

Randomization of penalties is a completely logical theory that against all odds turns out to be true in practice. As long as the penalty-taker is a pro, rather than some terrified Southgateian innocent roped in for a job that he doesn't understand, simple lists like Lehmann's are not much use.

All this shows the extraordinary amount of subconscious thought that goes into playing top-level soccer. Previous studies in game theory had shown that people could construct random sequences if the problem was first explained to them in some detail. Nobody is suggesting that soccer players have sat at home coming up with mixed-strategy equilibria. Rather, the best players intuitively grasp the truth of the theory and are able to execute it. That is what makes them good players.

Franck Ribéry takes penalties for Bayern Munich and France. Needless to say, the scar-faced little playmaker places his kicks according to a randomized mixed strategy. But more than that, one of his former managers explains, even once Ribéry has embarked on his jagged hither-and-thither run-up, he himself does not know which corner he will choose. When the born economist Arsène Wenger was told this, he gushed with admiration.

As good a player as Ribéry is, he might do even better as a game theorist.

THE ECONOMIST IN THE WORLD CUP FINAL

Ignacio Palacios-Huerta watched the World Cup of 2010 from his home in Spain's Basque country, in between bouts of child care. It baffled him, he told Simon over the phone during the tournament, that he probably knew more about the penalty-takers there than did any team in South Africa. "I have nothing at stake," he reflected. "They have lots: the whole nation."

Four years on from 2006, some teams did have crib sheets more sophisticated than Lehmann's. One team in the quarterfinals told us it had an hour's film of penalties taken by players of the country it was due to face, plus a penalty database. That's why it was silly of England's coach, Fabio Capello, to announce his designated penalty-takers before playing Germany. He potentially gave the opposition time to study their habits.

Still, Ignacio reckoned that even the smartest teams in South Africa probably just counted who shot how often to which corner. "I would be super-surprised if they do any kind of statistical test," he said. He himself runs two. The first: Does a particular kicker follow a truly random strategy? If the kicker does randomize, then the direction he chooses for his next kick—right of the keeper, through the middle, or left—cannot be predicted from his previous kicks.

But Ignacio had detected patterns in several of the penalty-takers at the World Cup. Argentina's Gonzalo Higuain, for instance, before the

World Cup had been kicking too often to the keeper's right. Germany's keeper Manuel Neuer had also been failing to randomize: too often in club games, Neuer had dived to the opposite corner from his previous dive, going first right, then left, then right, etc.

Next Ignacio tests the kicker's success rate with each strategy. The kicker should have an equally high scoring rate whether he shoots right, middle, or left. But going into the World Cup both Argentina's Sergio Agüero and Germany's Miroslav Klose were scoring more often when shooting right of the keeper. That would logically encourage them to aim right if they had to take a kick in South Africa.

Only rarely does Ignacio find a kicker with a very skewed strategy, but England's Frank Lampard was such a man. For years Lampard had randomized his kicks beautifully. But in the 2009–2010 season, Ignacio noted, "he kicked 13 out of 15 times to the right of the goalkeeper—and the two lefts were in the same game when he had to retake the same penalty three times."

No wonder Lampard had developed a habit of missing penalties. Keepers were figuring him out. Portsmouth's David James, for instance, had chosen the correct corner for Lampard's penalty for Chelsea in the FA Cup final held a month before the World Cup—perhaps with help from Ignacio, who had sent Portsmouth a briefing note before the game. As it happened, Lampard's shot went wide. Admittedly Kevin-Prince Boateng missed his penalty for Portsmouth in the match, but then he had ignored Ignacio's advice to kick left of Petr Cech. It is probably harder for penalty-takers than for goalkeepers to follow someone else's advice.

On the phone Ignacio told Simon, "I don't think serious analysis of the data has arrived yet in soccer, but it's coming. I think the world will be a different place in a decade or so."

That phone call got Simon thinking. When Holland and Spain made the World Cup final, Simon, a lifelong fan of the Dutch, e-mailed an official he knew in Holland's camp. Would the Dutch be interested in a penalty analysis of the Spaniards provided by a specialist? The official said they would. And so Ignacio began pulling all-nighters to draw up a report on his fellow countrymen ready for July 11, 2010. More on this later in the book.

9

THE SECRET OF CLAUDE MAKELELE

How "Match Data" Are Changing the Game on the Field

Early in 2011 one of us, Simon, visited Manchester City's tranquil training ground in the village of Carrington. It was a glorious sunny winter's morning, and outside the gates hired hands were washing soccer players' SUVs and sports cars. The defender Kolo Touré coasted past in a giant black contraption straight out of *The Godfather*. Carrington is used to cars like that: Manchester United trains in the village, too.

"Abu Dhabi Travellers Welcome," said the message on the facade of City's sky-blue training center. Abu Dhabi's ruling family owns Manchester City, and one thing it has done since buying the club in 2008 is hire a large team of data analysts. Inside the building was Gavin Fleig, City's head of performance analysis, a polite, sandy-haired man in a neat black City sweater. Hardly anyone outside Carrington has heard of him, and yet Fleig is a prime mover in English soccer's data revolution. Largely unseen by public and media, data on players have begun driving clubs' decisions—particularly decisions about whom to buy and sell. At many clubs, obscure statisticians in back rooms are helping shape transfers.

Fleig gave me the sort of professional presentation you'd expect from a "quant" in an investment bank. Lately, to his excitement, City had acquired stats on every player in the Premier League. Imagine, said Fleig, that you were thinking of signing an attacking midfielder. You wanted someone with a pass completion rate of 80 percent, who had played a good number of games. Fleig typed the two criteria into his laptop. Portraits of the handful of men in the Premier League who met them flashed up on a screen. A couple were obvious: Cesc Fabregas and Steven Gerrard. You didn't need data to know they were good. But beside them was a more surprising face: Kevin Nolan, then with Newcastle. The numbers wouldn't immediately spur you to sign him. But they might prompt you to take a closer look.

In recent years, after many false starts, the number crunchers at big English clubs have begun to unearth the stats that matter. For instance, said Fleig, "The top four teams consistently have a higher percentage of pass completion in the final third of the pitch. Since the recruitment of Carlos Tevez, David Silva, Adam Johnson, and Yaya Touré to our team, in six months, our ability to keep the ball in the final third has grown by 7.7 percent."

That stat had not necessarily driven their recruitment, Fleig cautioned. Indeed, some English clubs lean far more on stats than Manchester City does. Most of them rarely talk about it, though, for fear of sharing their secrets or getting ridiculed for relying on numbers. Few outsiders know just how far soccer's data revolution has progressed. "We've somewhere around 32 million data points over 12,000, 13,000 games now," said Mike Forde, Chelsea's then director of football operations, one morning in the empty stands of Stamford Bridge in 2011. Soccer on the field is starting to become clever.

II

Charles Reep, a wing commander in Britain's Royal Air Force, made possibly the first recorded attempt to log match data at a soccer game. Reep had become interested in the topic in the 1930s, recounts Jonathan Wilson in *Inverting the Pyramid.* He began collecting stats during the second half of a Swindon Town game in 1950. In that one half, he recorded 147 attacks by Swindon. Extrapolating from this small sample, Reep calculated that 99.29 percent of attacks in soccer failed.

He kept logging matches, and over time he developed a theory—based on extremely shaky numbers—that too much passing was a risky waste of time. Most goals came from very short moves, he said. The way to win, he concluded, was long balls forward.

Reep advised the strong Wolves team of the 1950s, and in the early 1980s influenced Graham Taylor, the future England manager, and Charles Hughes, the English Football Association's future director of education and coaching. Using his dodgy stats, Reep encouraged both men to develop the long-ball thinking that would eventually culminate in England's failure to qualify for the World Cup of 1994.

Reep's crude models probably did more to discredit the project of match data than to further it. However, one of his associates did put data to good use in the lower reaches of English soccer. Neil Lanham, a tidy mustached auctioneer, had gotten to know Reep in the Suffolk village where both men lived. In the 1960s Lanham began logging games, but with rather more rigor than the wing commander. "The findings that I talk of," Lanham wrote in a paper for *Soccer Journal* in 2008, "are based on hand-recording every possession for every team in more than 4,000 games. . . . When you sit in the stands and write down every possession by hand, you see and virtually kick every ball."

His methods led him to some startlingly exact findings. For instance, Lanham reckoned that teams scored on average once every 180 possessions, a figure that he said was "near constant" for any division of English soccer and for the World Cup. This finding, he added, was based on "328,018 hand-noted possessions."

Lanham came to the same conclusion as Reep: the secret of soccer was putting the ball near the other team's goal fast. "Two thirds of goals come from possessions won in the final third of the field," he lectured. The great sin, to him, was losing the ball near your own goal.

Sometime in the 1980s Lanham wrote to clubs offering his analysis. Many ignored him, but Wimbledon's manager, Dave Bassett, replied at once. Advised by Lanham, Wimbledon won two promotions. Generally, long-ball soccer seemed to work better at lower levels than it would in the early 1990s for Taylor's England. Lanham, billing himself with the startling twenty-first-century title "soccer performance analyst," went on to advise Sheffield United, Crystal Palace, and Cambridge United as they used long-ball tactics to climb the divisions. "Eight promotions," read the stat on Lanham's letterhead. He also did "various works for international managers," he told us in a letter in 2011.

Though Lanham was determinedly artisanal, in 1985 he began feeding his shorthand codes into what he called "a database computer system." Computers were about to revolutionize match data. In the late 1980s, the young French manager of Monaco, Arsène Wenger, a keen mathematician, began using a computer program called Top Score, developed by a friend, which gave marks for every act performed during a game. "Most players who had very high scores went on to have successful careers," Wenger said later.

A less likely pioneer of match data was the late, great vodka-sodden Ukrainian manager Valeri Lobanovsky. When Simon visited Kiev in 1992, Lobanovsky's pet scientist, professor Anatoly Zelentsov, had him play the computer games that Dynamo Kiev had developed to test players. When Lobanovsky said things like, "A team that commits errors in no more than 15 to 18 percent of its actions is unbeatable," he wasn't guessing. Zelentsov's team had run the numbers.

Meanwhile up in Norway, one of Reep's disciples was making great strides. The Marxist Egil Olsen and Wing Commander Reep had become unlikely allies. They shared a love of stats that went far beyond soccer. Olsen knows (and will sometimes name) the highest mountain of every country in the world. As manager of Norway, he used to gather his players before games to show them their latest individual stats on a big screen. It got to the point that when the midfielder Lars Bohinen mis-hit a pass at the World Cup of 1994, he'd instantly think, "Oh no—I've got an 'M'"—Olsen's code for a misplaced pass. Still, the methods seemed to work. Norway briefly rose to second place in FIFA's rankings. When Olsen became Wimbledon's manager in 1999, the ninety-five-year-old Reep—still billing himself as "wing commander"—offered his services as an analyst, writes Wilson. But Olsen, Wenger, and Lobanovsky were years ahead of their time. The broader breakthrough for stats came in 1996, when Opta Consulting in London began to collect match data for the English Premier League. The management consultancy's main aim was to build its own brand by creating soccer rankings. The Premier League's sponsor, Carling, paid for the so-called Opta Index. Clubs and media got the data for free. Each club received an Excel report with some basic statistics. By today's standards, it was primitive. But in soccer then, it was revolutionary.

Within just a few years, the game moved from a paucity of data to a state of too much information. Pretty soon Opta and its rivals were sending out thousands of new data points each week. Clubs learned facts they had never contemplated before: how many kilometers each player ran per match, and how many tackles and passes he made.

Collecting these numbers took—and still takes—meticulous work. Most people know the impact of computers on our lives, but the work of the grunts is often forgotten. They are like the farm laborers of the preindustrial age who were required to bring in the harvest. Opta's tenth-floor offices next to London's Waterloo station provide a spectacular view of the city, but the dozens of "analysts" barely notice.

Simon visited Opta's offices the day after Manchester City won 1–6 at Old Trafford in October 2011. Two young men were sitting side by side, each in front of a computer, both watching the same images from the game on a screen. One logged all of City's actions, and the other all of Manchester United's. Two other people had logged the game live the day before, with a third person watching for quality control, but Opta likes to repeat the process the next day "with a different set of eyes," said John Coulson, head of professional soccer services at the company. "We're collecting 2,000 events a game live as it happens, with every event logged with a time code and a pitch coordinate, so you have to keep up with it," he explained.

Opta's analysts type in the minutiae of every televised game they can find, from the Premier League to the MLS or the Montenegrin league. Most of the analysts work in London, but others sit in regional offices from just outside Venice to New York. All the ones we saw were men, generally in their twenties, kitted out in regulation grunge and looking wan. Most were college graduates who hadn't been able to resist the temptation of earning pitiful amounts of money to watch soccer. "We take on one person of the twenty or thirty who apply for these jobs," said Coulson. Not that the analysts can really watch the games, as they sit there logging every single event in endless detail (long pass, weight on the ball, origin of the ball, where the ball lands). In all, Opta now collects several hundred categories of data. Doing the analysis looks like a harder job than playing soccer. Most of the grunts are burned out after a couple of years, but then there are plenty more people willing to give it a go.

Gradually managers started to look at the stats being pumped out by the data companies. In 2001 Alex Ferguson of Manchester United suddenly sold his defender Jaap Stam to Lazio Roma. The move surprised everyone. Some thought Ferguson was punishing the Dutchman for a silly autobiography he had just published. In truth, although Ferguson didn't say this publicly, the sale was prompted partly by match data. Studying the numbers, Ferguson had spotted that Stam was tackling less often than before. He presumed the defender, then twenty-nine, was declining. So he sold him. It was a milestone in soccer's history: a major transfer driven largely by stats.

As Ferguson later admitted, it was also a mistake. Like many soccer men in the early days of match data, the Scot had studied the wrong numbers. Stam wasn't in decline at all: he would go on to have several excellent years in Italy. Nate Silver points out in his book *The Signal and the Noise* that as more data becomes available, we become more likely to use them to make mistaken decisions. Often, the masses of data seem to form a pattern that just isn't there. That's why you often see false positives for breast cancer in mammograms, or false assessments of soccer players.

Despite the dangers, Ferguson's rival Wenger embraced the new match data. He has said that the morning after the game he's like a junkie who needs his fix: he reaches for the spreadsheets. "Wenger always used to love the averages, the trends," Opta's chief executive, Aidan Cooney, told us. Dennis Bergkamp, in his book *Stillness and Speed*, describes how Wenger "used statistics on me" during the Dutchman's declining years as a player at Arsenal. Their conversations would go something like this:

BERGKAMP: Where in your statistics does it say that I changed the game with a killer pass?

WENGER: You run less in the last thirty minutes and you're more at risk of getting injured, and your pace is dropping.

Few would suspect it of West Ham's manager, "Big Sam" Allardyce, but his somewhat Neolithic appearance also conceals a professorial mind. As a player Allardyce spent a year with Tampa Bay, where he grew fascinated with the way American sports used science and data. In 1999 he became manager of little Bolton. Unable to afford the best players, he hired good statisticians instead. The analysts fixed upon one particular number that enchanted Allardyce. "The average game, the ball changes hands four hundred times," recited Chelsea's Forde, who got his start in soccer under Allardyce. Big Sam loved the figure and would drum it into his players. To him, it summed up the importance of switching instantly to defensive positions the moment the ball was lost.

More concretely, stats led Allardyce to a source of cheap goals: corners, throw-ins, and free kicks. Fleig, another Allardyce alumnus, recalled that Bolton used to score 45 to 50 percent of their goals from such "set pieces," compared with a league average of about a third. Fleig said, "We would be looking at, 'If a defender cleared the ball from a long throw, where would the ball land? Well, this is the area it most commonly lands. Right, well, that's where we'll put our man.'"

In 2003 soccer's data revolution got a new impetus when Michael Lewis published *Moneyball.* "I bought twenty copies and sent them out to all the Premier League managers," recalled Cooney. He pauses and chuckles. "Didn't get one response." Nonetheless, a few people in English soccer read the book and sat up. They began thinking about doing "a Moneyball of soccer": using stats to find new ways of valuing players.

It so happened that just as soccer executives were getting interested in *Moneyball*'s hero, Billy Beane, Beane was getting interested in soccer. On a London vacation with his wife, he'd encountered the game and fallen hard for it. Forde, who had studied in Beane's hometown of San Diego and followed American sports, made the pilgrimage to Oakland to quiz Beane about the uses of data. That proved tricky: Beane spent the first few hours of the conversation quizzing Forde about soccer. "In the last half an hour I managed to turn it around to talk about his role in baseball," Forde told us, laughing.

Early in 2011 Simon visited Beane in the Oakland Coliseum. We spoke in what looked like the junk room but in fact is the clubhouse. Beane can often be found sprawled on a dilapidated sofa here watching

European soccer matches while skeptical baseball players watch him. When Beane watches soccer, he sees a game full of emotion, and where there is emotion, he knows people will be making emotional decisions.

Soccer will follow baseball in turning into "more of a science," Beane predicted. "I always say, in a casino there's a reason guys who count cards get kicked out and guys who bet on gut feel don't." Beane agreed that data probably wouldn't transform soccer as they had baseball, but then they didn't need to, he said. If using statistics in soccer gives you an edge, then all clubs will end up having to use statistics. He explained, "If somebody's right 30 percent of the time using gut feel, and you can find a way to be right 35 percent, you create a 5 percent arbitrage, and in sports that can make the difference between winning and losing."

Beane's closest friend in soccer was the Frenchman Damien Comolli, a former assistant of Wenger's. Comolli had lived in Northern California for a year as a teenager. He became a baseball fan, and an A's fan, and the ideal reader of *Moneyball.* When he took over as director of soccer at Tottenham in 2005, he began using data to inform the club's decisions on transfers.

The surprise is not that this happened but that it happened so late. London has long since been taken over by highly educated professionals. Every other serious company in town uses data and computers. It just took London's soccer clubs awhile to catch up.

Yet Comolli's three years at Spurs encapsulated many of the early struggles of soccer's data revolution. British soccer had always been suspicious of educated people. The typical manager was an ex-player who had left school at sixteen and ruled his club like an autocrat. He relied on gut, not numbers. He would have noticed that in many other industries, lesser-educated working-class men like him had been replaced by people with degrees or by computers. He wasn't about to obey a bespectacled Frenchman who had never played professionally.

The manager's suspicion might sound perverse: after all, Comolli's numbers might have helped the club win games. However, many people in soccer clubs are less bothered about winning than about hanging on to their own job and power base.

In fact, the traditionalists shouldn't have been so worried. In soccer there will always be a place for gut alongside numbers. Fergus Connolly, a performance consultant whose clients include Premier League soccer and NBA teams, says, "Some coaches are afraid that data will tell them what to do. It can never tell them what to do. It can never be black and white." The work of data companies is "supplementary," agrees Rob Bateman of Opta. Data can support a decision about a player, but not determine it. As Silver says, an expert needs to use his judgment to interpret the stats, rather than imagine that the stats are speaking an unmistakable truth. No dataset will do away with the need for soccer managers.

Even so, the traditionalists worried. Comolli at Spurs was always having to fight "nerds versus jocks" battles. In hindsight, he unearthed some excellent players for Tottenham: Luka Modric, Dimitar Berbatov, and a seventeen-year-old left-back from Southampton named Gareth Bale. Some of his choices didn't pay off: using data can only raise your probability of finding the right player, not guarantee success. On balance, Comolli did pretty well. However, he was eventually forced out. The forces of tradition were too strong.

When it comes to knowledge, the world divides into liberals and conservatives. Conservatives tend to believe that we have reached the limits of what we can know and that delving further is not only futile but immoral—some things are better left unknown. Liberals, on the other hand, tend to believe that even if we don't know how something works, patient analysis will eventually reduce the problem to a manageable set of proven relationships. Ever since Renaissance scholars began figuring out where a cannonball would land, the conservatives have been on the retreat. So many things we once thought were beyond analysis are now well understood, from the aerodynamics of flight to the mechanisms of disease. Now neuroscientists are starting to find answers to questions about how we know what we like, how we fall in love, and what we achieve in life. The conservative's ultimate fear is that one day we may know so much about what happens next that there are no choices left to be made; the universe will seem so predetermined that no one will bother to get out of bed.

In soccer the conservatives fought back. There was one question the new nerds kept having to answer. Yes, the conservatives would say, stats may well be useful in a stop-start game like baseball. The pitcher pitches, the batter hits, and that event provides oodles of clear data for nerds to crunch. But surely soccer is too fluid a game to measure?

Forde responded, "Well, I think it's a really genuine question. It's one that we ask ourselves all the time." However, the nerds can answer it. For a start, good mathematicians can handle complex systems. At Chelsea, for instance, Forde employed a statistician who had a past in insurance modeling. Soccer—a game of twenty-two people played on a limited field with set rules—is not of unparalleled complexity.

Second, in recent years the fluid game of basketball has found excellent uses for data. Beane said, "If it can be done there, it can be done on the soccer field." And third, a third of all goals in soccer don't come from fluid situations at all. They come from corners, free kicks, penalties, and throw-ins—stop-start set pieces that you can analyze much like a pitch in baseball.

The nerds could point to so many obvious irrationalities in soccer, especially in the transfer market, so many areas where smart clubs could clean up. For instance, goalkeepers have longer careers than forwards, yet earn less and command much lower transfer fees. Clubs often sign large players but actually tend to use the smaller ones, having belatedly realized that they have overvalued size. And few clubs have asked themselves even basic questions, such as whether they earn more points when certain players are on the field.

Given that you can hire perhaps thirty statisticians for the approximately £1.5 million ($2.5 million) that the average player in the Premier League earns, you'd think it might be worth paying some nerds to study these questions. Yet soccer's distrust of numbers has not entirely faded. "Letting even a top-level statistician loose with a more traditional soccer manager is not really the right combination," said Forde.

Given the prevailing suspicion, the clubs that have led the data revolution are typically the ones where the manager himself has trusted numbers. By the early 2000s Wenger's Arsenal and Allardyce's then club Bolton were valuing players in much the way financial investors value cattle futures. Take Bolton's purchase of the thirty-four-year-old central midfielder Gary Speed in 2004. On paper, Speed looked too old. But Bolton, said Fleig, "was able to look at his physical data, to compare it against young players in his position at the time who were at the top of the game, the Steven Gerrards, the Frank Lampards. For a thirty-four-year-old to be consistently having the same levels of physical output as those players, and showing no decline over the previous two seasons, was a contributing factor to say: 'You know what, this isn't going to be a huge concern.'" Speed played for Bolton till he was thirty-eight (and, tragically, committed suicide at forty-two).

Just when Bolton was buying Speed, Wenger was searching for an heir to Arsenal's all-action midfielder Patrick Vieira. As Christoph Biermann recounts in his book *Die Fussball-Matrix,* Wenger wanted a player who could cover lots of ground. He scanned the data from different European leagues, and spotted an unknown teenager at Olympique Marseille named Mathieu Flamini who was running 14 kilometers a game. Alone, that stat wasn't enough. Did Flamini run in the right direction? Could he play soccer? Wenger went to look, established that he could, and signed him for peanuts. Flamini prospered at Arsenal, and after a few years with Milan is now back there prospering again. Wenger, said Beane, "is undoubtedly the sports executive I admire most."

Conversely, the clubs that stuck with "gut" rather than numbers began to suffer. In 2003, Real Madrid sold Claude Makelele to Chelsea for $27 million. It seemed a big fee for an unobtrusive thirty-year-old defensive midfielder. "We will not miss Makelele," said Madrid's president Florentino Pérez. "His technique is average, he lacks the speed and skill to take the ball past opponents, and 90 percent of his distribution either goes backwards or sideways. He wasn't a header of the ball and he rarely passed the ball more than three metres. Younger players will cause Makelele to be forgotten."

Pérez's critique wasn't totally wrong, and yet Madrid had made a terrible error. Makelele would have five excellent years at Chelsea. There's now even a position in soccer named after him: the "Makelele role." If only Madrid had studied the numbers, it might have spotted what made him unique. Forde explained: "Most players are very active when they're aimed towards the opposition's goal, in terms of high-intensity activity. Very few players are very strong going the other way. If you look at Claude, 84 percent of the time he did high-intensity work, it was when the opposition had the ball, which was twice as much as anyone else on the team."

If you watched the game, you could miss Makelele. If you looked at the data, there he was. Similarly, if you looked at Manchester City's Yaya

Touré, with his languid running style, you might think he was slow. If you looked at the numbers, you'd see that he wasn't. Beane said, "What stats allow you to do is not take things at face value. The idea that I trust my eyes more than the stats, I don't buy that because I've seen magicians pull rabbits out of hats and I just know that rabbit's not in there."

Yet by the mid-2000s, the numbers men in soccer were becoming uneasily aware that many of the stats they had been trusting for years were useless. In any industry, people use the data they have. The data companies had initially calculated passes, tackles, and kilometers per player, and so the clubs had used these numbers to judge players. However, it was becoming clear that these raw stats—which still sometimes get beamed up on TV during games—mean little.

Forde remembered the early hunt for meaning in the data on kilometers. "Can we find a correlation between total distance covered and winning? And the answer was invariably no." You might know how many passes a player had given, but that didn't tell you whether they were splitting through-balls or sideways shoves into a teammate's feet.

Tackles seemed a poor indicator too. There was the awkward case of the great Italian defender Paolo Maldini. "He made one tackle every two games," Forde noted ruefully. Maldini positioned himself so well that he didn't need to tackle. That rather argued against judging defenders on their number of tackles, the way Ferguson had when he sold Stam. Fleig said, "Tackles to me are a measure of being under pressure."

Forde reflected, "I sat in many meetings at Bolton, and I look back now and think 'Wow, we hammered the team over something that now we think is not relevant.'" Looking back at the early years of data, Fleig concluded, "We should be looking at something far more important."

| |

That is starting to happen now. Almost unseen by fans, some big clubs have arrived at statistical insights that are incrementally changing the game. Especially in England and Germany, where clubs have tended to look more at match data than in Spain or Italy, the "quants" are isolating the numbers that matter. "A lot of that is proprietary," Forde told us. "The club has been very supportive of this particular space, so we want to keep some of it back." But the quants will discuss certain findings that are becoming common knowledge in soccer. For instance, rather than looking at kilometers covered, clubs now prefer to look at distances run at top speed. "There is a correlation between the number of sprints and winning," Daniele Tognaccini, AC Milan's chief athletics coach, told us in 2008.

That's why Fleig cares about "a player's high-intensity output." Different data companies measured this quality differently, he said, "but ultimately it's a player's ability to reach a speed threshold of seven meters per second." If you valued this quality, you probably would never have made the mistake Juventus did in 1999 of selling Thierry Henry to Arsenal. "For Henry to reach seven meters per second, it's a relative coast," said Fleig admiringly. The Frenchman got there almost whenever he ran.

Equally crucial is the ability to make repeated sprints. Tevez, Manchester City's star player until he fell out with the club, was a bit like a windup doll: he'd sprint, briefly collapse, then very soon afterward be sprinting again. Fleig said, "If we want to press from the front, then we can look at Carlos's physical output and know that he's capable of doing that for ninety minutes plus." Fleig didn't mention it, but the data show that Tevez's successor, Sergio Agüero, does much less defensive running. The whole team needs to work harder to allow Agüero to score his goals.

The quants have also gotten better at valuing goalkeepers. They used to rank keepers by what percentage of shots each one stopped. However, that technique tended to favor keepers from big clubs, who play behind tight defenses and therefore see a higher proportion of easy shots from outside the penalty area. Once clubs started counting only shots from inside the area, the rankings became more telling.

By now statisticians have developed endless metrics for judging keepers. Columbia University in New York did a sophisticated analysis of the Premier League's keepers for the 2009–2010 season. In the tenth-floor office at Waterloo, the Opta men flashed it up on a screen for us. Columbia had worked out how many shots each goalkeeper faced from different parts of the field, measured the strength of those shots, clocked what proportion each keeper stopped, and ended up with a surprising number one: Craig Gordon of Scotland and Sunderland. Gordon was consistently above average in all areas, whereas all the other keepers seemed to have at least one significantly weaker spot. Second in the rankings was Liverpool's Jose Reina, and third was Heurelho Gomes of Spurs (another of Comolli's signings, later banished by the club into outer darkness). Our eyes flitted down the list, through great keepers from all over the world, until we reached the bottom four in the rankings: David James, Paul Robinson, Robert Green, and Chris Kirkland. All four were recent England goalkeepers. It should be noted that this was only one season of data, but English soccer probably needs to rethink how it develops goalkeepers; even the US seems to do a much better job.

Of course, not all clubs care about the same stats. Some managers request custom-made numbers from the data companies: how many players each team stations by each post at corner kicks, for instance. Favored stats differ per country, too. Italian clubs, said Cooney of Opta, don't use the concept "tackle." German clubs love what they call "duels" between players. They even track duels when there is no ball nearby. And the data providers have made it ever easier for clubs to use the stats. For instance, you can now crunch data in umpteen categories to identify the right-back in the German second Bundesliga who best meets your specifications, and then click on a button and watch video of every through-ball he has hit in the past month. Or, if you are Liverpool and looking for the next Gerrard, you can ask the computer to find the midfielders in Europe under age twenty-three whose attributes most closely resemble his.

Bit by bit, the data revolution in soccer progresses. Partly because number crunching succeeded in baseball (the New York Yankees recently hired twenty-one statisticians) and is now sweeping almost all ballgames, it has arrived in European soccer larded with prestige. And it keeps getting more useful. Just as clubs have learned to isolate sprints from other running, they have learned to isolate telling passes from meaningless square balls. On the screen in Carrington, Fleig flashed up a list of Manchester City's players, ranked by how many chances each had created. One name stood out: David Silva had passed for a third more goal-scoring opportunities (irrespective of whether the goal was actually scored) than any of his teammates.

THE MONEYBALL OF SOCCER: A TALE OF ONE CITY AND TWO CLUBS

The most telling statistics in the world aren't much use if you ignore them. At many clubs, the "data analyst" is still just a guy who has branched out from making videos. These clubs find the flood of data that arrives each week overwhelming. They are drowning in information. Opta has video of some games from Liechtenstein, Lesotho, and Nicaragua. Who has time to watch that? And even when a club's data analysts do come up with an insight, the manager is liable to ignore them. Knowledge is no use if people in power won't use it.

Manchester United under Ferguson was an example of a club with only limited use for statistics. Ferguson did employ a large data department, but then he was always vacuuming up information from all sources: from ex-managers he spoke to on the phone all day as well as from mathematics graduates. And he couldn't do what Wenger does and crunch numbers himself. "If you showed him a laptop," growled an employee of Ferguson's, "he'd think it was a place mat."

It's worse at some other clubs, where analysts get locked in computer-filled back rooms and never meet the manager. A key question in any company is, "Who controls the budget?" In English soccer, typically the manager does. The quants advise, but they almost never make the final decision on who gets bought or sold. Coulson of Opta thought in 2011 that data played a big role in recruitment at only "four or five teams" in the Premier League. As we described in Chapter 2, not all clubs have entirely perfected their transfer policies.

Lately, however, one city appears to have taken over the lead in English soccer's data revolution. In October 2010 Boston Red Sox owner John Henry bought Liverpool. Henry, who made his money trading commodities, believes in numbers. In 2002 he had tried to bring Billy Beane to Boston, and subsequently won two World Series using Moneyball methods. He wanted to do "a Moneyball of soccer" at Anfield. The only problem was that he knew nothing about soccer. He called Beane to ask for advice. Beane told him to hire Comolli. The Frenchman was made Liverpool's director of soccer. Often, during his time at Anfield, he'd exchange ideas with the father of Moneyball 5,000 miles away.

Beane told us, "You can call him anytime. I'll e-mail him and it will be two in the morning there and he'll be up, and he'll e-mail me and say, 'Hey, I'm watching the A's game,' because he watches a lot of A's games on the computer. The guy never sleeps."

Comolli became the poster boy for the "Moneyball of soccer." When he was sacked in April 2012, the experiment accordingly appeared discredited. His experience at Anfield tarnished the image of stats in soccer. But it would be wrong to write off the whole project based on his case alone. While Comolli was floundering at Anfield, just across town, almost unnoticed, Liverpool's rivals Everton were doing very well playing Moneyball. The story of Liverpool and Everton illustrates both the scope and the shortcomings of Moneyball in soccer.

At Liverpool, Comolli had the power to use data to shape club policy. In January 2011 he bought Andy Carroll and Luis Suarez for a combined $93 million, and sold Fernando Torres to Chelsea for $80 million. "When you find yourself handling three of the biggest transfers in English football history in the last days of the market," Comolli said at the time, "precise figures allow you not to do that blind." He didn't say much more than that, but before selling Torres, he undoubtedly would have tracked the player's rate of decline. With older players—and at twenty-six a pacy striker is getting old—the key question is, "How fast is he fading?" You can measure that by comparing the player's key outputs from year to year. If, for instance, his top sprinting pace, number of shots on goal, and number of completed passes in the final third are gradually declining, you can probably see his future. (Comolli presumably knew that Steven Gerrard's number of shots on target—a key stat—had been falling since he was twenty-six. A canny unsentimental Liverpool might have sold Gerrard at twenty-eight, before others noticed his decline.)

Getting a statistical take on Suarez was harder. The forward had never played in the Premier League. What formula do you use to translate goals, shots, or assists in the easy Dutch league into their equivalents in tougher England? Luckily, Suarez's Dutch numbers spoke loudly. Beane told us a few days after Suarez moved: "He was so dominant there that even though he was jumping into a bigger league, I think they felt like they were going to have at least a certain caliber of player no matter what." One day there will be so many years of statistical analysis on players from every big foreign league that English clubs will be much better able to predict how well a newcomer from, say, the MLS will make the jump.

In the summer of 2011, numbers guided Comolli again. Few followers of soccer had identified Stewart Downing as a great talent, but the data showed that he was one of the most prolific dribblers and creators of chances in the Premier League. According to rankings produced by Opta with the CIES Football Observatory in Switzerland, the midfielder was responsible for 17 percent of Aston Villa's "overall club production" in the 2010–2011 season, a greater share than any other player at any other club in the Premier League. Comolli bought him and Jordan Henderson, who, age just twenty, was already Sunderland's link man, responsible for 13.6 percent of the team's passing. Together, Henderson and Downing were supposed to provide the crosses for Carroll to head home.

It didn't work out. Just as previous Liverpool managers Gérard Houllier and Rafael Benitez had relied on experience and gut feel to make bad transfers (as discussed in Chapter 2), Comolli's data-driven purchase of the Carroll-Henderson-Downing trio went horribly wrong. It begged the question: Can Moneyball thinking work in soccer? Even John Henry has said soccer is "too dynamic" to allow stats to guide recruitment.

Yet Comolli's experiences need to be examined more carefully—and then set alongside what Everton's then manager David Moyes was simultaneously doing with stats at Liverpool's crosstown rival.

What the Comolli experiment showed is that the Moneyball of soccer is still in its infancy. He had assembled the best possible players for a crossing strategy. The problem is that as we learn more about match data, we are learning that crosses from open play are a poor way to score goals. Much of the best work on match data is done not in soccer clubs but by amateurs on the sofa. Many of these amateurs have day jobs in statistics—working in insurance, doing math PhDs, and the like. One excellent blogger who identifies himself merely as "a Liverpool-supporting atmospheric scientist who spends far too much time looking at numbers" analyzed Liverpool's play in the 2011–2012 season. He found that Liverpool had hit more crosses than any other team in the Premier League. However, he wrote: "Their conversion from crosses was simply atrocious. They required a staggering 421 open-play crosses to score a single goal in open-play on average last season. This was the worst rate in the whole league."

It turns out that crossing is not the way to victory. Comolli had bet the company on a bad strategy. A cross from a free kick makes sense, because the player hitting it has time and space to achieve precision. But to send a man sprinting down the wing with a defender in his face, and then count on his cross being nodded in, is usually hopeless.

Another problem for soccer's Moneyballers has to do with the game theory that we discussed in the last chapter. It's one thing to plan a strategy—for instance, of heading in crosses—and to show statistically that this strategy has produced goals in the past. It's quite another to declare that this strategy will keep working in the future. Once you have signed a good crosser and a tall striker, it is perfectly obvious to your opponents what you are going to do and therefore how they should set about defending against your strategy. In some extreme cases (Messi and Cristiano Ronaldo spring to mind), defending may be impossible even if you know what your opponents are planning, but generally this is not the case. Telegraphing your strategy may be the biggest pitfall when it comes to using big data in soccer.

At least the Liverpool experiment taught us more about which data matter: crosses rarely work. That knowledge is progress of sorts. It's also wrong to dismiss Comolli as a failure: this, after all, is the man who recruited Bale and Suarez to the Premier League, and sold the declining Torres for the largest fee ever paid by an English club. In part, Comolli got scapegoated because he's exactly the type of person media, fans, and ex-players–turned pundits are quick to scapegoat: a bespectacled Frenchman who never played professionally and isn't very easygoing or clubbable. His habit of claiming credit for good decisions can also bite him in the leg when there's a bad decision looking for an owner.

But there's more to Moneyball in soccer than Comolli. Everton is the smaller and poorer of Liverpool's two clubs, yet in both 2012 and 2013, it finished the season above Liverpool in the table. In part at least, this was thanks to data analysis. One day in March 2013, Simon visited the club's training ground at Finch Farm, on the city's semi-rural outskirts. It was a Monday morning, two days after Everton had beaten Manchester City, possibly the world's richest club, yet there weren't hordes of fans waiting outside Finch Farm. In fact there was nobody waiting there at all.

In the dining room a few players in shorts were eating lunch. At the other end of the room was a table with four members of manager David Moyes's support staff. One of the men, David Weir, a quiet Scotsman in a cardigan, had played for Everton for years before becoming a coach there; but the other three were unknown outside Finch Farm. Steve Brown, James Smith, and Dan Hargreaves, in their blue elephant-adorned training kit, were Everton's unheralded assets, who earn dozens of times less than the players they work with. Yet Moyes obviously took them seriously. Smith and Brown, the club's main performance analysts, weren't hidden away in some back room where nobody could hear them scream. Their offices were on the corridor directly opposite Moyes's.

Often Moyes would march into their rooms firing out questions: How efficient was next Saturday's opponent at scoring from crosses, or throw-ins? What types of passes did their midfielders make? When Everton faced Gareth Bale at Tottenham, Moyes wanted "an assessment of where Bale is actually picking up the ball compared to the areas where you think he is working," said Brown. Smith added: "He [Moyes] is quite demanding in terms of data. In terms of managers, he is probably as into it as any." (A measure of the staff's awe for Moyes is that they rarely referred to him by name—what to call him? "Moyes"? "Mr. Moyes"? "David"?)

Moyes had no particular ideology of how he wanted to play soccer. Instead he tailored Everton's style to each new opponent. He worked out what the opposition did, and then tried to stop it. Before facing Manchester City, for instance, he found the positions where City's playmaker Silva usually received the ball, and put men there (this, incidentally, is excellent game theory).

The insights that Moyes and his staff gleaned from video and statistics were constantly transmitted to Everton's players. Brown said, "There is a post-match data sheet that goes up in the changing room. Some players will actually sit down and look at the Prozone data with us; they will look at pass-maps and their 'receive positions,' their crossing data. We have one central midfielder who comes in every week and looks at his pass completion." The analysts cautioned that you always need to understand the context of any piece of data. For instance, what was a player's role in a particular game? Who was he playing alongside? Match data without context is meaningless.

Weren't some players skeptical of numbers? "There is a bit of that," agreed Brown. But mostly, the analysts said, Everton's players appreciated the help. Many players considered stats (about themselves and about opponents) a survival tool that could help keep them afloat a little longer in the lucrative higher reaches of soccer. Smith said, "Going out to play in the Premier League is a daunting thing. They want David Moyes to tell them what to do. That's reassuring. One player once said to me, 'They might complain about a meeting, but if it wasn't there they would be the first to say, 'Where is the meeting?'"

The staffers noted that most fans and media seem unaware of all the analysis that went into preparing games. Often, in pubs and TV studios, a game is discussed as if it were a mix of bursts of inspiration, individual blunders, and a manager's motivational powers. Hargreaves said, "What the public sees isn't necessarily what's happening. The level of ex-player punditry doesn't lend itself to what's happening behind the scenes." In part, that's because managers like Moyes won't reveal their tactical secrets. So journalists end up writing about how a winning manager "psyched out" his opponent with "mind games."

It's not that Moyes at Everton based his every decision on data. Rather, data was one of the things he considered. It made signing a player, for instance, a little less of a leap in the dark. "Watching players is actually a very subjective thing, an inexact science," said Smith. "There are all kinds of inputs: live player reports, extensive video analysis, speaking to people who have worked with them, and data is one of those layers. Data plays a role—not a massive role at the moment."

One occasion when data did matter was in 2008, when Everton was trying to replace midfielder Lee Carsley. Smith said, "We needed someone to replace things that he had been doing: possession regains, winning tackles and headers, protecting the back four." The club's eye fell on a twenty-year-old Belgian, obscure but for his enormous mane of hair, named Marouane Fellaini. "We'd followed him at the 2008 Olympics but he didn't have a great tournament, and actually he got sent off quite early on," Smith recalled. There were few match stats for Fellaini, because at the time there was no data available for Belgian league matches. And so

Everton watched videos of him to compile their own set of stats, using key performance indicators that seemed relevant. Smith said, "Fellaini was one of those where everything said, 'Yes, do it': the data, the subjective reports, the age, the fact that he was already playing for Belgium, his size." And so Everton gambled $28 million on him—still the club's record transfer fee. It paid off. In September 2013, after Moyes had moved to Manchester United (undoubtedly bringing his data-driven methods with him), he bought Fellaini for $43 million.

Everton's performance analysts wanted to improve their use of data. They had been picking brains inside and outside soccer for new insights. They were painfully aware, for instance, that no one in their group had so much as a math degree. Still, soccer clubs may now be more advanced than most corporations in using data to recruit employees. In the typical corporation, very few human-resources staff have college degrees involving numbers, says Rob Symes, who made the documentary film *Outside View* on sports and data. Daniel Kahneman, the psychologist who won the Nobel Prize for economics in 2002, says in the film that a key to good decision-making is to let statistics "not humans make the final decision." Increasingly, that is happening in soccer.

Soccer's data revolution is only just getting started. Clubs still have great room for improvement. For instance, you still constantly see players shoot at goal from outside the penalty area. Yet Opta's data show that in the Premier League, only 2 percent of shots from just outside the area produce goals. Presumably the players have in their minds images of crackers flying into the top corner: these are the beautiful goals that stick in the memory long after all the balls that disappear into the crowd have been forgotten. Statisticians have a lobbying job to do here.

There's a particular problem with direct free kicks. Whenever a team gets one anywhere near the penalty area, the team's biggest name generally grabs the ball, makes a great show of placing it, and then whams it into the crowd. It's a superstar's perk, rather like the film star's trailer with his name on it in Hollywood. In the 2010–2011 season, write Anderson and Sally in *The Numbers Game,* the average team in the Premier League scored from just one of every 35 direct free kicks. Yet a free kick should be the perfect opportunity to pass. Your opponents have to retreat nine yards, and they need to put two or three people in the wall in case you shoot. That leaves vast spaces to pass to runners in the penalty area. Almost inevitably, teams will start to do that instead of shooting from free kicks.

Someone who has thought harder than most about what shape a Moneyball of soccer might take is the director of baseball operations at the Oakland A's. Farhan Zaidi is a little round MIT economics graduate with a sense of humor. He's the sort of guy you'd expect to meet late one night in a bar in a college town after a gig, not at a professional sports club. For work, Zaidi crunches baseball stats. But he and Beane spend much of their time arguing about their other loves: the British band Oasis and soccer. In 2006, in the middle of the baseball season, he and Beane traveled to the World Cup in Germany together. "We spend so much time together," chuckles Zaidi, "that if all we ever talked about was the numbers on these spreadsheets, we would have killed each other a long time ago."

Because Zaidi knows where the data revolution in baseball has gone, he can make predictions for soccer, which lags baseball by perhaps a decade. Soccer's holy grail, he thinks, is a stat he calls "goal probability added." That stat would capture how much each player's actions over his career increased the chance of his team scoring, or decreased it. Zaidi explains, "With some of the tools that are being created now to track everything that's happening on the soccer field, I really feel like this is the next frontier: having enough data so that whenever a player advances the ball from point A to point B on the field, you know that play has happened a hundred times before, and you know exactly how valuable it is. So if a ball is in grid one of the field, you know that the team over the next five minutes scores a goal 0.5 percent of the time. Now that player advances it to grid six, say. You know that the team from there scores a goal in the next five minutes with a probability of 2 percent. He's raised the probability of scoring by 1.5 percent."

Does this mean that one day pundits might say things like, "Luis Suarez has a goal probability added of 0.60, but Carroll's GPA is only 0.56"?

Zaidi replies, "I tend to think that will happen, because that's what happened in baseball. We talk now about players in ways that we wouldn't have dreamed of ten or fifteen years ago." In their ancient battle against the jocks, the nerds are finally taking revenge.

10

THE SUBURBAN NEWSAGENTS

City Sizes and Soccer Prizes

The scene: the VIP room at the Athens Olympic Stadium, a couple of hours before the 2007 Champions League final between Milan and Liverpool kicks off. Michel Platini and Franz Beckenbauer are being buttonholed every couple of yards by other middle-age men in expensive suits. There is a crush at the buffet, and another across the room, where a familiar silver cup with "big ears" stands on a dais. You line up, assume a conquering pose beside the Champions League trophy, and grin. Nice young ladies from UEFA slip the picture into a frame for you.

An Englishman watching the scene, a soccer official, confides that he first got this close to the cup thirty years ago. Where? In Bramcote, a suburb of Nottingham. One of Brian Clough's brothers ran the local post office–cum–newsagents, and Clough himself would sometimes pop in and serve customers, or just stand behind the counter reading the papers. One Sunday morning when the future official went in with his grandfather, there was the European Cup freshly won by Forest, plunked on top of a pile of *Nottingham Evening Posts*. Behind it stood Brian Clough, holding an open newspaper in front of his face. He neither moved nor spoke, but he knew the boy would remember the scene forever. The official remembers, "I was too young and shy to speak to the man, which I regret to this day."

It's odd to think of the game's biggest club trophy ending up in a place like Bramcote (population 7,318). Yet it's not that exceptional. Provincial towns like Nottingham, Glasgow, Dortmund, Birmingham, and Rotterdam have all won European Cups, while the four biggest metropolitan areas in Europe—Istanbul, Paris, Moscow, and London—never had until Chelsea finally got one in 2012. This points to an odd connection between city size, capital cities, and soccer success. Here's why London took so long to win the Champions League—and why Europe's biggest cities might now start adding some trophies.

GENERAL FRANCO'S TRANSISTOR RADIO: THE ERA OF TOTALITARIAN SOCCER

The best measure of success in club soccer is a simple list: the names of the clubs that have won the European Cup since the competition began in 1956. Study this list, and you'll see that the history of the European Cup breaks down into three periods.

The first, from 1956 through the late 1960s, is dominated by the capital cities of fascist regimes. Of the first eleven European Cups, eight were won by either Real Madrid (favorite club of General Francisco Franco) or Benfica (from the capital of the Portuguese dictator Salazar). In seven of the first sixteen finals, the losing teams also came from fascist capitals: Real, Benfica, and in 1971, Panathinaikos from the Athens of the colonels' regime.

But by the start of the 1970s, the dominance of fascist capitals was eroding. Fascist governments seldom outlast their leaders, and Portugal's had entered a twilight after Salazar died in 1970. Meanwhile, everyone was waiting for Franco to go, too.

Yet even after fascism disappeared, teams from Europe's remaining dictatorial capitals continued to thrive. Steaua Bucharest, run by a son of the Romanian dictator Nicolae Ceauşescu, won the cup in 1986. Red Star Belgrade triumphed in 1991 just as Yugoslavia was breaking into pieces. The same phenomenon was at work in the communist countries as in the fascist capitals before them. Dictators send resources to the capital because that is where they and their senior bureaucrats and soldiers and secret policemen live. So the dictators do up the main buildings, boost the local economy, and help the soccer club. That's totalitarian soccer.

A communist takeover of Britain could have done wonders for a capital team like Arsenal. Just look at the triumphs of Dynamo Berlin, founded in the former East Germany with the express purpose of keeping the league title in the capital. The club president until the Berlin Wall fell was Erich Mielke, feared octogenarian chief of the East German secret police, the Stasi. Mielke loved Dynamo. He made all the best East German players play for it. He also talked to referees, and Dynamo won a lot of matches with penalties in the ninety-fifth minute. Dynamo was popularly known as the *Elf Schweine,* the eleven pigs, but it did win the East German league title every year from 1979 to 1988. This was possibly Europe's most extreme case of politicians rigging the soccer market.

Dynamo never got far in the European Cup, but General Franco's local team did. The general made a point of catching Real Madrid's games on the radio, taking a transistor along with him if he was out partridge shooting, writes Jimmy Burns in *When Beckham Went to Spain.* It wasn't so much that Franco fixed referees or gave Real money. Rather, he helped the club indirectly, by centralizing Spain's power and resources. And he believed that Real's European Cups helped him. Fernando María Castiella, foreign minister under Franco, called Real Madrid "the best embassy we have ever had."

DOWN AND OUT, PARIS AND LONDON: THE FAILURE OF DEMOCRATIC CAPITALS

Totalitarian capitals got off to a great start in the European Cup. But for the first forty-two years of the trophy's life, the democratic capitals of Europe never won it.

There is only one caveat: Amsterdam is nominally the Dutch capital, and Ajax of that city won the Champions cup four times. However, Amsterdam really is only nominally the capital. The government, parliament, the king's palace, and the embassies are all in The Hague, a city that has often gone years at a stretch without having a team in the Dutch premier division. The Hague's only professional club, ADO, traditionally plays its games in front of a few thousand people, a large proportion of whom are nuts. Little happens on the field beyond the occasional smoke bomb or plague of rabbits. Only in the last few seasons has ADO even established itself as a regular in the top Dutch division. This is the curse of the democratic capital.

Instead of western capitals, provincial western European cities have dominated the European Cup and Champions League. The rule of the provinces holds true even in the most obsessively centralized countries. Teams from five provincial British cities won the European Cup before London finally got one. (The town of Nottingham still has more trophies—two—than London, Paris, Istanbul, Berlin, and Moscow combined.) Olympique Marseille won the cup in 1993, but Paris Saint-Germain never has. Porto has won it twice since Portugal went democratic, while the Lisbon clubs have been winless since 1962. Clubs from Milan and Turin have won a combined total of twelve trophies; Roman clubs, zero. The cup has gone to Munich and Hamburg, but never to Bonn or Berlin. For many years, in fact, neither of those cities even had a team in the Bundesliga. Hertha Berlin, the only big club in the current capital, has not been champion of Germany since the Weimar Republic.

Capitals—especially London, Paris, and Moscow—tend to have the greatest concentrations of national resources. It's therefore striking how badly their clubs seem to underperform. We can speculate about why this is. But perhaps the main reason teams from democratic capital cities are not up to much is psychological. In capital cities, no soccer club can matter all that much. There was an instructive sight, sometime in the late 1990s, of a group of visiting fans from an English provincial town wandering down London's Baker Street yelling their club songs at passersby. In their minds, they were shaming the Londoners, invading the city for a day, making all the noise. But the Londoners they were shouting at—many of them foreigners anyway—didn't care, or even understand the point they were making.

Capitals simply have less to prove than provincial cities. They have bigger sources of pride than their soccer teams. Londoners don't go around singing songs about their city, and they don't believe that a prize for Arsenal or Chelsea would enhance London's status. Roman Abramovich and David Dein helped bring trophies to Chelsea and Arsenal, but neither ever could have been voted mayor of London. Soccer matters even less in Paris, where it's possible to spend a lifetime without ever knowing that soccer exists. Paris Saint-Germain, whose ground is only just inside the city's Péripherique ring road, is hardly going to become the main focus of Parisian pride.

London, Paris, and Moscow don't need to win the Champions League. It is a different type of city where a soccer club can mean everything: the provincial industrial town. These are the places that have ousted the fascist capitals as rulers of European soccer.

DARK SATANIC MILLS: WHY FACTORY TOWNS BECAME SOCCER TOWNS

In 1878 a soccer club started up just by the newish railway line in Manchester. Because the players worked at the Newton Heath carriage works of the Lancashire and Yorkshire Railway Company, their team was called Newton Heath. They played in work clogs against other work teams.

Famously, Newton Heath became Manchester United. But what matters here are the club's origins, well recounted in Jim White's *Manchester United: The Biography*. White describes the L&YR's workers, "sucked in from all over the country to service the growing need for locomotives and carriages." Life in Manchester then was neither fun nor healthy, he writes. "In the middle of the nineteenth century the average male life expectancy in Little Ireland, the notorious part of Manchester . . . was as low as seventeen." This was still the same brutal Manchester where a few decades before, Karl Marx's pal Friedrich Engels had run his father's factory, the industrial city so awful it inspired communism.

Industrial Manchester had grown like no other city on earth. In 1800 it had been a tranquil little place of 84,000 inhabitants, so insignificant that as late as 1832 it did not even have a member of Parliament. It was the Industrial Revolution that changed everything. Workers poured in from English villages, from Ireland, from feeble economies everywhere. For instance, the great-grandparents of Simon, one of this book's authors, came to Manchester from Lithuania.

By 1900 all these newcomers had made Manchester the sixth-biggest city in Europe, with 1.25 million inhabitants, more than Moscow at the time. It was still a hard city. In the early twentieth century Simon's great-grandparents emigrated on to much healthier southern Africa, after two of their children had died in Manchester of scarlet fever.

Inevitably, most of the early "Mancunians" were rootless migrants. Unmoored in their new home, many of them embraced the local soccer clubs. Soccer must have given them something of the sense of the community that they had previously known in their villages.

The same thing happened in Britain's other new industrial cities: the migrants attached themselves to soccer clubs with a fervor unknown in more established towns. When the English Football League was founded in 1888, six of the twelve founding members came from industrial Lancashire, while the other six were from the industrial Midlands. Montague Shearman wrote that year, "No words of ours can adequately describe the present popularity [of soccer] which, though great in the metropolis, is infinitely greater in the large provincial towns. . . . It is no rare thing in the north and midlands for 10,000 people to pay money to watch an ordinary club match, or for half as many again to assemble for a 'Cup Tie.'" It helped that workers in the textile industry in the Northwest began to get Saturdays off in the 1890s, a luxury that workers elsewhere in Britain did not enjoy.

By 1892, all twenty-eight English professional clubs were from the North or the Midlands. Soccer was as northern a game as rugby league. The champions in the Victorian era came from northern industrial towns such as Preston, Sheffield, or Sunderland, then still among the richest spots on earth. When these places became too poor and small to support successful clubs, the league title merely migrated to larger northern cities.

The legacy of the Industrial Revolution still shapes English fandom. Today the combined population of Greater Merseyside, Greater Manchester, and Lancashire County is less than 5.5 million, or a little more than 10 percent of the English population. Nonetheless, as we write, in January 2014, four of the top seven clubs in the Premier League table—the two Manchester teams, Liverpool, and Everton—are based in this region. Their advantage: more than a century of brand building. Manchester United became arguably the most popular club on earth largely because Manchester had been the first industrial city on earth. The club is only the biggest local soccer relic of that era. The forty-three professional

FIGURE 10.1. Europe's preferred clubs

Club	*Estimated number of fans (in millions)*
Barcelona	44.2
Real Madrid	41.9
Manchester United	37.6
Chelsea	25.6
Zenit St Petersburg	23.9
Liverpool	23.0
Arsenal	21.3
AC Milan	21.0
Bayern Munich	19.8
Juventus	17.5
CSKA Moscow	11.1
Inter Milan	10.3
Olympique Lyon	9.4
Olympique Marseille	9.4
Galatasaray	9.0
Spartak Moscow	8.1
Fenerbahce	7.3
Wisła Kraków	6.5
Ajax Amsterdam	6.5
Dynamo Moscow	5.7

clubs within ninety miles of Manchester probably represent the greatest soccer density in the world.

Almost all of Europe's best soccer cities have a profile like Manchester's. They were once new industrial centers that sucked in hapless villagers. The newcomers cast around for something to belong to, and settled on soccer. Supporting a local club helped them make a place for themselves in the city. So clubs mattered more here, and grew bigger, than in capital cities or ancient cathedral towns with old-established hierarchies.

The market research company Sport+Markt has been studying fandom since 1994. In 2008 it asked 9,600 people interested in soccer, spread over sixteen European countries, to name their "preferred" club. The top twenty are shown in figure 10.1.

It would be wrong to treat the results as at all precise. The figures differed significantly from those in Sport+Markt's survey of the previous year. In that one year Chelsea, for instance, had supposedly gained

FIGURE 10.2. Favorite teams of each large country

Country	*Best-supported club*
England	Manchester United
France	Olympique Lyon
Germany	Bayern Munich
Italy	AC Milan
Poland	Wisła Kraków
Russia	Zenit St Petersburg
Spain	Barcelona

almost 6 million fans. Enormous numbers of people change their answers to the question, "Which is your preferred team?" depending on who just won the league or where Cristiano Ronaldo happens to be playing. However, the survey does tell us something. Few would dispute that this top twenty includes most of Europe's best-supported clubs. And there is something remarkable about this list: the biggest clubs are not in the biggest cities. They are in the formerly industrial ones.

Of course, some teams from capitals are popular. They would be, given that London, Paris, Rome, and Moscow are by far the largest cities in their countries. Clubs in capitals have unparalleled catchment areas, even given the profusion of local teams. But in none of the seven largest European countries surveyed does the best-supported club come from a capital city. Figure 10.2 shows the favorite team of each large country, according to Sport+Markt.

In six out of seven countries, the number-one team comes from a provincial town with a strong industrial history. The sole exception is France, where Lyon is a provincial town but was mostly bypassed by the Industrial Revolution. We saw how the club's popularity came from nowhere after just 2002, thanks to Lyon's clever gaming of the transfer market under president Jean-Michel Aulas.

Taken together, the provincial industrial towns in Sport+Markt's top twenty dominate European soccer. Between them they won thirty out of fifty-one European Cups from 1963 through 2013. The smaller industrial or port cities Glasgow, Nottingham, Birmingham, Porto, Dortmund, Eindhoven, and Rotterdam have won an additional nine between them. And all these industrial cities have a story much like Manchester's, although their growth spurts happened later. Peasants arrived from the countryside, leaving all their roots behind. Needing something to belong to in their new cities, they chose soccer. That's why in all these places, the soccer clubs arose soon after the factories.

In most of the cities on Sport+Markt's list, the industrial migrants arrived in a whoosh in the late nineteenth century. Munich had 100,000 inhabitants in 1852, and five times as many by 1901. Barcelona's population trebled in the same period to 533,000. Turin, for centuries a quiet Piedmontese town, began acquiring factories in the 1870s. Milan surged with the new railways that followed Italian reunification.

Once the local merchants had grown wealthy and discovered English ways, they founded soccer clubs: Juventus in 1897, Barcelona and AC Milan two years later, Bayern in 1900. The clubs then grew with their cities. Newly industrial Milan, for instance, sucked in so many migrants that it could eventually support two of the three most popular teams in the country.

The second stage of the soccer boom in the continent's industrial cities happened after the war. The 1950s and 1960s were the years of Italy's "economic miracle," when flocks of poor southern Italian peasants took the "train of the sun" north. Many of these people ended up in Turin, making cars for Fiat. The historian Paul Ginsborg writes, "So great and persistent was the flow from the South, that by the end of the sixties Turin had become the third largest 'southern' city in Italy, after Naples and Palermo." The migrants found jobs, but not enough schools or hospitals or apartments. Often there was so little space that roommates had to take turns sleeping. Amid such dislocation, soccer mattered all the more. Goffredo Fofi, author of a study of southern immigration to Turin in the 1960s, said that "during a Juventus-Palermo match, there were many enthusiastic immigrant Sicilian fans whose sons, by now, like every respectable FIAT worker, backed the home team."

It's one of the flukes of history that this mass migration to Turin began soon after the Superga air disaster of 1949 had decimated the city's previous most popular team, Torino. The migrants arrived soon after Juve had established itself as the local top dog, and they helped make it a global top dog. For starters, they transmitted the passion to their relatives down south.

Barcelona experienced the same sort of growth spurt at about the same time as Turin. In the 1950s and 1960s perhaps 1.5 million Spaniards moved to the Barcelona area. Entire villages in the country's interior were left almost empty. On wastelands outside Barcelona, self-built shantytowns sprang up—the sort of thing you might now see on the outskirts of Jakarta—packed with peasants who had left behind everything they knew. Many were illiterate. Hardly any spoke the local language, Catalan. A lot of them attached themselves to Barça. In Spain's new Manchester, it was the quickest way to belong.

The link between industry and soccer is almost universal across Europe. The largest average crowds in Europe in the 2012–2013 season were at Borussia Dortmund (average: 80,558), one of many clubs in the industrial German Ruhr region. In France, too, it is the industrial cities that have historically loved their clubs best. The country's few traditional hotbeds of soccer are the mining towns of Lens and Saint-Étienne, and the port of Marseille.

All these industrial cities were products of a particular era. In all of them the Industrial Revolution ended, often painfully. But besides the empty docks and factory buildings, the other legacy of industrialization was beloved soccer clubs. The quirk of a particular era gave Manchester United, Barcelona, Juventus, Bayern Munich, and the Milan clubs enough fans to dominate first their own countries, and then Europe.

If Sport+Markt had polled the popularity of soccer clubs in Turkey, it would have found the universal principle holding there, too. The country's capital of soccer is not the capital city, Ankara, but the new industrial powerhouse, Istanbul. The city is home to all three of Turkey's most popular clubs: Galatasaray, Fenerbahce, and Besiktas.

It's true that Istanbul, like Saint Petersburg, was once the seat of government, but both cities lost that role more than ninety years ago, long before soccer amounted to anything in their countries. Even as late as 1950, Istanbul was a sleepy place with barely a million inhabitants. Then it became possibly the last big European city to experience an industrial revolution. Migrants were sucked in from all over Anatolia. Between 1980 and 1985 alone, Istanbul's population doubled. Today it is the largest metropolitan area in Europe, with nearly 14 million inhabitants. The rootless peasants needed somehow to belong in their new home, and so they attached themselves to one of the city's great clubs. Often, soccer provided their strongest loyalties in Istanbul.

Admittedly, almost all cities in Europe have some experience of industrialization. But very few have had as much as Manchester, Turin, Milan, Istanbul, or Barcelona. These were the European cities with the most flux, the fewest long-standing hierarchies, the weakest ties between people and place. Here, there were emotional gaps to fill. This becomes obvious when we contrast the industrial cities with old towns that have a traditional upper-class streak. In England, Oxford, Cambridge, Cheltenham, Canterbury, York, and Bath (including its rural outskirts) are all decent-sized places, with somewhere between 100,000 and 175,000 inhabitants each. Many industrial towns of that size or even smaller—Middlesbrough, Reading, Ipswich, Blackburn, Watford, Burnley—have serious soccer traditions. Yet Oxford, Cambridge, Bath, Canterbury, York, and Cheltenham between them currently have just three small teams in the English Football League: Cheltenham Town, which joined it only in 1999, Oxford United, which reentered the league only in 2010, and York City, which returned in 2012. All three clubs play in the fourth (or bottom) tier of the English league. In towns like these, with age-old hierarchies and few incoming peasants, people simply didn't need soccer clubs to root themselves.

Oxford's face to the world is the university. In industrial cities it is the soccer club. Barcelona, Marseille, and (until recently) Newcastle are the pride of their cities, a symbolic two fingers up at the capital. When Barcelona wins something, the president of Catalonia traditionally hoists himself up on the balcony of his palace on the Plaça Sant Jaume and shouts at the crowds below, "Barça wins, Catalonia wins!"

These provincial clubs have armies of fans, players who will bleed for the club, and backing from local plutocrats. Bernard Tapie put money into Olympique Marseille, the Agnelli family into Juventus, and Sir John Hall into Newcastle because they wanted to be kings of their towns. Local fans and sponsors invest in these clubs partly because they feel civic pride is at stake. In the Middle Ages they would have built a cathedral instead.

Usually, provincial cities such as these have only one major club, which often becomes the only thing many outsiders know about the place. For instance, there must be many Manchester United fans around the world

FIGURE 10.3. European Cup winners

Club	*Year(s) they won it*	*Metropolitan area*
Feyenoord Rotterdam	1970	1 million
Ajax Amsterdam	1971–1973	1 million
Bayern Munich	1974–1976	2.9 million
Liverpool	1977–1978 and 1981	1.4 million
Nottingham Forest	1979–1980	470,000

who don't know that Manchester is a city in England. True, most provincial cities have two teams that compete for top-dog status: United and City in Manchester, Inter and Milan in Milan, Torino and Juventus in Turin, United and Wednesday in Sheffield, Celtic and Rangers in Glasgow, Forest and County in Nottingham, Everton and Liverpool FC in Liverpool, Bayern and 1860 in Munich, Barça and Espanyol in Barcelona. Many of these rivalries have something to do with religion or politics or both. But usually one team struggles. Manchester City, Torino, and 1860 Munich have all spent long phases in the lower divisions. City only reached the top thanks to the arrival of a billionaire Arab sheikh in 2008. Everton last won the league in 1987. FC Amsterdam went bust. Midsize provincial cities are simply not big enough to sustain two big clubs for long. Almost always, one club pulls ahead.

"THEY MOVED THE HIGHWAY": THE RISE AND FALL OF SMALL TOWNS

Provincial industrial towns began to dominate the European Cup in the late 1960s. But their rule breaks down into two main periods. The first, from 1970 to 1981, is the small-town era, when clubs from some very modest places won the European Cup. Figure 10.3 shows them, with the populations not just of the cities themselves but of their entire metropolitan areas, including people in all the local suburbs.

Note that we are estimating the size of these places very generously, going way beyond the city borders. The figure for Liverpool, for instance, includes all of the local Merseyside region.

The rule of the small is even more striking when you consider some of the losing teams in European Cup finals in this era. In a remarkable four-year

FIGURE 10.4. Winning towns

Club	*Size of town*	*Size of total metropolitan area*
Saint-Étienne	175,000	320,000
Mönchengladbach	260,000	260,000
Bruges	115,000	270,000
Malmö	240,000	600,000

period from 1976 to 1979, the towns of Saint-Étienne, Mönchengladbach, Bruges, and Malmö all had teams in the final.

Perhaps the emblematic small-town team of the seventies is Borussia Mönchengladbach, whose rise and fall encapsulates that of all these towns.

In the 1970s Gladbach won five German titles and reached four European finals. The Bökelberg stadium, perched on a hill among the gardens of smart houses, saw the best years of Gunter Netzer, Rainer Bonhof, and Alan Simonsen. Fans drove in from neighboring Holland and Belgium, as well as from the town's British army barracks. Decades later, a German marketing company showed that the knee-jerk response of the country's fans to the word *counterattack* was still *Gladbach*.

It was a cozy little club: Berti Vogts spent his whole career here, and when Netzer later played in Zurich he often used to drive up, sometimes to scout players for Spanish clubs, but often just to eat sausages in the canteen.

Like David Cassidy, Gladbach would have done well to combust spontaneously at the end of the seventies. In 1980 the club lost its last UEFA Cup final to Eintracht Frankfurt, and the decades since have been disappointing. There was the spell in 1998, for instance, when it just couldn't stop getting thrashed. "We can only get better," announced Gladbach's coach, Friedel Rausch, just before his team lost 8–2 to Bayer Leverkusen. "I feel I can solve our problems," he said afterward. When Gladbach lost its next match 7–1 to Wolfsburg, Rausch was sacked. Gladbach spent time in Germany's second division, and has never regained its former heights.

This upsets leftist, educated fiftysomethings all over Germany, who still dislike Bayern, revere the socialist Netzer, and on Saturday afternoons check the Gladbach result first. But there is nothing to be done.

The glory days cannot come back, because what did in Gladbach was the modern era.

In the words of Norman Bates in Hitchcock's *Psycho*: "They moved the highway." In the seventies Gladbach's coach, Hennes Weisweiler, was able to build a team of boys from the local towns. The part-Dutch Bonhof came from nearby Emmerich, Vogts was an orphan from Neuss-Buttgen, and Hacki Wimmer, who did Netzer's dirty work, spent decades after his playing career running his parents' stationery shop just down the road in Aachen.

These stars stayed at Gladbach for years because there was little more money to be earned anywhere else in soccer, because most rich clubs were allowed only a couple of foreign players at most, and because their own club could generally stop them from leaving. In short, there were market restraints. That's why Gladbach, Nottingham Forest, Bruges, and Saint-Étienne could thrive in the 1970s. Even then, big cities had more resources, but they had limited freedom, or limited desire, to use them.

The beginning of the end for small towns was the day in February 1979 when Trevor Francis became soccer's first "million-pound man." In fact, Clough agreed to a fee of only £999,999 (then about $2 million) to bring him from Birmingham to Forest, but there were taxes on top. Three months later Francis headed the goal (against Malmö) that gave Forest the European Cup. But the swelling of the soccer economy that he embodied would eventually do in small clubs like Forest.

In the 1980s TV contracts grew, and Italy opened its borders to foreigners. Later, teams around Europe began renovating their stadiums, which allowed the ones with a lot of fans to make more money. After the European court of justice's "Bosman ruling" in 1995, big clubs could easily sign the best players from any country in the European Union. Around the same time, the clubs with the most fans began earning much more from their television rights. Big clubs everywhere got bigger. Bayern Munich, previously Gladbach's main rival, mushroomed into "FC Hollywood."

After that, clubs like Gladbach could no longer keep their best players. Lothar Matthäus made his debut for "*Die Fohlen*" at the end of the golden era, but when he was only twenty-three he graduated to Bayern. The next great white hope, the local lad Sebastian Deisler, left Gladbach for Hertha at age nineteen in 1999, as soon as he distantly began to resemble Netzer. Small towns couldn't afford the new soccer.

"THAT'S NOT COCAINE, IT'S SAFFRON": THE DEMISE OF THE CATHEDRAL CITIES

Wandering around Florence, you can still imagine it as the center of the universe. It is the effect of the great cathedral, the endless Michelangelos, and all the tourists paying $10 for an orange juice. A Medici ruler returning from the dead, as in one of Florence's umpteen paintings of the Day of Judgment, might feel his city had won the battle of prestige among European city-states.

But he would be wrong. These days a midsize city in Europe derives its status less from its cathedral than from its soccer club. Here towns the size of Florence (600,000 people in its metropolitan area) have slipped up.

Fiorentina's last flurry came in 1999, when it beat Arsenal in a Champions League match at Wembley thanks to a goal by Gabriel Batistuta, with Giovanni Trapattoni sitting on the bench. In those days "Trap's" biggest problems were his players' insistence on busing the 150 yards from the locker room to the training ground and Brazilian Edmundo's ritual late return from the Rio Carnaval. But those days will never return. In the Champions League, the midsize cities are now finished.

Fiorentina's demise can be dated to the day in July 2001 that the Italian police raided the home of the team's owner, the Italian film baron Vittorio Cecchi Gori. What happened was exactly what should happen when police raid a film baron's home, as if Cecchi Gori had read up on Jackie Collins beforehand.

The police broke into his apartment in the Palazzo Borghese in Rome, but then took ninety minutes to find him. This was because his bedroom door was concealed inside a mirrored wall. Only after the Filipina maid had pointed this out did they enter the bedroom to find Cecchi Gori asleep with his girlfriend, Valeria Marini, a Caprice-like figure who calls herself a singer-actress but in fact can do neither.

The police told Cecchi Gori to open his safe. Donning his silk dressing gown, he did so. When the police remarked on the stash of cocaine stored inside, Cecchi Gori replied nonchalantly, "Cocaine? That's not cocaine, it's saffron!"

Meanwhile, his business empire was unraveling. It should be said that he acquired the empire only by inheritance from his father, Mario, who before dying in 1993 had warned his old business partner, Silvio Berlusconi, "Take care of Vittorio, he is so impulsive and naive."

Vittorio's problem was that he wanted to be Berlusconi. He bought commercial TV channels (a failure), pumped fortunes into his soccer team (no titles), and dabbled in politics (getting no further than senator), but might have been okay had he not gotten caught in a divorce expected to be so expensive that it alone could have funded Fiorentina for years. Cecchi Gori remained admirably upbeat even after all this, leaning out of the window of his Mercedes limousine on Rome's Via Veneto to shout "*La dolce vita!*" to friends. However, he ruined Fiorentina.

It was hard to work out which bit of Cecchi Gori's empire owed what to which, but it was clear that he had borrowed tens of millions of dollars from the club. After everything went wrong, he tried the traditional Italian remedy, putting his eighty-two-year-old mother in charge, but even she could not save Fiorentina. A fax from a Colombian bank offering to pay off the club's entire debt proved, amazingly, to be a forgery.

In 2002 Fiorentina went bankrupt, slipping into Italy's fourth division, where it had to visit Tuscan village teams whose players were mostly Fiorentina fans. Now it is back in Serie A, but the days of Trap, Batistuta, and "The Animal" Edmundo won't return. Florence is just too small now.

Florence is typical. Midsize European cities (between 150,000 and 1 million inhabitants) have all but dropped off the map of European soccer. They can no longer afford to compete with clubs from bigger places. In early 2004 it was the turn of Parma, whose owners, the dairy company Parmalat, turned out to have mislaid 10 billion euros. Leeds United is the great English example. In Spain Deportivo La Coruña, pride of a midsize Galician city, suddenly discovered that its debt had hit the strictly notional figure of 178 million euros. Valencia followed a few years later. These clubs fell short because they had hardly any supporters outside their own city walls. Other midsize cities—Glasgow, Amsterdam, Nottingham—have retreated with less fanfare, but they too must know they will never again produce a European champion. Even Newcastle has slowly emerged from denial.

The third period of the European Cup began in 1982 and hasn't ended yet: rule by sturdy provincial city. There were still a few undersize winners: Porto and Liverpool twice each, and Eindhoven, Marseille, and Dortmund. However, these towns are not exactly midgets. Four of the five are agglomerations of 1.2 million inhabitants or more. Only Eindhoven has just 210,000 people and a metropolitan area—if you draw it very generously—of only 750,000. In general, European champions are getting bigger. In modern times, the race has usually gone to the rich.

The swelling of the soccer economy—the bigger TV contracts, the new stadiums, the freer movement of players, and so on—favored the most popular clubs. For historical reasons, these tended to be the ones in big provincial cities. Their teams came to dominate the Champions League in a sort of endless loop. Every club that won the trophy from 1998 through 2011 had won it at least once before. Most had won it several times before. Are their fans growing blasé? When you have won the thing nine times, the buzz probably starts to fade.

The dominant clubs until now haven't been from the megacities of Moscow, London, Paris, or Istanbul but from urban areas with about 2 million to 5 million inhabitants: Milan, Manchester, Munich, Madrid, and of course Barcelona. These cities are big enough to produce the required fan base yet provincial enough to generate a yearning for global recognition.

Strangely, one of these cities, Madrid, is a democratic capital. How could Real break the golden rule of the Champions League and win the trophy in 1998, 2000, and 2002? Because it had built its mammoth stadium, brand, and support in the days when Madrid was the capital of a dictatorship. Spain may have gone social democratic, but Real's players still enter the Santiago Bernabeu in those white "meringue" shirts as if it were 1955. The club's global standing is a relic of the fascist era.

GEORGE ZIPF COMES TO LONDON: THE FUTURE METROPOLITAN ERA?

George Kingsley Zipf is an almost forgotten Harvard linguist. Born in 1902, died in 1950 just as he was starting to make a name, Zipf is now known only for having formulated a law that explains almost everything. Among other things, Zipf's law tells us that London or Moscow should start winning Champions Leagues soon.

Consider the following: if you rank every American city by the size of its population, the difference in population between two consecutive cities is simply the ratio of their ranks. So if you compare cities number 1 and 2, city 2 has half (or 1/2) the population of city 1. If you compare cities number 2 and 3, city 3 has two-thirds (2/3) the population of city 2. City 100 has 99/100ths the population of city 99 and so on down the list. Statistically speaking, the fit of this relationship is almost as perfect as it is possible to be.

This is a particularly elegant example of a more general relationship known as Zipf's law, and it applies to a lot more than city sizes. For instance, it is also true of the frequency with which words are used in English. *The* is the most commonly used word in the language, *of* is second, and so *of* is used about half (1/2) as often as *the*. All in all, Zipf's law has been called possibly "the most accurate regularity in economics." (The Nobel Prize–winning economist Paul Krugman says, "Anyone who spends too much time thinking about Zipf's law goes mad," but we hope that is a joke.)

Zipf's law works for European cities, too, though not quite as neatly as for American ones. City sizes in most European countries are more closely bunched, and so the second city is closer to the first city's size than in the United States, the third closer to the second, and so on.

Why might this be? Zipf's law must have something to do with migration. People will always try to migrate to where the money is. In the United States, with its open markets and very high mobility of labor, they generally do. But in Europe, political and cultural barriers have curbed migration. That might explain why city sizes are more compressed there. Nonetheless, the academics Matthieu Cristelli, Michael Batty, and Luciano Pietronero showed in an article in the prestigious journal *Nature* in 2012 that "Zipf's Law holds approximately for the city sizes of each European country (France, Italy, Germany, Spain, etc)." They add that the law "completely falls apart" if you rank them as cities within a single state, i.e., the European Union, but then that is no surprise—these cities grew big in their nation-states long before the EU was ever thought of.

For a long time, nobody could understand why Zipf's law should hold for so many different phenomena. Now, though, economists and scientists are starting to generate models of growth in which the natural outcome of a process is distribution obeying Zipf's law. Recently the economist Xavier Gabaix of New York University came up with an explanation for why Zipf's law applies to city sizes. He said Zipf's law emerges when all cities grow at the same rate, regardless of their size and their history, but subject to random variation. This implies that common factors drive the growth of cities within a country, while the differences in growth are due to a series of random events ("shocks," in the economic jargon), such as bombing during the war, which in principle could occur anywhere. A story this simple is enough to explain the city sizes that Zipf's law predicts.

Two consequences of Zipf's law are crucial to soccer. First, giants—whether giant cities, giant soccer clubs, or giants of any other kind—are rare. That is because becoming a giant requires a long sequence of positive shocks, like tossing a coin fifty times and coming up "heads" every time. It can happen, but it is rare. Second, once a city becomes a giant, it is unlikely to shrink into the middle ranks unless it experiences a long series of repeated misfortunes (fifty "tails" in a row). By contrast, small cities are unlikely ever to become giants. In other words, the hierarchy of cities, which has established itself over centuries, probably won't change much in the foreseeable future.

This "law of proportionate growth" has some other consequences. What's true for cities is also true for many other social phenomena. For example, if your kid is behind at school, don't worry: he or she will almost certainly catch up, since all children tend to learn at the same rate, plus or minus a few shocks. Likewise, if you think your brilliant six-year-old soccer player is going to become another Beckham or Rooney, don't. More likely the boy had a few positive shocks in his early years, which will cancel out. Rooneys and Beckhams almost never happen. The distribution of talent is thus a bit like the distribution of city sizes: a few great talents stand out at the top, the Maradonas and Messis, but as you go down the list, the differences become smaller and smaller.

This brings us back to European cities: there are only a few giants, chiefly Moscow, Istanbul, Paris, and London. You would expect these giant cities to produce the biggest clubs, yet they have won just one single Champions League between them.

But soon they might win more. Soccer is changing. It is becoming more of a free market, as fascist dictators no longer interfere and the best players can move between clubs almost at will. Inevitably, the best players are starting to move to the biggest markets, as happens in Major League Baseball. And so you would expect dominance in European soccer to move, too: after rule by dictatorial capitals, midsize provincial towns, and big provincial cities, now London and possibly Moscow and Paris should get in on the action at last.

Moscow might, because it is Europe's last large nondemocratic capital. Russia's resources are being sent to the center, and with all that oil and gas under the soil, that's a lot of resources. Paris might, because it has nearly 12 million inhabitants and only one top-division soccer club, Paris Saint-Germain, which was appallingly run for years but has now been taken over by Qataris who have converted oil into soccer players. And with Chelsea's victory over Bayern on penalties in 2012, London has already gotten there. (This is one prediction we got right in the original 2009 edition of *Soccernomics*. We wrote then that "soon" Arsenal or Chelsea "could become the first London team to be champions of Europe.")

It's little surprise that London has finally become a front-rank soccer city. Even after the implosion of British banks, it has the largest local economy in Europe. It already supports two of Europe's biggest soccer teams and could probably cope with more. This represents quite a change. In the early 1990s London rather resembled Moscow circa 1973. Tired people in gray clothes waited on packed platforms for 1950s Tube trains. Coffee was an exotic drink that barely existed. Eating a meal outside was forbidden. The city center was almost uninhabited, and closed at 11 P.M. anyway. There was a sense of permanent decline.

Nor had London ever been the soccer capital of Britain. Only in 1931 did a southern club—Arsenal—first win the league. Even after that, though, the title generally went north.

But in the 1990s London transformed. Cheap flights from five airports took Londoners around Europe. Trains began running to Paris and Brussels. Today it is quicker to get there than to the shrinking northern cities of Liverpool and Manchester, and less of a culture shock when you arrive. London became a European city, detached from the rest of Britain. The geographer Daniel Dorling said Britain was starting to look like a city-state. Moreover, the city was starting to grow again. Greater London had been losing inhabitants from the Second World War until the 1980s, but boom-time London changed that. Just between 2001 and

2011, the city's population jumped 12 percent to 8.17 million—the fastest growth of any region of England or Wales in that period.

From the late 1990s until today, even through the financial crisis, London has offered a Technicolor vista of raucous young people from all over the world dressed in weird youth-culture outfits chucking cash at each other. The Tube trains have ceased to be antique curios. The place smells of money. All this has raised London's status in soccer.

At the same time as the city became fully international, so did the market in soccer players. The best ones can now work wherever they want. Many of them—like many investment bankers and actors—have chosen London.

Black and foreign players like living in a city where 95 percent of the inhabitants agree with the statement, "It is a good thing that Britain is a multicultural society." When Thierry Henry was spending his best years at Arsenal, he said, "I love this open, cosmopolitan city. Whatever your race, you never feel people's gaze on you." In a virtuous cycle, foreigners attract foreigners. The Frenchman Jacques Santini, Tottenham's manager for about five minutes, wanted to come to London because his son Sebastien already lived there—a classic example of chain migration.

Equally to the point, even in the current economic crisis a soccer player can still earn a living in London. The capital's clubs have been coining it. First, their customers can still afford to pay the highest ticket prices in global soccer. In 2013–2014 Arsenal charged £985 (nearly $1,600) for its cheapest season ticket, which was the highest rate in English and probably in global soccer. So many Londoners are happy to fork out this kind of money that Arsenal has been able to build a new stadium with 60,000 seats and sell it out. No club in London's history has drawn such a large regular crowd. In 2012–2013 Arsenal and Chelsea achieved revenues per seat per game of over £50 (about $80), according to the financial analyst Stephen Clapham of the London-based research consultancy Behind the Balance Sheet. Those were the highest figures in England, and probably in Europe. Over the 2011–2012 season, the business advisory firm Deloitte ranked Arsenal and Chelsea among Europe's six richest clubs.

No other European city has as many investors. When Abramovich decided to buy an English soccer club, it was always likely that he would end up owning Chelsea in his adopted city rather than, say, Bolton.

When the American billionaire Shahid Khan bought Fulham in 2013, it mattered to him that it was a London club. Even Queens Park Rangers are owned by the Malaysian Tony Fernandes and Indian Lakshmi Mittal, the world's forty-first-richest man, according to *Forbes,* who of course lives around the corner from the club in Kensington. Yes, other rich foreigners have bought Liverpool, Manchester City, Blackburn, and Aston Villa, but London is still a touch more appealing to billionaires.

The handful of the biggest provincial clubs—Manchester United, Liverpool, Bayern, Barcelona, the two in Milan—have built up such strong brands that they will remain at the top of European soccer. However, their new challengers probably will not be other provincial clubs but teams from London, Paris, and Moscow.

At last, being in a giant capital city is becoming a strategic asset to a soccer club. No London team had ever reached the Champions League final before 2006. From 2006 through 2012, Arsenal got there once and Chelsea twice, winning one. Soon, if we're not careful, the city will dominate every aspect of British life.

11

FOOTBALL VERSUS FOOTBALL

When Nelson Mandela was a teenager in the Transkei region of South Africa, he was sent to a mock British boarding school. The Clarkebury Institute taught black students but was of course run by a white man, the Reverend C. Harris. "The school itself consisted of a cluster of two dozen or so graceful, colonial-style buildings," Mandela recalled in his autobiography, *Long Walk to Freedom*. "It was the first place I'd lived in that was western, not African, and I felt I was entering a new world whose rules were not yet clear to me."

Like the Victorian British schools that it imitated, Clarkebury aimed to turn its pupils into Christian gentlemen. A gentleman, to Victorian Britons, was someone with posh manners who spoke English and played British games. As Mandela described his school days, "I participated in sports and games as often as I could, but my performances were no more than mediocre. . . . We played lawn tennis with home-made wooden rackets and soccer with bare feet on a field of dust."

He had encountered the British Empire. The British colonial officers, merchants, and sailors who went around the world in the nineteenth century didn't merely aim to exploit the natives. They also tried to teach them British values. They succeeded spectacularly with Mandela, who at an earlier school had acquired a new first name (Admiral Nelson was a British naval hero) and eventually became the epitome of the courtly British gentleman. However, his story is exemplary of millions of people around the world, both in Britain's official colonies and in the "informal empire," the countries where the Brits supposedly didn't rule.

From about 1917 to 1947, the British gradually stopped running the world and handed over the keys to the Americans. But the American empire was much less ambitious. It barely spread Americanism. Football, the American empire's most popular sport, still hardly exists outside the home country. In fact, when American troops in Afghanistan wanted to woo natives, they were reduced to handing out soccer balls. (The exercise failed: Allah's name was found to be printed on a ball, a blasphemy for an object designed for kicking.)

At this point, let's agree to call the global game "soccer" and the American game "football." Many people, both in America and in Europe, imagine that *soccer* is an American term invented in the late twentieth century to distinguish it from gridiron. Indeed, anti-American Europeans often frown on the use of the word. They consider it a mark of American imperialism. Even some American soccer fans seem embarrassed by the word. This is a silly position. "Soccer" was the most common name for the game in Britain from the 1890s until the 1970s. As far as one can tell, when the North American Soccer League brought soccer to the Americans in the 1970s, and Americans quite reasonably adopted the English word, the British stopped using it and reverted to the word *football.*

It's actually possible to show this little bit of linguistic snobbery on a chart. To do this we engaged the help of Antoinette Renouf, professor of English language and linguistics at Birmingham City University in the UK. Renouf is a "corpus" linguist, which means that she trawls electronic "text collections" for the purpose of empirical language study. Corpora come in all sizes and shapes, but she works mainly on a corpus derived from two British national newspapers, the *Guardian* and *Independent,* which she has been building with successive software research teams since 1984. So far her corpus contains approximately 1.3 billion words of running text. This supports a short-term diachronic approach to language research and lexico-semantic language use—or to say it in English, we can see from the corpus how the use of words changes over time. Renouf generated two charts for us, one showing the frequency of use of the word *football,* the other of *soccer,* from 1984 to 2011.

Back in 1984 the word *football* appeared about fifty times per million words used, while *soccer* appeared about ten times per million. The year

1984 is close to the nadir of the game in England: the time of hooligans, collapsing stadiums, and cheap tickets. Since then English soccer's renaissance has brought millions of new fans and billions of dollars into the game. The game became a talking point in all walks of life from politics to fashion. As result, the frequency of use of *football* rose steadily up to the year 2000 to about two hundred times per million, where it has stabilized for the past decade or so. By contrast, the relative use of the word *soccer* didn't increase in the '80s, '90s, and noughties, but remained at around ten times per million until around 2008. Since then, its usage has actually fallen to about five times per million words. Another way to express this is as follows: in 1984 about 17 percent of references to the English game ("football" or "soccer") employed the word *soccer,* but by 2011 only about 2 percent did. In the space of thirty years *soccer* has become a bad word in Britain. We, however, will compare soccer with football, and the readers will know what we mean.

What follows is a tale of two games and two empires. Soccer spread around the world whereas football did not, largely because Victorian Britons were instinctive colonialists whereas today's Americans are not. But now, for the first time, the empires are going head-to-head as if in a kid's computer game. Both the Premier League and the NFL want to conquer new territories. This is a struggle between two very different types of empire: the British (which contrary to popular opinion still exists) and the American (which contrary to popular opinion may never have existed). Emerging from the struggle is a new breed of sports fan.

GENTLEMEN WITH LEATHER BALLS

In 1884 a nine-year-old boy named Charles Miller embarked on the SS *Elbe* in Brazil and set off for England. Miller's father had emigrated from Britain to Brazil, to work as an engineer for the São Paulo Railway Company. Now Charles was making the return journey, to enroll at an English boarding school. Like Mandela at Clarkebury, Miller at Banister Court learned games. "Just as a schoolboy, in the Garden of Childhood, listens to the teacher, so I, fascinated, saw my first game of Association Football," he later wrote.

In 1894 Miller returned to Brazil with a leather ball and a set of rules in his luggage. He set up the first Brazilian soccer league. He also introduced rugby to Brazil, though with rather less success. He died in 1953, having lived long enough to see Brazil host the World Cup of 1950 and reach the final.

Miller's story was typical of soccer pioneers in many countries. First, he was posh, or at least posh enough to go to boarding school. (Contrary to myth, it wasn't on the whole British sailors who gave the world soccer. The upper classes had considerably more soft power.) Second, Miller was typical in that he spread soccer to a country that wasn't a British colony. In the colonies, places like Australia or India, British schoolteachers and administrators mostly taught the natives cricket and rugby. Soccer did best in the informal empire, the non-colonies: most of Europe, Latin America, and parts of Asia. Here, it probably benefited from not being seen as a colonial ruler's game. Brits in the informal empire were supposedly just businesspeople, even if in practice their commercial clout gave the British prime minister vast influence over many unlikely countries.

From about 1850 until the First World War, Britain was the sole economic superpower. As late as 1914, Britons still owned about 42 percent of all the world's foreign investment. The British expats who inhabited the informal empire represented the empire's economic might. The men tended to work in the railways (like Miller's father), or as businessmen (like the Charnock brothers, who set up Russia's first soccer club, the future Dynamo Moscow, for their mill employees outside Moscow), or as schoolteachers (like Alexander Watson Hutton, the Scottish teacher who in the early 1880s introduced soccer in Argentina).

These people had only soft power: the wealth and prestige of the British gentleman. That was enough to spread their games. Men like Hutton taught foreigners to see sports as a British upper-class and hence aspirational product. If you were a young man like Mandela who wanted to become a British gentleman, one of the things you did was play soccer. That's why the game's early adopters in the informal empire tended to be rich people who had contact with British gentlemen. Pim Mulier, for instance, who introduced a whole list of sports to the Netherlands, first encountered soccer as a five-year-old at a Dutch boarding school that had some British pupils. In 1879, when Mulier was fourteen, he founded the first Dutch soccer club.

Soccer conquered the world so fast largely because the British gentleman was such an attractive ideal. A century later a new British archetype, the hooligan, in his own way probably added to the game's glamour.

By the 1930s, when Mandela went to Clarkebury, the British Empire had already begun to fade. However, many of the empire's global networks outlived the loss of the colonies. The most important survivor would be the English language, even if it sustained its global reach largely thanks to the Americans. English gave people around the world an easy connection with Britain. Steven Stark, an American soccer fan, former speechwriter of Jimmy Carter, and a teacher of English rhetoric, asks, "Isn't the best thing the Premiership has going for it is that it's in English? I mean, if everyone in France spoke English and everyone in England spoke French, we'd all be following the French league. In an international economy, English trumps the competition."

Many people in former British colonies grew up absorbing British soccer from British media outlets that had also outlived the empire. Peter Draper, when he was marketing director of Manchester United, noted that English soccer has been televised for decades in many Asian countries. That had built loyalty. Real Madrid, Draper told us, "didn't have the platform. Spanish television is nowhere in Asia. Best team of the 1950s? Sorry, didn't see them in Asia."

Mike Abrahams is a gangster-turned-intellectual who grew up in a poor, nonwhite Cape Flats township outside Cape Town. As a child he used to sit in the local library reading British boys' magazines like *Shoot* and *Tiger*. He admits that classic British soccer cartoons like *Billy's Magic Boots* shaped him.

Abrahams was a leftist who identified with only one product of white capitalist imperialist Britain: soccer. He says, "People in the Cape follow English football very seriously. One of my friends, his first child's name is Shankly [after Bill Shankly, the former Liverpool manager]. And this is an activist! You can say England is a bitch on Friday night, and on Saturday afternoon you go to a sports pub to watch English soccer."

People are always complaining that American culture has conquered the world. In fact, British culture probably remains more dominant. This fading midsize island has kept a bizarre grip on the global imagination. It's not only their sports that the Brits have exported. The world's six best-selling novels of the past hundred years are all British: four Harry Potters, one Agatha Christie, and one J. R. R. Tolkien. The world's best-selling band ever is the Beatles. And the sports league with the biggest global impact is surely the Premier League. England has produced few great soccer players, yet on an average Saturday people in San Francisco and Shanghai gather in bars for the kickoff at White Hart Lane rather than for anything from Germany.

They certainly aren't watching the NFL. In fact, the United States has rarely even aspired to vast cultural reach. The Americans fought wars, but mostly tried to avoid creating long-term colonies, notes John Gray, emeritus professor at the London School of Economics. In Vietnam and Iraq, for instance, the aim was to "go in, do the job, get out." Unlike Britons, Americans generally didn't want to be in the business of empire. We know an American lawyer who spent a few months working for the British government during the occupation of Iraq. In the "Green Zone" in Baghdad he noticed a difference between the way Brits and Americans worked. When American officials wanted an Iraqi to do something, the lawyer said, they would generally call the person into the Green Zone and if necessary "bawl him out." Sometimes this strategy worked. Sometimes it didn't. But the Americans summoned Iraqis only when something needed fixing. British officials worked differently, said the lawyer. They were always inviting Iraqis in, for parties or just for chats, even when there was nothing in particular to discuss. This was exactly how the British had operated both in their colonies and in their "informal empire": they made long-term contacts. The Reverend Harris at Clarkebury school may not entirely have known it, but in effect he was a British agent charged with teaching Mandela Britishness.

By contrast, few American Harrises ever taught baseball or football to budding foreign rulers. There have been a handful of prominent American colonialists, but they are so rare as to stand out. Douglas MacArthur ruled Japan for years. Hollywood makes its blockbusters chiefly for the global market. And in sports, the NBA's former commissioner, David Stern, spent thirty years interesting foreigners in basketball. But most American sporting moguls, like most American producers in general, have been satisfied with their giant domestic market. Baseball's last great overseas tour was in 1913–1914, after which Americans barely even tried to spread baseball or football abroad until the 1990s.

The American empire's favorite games have been no good at cultural imperialism. It's a story told in one statistic: Super Bowl XLIV in 2010 briefly became the most popular TV program in American history, with 106.5 million domestic viewers, yet the media agency Futures Sport + Entertainment estimates that only 4 million people outside North America watched it.

WHILE AMERICA SLEPT: HOW SOCCER INVADED THE US

After the British Victorians spread their games, sports experienced a century of relative stability. The Indians played cricket, the US resisted soccer, and the isolated town of Melbourne favored Australian Rules football, which barely existed even in some other parts of Australia. But from the 1980s, new TV channels—free, cable, and satellite—began mushrooming almost everywhere. They took up the burden of carrying sports around the world. When Britain's Channel Four was created in 1982, for instance, it began broadcasting NFL games. They were a hit. Suddenly there were people in Norwich or Manchester who called themselves 49ers fans. William "the Refrigerator" Perry, the supersize Chicago Bears lineman, became a cult hero in Britain. Alistair Kirkwood, the NFL's UK managing director, fondly recalls that for a year or two in the 1980s, the Super Bowl had higher ratings in Britain than the beloved soccer program Match of the Day on the same weekend.

It didn't last. English soccer cleaned up its stadiums, kicked out most of its hooligans, sold its rights to Rupert Murdoch's Sky Television, and revived. Eventually Channel Four dropped the NFL. The halfhearted American invasion—albeit led by British TV—had been repelled.

Meanwhile, across the ocean, soccer was slowly infecting American life. Even though the US already had four big team sports and seemed to have no need of another, in the 1970s the game came from almost nowhere to conquer American childhoods. It turned out there was a gap in the American sports market after all. The most popular sport in the US, football, was too dangerous, too male, and too expensive for mass participation. Fitting out a kid with all the necessary equipment for football costs around $300 to $400, a significant expense, especially if the child quickly decides that he doesn't like being beaten up. Today, probably fewer than 1 million people in the world play tackle football, compared to the 265 million who (according to FIFA) played soccer in 2006.

Victorian Britons had conceived of soccer as a "man's game." But Americans saw that it was a soft sport, safe for girls as well as boys. So soccer in the US became an unlikely beneficiary of feminism. It did almost as well out of another post-1960s social trend, Mexican immigration. The estimated 53 million people of Hispanic origin now living in the US (up more than threefold since 1980) outnumber the population of Spain.

The upshot is that more American children under twelve play soccer than baseball, football, and ice hockey put together. Contrary to popular opinion, soccer in America has been a success. When David Beckham joined the LA Galaxy, the cliché was that his task was to "put soccer on the map" in America. In fact, this was impossible, because soccer was already "on the map" in America. The US has a strong soccer culture. It's just different from any other country's soccer culture. In particular, it doesn't require a strong domestic men's professional league.

Major League Soccer is not American soccer. It's just a tiny piece of the mosaic. Kids' soccer, college soccer, women's soccer, indoor soccer, Mexican, English, and Spanish soccer, the Champions League, and the World Cup between them dwarf the MLS. To cite just one example: 19.4 million Americans saw their country lose to Ghana at the World Cup of 2010. In American daytime on a Saturday, for a round of sixteen game, that was a bigger audience than the Fox network averaged for five baseball World Series games played in prime time later that year. That summer of 2010, US-Ghana also outdrew the average game in the NBA finals between the Boston Celtics and the LA Lakers—itself the most popular NBA matchup in many years. Moreover, soccer has penetrated most branches of the American entertainment industry, from *The Sopranos* to presidential elections in which "soccer moms" have been touted as pivotal figures.

American soccer people often fret over the MLS's marginality. As American writer Dave Eggers has noted, "Newspaper coverage of the games usually is found in the nether regions of the sports section, near the car ads and the biathlon roundups." Some TV ratings for MLS games "are in the realm of—or, in some cases, actually below—tractor pulls, skateboarding competitions, and bass fishing tournaments," writes Andrei Markovits, politics professor at the University of Michigan. The lowliest MLS players earned a modest $35,125 a year in 2013.

But to worry about the MLS—which is growing in popularity anyway—is to misunderstand why so many American suburban families like soccer. The game has thrived as a pastime for upscale kids in part precisely because there is no big soccer in the US. Many soccer moms are glad that soccer is not a big professional American sport like basketball or football. Like a lot of other Americans, they are wary of big-time American sports, whose stars do lousy and unethical things like shooting their limousine drivers.

By contrast, many moms see soccer as an innocent game, free of certain aspects of modern America: not violent, not drenched in money, and not very black. A large number of MLS players are white college boys. American soccer has no Charles Barkley.

ANY GIVEN SUNDAY: IS THE NFL REALLY SO EQUAL?

Clearly, though, the NFL is doing something right. Here are the average attendance rates of the most-watched leagues of all the world's ball games:

	Average attendance per game	*Full-season attendance*
1. NFL (2011)	67,358	17.1 million
2. German soccer, Bundesliga (2012–2013)	42,609	13.0 million
3. English Premier League (2012–2013)	35,931	13.7 million
4. Australian Football League (2013) (Australian Rules football)	33,461	6.9 million
5. Major League Baseball (2013)	30,504	74.0 million

The NFL comes top measured by attendance per game, while MLB is way ahead in terms of attendance for the whole season. Aussie Rules clearly dominates in terms of attendance per capita (i.e., attendance divided by the country's population) but the Premier League is not far behind with a rate of 26 percent for the season, compared to only 5 percent for the NFL (and only 16 percent for the much-feted Bundesliga). But measured by the number of fans inside the stadium for any given game, no professional league can begin to rival the NFL. When people try to explain the NFL's popularity, they often mention its famous slogan: "On any given Sunday any team in our league can beat any other team." This is a boast the Premier League would never dare make. English soccer looks horribly unbalanced, with a few rich teams perennially dominating at the top, whereas the NFL claims to be a league of equals.

Indeed, the NFL is often called "the socialist league." Its clubs share TV income equally, and 40 percent of each game's gate receipts goes to the visiting team. This aspiration to equality is a general American sporting trait. Clubs in American baseball, basketball, and the MLS also share far more of their income than European soccer does. Take the ubiquitous New York Yankees baseball cap. Outside of New York, the Yankees receive only one-thirtieth of the profit on each cap sold, the same as every other team in baseball. By contrast, Manchester United wouldn't dream of giving Norwich or Sunderland a cut of its shirts.

Many in European soccer, and particularly in England, have come to envy the NFL. English fans often complain that their sport is getting boring because the big clubs win everything. A handful of clubs—chiefly Manchester United, Chelsea, Arsenal, and now Manchester City—dominate the Premier League. In the Champions League, only Barcelona and Bayern Munich usually beat them. Even Emilio Butragueño, when he was sporting director of plucky little Real Madrid, told the BBC, "You need uncertainty at the core of every competition. . . . We may eventually have something similar to the [salary cap] system in the US, to give a chance to all the clubs."

In 2008 Andy Burnham, Britain's then culture secretary, warned that although the Premier League was "the world's most successful domestic sporting competition," it risked becoming "too predictable." He added, "I keep referring to the NFL, which has equal sharing. . . . In the US, the most free-market country in the world, they understand that equal distribution of money creates genuine competition."

UEFA's president Platini seems to agree. Searching for a way to even things out in European soccer, he once put a team of UEFA officials on a plane to the US. Perhaps there was something over there that soccer could copy.

People who think like this tend to accept two truisms: The NFL is much more equal than European soccer. And sports fans like equality. Unfortunately, neither of these truisms is true. First, the NFL isn't nearly as balanced as it pretends. Second, we have data to show that overall, fans prefer unbalanced leagues.

At first glance, you could be forgiven for believing that the NFL really is much more equal than the Premier League. In the decade through 2011, seven different teams won the Super Bowl. In the same period, only three teams won the Premier League, with Manchester United bagging a snore-inducing five titles. On any given Sunday (or Saturday lunchtime, Tuesday night, whenever), Sunderland or Cardiff can beat United, but the fact is that they usually don't.

Yet is the NFL much more equal than the Premier League? Does it have a more even distribution of wins? Measuring the level of equality in both leagues is tricky, first because there are no ties in the NFL and second because the NFL's regular season consists of just sixteen games and the Premier League's of thirty-eight. In any given season, a weak English team has many more chances to get lucky.

Happily, there is a way to allow for these differences so that we can compare the two leagues. We will do this by dreaming up another league, a totally equal one in which every team always has an equal chance of winning any given game. This equal league would be a league of coin flips. Obviously, in the coin-flip league each team would be expected to win an average of 50 percent of its games. Even so, the outcome of any sixteen- or thirty-eight-game sequence would produce some random inequalities. Hardly any team in the coin-flip league would win exactly half its games. Rather, the win percentages for the season would be randomly dispersed around 50 percent. The question then is: Which looks more like the totally equal coin-flip league, the NFL or the Premier League?

To work this out, we must calculate how random the dispersion of wins is in each of our three leagues. The measure of dispersion is commonly called the standard deviation. Let's calculate standard deviation for the coin-flip league, and then for the NFL and the Premier League. (And please feel free to skip the next few paragraphs if you aren't interested in the math.)

The standard deviation of win percentages for any league is calculated by first taking the difference between each team's win percentage and 50 percent (the difference will be positive when the team has a winning season, negative for a losing season). Then we square the difference, to make sure pluses and minuses don't cancel out. Next we add up the difference for all teams in the league, and take the square root. That gives a number that is comparable to the average win percentage.

Now we are ready to find the figure we want: the standard deviation, or dispersion of win percentages. If our average win percentage is 50, a standard deviation of 1 would mean that most teams are close to the average. If the standard deviation were 20, it would mean that there is quite a lot of dispersion. In coin-tossing leagues, we know what the standard deviation should be: close to half of the reciprocal of the square root of the number of games played. This is easy to calculate. If you play sixteen games, the square root is four, the reciprocal is one-quarter, and half of that is one-eighth, or 12.5 percent.

That is what the standard deviation of win percentage in the NFL would be if on any given Sunday any team in the league really had a fifty-fifty chance of beating its opponent. Well, the NFL is not a coin-tossing league. In the decade from 2002 through 2011, the standard deviation of win-loss records has fluctuated between 16 percent and 21 percent, and has averaged 19 percent. That's well above the 12.5 percent of the coin-tossing league.

The Premier League is only slightly less equal than the NFL. If the Premier League were a coin-tossing league, the expected standard deviation would be just over 8 percent. In fact, in the decade from 2002 through 2011 the Premier League's standard deviation averaged 14 percent. So it's not a coin-tossing league, either, but the difference is not much greater than for the NFL. To put it another way, the NFL has a standard deviation about 54 percent larger than a coin-tossing league, while the English Premier League is about 74 percent larger than a coin-tossing league. This is a difference, but in the scale of things not a very big one.

You might object that even if there isn't a huge difference in the statistical balance of the NFL and Premier League, the identity of the dominant teams and doormats changes each season in the NFL but not in the Premier League. After all, each season the worst NFL team gets the first draft pick, a very large human being who is in fact a device for bouncing back. Sudden reversals of fortune are much more likely in the NFL. In 2011 the Indianapolis Colts, having been dominant for a decade, endured a season with only two wins after their star quarterback, Peyton Manning, was injured. This dismal record was rewarded with first pick of the 2012 draft. Naturally they chose the Stanford graduate Andrew Luck, thought to be one of the best quarterback prospects to come out of college in recent years. This allowed them to return to their winning ways the following season. As the distinguished "Chicago school" economists Sherwin Rosen and Allen Sanderson have pointed out, the Premier League punishes failure, while the NFL rewards it.

But for all the NFL's efforts, the identity of winners and losers is pretty stable in both leagues. The best team in the NFL, the New England Patriots, won 77 percent of its regular-season games from 2002 through 2011. The Colts won 69 percent in that period, and the Pittsburgh Steelers 66 percent. Well, in the same decade in the Premier League, Manchester United won 76 percent, Chelsea 74 percent, Arsenal 71 percent, and Liverpool 65 percent. In other words, in the NFL three teams out of thirty-two dominated. In the Premier League four out of twenty dominated marginally more. It's hard to say on that basis which league is more balanced.

Likewise, there are as many losers in the NFL as in the Premier League. From 2001 through 2010, the Detroit Lions won fewer than a quarter of their games. A very few teams in the Premier League have been as bad or worse—Derby County in 2007–2008 managed to win one match all season—but there's a difference. Calamitous teams in the Premier League get relegated, whereas the Lions sustained their peculiar brand of misery for a decade.

So the NFL isn't much more equal than the Premier League. It just looks like it is. It manages to look more equal thanks largely to randomization devices that ensure that the best team doesn't always win the Super Bowl: first, the small number of regular-season games; second, the playoffs. Both these devices ensure that no NFL team is likely to dominate for years like Manchester United has. However, this randomization comes at the expense of justice. Fans often feel that the best team in the NFL did not win the Super Bowl. In fact, the NFL looks a lot like the Champions League, where the knockout rounds add a random element that often ambushes the best team.

This disposes of our first truism: the claim that the NFL is much more equal than the Premier League. What about the second one, the notion that sports fans, like French revolutionaries, desire equality?

If fans want all teams to be equal, then they will shun games in which results are predictable. If so, more of them will watch games whose outcome is very uncertain. How to test whether fans really behave like that? Researchers have tried to gauge expected outcomes of games either by using prematch betting odds or the form of both teams over the previous half-dozen games. Studies of soccer, mostly in England, show mixed results. Some studies find that more balanced games attract more fans. Others find the reverse.

The British economists David Forrest of Salford Business School and Robert Simmons of Lancaster University have done some of the best work in this field. They found that a balanced English game could sometimes increase attendance. However, they also carried out a simulation to show that if the English leagues became more balanced, they would attract *fewer* fans. That is because a balanced league, in which all teams are equally good, would turn into an almost interminable procession of home wins. By contrast, in real existing soccer, some of the most balanced games occur when a weak team plays at home against a strong team (Stoke versus Manchester United, for instance).

Forrest and Simmons found that the people who care most about competitive balance are television viewers. The spectators at the grounds tend to be the hard core: they simply want to see their team. However, most TV viewers are "floating voters." When the outcome of a game seems too predictable, they switch off. The two economists found that the closer a televised English soccer game was expected to be (measured by the form of both teams going into the game), the higher the viewing figures on Sky TV in Britain. Still, the size of this effect was modest. Forrest and Simmons said that even if the Premier League were perfectly balanced (in the sense that each team had an equal probability of winning each game), TV audiences would rise by only 6 percent. That would be a small effect for such a revolutionary change.

A moment's thought suggests why some unequal games might be very attractive. Most fans in the stadium are fans of the home team, and so they do not really want a balanced outcome. Often the most attractive games involve strong home teams playing weak visiting teams (Manchester United versus Stoke, again), in which case the home team typically has a lot of supporters who enjoy watching their heroes score a lot of goals, or they are games between weak home teams and strong away teams (Stoke versus Manchester United), in which local fans come to see the visiting stars.

Furthermore, big teams have more fans than small ones, and so if Manchester United beats Stoke, more people are happy than if Stoke wins. Also, fans are surprisingly good at losing. Psychological studies show that they are skilled at transferring blame: "We played well, but the referee was garbage." This means that fans will often stick with a team even if it always loses. It also explains why, the morning after their team gets knocked out of the World Cup, people don't sink into depression but get on with their lives.

Last, dominant teams create a special interest of their own. Millions of people support Manchester United, and millions of others despise it. In a way, both groups are following the club. United is the star of English soccer's soap opera. Everyone else dreams of beating it. Much of the meaning of supporting a smaller club like West Ham, for instance, derives from disliking Manchester United. Kevin Keegan, when he was chasing the title as manager of Newcastle in 1996, thrillingly captured that national sentiment with his famous, "I will love it if we beat them! Love it!" monologue. (United beat him instead.) Big bad United makes the Premier League more fun.

Another way of looking at competitive balance is to view the league as a whole, rather than match by match. Do more spectators come when the title race is exciting than when one team runs away with it?

It turns out that a thrilling title race does little to improve attendance. English fans will watch their teams play in the league even when they haven't a hope of winning it (or else dozens of English clubs would not exist).

It is true that a game has to be significant to draw fans, but that significance need not have anything to do with winning the title. A study by Stephen Dobson and John Goddard showed that when a match matters more either for winning the league or for avoiding relegation to a lower league, then attendance tends to rise. In every soccer league in Europe, the bottom few teams are "relegated" at the end of the season to a lower tier. The worst three teams in the Premier League, for instance, drop to the Championship. It's as if the cellar teams in Major League Baseball got exiled to Triple A. Relegation is brutal, but the device has a genius to it. The annual English relegation battle boosts fans' interest to the point that teams at the bottom often outdraw teams at the top as the season comes to an end. The NFL, too, could do with a system of relegation. It would replace losers with rising teams. This would be in the fans' interest, but not in the owners'.

Fans need a reason to care. Most matches in the Premier League are significant for something or other, even if it's only qualifying for European competition. Given that games can be significant in many different ways, it is unclear why a more balanced Premier League would create more significance.

There is a third way of looking at balance: the long term. Does the dominance of the same teams year in, year out turn fans off?

Let's compare a long period with dominance in English soccer to a long period without dominance: the fairly equal era that ran from 1949 to 1968, and the "unfair" era of the Premier League from 1993 to 2012.

In the first, "equal" twenty-year period, eleven different teams won the English league. The most frequent champion, Manchester United, won five titles in the period. The second period was far more predictable: only five teams won the title, with United taking it thirteen times. Yet during the first "equal" period, total annual attendance in the top division fell from an all-time high of 18 million in 1949 to only 15 million in 1968 (and even that figure got a temporary boost from England winning the World Cup in 1966). During the second, "unequal" period, total attendance rose from below 10 million to over 13 million, even though tickets became much more expensive and people had many more choices of how to spend their free time.

Anyone who dismisses the Premier League as "one of the most boring leagues in the world" (in the words of Kevin Keegan), a closed shop that shuts out smaller clubs from the lower divisions, has to explain why so many people now watch all levels of English league football. In the 2009–2010 season, in the pits of recession, more than 30 million spectators paid to see professional games in England, "a level not seen since well before the introduction of all seated stadia [in the early 1990s]," commented Dan Jones of Deloitte's Sports Business Group. The Premier League pulled fans even though, as Keegan has noted, everyone knew the top finishers in advance. Yet more than half of those 30 million–plus spectators watched the Football League, the three divisions below the Premier League. In fact, the Football League that season drew its biggest crowds in fifty years. The clubs in the Championship, the second tier of English soccer, have supposedly been doomed to irrelevance by Manchester United and can only dream of one day clinging on at the bottom of the Premier League, yet their division in 2010–2011 was the fourth-best attended league in Europe, ranked by total number of spectators.

The Premier League's inequality coexists with rising crowds, revenues, and global interest, not least from North American businessmen schooled in American major league sports: notably, the Glazer family at United itself, Stan Kroenke at Arsenal, and John Henry at Liverpool. These people do not seem too worried about competitive balance in English soccer.

They have reasons to feel relaxed. The Premier League's TV income is starting to catch up with the NFL's. In the 1970s the NFL generated hundreds of millions of dollars annually when soccer in Europe was generating almost nothing. By 1980 the average NFL team still had nearly as much income a year as all the clubs in the English top division put together. In 2010–2011 the average Premier League team earned about $80 million a year from TV, while its NFL counterpart did only slightly better with $95.8 million. That's pretty good given that England has about 265 million fewer inhabitants than the US. Moreover, the gap between the two leagues has been closing fast, and before long the English might even pull ahead as they finally start making big money out of the global market. One day we might see English soccer chairmen buying NFL teams.

Some of English soccer's critics have not digested these figures. When we pointed out to Platini at UEFA's headquarters on Lake Geneva that English stadiums are full nowadays, he replied, "Not all. They're full at the teams that win." This argument is often made but flawed nonetheless. Whenever rows of empty seats appear at struggling teams like Blackburn, it is back-page news, and regarded as ominous for the Premier League as a whole. Yet it's natural that some fans should desert disappointing teams in small towns (especially during a recession), while others flock to exciting ones. Sunderland, Arsenal, Manchester United, and other clubs have built bigger stadiums and filled them. Not every English team has gained spectators since 1992–1993, but most have. All twenty clubs in the Premier League in 2011–2012 had a higher average attendance than in 1992–1993. If the team had been in the Premier League in 1992, the average increase was 48 percent; if it had risen from a lower division, the average increase was an even more handsome 93 percent. Even teams that were in the Premier League in '92–'93 but not in '11–'12 usually had higher attendance—only Leeds United, Sheffield Wednesday, and Oldham Athletic lost spectators. The rising English tide had lifted almost every boat.

Admittedly, today's large crowds don't in themselves prove that dominance attracts fans. After all, many other things have changed in England since the more equal 1949–1968 period. Crucially, the country's stadiums have improved. However, the rising attendance rates do make it hard to believe that dominance in itself significantly undermines interest. Indeed, pretty much every soccer league in Europe exhibits more dominance than the American major leagues, yet fans still go.

WHY DAVID BEAT GOLIATH

Strangely, it was the British fanzine *When Saturday Comes* that best expressed the joys of an unbalanced league. *WSC* is, in large part, the journal of small clubs. It publishes moving and funny pieces by fans of minnows like Crewe or Swansea. Few of its readers have much sympathy with Manchester United (though some, inevitably, are United fans). Many of WSC's writers have argued for a fairer league. Yet in September 2008 Ian Plenderleith, a contributor living outside Washington, DC, argued in *WSC* that America's MLS, in which "all teams started equal, with the same squad size, and the same amount of money to spread among its players' wages," was boring. The reason: "No truly memorable teams have the space to develop." The "MLS is crying out for a couple of big, successful teams," Plenderleith admitted. "Teams you can hate. Dynasties you really, really want to beat. Right now, as LA Galaxy coach Bruce Arena once memorably said: 'It's a crapshoot.'"

In short, the MLS lacks one of the joys of an unbalanced league: the David versus Goliath match. And one reason fans enjoy those encounters is that surprisingly often, given their respective budgets, the Davids win. The economist Jack Hirshleifer called this phenomenon "the paradox of power." Imagine, he said, that there were two tribes, one large, one small. Each can devote its efforts to just two activities, farming and fighting. Each tribe produces its own food through farming, and steals the other tribe's food through fighting. Which tribe will devote a larger share of its efforts to fighting?

The answer is the small tribe. The best way to understand this is to imagine that the small tribe is very small indeed. It would then have to devote almost all its limited resources to either fighting or farming. If it chose farming, it would be vulnerable to attack. Everything it produced could be stolen. On the other hand, if the tribe devoted all its resources to fighting, it would have at least a chance of stealing some resources. So Hirshleifer concludes—and proves with a mathematical model—that smaller competitors will tend to devote a greater share of resources to competitive activities.

He found many real-world examples of the paradox of power. He liked citing Vietnam's defeat of the US, but one might also add the Afghan resistance to the Soviet Union in the 1980s, the Dutch resistance to the Spanish in the sixteenth century, or the American resistance to the British in the Revolutionary War. In these cases the little guy actually defeated the big guy. In many other cases, the little guy was eventually defeated, but at much greater cost than might have been expected based on physical resources (the Spartans at Thermopylae, the Afrikaners in the Boer War, the Texans at the Alamo).

In soccer as in war, the underdog tends to try harder. Big teams fight more big battles, and so each big contest weighs slightly less heavily than it does for their smaller rivals. Little teams understand that they may have few opportunities to compete at the highest level, and so they give it everything. They therefore probably win more often than you would predict based on ability alone.

NOTHING WORSE THAN NEW MONEY

Fans enjoy unbalanced modern soccer. Yet the complaints about its imbalance continue. The curious thing is that these complaints are relatively new, a product of the past fifteen or so years. Contrary to popular opinion, soccer was unbalanced in the past, too, but before the 1990s fewer people complained.

It is a fantasy that Europe was ever a very balanced soccer continent. In smaller countries, clubs from the capital have tended to rule. The Italian league was always dominated by Juventus, Milan, and Inter, and the Spanish league by Barcelona and Real Madrid. By the 1980s Bayern Munich controlled the Bundesliga, and in the postwar era English soccer has mostly been dominated by Manchester United, Arsenal, and Liverpool. United's thirteen titles in the twenty seasons through 2013 may sound boring, but Liverpool won ten in twenty between 1969 and 1988. Almost all other clubs are so firmly excluded from power that even very big Newcastle has not won the title since 1927. The imbalance in England as in all European leagues was reinforced by the European Cup (now the Champions League), which handed the dominant teams more money.

The old European Cup was seldom much fairer than the Champions League is now. We saw earlier in the book that only between 1970 and 1981 did clubs from modest-size towns regularly win the trophy. Usually the cup went to the biggest provincial cities, or to Madrid. Even Platini admits, "For forty years it's been the biggest clubs that won the Champions League; when I played, too. With or without homegrown players, it was Real Madrid, Liverpool, Manchester, Juventus who won. English clubs won the cup ten times in a row, I think. No? In the 1980s."

Oh, dear. Platini is not going to win any bar quizzes anytime soon. In fact, English clubs won six straight European Cups from 1977 through 1982. But his point stands: inequality in European soccer is nothing new.

Platini smiles, thinking again of that English dominance in the 1980s: "It's funny. There were no great debates then, saying, 'We have to change everything.' Today it's the money that makes the difference."

That is precisely the point. Today's inequality in soccer bothers people not because it is unprecedented, but because it is more driven by money than it used to be. In the old days, a middling soccer team could suddenly enjoy years of dominance if it happened to hire an excellent manager who signed excellent players. That's what happened in the 1970s to Liverpool under Bill Shankly, or to Nottingham Forest under Brian Clough. Today a middling team can suddenly enjoy years of dominance if it happens to be bought by a billionaire who hires an excellent manager who signs excellent players. That is what happened to Chelsea under Abramovich, and what may happen to Manchester City under Abu Dhabian rule. So inequality in soccer, as well as not being boring, is not even new. All that's new is the money.

Many people tend to feel that inequality becomes unfair when it is bought with money. It disgusts them that Chelsea (or the New York Yankees) can sign the best players simply because it is a rich club. This is a moral argument. It's a form of idealistic egalitarianism, which says that all teams should have more or less equal resources. This stance may be morally right (we cannot judge), but it is not a practical political agenda, and it probably doesn't reflect what most soccer fans want. Spectators vote with their feet. It's certainly not the case that millions of them are abandoning the Premier League because the money offends them. Based on the evidence of what they go to watch, they want to see the best players competing against each other. Many people will say they find Manchester United evil. Not many seem to find them boring.

COUCH POTATOES AND THE STRUGGLE FOR WORLD DOMINATION

Sometime in the early 2000s, when Paul Tagliabue was NFL commissioner, he told the team owners something like this: "You have to ask yourself, 'Do you want a potential fan base of 400 million or 4 billion in twenty or thirty years?'" His point was that if they wanted 4 billion, they'd have to find them abroad.

That was when the sporting struggle between the American and British empires finally got serious. The NBA had been trying to conquer the world since the 1980s, but at last the NFL plunged in, too. In recent seasons it has played games in London and Toronto, and that may be just a first step.

The market in sports fans is becoming more global. This means that a century-old model of fandom—the man who supports the hometown team he inherited from his father—is collapsing. The new globalized sports fan will happily snub his local domestic league. If you live in London and you like football, you probably support an NFL team rather than some bunch of no-hopers playing on a converted rugby field a few miles from your house. Similarly, if you live in the US and like soccer, you are more likely to support Manchester United than your local MLS team, which in any case may be hundreds of miles from your house. Even in Argentina, with its great historic soccer clubs, people increasingly watch United on TV. That's all the more true in the US, China, or Japan, countries whose soccer fans mostly came of age during the second wave of sporting globalization.

These people want to see the real thing. Global fans want global leagues. For most of them, that means the NBA, the NFL, or the Premier League. It was therefore wrong to imagine that Beckham could save American soccer by playing for the Galaxy. American soccer is alive and well and lying on the sofa watching Manchester United on NBC.

The Premier League is going to spread ever further, and the NFL will try to. This struggle won't be fought to the death. There is room for them both. "I personally don't know anybody who follows only one sport and nothing else," Kirkwood, the NFL's UK managing director, told us. "I don't think it's as competitive as it looks. We don't have a vision of being a top-three sport in Britain. If you go into a big enough market, you can carve a niche. So you can be an Arsenal fan and a New York Giants fan."

Some Arsenal fans have probably become Giants fans, but we suspect that a lot more Giants fans are becoming Arsenal fans. Long after the sun set on the British Empire, it is achieving a posthumous victory in sports.

PART II
The Fans

Loyalty, Suicides, Happiness,
and the Country with the Best Supporters

12

THE COUNTRY THAT LOVES SOCCER MOST

Which country loves soccer most?

This might sound like a matter of the heart that is hard to measure, but in fact the data exist. Loving soccer expresses itself in three main ways: playing the game, going to the stadium, and watching soccer on television. We have international figures for all three.

First, a caveat: not all the numbers are reliable. There are lies, damned lies, and statistics, and statistics from outside the Western world tend to be even worse. We will therefore limit our quest to Europe. Using a bit of judgment, by the end of the chapter we will be able to say with some confidence which European country cares most about the game.

PLAYERS: OH, TO BE A TINY ISLAND

In 2006 FIFA tried to count how many people in the world played soccer. The "Big Count" came up with 265 million soccer players, more than 90 percent of them males. Some were registered with proper clubs. The overwhelming majority, though, were "unregistered occasional players" who kicked around with friends on playgrounds and beaches and five-a-side courts. The only way to find out whether these people played soccer was by asking them—or at least a tiny representative sample of them.

None of these obstacles put off FIFA. The organization is a bit vague about exactly how it got ahold of the figures, saying it used "the standard practice of a questionnaire as well as an online tool." It also threw in its Big Count 2000, plus a UEFA survey and other "internal analyses,"

FIGURE 12.1. **Most enthusiastic soccer-playing countries**

Country	*Percentage of population that plays soccer*
Costa Rica	27
Germany	20
Faeroe Islands	17
Guatemala	16
Chile	16
Paraguay	16
Aruba	15
Barbados	13
Vanuatu	13
Mali	12
Anguilla	12
Austria	12
Norway	12
Slovakia	11
Sweden	11
Bermuda	11
Iceland	11
Netherlands	11
Ireland	10
Cook Islands	10

to "supplement missing data from associations and for plausibility purposes." Reading between the lines of the survey, it seems that more than a fifth of national FAs didn't even bother to take part. The whole endeavor was "scientifically observed by Lamprecht & Stamm SFB AG, a social research company based [handily] in Zurich."

Anyway, the most ambitious survey of soccer participation in history came up with a list of the most enthusiastic soccer-playing countries. China and the US were found to have the most players (26 million and 24 million, respectively), but of course the key question is which countries had the largest proportion of their inhabitants playing. Figure 12.1 shows FIFA's list.

It's striking how many of the most enthusiastic soccer players live on little islands where there presumably isn't much else to do but play soccer and watch the waves roll in. The Faeroe Islands, Aruba, Barbados,

Vanuatu, Anguilla, Bermuda, Iceland, and the Cook Islands (combined population about 1 million) all make the top twenty.

FIFA's list is interesting if true. Let's take the case of Mali, tenth on the list. This is a vast unstable country with poor or nonexistent roads. It stretches much of the way across the Sahara. The average inhabitant has a daily income of about three dollars. Who worked out that 11 percent of the 12 million Malians play soccer?

Even the European figures are dubious. When the Mulier Instituut in the Netherlands set out to collate data on sports participation in the EU, it began its report with a series of caveats. Different countries use different methods to establish how many people play sports, it said. "Even within a single year, research conducted in one and the same country can result in significant differences in the recorded figures for sport participation for up to 40 percent."

Still, when it comes to European countries at least, FIFA's list probably has some value. That's because Europe is an organized sort of continent where a high proportion of the people who play soccer are actually registered with a club. We have a good idea of how many registered soccer players there are, because every one of them belongs to the country's soccer federation. So the number of registered players in a European country is a fair indicator of the total of all its soccer players. By way of reality check, let's see whether the European countries on FIFA's overall list of most enthusiastic players had a lot of registered soccer players, too.

It turns out that Germany, Holland, Austria, and Sweden—all in the top twenty of most enthusiastic soccer countries per capita—also figured in FIFA's top twenty countries with the most registered players. Furthermore, Slovakia was in the top twenty countries with the most registered male players, even though it has only 5.4 million inhabitants. In the Faeroes, Norway, and Ireland, also on FIFA's list of enthusiastic countries, a mammoth 10 percent or so of the population were registered players. Of the most enthusiastic European countries identified by FIFA, only Iceland lagged a bit in registration: just 7 percent of Icelanders were registered players. However, as we'll see, Iceland—with artificial minipitches at most of its schools, and indoor arenas all over the place—now seems to harbor an unusually high amount of casual kick-around soccer.

So it seems that the European countries in FIFA's top twenty per capita might really play a lot of soccer. Without treating the Big Count as gospel, let's give those nine European countries on FIFA's list a little star each, and continue our quest to find the most enthusiastic of them all.

SPECTATORS: GREAT HORDES OF PEOPLE NOT GOING TO SOCCER MATCHES

Playing is one way of expressing a love of soccer. Going to watch matches is another.

When you think of packed soccer stadiums, you think of England. Visually, soccer crowds are one of the things that the English do best. And everyone knows that the Premier League has the biggest crowds in the world.

Well, the second-biggest crowds, anyway. The average attendance in the Premier League in 2012–2013 (the season for which we have compared attendances around Europe) was 35,921. That was nearly 7,000 fewer than went to see the average Bundesliga game that same year.

This fact comes from a weirdly addictive statistics website. The best thing about European-football-statistics.co.uk is its collection of average attendance rates for almost every soccer league in Europe. These stats give surprising insights into fandom and help reveal which European country is maddest about the game.

The first thing you notice on the website is how much attendance figures fluctuate over time. The data on the site go back decades. Back in the 1980s, when Italian stadiums were as safe as family restaurants and Serie A was the world's best league, Italians watched far more soccer than the English. In the 1984–1985 season the average crowd in Serie A was 38,872. Meanwhile, in the English first division in that year of the Heysel disaster and the fatal fire at Bradford City, only 21,080 braved the average league match.

How times change. By the 2012–2013 season, Serie A and the Premier League had pretty much changed places: the average Italian game drew only 23,234 people, a good 12,000 fewer than the Premier League.

Many other European leagues also have sharp trends in attendance over time, further evidence that fans behave much more like consumers than like addicts. French, German, and Dutch attendance rates have soared since the 1990s. In eastern Europe, by contrast, we see what Brian Clough once called the great hordes of people not going to soccer matches. These empty stadiums are a post-communist phenomenon. Back in 1989, Nicolae Ceauşescu's last year in power, the average crowd at a Romanian first-division match was officially 17,000, nearly as many as in England at the time. In 2012–2013 it was just 5,184.

The least popular league in Europe was Estonia's, with an average attendance in the country's top division of 215 (presumably not so hard to count). And even given that Russian men are dying at such a startling rate, it's disappointing that only 13,180 on average bothered to turn up to Premier League matches there. The English Championship, the level below the Premier League (average: 17,488), was more popular, and in fact outdrew every league in Europe east of Germany. The English and Germans are the only Europeans who go to watch mediocre soccer in numbers.

However, as a friend of ours in Moscow once advised, "Never believe any Russian statistic." Paul in 't Hout, longtime boss of European-football-statistics.co.uk, told us he doubted the stats for certain eastern European countries. He got particularly suspicious when the official attendance for a game was reported as a round number—3,000, for instance—as opposed to a precise one, like 3,142. He e-mailed: "In some leagues I found figures for one game of for example 2,000 and 5,000." His doubts recall Benford's Law, a theory about the frequency with which digits will appear in data. One implication of this law is that datasets with lots of zeroes at the end often turn out to be fraudulent.

The western European data on attendances tend to be more reliable. Even there, though, there are doubts. In England, is the attendance the number of people who actually went to the game or the number who held tickets for it? After all, many season-ticket holders skip some matches. At a small club at the end of a disappointing season, they might have trouble passing on their tickets. In countries such as Italy, ticket sellers have been known to wave through hundreds of scary-looking away fans without anyone paying. Some turnstile attendants might slip the odd bribe into their pockets and click somebody through, or let in friends for free. Clubs in some countries might report a lower attendance number than the real figure, to reduce the tax they pay on their ticket income. Anyway, there's often nobody assiduously counting butts in seats.

Still, the figures on European-football-statistics.co.uk do tell us something. Most of them are not made up. Especially in western Europe, they probably correlate to a large degree with the number of people who actually went to games. And we can accept the general finding that eastern European crowds are low. A glance at the pictures on TV tells us that. Admittedly, we can't make a precise ranking of average crowds in all European countries, but we can identify a few countries where attendance at soccer seems to be particularly high as a share of their populations.

The way to identify these hot spots is first to count the combined average crowds for the main professional divisions in each country. Let's start with the largest European countries, which typically have three serious divisions each. England has four, but so as to compare it to France, Germany, Italy, and Spain, we will analyze only its top three divisions.

The sixty-eight English league clubs in those three divisions averaged about 1.29 million spectators between them in 2012–2013. (The clubs in League Two, the English fourth tier, averaged an additional 105,000 combined, too few to make much difference to the national total.) That is, over two normal match days, in which every club played at home at least once, you would expect 1.29 million people to show up in England's top three divisions. That is by no means a precise figure, but it is probably a decent indication.

We then divided that spectator average by the country's population. England has 53 million inhabitants; 1.29 divided by 53 = 0.024. That means that the total combined spectator average of English clubs equaled 2.4 percent of the English population.

It turns out the English were the most enthusiastic stadium-goers of all the large European countries. Figure 12.2 shows the (very rough) stats for the top three divisions of each big country.

Spain has experienced a sharp fall since 2007–2008, when we last calculated these numbers. Probably because of the recession, its percentage dropped from 1.9 percent then to 1.5 percent today. Spain's average in both cases included only the top two divisions—all that European-football-statistics.co.uk had. However, in the other large countries the crowds for the third division added only between 0.1 and 0.2 percentage points to the national total.

FIGURE 12.2. Total spectator average as percentage of population, part 1

Country	*Total spectator average as percentage of population*
England	2.4
Spain	1.5
Germany	1.5
Italy	1.0
France	0.9

FIGURE 12.3. Total spectator average as percentage of population, part 2

Country	*Total spectator average as percentage of population*
Faeroes	10.0
Iceland	4.0
Scotland	3.8
Cyprus	3.6
Norway	2.6
Netherlands	2.5

So far the English have lived up to their reputation as great consumers (if not players) of soccer. But when we compare them to the smaller western European nations, their spectating becomes less spectacular. The Scots, for one, are much more eager watchers of soccer. Celtic and Rangers between them drew average crowds of over 92,000 in 2012–2013. That's not bad in a nation of 5.3 million, particularly in a season when Rangers were playing in the third division. In the typical fortnight that year, a combined total of 1.7 percent of Scots watched either Celtic or Rangers play at home. The two most watched clubs in England, Manchester United and Arsenal, would need home crowds of 450,000 each to draw the same proportion of the English population. You might even say that the English are somewhat lackluster fans, given that they have the best teams on earth playing on their doorsteps. On the other hand, they also have to pay the highest ticket prices on earth.

The Scots are among the European spectating elite, if not at the very top. Figure 12.3 shows the European countries whose inhabitants, according to European-football-statistics.co.uk, were most inclined to watch professional soccer in 2012–2013.

For Scotland, Norway, and the Netherlands, we counted attendance figures in the top two divisions; for even smaller Cyprus, Iceland, and the Faeroes, only the top one. All twelve clubs in the Icelandic top division put together had a total average attendance of just 12,684 in 2013, a bit less than the San Jose Earthquakes all by themselves. However, that was pretty good for a country of about 320,000 people who had just decimated their own economy by buying up half the world's toxic assets.

But even among these high-flying countries, one stands out: the freezing windswept Faeroe Islands of the north Atlantic. The Faeroes' ten first-division clubs, staffed mostly by men who work in fishing or whaling, have combined average home crowds of 5,070 people. That figure may not sound mammoth, but it amounts to a whopping 10 percent of the Faeroes' population. By tradition, the crowd invades the artificial pitch at halftime and after the game.

International games draw about 5,000 people to the national stadium (which handily houses a bed-and-breakfast). However, Virgar Hvidbro, general secretary of the Faeroe Islands Football Association, recalls 8,000 cramming in for a game against Malta in the good old days when regulations were less strict. A rare foreign observer of Faeroese soccer, the British photographer Andrew Tobin explains: "Watching the local team is one of the main activities available in the small towns which, while often very picturesque, lack many other forms of entertainment." According to Tobin, many Faeroese introduce themselves first with their own name, and second with the name of the English club they support.

When it comes to watching live soccer, no other country in Europe even comes close to the Faeroes. We've already seen that 17 percent of the islanders played the game in 2006. These fishing folk sure do like their soccer. "The importance of football to the Faeroes is almost the same as it is for the Brazilians," says prime minister Kaj Leo Johannesen, who is of course a former international soccer goalkeeper.

It would be silly to treat the attendance figures for these top six nations as exact to the decimal point. On the other hand, these are countries that tend to produce fairly reliable statistics. Norway and the Netherlands are wealthy and hyperorganized. Iceland was wealthy until it discovered toxic assets and remains hyperorganized. The Faeroes are fairly well off, and those 5,070 spectators can't be very difficult to count. Scottish soccer has some modern stadiums and voracious marketing officials, who keep elaborate electronic databases of their supporters. They have a pretty good idea of how many come to matches. In 't Hout told us that he considered the Norwegian, Icelandic, and Scottish attendance data quite reliable, because they were reported as exact figures—3,921 or 5,812 spectators. He was more suspicious of Cyprus, where (as in eastern Europe) the figures were reported as round numbers like 2,000 or 9,000.

Still, we can say with some confidence that all these top six nations love going to watch soccer. Their position at the top of these rankings is not a one-shot deal. When we did this exercise in 2008, Cyprus, Iceland, Scotland, and Norway were all in the top four (the website had no attendance figures for the Faeroes back then). People in these countries watch in astonishing numbers, given how poor their leagues are. To quote Nick Hornby, marveling at the thousands of people who watch even the most pathetic English clubs, "Why, really, should anyone have gone at all?"

In the case of Norway in particular, it should be noted that Norwegians don't just go to watch their own soccer. They go and watch England's, too. Obsession with English soccer is now almost a human universal—South African cabinet meetings have occasionally been interrupted by quarrels over the previous night's English games—but Norway got there first. On Saturday, November 29, 1969, decades before the Premier League hatched its secret plans for world domination, Norwegian TV broadcast its first-ever live English soccer match: Wolves 1, Sunderland 0. Naturally, the nation was hooked. The Saturday game from England fast became an institution. "The most important thing in Norway when it comes to affection for soccer is the Saturday TV games," says Andreas Selliaas, who works for Norsk Tipping, the Norwegian national lottery. "My father supports Leyton Orient. Why?"

Orient isn't even the worst of it. Tiny British neighborhood teams like Barnet and Rushden and Diamonds have Norwegian fan clubs (King Harald is an honorary member of the Spurs supporters' club). Then there are the planeloads of Norwegians who commute to Old Trafford. According to the British national tourist agency VisitBritain, 80,000 Norwegians came to see a soccer match in Britain in 2011, more than any other visiting nationality except the Irish. And while doing all this, the Norwegians still find time to lead the world at winter sports.

Norway and the other five leading spectating countries each get a star in our quest to find Europe's most enthusiastic soccer nation. Four of the top six—Faeroes, Norway, Iceland, and the Netherlands—also appeared in our very cautious list of the countries that played the most soccer. The Faeroes were ahead of their nearest rivals in both categories, so they currently lead the European pack. But the Norwegians, Icelanders, and Dutch also enter the final round of our contest with two stars each.

NATIONS OF COUCH POTATOES: THE MOST POPULAR TV PROGRAMS IN HISTORY

In our quest to establish which country cares most about soccer, one statistic towers over all the others: TV viewing figures. After all, relatively few people actually play soccer—seldom more than 10 percent of a country's inhabitants—and even fewer watch it in stadiums. In any case, we have seen the flaws in the data for playing and spectating. But we do have good figures for the most popular way to consume soccer: watching World Cups and European championships on TV. Viewing figures are the final piece of evidence to assess before we can name the most soccer-mad country in Europe.

TV ratings have plunged over the past thirty-odd years. Once upon a time only the BBC broadcast in Britain, and so every program the BBC aired had a market share of 100 percent of viewers. Then television expanded: first came other free channels like ITV and Channel Four, and later satellite and broadband cable. Audiences in all rich countries splintered among the different channels. The share that any one show could command slumped. In the US, for instance, thirty-six of the top forty-five shows ever aired were shown before 1990. No longer does the whole family sit down together to watch *M*A*S*H* or *Cheers*. But here's the thing: all the top nine American programs from 1990 through 2008 were sports events. Seven were Super Bowls, and the other two were ladies' figure skating events from the 1994 Winter Olympics, which people watched largely because they knew that one American skater had paid someone to hobble her rival on the national team. Only sports could still unite Americans on the sofa.

It is the same in Germany, where seven out of the eight highest-rated programs from the start of TV viewing data through 2008 involved the German soccer team playing in a major tournament. In Britain only the

1966 World Cup final and the 1970 FA Cup final replay between Leeds and Chelsea made the top ten. Still, here too big soccer tournaments provide some of the communal glue once supplied by trade unions, churches, and royal weddings. Possibly the best chance English people get to bond with each other nowadays, unless they are weeping over the passing of a royal or a reality-TV star, is during a World Cup. Big soccer matches have that sort of unifying role in most European countries.

Before we can work out which country watches the most international soccer on TV, we need to separate the reliable viewing data from the false ones. Organizations like FIFA and the International Olympic Committee report the highest numbers they can. The more TV viewers an event attracts, the more advertising will flow to the event, and the more broadcasters will pay to screen it. Hence the improbable tallies that organizers sometimes cite for their events. According to FIFA, a cool 715 million people watched the World Cup final in 2006. Even this claim looks modest compared to the 1.5 billion who supposedly saw the opening ceremony of the Commonwealth Games in Melbourne in 2006. What to believe?

This is where Kevin Alavy comes in. Alavy is managing director of the Futures Sport + Entertainment consultancy. His job is to sit in London working out how many people really watch different sporting events, though in fact he is far more charming than that description implies. This is how he defines his work: "Very simply, are these sports events worth the massive investment that they typically cost, and how can my clients get even more value from their association with sport?"

Alavy can both explain how the inflated numbers were invented and give advertisers (and some of the rights holders) the more reliable estimates they need. He also extracts trends from the mountains of broadcasting data that exist nowadays. For this book, he gave us some insight into the data he has been gathering on World Cups and European championships since 1998. Using it, we can identify the most fanatical soccer nation in Europe.

Around the world, TV data are extrapolated from the viewing habits of a sample of the population—in the US, about 10,000 people. Individuals used to get paid a small fee to keep a diary of their TV consumption. Then came the "people meter": a little electronic box attached to a TV set that allows each person in a household to indicate when they are watching. Invented in Britain, the people meter is now used in most wealthy countries to measure viewing. Alavy calls it "the gold standard of global media research."

To see how people-meter data differ from the inflated data, consider the Super Bowl. It is indisputably the most watched event in the US. The ten Super Bowls through 2008 were the ten most watched American TV programs of that decade. But exactly how watched were they? Figures of 750 million to 1 billion global viewers per game are cited. Instead, using the people-meter data, Alavy puts a typical Super Bowl's average live audience in those years at about 100 million viewers, or about one-third of all Americans excluding the under-five set. (That is a mammoth figure, except when compared to the viewing figures for big soccer games. For instance, six matches at Euro 2004 drew a larger live global audience than that year's Super Bowl.) The inflated figure of "750 million to 1 billion" is not an outright lie. Rather, it is a reasonable guess as to the number of people in the world who could have watched the Super Bowl on TV because they subscribe to the right channels.

Using the people meter, Alavy has collected verifiable viewing figures for sports in fifty-four countries. Thirty-one of the countries on his list are in Europe, twelve in Asia, ten in the Americas, and only one (South Africa) in Africa, a continent where there is almost no serious measurement of viewing habits. Many poorer countries still use diaries rather than people meters. Even so, for thirty-three of Alavy's fifty-four countries, we have figures for at least four of the six major soccer tournaments covered from the World Cup of 1998 through Euro 2008.

The viewing figure Alavy uses for any given game or event is the "average program audience." That is the average number of viewers during the entire event, rather than the peak figure, which would typically be one and a half times higher, or the "reach," which includes anyone who caught at least three minutes. The average audience for many TV programs is frighteningly low. In fact, Alavy estimates that on current trends, over a quarter of sports programs around the world are now *watched by nobody*. That is, they have no measurable audience.

Happily, big international soccer tournaments are watched by many people, and not only by men. Forty percent of the global audience for

Euro 2004 was female, for instance. It's precisely the long-term rise in female viewers that has made televised soccer more popular than ever before. Almost any game at a World Cup and many in the European Championship nowadays will beat the magic mark of 100 million global viewers. Hardly anything else on television can match that, not even iconic events like the Oscars or Barack Obama's inauguration or Princess Diana's funeral, says Alavy.

He reports the viewing figure for any game at these tournaments as a percentage of all the people in each country who live in households with TV sets. In most European nations almost every household has owned a set since the 1970s. However, that is not true in less developed nations. Only about a quarter of India's population of 1.2 billion, for instance, lived in households with TVs in 2008.

Alavy's collection is a treasure chest: thousands of TV ratings covering hundreds of games between national teams screened in fifty-four countries since 1998. But there is an obvious problem: Germans probably watch a lot of games involving Germany, and Germany has a pretty good record; how to compare the viewing figures of the successful Germans with the not-quite-so-successful English? Indeed, how to compare German viewing of Euro 2008, where their team made the final, to viewing by the English, whose team didn't even qualify? Or to cite another complication: a casual fan who watches only his own national team is surely not to be compared to the fanatic who glues herself to the sofa for every match of the tournament. Going one step further, viewers in Malaysia or Colombia who follow the Euro must surely be considered to have reached the acme of perfection in fandom.

There are other problems. The World Cup in Japan and Korea had disastrous TV ratings in Europe, because most games were played in the European late morning or at lunchtime. That is why FIFA was so eager to keep the World Cup of 2010 in South Africa despite all the problems there: Johannesburg is usually on the same time as central Europe, making it ideal for European viewers. It's less convenient for Americans. In all the agonizing over the refusal of Americans to watch soccer on TV (as opposed to playing it, which American children do in great numbers), an obvious but overlooked explanation is that most of the best games are played in Europe at times when most Americans are working. In 2014, for the first time in twenty years, Americans will have a World Cup more or less in their own time zones (but even then most kickoff times have been scheduled to suit Europeans).

We also need to control for the significance of each match. Obviously the final will draw more viewers than a group match, but how many more?

In short, no two of our thousands of ratings are strictly comparable. Happily, there is a way to control for the differences, and so to strip down to the essence of TV fandom. We can expect viewing levels in every country to rise for the final of a tournament. We can also expect an uplift when the country's own national team plays, or when a game is shown in prime time. We need to wheel out the technique of multiple regression. Quite simply, multiple regression is a mathematical formula (first identified by the mathematician Carl Friedrich Gauss in 1801) for finding the closest statistical fit between one thing (in this case TV viewing figures) and any other collection of things (time of match, who is playing, and so forth). The idea is beautifully simple. The problem used to be the endless amount of computation required to find the closest fit. Luckily, modern computers have reduced this process to the press of a button (just look up "regression" on your spreadsheet package).

When you have many observations—like the thousands we have here—the regression technique is extremely powerful. Not only does it give you a precise figure for the influence of one factor on another, but it can also tell you how reliable that statistical estimate is. For example, the regression can show that playing a game in prime time will add, say, 4 percent to the size of the audience, and it can also say that the probability that this estimate is mistaken is less than 1 percent.

Running a regression will allow us to isolate each contributory factor—such as kickoff time—and measure its impact on attendance. Not only will this tell us a great deal about what attracts viewers to televised soccer, but the final figure we are left with after these regressions consists of two parts. One part is what is called a "random error": that which we cannot explain because we know too little about what happened on the day. The other part, though, is a "fixed effect": an estimate of the viewing share that a soccer match will achieve in a given country, stripped of all other characteristics like kickoff time, identity of teams, stage in the tournament, and so on. The fixed effect is what we are after. The size of the fixed effect in each country will tell us how eager that country is to watch international soccer on TV.

The method works like this: our data show that the fixed effect for the UK is 6.98. This means that just under 7 percent of all British households with TV sets will watch a World Cup or European championship game, regardless of its characteristics. Seven percent is the proportion of Brits that we can expect to have watched, say, Tunisia versus Saudi Arabia at the World Cup of 2006. However, if the game is played in the middle of prime time (meaning a kickoff between 7 and 8:45 P.M.), the total of British viewers rises by about 4.3 percent. If the game is a semifinal, viewing goes up an additional 5.6 percent.

So our regressions would lead us to estimate the British audience for each World Cup semifinal in 2006 at 16.9 percent: the core audience of 7 percent would have risen by 4.3 percent because each game kicked off in prime time, and by an additional 5.6 percent because it was a semifinal. The actual viewing figures for each game were within 2 percentage points of our estimates.

By no means perfect, but over the hundreds of games seen in fifty-four countries, the errors are relatively small. The average rating figure for each game taken across all fifty-four countries is 8.6 percent. Again: that is the proportion of households with TV sets that watched the game. For more than three-quarters of our estimates, the error was smaller than half this number. So while we cannot place too much weight on any single estimate for a particular match seen in a specific country, overall the regression summarizes the data pretty well. The regression captures just over two-thirds of the variation in viewing figures. The remaining third of the variation is due to unexplained random factors.

Before we ask which countries are the biggest soccer couch potatoes, let's pick apart the other regression effects for what they tell us about fandom. We found that only two time-of-day effects mattered: games played during "sleep time" (midnight to 5:40 A.M.) reduced the average audience by 3.6 percentage points, while prime time added about 4 percentage points depending on the exact time.

The significance of a match was crucial. In the group stages, if one or both teams playing in the third match were already knocked out, the TV rating fell. If both teams were out, the game lost 4.7 percentage points of its rating—a giant loss, since a rating of 4.7 percent is usually enough to keep a series on TV in the first place.

Yet when one or both teams in a third group game had nothing much to play for because they had already qualified for the next round, viewing figures barely fell. Soccer is soap opera. We watch it because of the story that unfolds after the game, not just because of the game itself. As long as a team is still in the tournament, its story continues.

Viewing figures rise steadily for each round of a tournament. The World Cup's round of sixteen adds 1.4 percent to the audience, while quarterfinals add 2.5 percent, semifinals 5.6 percent, and the final itself 10.1 percent. Even the match for third place, often mocked as meaningless, raises audiences by 4.9 percent—only slightly less than the semifinal effect. UEFA dropped the third-place playoff from the European Championship in 1984 because the game was thought to be boring. Perhaps UEFA should reconsider.

Besides time and significance of the match, a third effect sometimes matters: who is playing. Brazil is everybody's "second team." Despite getting duller since 1970, the team continued to command a viewing premium of 2.2 percent whenever it played. Weirdly, only one other national team consistently enhanced viewing figures across all fifty-four nations in Alavy's database: not Italy or Holland or Argentina but, yes, England. Its games boosted global TV ratings by 1.4 percent.

To sum up, imagine a World Cup final played in mid–prime time between England and Brazil. This would add 10.1 (the final effect) + 4 (prime-time effect) + 1.4 (England effect) + 2.2 (Brazil effect) = 17.7 percent to average viewership expected in any country.

There is one last factor to consider: nationalism. Its effect is enormous. For any game, for any country, broadcasting the national team added an average of 17.9 percent to the audience. It appears that for the average person on earth, simply watching his own national team in a humdrum group match is more attractive than watching England versus Brazil in the World Cup final. People who love soccer are vastly outnumbered by nationalists who tune in only for "our boys."

If England did play Brazil in a World Cup final in prime time, how many Britons would watch? Our model would predict 7 percent (the core

FIGURE 12.4. **The biggest soccer couch potatoes**

Team	*Core TV viewing rating for soccer as percentage of households with TV sets*
Croatia	12.4
Norway	11.9
Netherlands	11.5
Uruguay	10.7
Denmark	9.1
Serbia	9.0
Ecuador	9.0
Brazil	8.8
Korea	8.7
Sweden	8.6
Germany	8.6
Hungary	7.9
Italy	7.8
Argentina	7.4
Indonesia	7.3
Singapore	7.1
Romania	7.1
UK	7.0
Lebanon	7.0

audience) + 17.9 (the nationalist effect) + 16.3 (the prime time, final, and "Brazil" effects) = 41.2 percent. That would equal about 25 million viewers. In fact, this is almost certainly an underestimate, partly because it wouldn't count the people watching in pubs and other public places. Predictions about events that are both extremely rare and important are inevitably subject to wide margins of error. The same problem afflicts forecasting in financial markets: no statistical model can accurately predict a meltdown of the stock market like the one that happened in 2008. We have a good idea of how regular "small" factors like the time of day will affect viewing figures. We are much less precise about the effect of big one-shot deals like the country's own national team playing a final.

Now we can finally open the last door: After correcting for all incidental factors, which country has the highest TV ratings for World Cups and European championships?

And the winner is: Croatia! Alavy notes that Croat passion goes beyond soccer. "They also have very high ratings in other major sporting events," he says. For instance, when Croatia and Spain met in the world handball final in 2005, average ratings in Croatia were nearly four times higher than in Spain. This enthusiasm may stem from having recently fought for independence in a nationalist war, or it may just be because Croatia has very good sports teams.

The other European countries that watch the most international soccer—the Norwegians, Dutch, Danes, and Serbs—also have relatively small populations and relatively big soccer reputations. Quite likely, small nations score high in our rankings because they tend to be more interested in what is going on outside their borders than big nations like France or Mexico. Alavy notes, "To have high average ratings, it's all about having a high tendency to watch when your local heroes are *not* playing."

Britain, for all its claims of soccer obsession, is stuck in what Alavy calls "a kind of midtable mediocrity," sandwiched in eighteenth place between Romania and Lebanon. Germany has the most eager couch potatoes among Europe's big countries. Eleventh in the table, the Germans would be even higher but for their new custom of "Public Viewing," as they call it in their impenetrable language. Since 2006, they have taken to watching games in huge crowds on big screens outside. About 12 million Germans are estimated to have chosen this method to watch their team lose to Italy in that year's World Cup semifinal. The figure was particularly impressive given that the 30 million other Germans who watched at home were by themselves the country's largest-ever TV audience up to that point. During Euro 2008, the "Fan Mile" by the Brandenburg Gate in Berlin had to be closed nearly three hours before the final because it was already packed with nearly half a million singing and dancing "public viewers." Yet these people do not show up in Germany's people-meter data.

Generally, European countries dominate at the top of Alavy's table. Partly this is because most World Cup games are played at times designed to suit them. There is a vicious (or virtuous) cycle here: because Europe has high viewing figures for soccer, World Cups are often held in Europe, and so European teams do well, and so European viewing figures are high. Only as Asians become richer and more enthusiastic about

FIGURE 12.5. **Least-enthusiastic nations**

Team	*Core TV viewing rating for soccer as percentage of households with TV sets*
Australia	2.7
New Zealand	2.5
Ukraine	2.1
Mexico	2.0
Lithuania	1.8
Canada	1.7
Latvia	1.6
India	1.2
US	0.6
Taiwan	–0.8

soccer might this change. Chinese prime time could be a very lucrative market one day.

The Asian figures in our table need a pinch of salt. The Korean figures are for 2002 to 2008, so they benefited from the "halo effect" created by South Korea's run to the semifinal in 2002. Moreover, in Korea and Indonesia the World Cup is hard to escape because it is often shown "wall-to-wall" on several channels simultaneously. By contrast, Singapore scores high partly because only the best World Cup matches are shown there—and partly because Singaporeans love betting on soccer the way other people love soccer.

Figure 12.5 shows Alavy's least enthusiastic nations.

The Taiwanese must really not like soccer. Of course, even they cannot achieve a negative rating in practice, but our data combine the actual viewing figures with the specific characteristics of each game (time of day, group match, and so forth) to produce a final figure. In real life the Taiwanese numbers did not come out far from zero. Nor did the ratings for the US and India, though viewing rose sharply in both countries for the World Cup of 2010. An oddity of the US is that it is the only country where the nominal national team often does not draw the highest ratings. At the World Cup of 2006, viewers there preferred watching Brazil, Italy, and Mexico. For many people living in the US, of course, these are their true "home" teams.

Americans, Indians, and Taiwanese at least have an excuse for not watching soccer: they prefer other sports. The nations that stand out among Alavy's least enthusiastic are Mexico and Ukraine, which both have respectable traditions in soccer. Indeed, several other countries that don't care much—Spain, Portugal, and France—have some of the best soccer teams on earth. Alavy notes that Spanish audiences for international sports have traditionally tended to be relatively low, perhaps because of the country's regional divides. Many Basques, for instance, did not want to follow a Spanish "national" team. That is now changing: Spanish viewing figures shot up during Euro 2008 even before Spain reached the final, and then again, for obvious reasons, at the World Cup of 2010.

The problem, in terms of our quest for Europe's most soccer-crazy nation, is that Alavy didn't have TV viewing figures for two of our contenders, Iceland and the Faeroe Islands. It may be that the entire population of both countries watches every game of every international soccer tournament, even the goalless tie between Bolivia and South Korea in the World Cup of 1994, but he just doesn't know. We checked with some high-powered Faeroes television executives (the place has had TV since the early 1980s), and even they don't have any viewing figures. "The islands pretty much sit down for World Cup and European finals," Hvidbro of the Faeroes FA assured us. However, in the absence of hard numbers we have to rule the islanders out of our quest. They can content themselves with a very honorable mention.

Iceland is a different matter. It introduced people meters only in 2007, and anyway is too small a market for Futures Sport + Entertainment to have bothered to track its viewing habits. But we went and found some Icelandic figures. FIFA produced an unprecedentedly rigorous report on worldwide viewing of the 2010 World Cup. The report, written by the research consultancy KantarSport, drew on well-sourced viewing figures from national TV stations around the world. Again, we'll just look at the European figures. The key number, for us, is the average TV ratings for live matches—i.e., the percentage of the possible total audience that watched the average match. The leading European countries as ranked by KantarSport and FIFA are shown in Figure 12.6.

FIGURE 12.6. Viewing of World Cup 2010 (European countries only)

Country	*Average live TV rating (as percentage of possible in-home audience)*
Iceland	18.8
Netherlands	16.1
Germany	12.4
Serbia	11.1
Croatia	10.8
Montenegro	9.7
Norway	9.7
Switzerland	9.6
United Kingdom	9.0

Iceland's first place is impressive given that the country's TV broadcast 250 hours of live matches from South Africa, more than twice as much as Norwegian TV, and 90 hours more than Dutch TV. Icelanders did particularly well to outwatch the Dutch, given that they themselves didn't have a dog in the fight whereas Holland went all the way to the final.

THE COUNTRY THAT BOUGHT WEST HAM

Iceland, the land of fish, volcanoes, and endless winters, is officially Europe's kookiest nation about soccer.

Just to recap: here is how it won our award. In our first category, playing soccer, Germany and the Faeroes scored highest in Europe, at least according to FIFA. Austria, Norway, Slovakia, Sweden, Iceland, Holland, and Ireland followed at some distance.

Of these enthusiastic playing countries, the most enthusiastic about spectating were the Faeroes, with Iceland a distant second. Somewhat further behind, the Dutch and Norwegians also went to lots of games, as did the Scots and Cypriots.

So our third category, TV viewing, had to provide the decider between the front-runners: the Faeroes, Norway, the Netherlands, and

Iceland. Norway and Holland registered among the Continent's leading couch potatoes as compiled by Kevin Alavy, alongside Denmark and Croatia. (In the previous edition of this book, when we didn't yet have viewing figures for Iceland, we named Norway as the most soccer-loving country in Europe.)

There are no TV data for the Faeroes. But Iceland's viewing of the 2010 World Cup blew away even the Dutch and Norwegians. Given that the Icelanders also led these two nations in going to the stadium, they clearly have an unhealthy obsession with soccer.

In some ways, Iceland's story is very like Norway's or the Faeroes'. Iceland too is a social democracy, whose government does its best to give all inhabitants the chance to play sport. It's also a cold country, with long winters, which Icelanders tend to spend hunkered down inside, either working hard or drinking hard while they wait for the summer partying season. What to do while hibernating? Vidar Halldórsson, an Icelandic sports sociologist, says: "We grew up watching English football on TV, from the 1970s. The only TV station in Iceland showed English games once a week, on Saturdays (not live, but a week later). They were the only professional sports we saw then." In a survey of Icelandic men in 2003, Halldórsson found that 88 percent could name a favorite English soccer team. Aron Jóhansson (raised in Iceland but now an American international) recalls boys fighting in the streets of Reykjavik over English soccer results. "That passion was very deep," he says. It's a passion that arguably reached its apogee in 2006 when the billionaire Björgólfur Guðmundsson—then Iceland's second-richest man after his son, Björgólfur Thor—bought West Ham United. After the financial crisis struck Iceland in 2008, *Forbes* magazine revalued Guðmundsson's estimated net worth from $1.1 billion to zero. In 2009 he was declared bankrupt. Still, no doubt the passion remained.

By then, also, Icelanders were finally playing soccer year-round. Iceland's league runs from May to September—"the shortest football season in the world," the country's soccer federation proudly calls it. But in the late 1990s, Iceland began building an all-weather soccer infrastructure that may be unparalleled on earth. Over 110 Icelandic schools got artificial mini-fields, and there are now seven heated indoor halls with full-size soccer grounds. Nowadays Icelanders can play even in winter, whether they belong to a club or not.

Playing sport is a part of life in Iceland, especially in the villages. Gender barely matters: nearly a quarter of the country's registered soccer players are girls aged under eighteen. Even six-year-old kids are trained by qualified paid soccer coaches. And they usually play other sports besides.

Sport in Iceland is something you do very seriously, for fun, while continuing real life on the side. There can't be many countries where the national team's goalkeeper is also a professional filmmaker. Hannes Thor Halldórsson actually shot the commercial for Icelandair that featured his own team. "It was weird," he told *Sports Illustrated.* "I had to act in the commercial as well, so I was directing the commercial in the national kit and boots." Meanwhile Iceland's legendary handball captain, Olafur Stefansson, seemed to regard himself primarily as an existentialist philosopher. When we asked him during the London Olympics what a handball gold would mean for the little country, he replied that he was unable to answer: "You have so many different realities. The game is—what is it? a simulacrum of life itself, maybe in simplified terms."

In Beijing in 2008, Stefansson's team had beaten Spain in the Olympic semifinal. During that game, "there was not a single transaction made on the Icelandic stock exchange," says the sociologist Halldórsson. Stefansson's men ended up with silver. No country that small had ever won an Olympic medal in a team sport.

Icelanders excel in many different competitions—they have won Miss World three times—but soccer is what really does it for them. In November 2013 Iceland only had to beat Croatia in a playoff to become the smallest nation ever to reach the World Cup. Before the home match, the soccer federation put the 9,800 tickets available to Icelanders up for sale at 4 A.M., worried that its website would crash if it opened sales in daytime. The tickets were gone before the sun rose (admittedly not difficult in an Icelandic winter). Sadly, Iceland lost 2–0 over two legs. But if these people ever make it to the World Cup, they might really start to like soccer.

13

ARE SOCCER FANS POLYGAMISTS?

A Critique of the Nick Hornby Model of Fandom

> Just this one afternoon started the whole thing off—there was no prolonged courtship. . . . In a desperate and percipient attempt to stop the inevitable, Dad quickly took me to Spurs to see Jimmy Greaves score four against Sunderland in a 5–1 win, but the damage had been done, and the six goals and all the great players left me cold: I'd already fallen for the team that beat Stoke 1–0 from a penalty rebound.
>
> —Nick Hornby in *Fever Pitch* (1992), on the origin of his lifelong love of Arsenal

Fever Pitch is a wonderful memoir, the most influential soccer book ever written, and an important source for our image of the soccer fan. The "Fan," as most Britons have come to think of him, is a creature tied for life to the club he first "fell for" as a child. Hornby says his love of Arsenal has lasted "longer than any relationship I have made of my own free will." But is Hornby's "Fan" found much in real life? Or are most British soccer supporters much less loyal than the world imagines them to be?

Let's start with Hornby's version, because it is the accepted story of the British Fan. As far as life allows, the Hornbyesque Fan sees all his club's home games. (It's accepted even in the rhetoric of fandom that traveling to away games is best left to unmarried men under the age of twenty-five.) No matter how bad his team gets, the Fan cannot abandon it. When Hornby watched the Arsenal of the late 1960s with his dad, the team's incompetence shamed him but he could not leave: "I was chained to Arsenal and my dad was chained to me, and there was no way out for any of us."

"Chained" is a very Hornbyesque word for a Fan's feelings for his club. Often the Fan uses metaphors from drugs ("hooked") or romantic love ("relationship," "fell for"). Indeed, some adult Englishmen who would hardly dare tell their wives that they love them will happily appear in public singing of their love for a club, or for a player who would snub them in a nightclub if they ever managed to sneak past his entourage.

No wonder the Fan's loyalty to his club is sometimes described as a bond stronger than marriage. Rick Parry, as chief executive of the Premier League in the 1990s, recited the then dominant cliché about fandom: "You can change your job, you can change your wife, but you can't change your soccer team. . . . You can move from one end of the country to another, but you never, ever lose your allegiance to your first team. That's what English soccer is all about. It's about fierce loyalty, about dedication." (The Argentine variant: "You can change your wife—but your club and your mother, never.") Recently, in more metrosexual times, soccer officials trying to emphasize the strength of club brands have extended the cliché by one more attachment: you can even change your gender, the officials say, but not your club.

Ideally, the Hornbyesque Fan supports his local team (even if Hornby did not). This gives the Fan roots, a sense of belonging. In a wonderful essay on fandom in the highbrow journal *Prospect,* Gideon Rachman quotes an archetypal declaration of faith from a Carlisle Fan named Charles Burgess, who wrote in *The Guardian,* "There never was any choice. My dad . . . took me down to Brunton Park to watch the derby match against Workington Town just after Christmas 41 years ago—I was hooked and have been ever since. . . . My support has been about who we are and where we are from."

In real life Rachman is a commentator on international politics in the *Financial Times,* but his essay in *Prospect* is a key text in the British debate about fandom. It is the anti–*Fever Pitch.* In it, Rachman outs himself as a "fair-weather fan, an allegiance-switcher," who at different times in his life has supported Chelsea, QPR, and Spurs. So casual are his allegiances that he registered with FIFA for the World Cup of 2006 as an Ivory Coast supporter, figuring that he wouldn't face as much competition for tickets. He got into every round including the final. He went to the World Cup in South Africa as a registered Paraguay fan.

Rachman treats the passions of Hornbyesque Fans as slightly bizarre. After all, in England a Fan's choice of team is largely random. Few clubs have particular religious or class affiliations, and few English people have an attachment dating back generations to any particular location. Some children become fans of their local team, however terrible it might be, but if you live in a rural part of England like Cornwall you may have no local team, while if you live in London or around Manchester you will have many. As Rachman asks, "Why devote a huge amount of emotion to favoring one part of west London over another?"

Nonetheless, the Hornbyesque Fan is a widely admired figure in Britain, at least among men. Whereas *fanatic* is usually a pejorative word, a *Fan* is someone who has roots somewhere. As we will argue later, this respect is connected to the quirks of British history: in Britain, roots of any kind are in short supply.

However, our first question is: How true is the Hornby model of fandom? Does it really describe the way most British fans feel about their clubs?

THE CHINESE SERIAL FAN

Very little is known about sports fans who are not hooligans. The academics D. L. Wann and M. A. Hamlet estimated in 1995 that only 4 percent of research on sports concentrated on the spectator.

So we start our quest into the nature of fandom with only one or two fairly safe premises. One is that foreign fans of English clubs, at least, are not all monogamous in their devotion. Rowan Simons explains in *Bamboo Goalposts,* his book about Chinese soccer, that many Chinese fans support "a number of rival teams at the same time" and are always changing their favorite club. Simons adds, "So dominant is the serial supporter in China that it is quite rare to find a fan with a real unflinching loyalty to one team."

FIGURE 13.1. Fan estimates for Manchester United

Year	*Estimated fans*	*Source*
2003	75 million	Mori
2007	About 90 million	Manchester United
2008	333 million (including 139 million "core fans")	TNS Sport
2011	659 million	Kantar

Stephanus Tekle, senior consultant at the market researchers Sport+Markt, has polling data to back up Simons's claim. Tekle says that since the late 1990s hordes of new fans around the world—particularly women—have come to soccer without long-standing loyalties. Many of these people appear to be "serial supporters" who probably support Manchester United and Liverpool, or Real Madrid and Barcelona, simultaneously. No wonder that clubs like United or Real keep changing their guesses as to how many fans they have worldwide. Figure 13.1 presents a few of United's estimates of the past few years.

None of these estimates is necessarily wrong. There may well be 659 million people on earth who have feelings for Manchester United. However, few of these "fans" are likely to be lifelong Hornbyesque devotees. Jose Angel Sanchez, now director general of Real Madrid, a club with its own share of foreign serial supporters, thought many of these serial fans might eventually evolve into Hornbys. He told us in 2003, "We used to say that the chances of changing your team is less than changing your partner or even your sex. But the way that people enter soccer in Asia is different: they enter through the stars. But this will not stay this way, in my opinion." Well, perhaps.

Still, surely British fans are a lot more loyal than those fickle Chinese, right? Unfortunately, polling suggests otherwise. In 2008 Sport+Markt found that Chelsea had 2.4 million "fans" in Britain. Again according to Sport+Markt, that represented a rise of 523 percent in the five years since Roman Abramovich had bought the club. Yet even that figure of 2.4 million represented a swift decline: in 2006, when, no doubt coincidentally, Chelsea had just won the league twice running, Sport+Markt credited the club with a mammoth 3.8 million British fans.

Again, we are not saying that Sport+Markt's figures were wrong. Rather, its premise was. To serial supporters, the question "Which is your preferred soccer club?" does not make sense. It presumes that everyone who likes soccer is a one-club Hornbyesque Fan. Instead, researchers should be asking, "Which are your preferred soccer clubs?" After all, a very large proportion of people who like soccer are polygamous consumers. One of the authors of this book, Stefan, as a Saturday-morning coach of grade-school children saw the color of the shirts switch from red to blue and back again depending on who last won the league. Newly rising clubs like Chelsea are particularly prone to attracting short-term fans, says Tekle of Sport+Markt. Clubs like Liverpool or Manchester United with stronger brands tend to have more loyal long-term supporters, he adds. In fact, the likes of Manchester United are likely to have both far more Hornbys and far more casual fans than other clubs. But detractors of United tend to seize upon the hordes of casual fans and don't mention the Hornbys.

Hornby himself recognized the prevalence of casual fans in soccer. Many of the people who pop up briefly in the pages of *Fever Pitch* enjoy the game but are not wedded to a particular club. Hornby calls this type the "sod-that-for-a-lark floating punter," and speaks of it with admiration: "I would like to be one of those people who treat their local team like their local restaurant, and thus withdraw their patronage if they are being served up noxious rubbish."

SPECTATORS: THE HARD CORE

We know there are, broadly speaking, two types of soccer fan: the Hornbys and the sod-that-for-a-lark floating punters. We know that the sod-that-for-a-lark people are heavily represented among foreign fans of clubs like United, and even seem to be pretty common in Britain. By 2006, if we can believe Sport+Markt's figures, about 90 percent of Chelsea's British fans were people who had not supported them in 2003. No doubt a club like Hartlepool has a higher percentage of devoted Hornbys among its fans, but then clubs like Hartlepool don't have many fans anyway.

One might carp that the sod-that-for-a-lark lot are mostly just armchair fans, and that "real" fans tend to be Hornbys. However, it would be wrong to dismiss armchair fans as irrelevant. The overwhelming majority of soccer fans in Britain are armchair fans, in the sense that they hardly ever go to games. In a survey by the pollsters Mori in 2003, 45 percent of British adults expressed an interest in soccer. But we've seen that the total average weekly attendance figures of all professional clubs in England and Scotland equal only about 3 percent of the population. In other words, most of the country's soccer fans rarely or never enter soccer stadiums.

Fletcher Research, in one of the first serious market analyses of English soccer in 1997, found that only about 5 percent of supporters of Premier League clubs attend even one match in an average season. If only a small minority of soccer fans get to the stadium at all, even fewer see every single home game for years on end, as Hornby did.

Most soccer fans are armchair supporters. If we want to unearth the Hornbys, we need to concentrate on the elite of fans who actually go to games: the spectators.

We know that in the Premier League at least, most spectators now watch every home game their club plays. Often they have to: at the most successful clubs, only season-ticket holders can get seats. Many of these regular spectators may be sod-that-for-a-lark punters at heart, who have been enticed by ticketing policies to show up every week. However, it's among this group of week-in and week-out spectators that we must look for the small hard core of lifelong Hornbys in English soccer. At moments of high emotion, the TV cameras like to zoom in on spectators in the stands—heads in hands, or hugging their friends—as if these people incarnated the feelings of the club's millions of supporters. They don't. Rather, they are the exceptions, the fanatical few who bother to go to games. Some of these spectators presumably support their club "through thick and thin," watching them unto eternity like Hornby does.

At least, that is the theory. But we studied attendance numbers in English soccer over the past sixty years and found that even among the actual spectators, a startlingly high proportion appeared to be sod-that-for-a-lark types.

II

Nobody seems to have tried before to calculate how many British fans are Hornbys. Yet the figures required to make some sort of estimate do exist.

That marvelous website, European-football-statistics.co.uk, has statistics on attendance rates and league performance for all clubs in the top four divisions of English soccer since 1947. Using these data we can find out (a) the annual mortality rate of soccer spectators; that is, how many of the people who watched last season don't come back the next? and (b) the sensitivity of new spectators to the success of teams. Do most newcomers flock to Chelsea when Chelsea wins the league?

Our model is based on some fundamental truths of soccer fandom. Generally speaking, teams cannot have very loyal Hornbyesque Fans (that is, a low mortality rate) and at the same time be capable of attracting large numbers of new spectators when they are successful. If most of the crowd consisted of Hornbys who never gave up their seats, then when a team did well, there would be no room in the stadium for all the new fans who wanted to watch them. So floating supporters can get tickets only if the mortality rate of the existing spectators is high enough.

Previous studies have shown that a club's attendance tends to rise and fall with its league position. (The rare exceptions include Newcastle, Sunderland, and the Manchester City of the late 1990s, when bad results failed to deter spectators.) In our data for the sixty-one-year period from 1947 through 2008, there were 4,454 changes in clubs' final league position. The average club moves six or seven league positions a year. In 64 percent of the cases where the club rose in the league, its home crowd increased, too. In 74 percent of the "down" years, home attendance fell. This means that 69 percent of all cases confirmed the simple hypothesis that fans respond to performance. Simply put: there is a market in soccer spectators. The few academics who study fandom—most of them in the US—explain the fans' motives through the psychological phenomenon of "BIRGing," or "basking in reflected glory."

To account for the ebb and flow of English soccer fans, we have constructed a very simple model. It consists of two elements that are logically connected to one another. First, there are the "new fans" coming into the game. New fans are estimated as the difference between the total attendance for the season and the number of loyal fans left over from the previous season. We divide new fans into two groups: the BIRGers, who come to watch the team depending on its success, and those who come for reasons we can't explain. We will treat these reasons as random factors, although each person probably had a good reason to come to the game at the time—a friend invited him, a girlfriend left him, or some such.

The second element of our model is the "loyal fans": those who came back from the previous season. Loyal fans are estimated as the difference between the total attendance for the season and the new fans entering the game. Of course, the difference between the loyal fans plus the new fans and last season's attendance is the "lost fans." We can think of these lost fans as falling into two groups as well: the BIRGers who were lost to the club because its performance declined, and those who were lost for other reasons that we cannot measure (got back together with girlfriend, took up DIY, or whatever).

So,

Total fans = loyal fans from last year
+ fans sensitive to winning
+ random fans

In our model we estimate the shares of loyal fans and fans sensitive to winning by minimizing the number of random fans. We minimize random fans precisely because we think most fans go for a reason: either loyalty or BIRGing. Randomness surely plays a relatively small role.

Now, we are not claiming that we can identify new fans, loyal fans, and lost fans *individually*. However, we can identify these categories *in a statistical sense,* as groups. We know how many people are in each group, even if we do not know their names.

Our model produces two results. First, it gives us an estimate of the BIRGers: the fraction of new fans that a team can expect to attract as a result of the position it achieves in the league. Looking at the annual changes in attendance figures, we found that spectators are only mildly sensitive to a team's performance. Our estimates implied that the club that won the Premier League would attract 2.5 percent of all new spectators entering the league the next season. However, a team that finished at the bottom of the Premier League, or at the top of the Championship (English soccer's second tier), does almost as well: it attracts 2 percent of all the league's new spectators. Teams in the middle of the four divisions (that is, those ranked around forty-sixth in England) would attract 1 percent of all new spectators, while teams at the very bottom of the fourth tier would attract almost nobody. In short, while new spectators do like success, the vast majority of them are not simple BIRGers, glory hunters. Judging by the ebb and flow of crowds over the sixty-one years through 2008, most people seem to go to a plausible club playing near their home.

That is the profile of the newcomers. But how many of last year's crowd do they replace? What is the mortality rate of the existing spectators?

We know how many spectators each club lost or gained, season by season for sixty-one years. We also know how many spectators the league as a whole lost or gained. That means that for every club we can calculate the average percentage of spectators at a given game one season who would not attend that same fixture the next season. And the percentage that fits the data best: 50. Yes: on average in the postwar era, half of all spectators in English soccer did not take their seats again for the equivalent match the next season.

Let's be clear about what exactly we are saying. Imagine that Bristol City plays Wolves one season, in front of 15,000 spectators. The next season, for the same fixture, even if there are again 15,000 spectators, half of them would typically be people who had not seen the previous year's match. Seven thousand five hundred of last year's crowd would be gone. Now, many of those 7,500 people might well see other games in the new season. Many of the "newcomers" might be people who had seen Bristol City–Wolves two years before, or ten years before, but had then gone missing at that fixture for a while. However, the point still stands: at any given match in England, half the spectators would be new compared with the same match the season before.

Here's an example of how the model works (for the sake of simplicity, we have rounded up all numbers):

Bristol City finished the 2006–2007 season in second place in League One, the English third tier. The team's total attendance that season was 295,000. Note that that doesn't mean 295,000 different people. Rather, 295,000 tickets were sold for all City's matches combined. Most fans would have attended multiple matches. The total attendance for all four divisions was 29.5 million.

The next season,

(a) The total attendance for all four divisions rose by 400,000, to 29.9 million
(b) Bristol City came in fourth in the championship—a rise of twenty-two places

So to calculate Bristol City's expected attendance in 2007–2008, we estimate its number of loyal "returning" fans and of new fans:

(c) Loyal fans are 50 percent of the previous season's total: 148,000
(d) New fans are calculated by estimating Bristol City's share (based on league performance) of new fans of the entire league
(e) We predict 15.1 million new spectators for English soccer as a whole. That equals this year's total attendance (29.9 million) minus loyal fans from last year (50 percent of 29.5 million = 14.8 million) = 15.1 million
(f) Given that Bristol City finished twenty-fourth out of ninety-two clubs, we estimate its share of all new fans in the country at 1.7 percent. Its number of new fans should therefore equal .017 x 15.1 million = 257,000
(g) So Bristol City's loyal + new spectators = 148,000 + 257,000 = 405,000
(h) Bristol City's actual number for 2007–2008 was 374,000, so our model overestimated their support by 31,000, or 8 percent

Obviously the model does not work perfectly for every club. At big clubs, such as Arsenal or Manchester United, there is very little flux in the stands. Their stadiums are pretty much always full, and total attendance therefore always the same. Most of their spectators are season ticket holders who see every game. These people generally renew their season tickets each year, because they know that if they don't their seats will be snapped up by others and they might never get back into the stadium again.

However, taking all ninety-two clubs together, the estimate that fits the data best is that 50 percent of the fans who saw a game last season do not see it again the next season. To quote one analysis of the English game, "One Third Division club in the London area, for example, has an estimated 'hard core' support of about 10,000; this rises to 20,000 according to the team's success and the standing of the visiting team." These words were written in 1951 in an economic study of soccer published by the London-based Political and Economic Planning think tank. They remain a good summary of English fandom as a whole since the war.

The discovery that half of all spectators—supposedly the hardest of hard-core Fans—are not there when the same fixture rolls around the next season conflicts with the Hornby version of loyal one-club fandom. Yet it has to be true, to explain the churn we see in attendance numbers. Even a club like Leeds, noted for its devoted fans—while stuck in League One it drew significantly larger crowds than Juventus—saw attendance fall from a peak of 755,000 in the 2001–2002 season to only 479,000 in 2006–2007.

Nor is this high mortality rate a new phenomenon. The sixty-one years of attendance data suggest that habits of English spectators have changed little over the years. While there has always been a hard core of Hornbys, it seems it has also always been the case that the majority of people who go to English soccer matches go only once in a while, and are often quite fluid about whom they choose to watch. And given that spectators are the fans who commit the most time and money to the game, their devotion is in most cases really rather limited. The long-term devoted spectator of the kind that Hornby described in *Fever Pitch*, far from being typical, is a rare species. Committed one-club lifelong fandom is a beautiful theory—or as Gandhi supposedly said of Western civilization, "It would be a good idea." The reality is that in English soccer, the loyal Hornbys are a small shoal in an ocean of casual Rachmans. England may be a nation of fans, but it's scarcely a nation of Hornbys.

CALL YOURSELVES "LOYAL SUPPORTERS"

In 1996 Alan Tapp, a professor of marketing at Bristol Business School, started to develop a relationship with a struggling club in the Premier League. Over the next four years he met the club's executives, got to see the data they had on their supporters, and assembled a team of researchers who conducted hundreds of interviews with the club's fans. Tapp eventually published two papers about his work in academic marketing journals.

Together they add up to a rare, marvelous study of how the spectators of one club actually behave. Tapp titled his second paper, published in 2004, "The Loyalty of Soccer Fans—We'll Support You Evermore?" with a very pregnant question mark. What he found was that fans talk loyal but don't always act it.

The club Tapp and his colleague Jeff Clowes studied—based in a Midlands town that is quite easy to identify—was not very good. It wasn't the sort of outfit to attract many BIRGing glory hunters. Most of the club's spectators lived locally. In a survey in 1998, a massive 87 percent of them agreed slightly or strongly with the phrase, "I would describe myself as a loyal supporter."

Well, they would say that, wouldn't they? Tapp cautions that many of those 87 percent might have been engaging in "socially desirable responding." After all, almost nobody in English soccer calls himself a "sod-that-for-a-lark floating punter." That would be socially taboo. Most fans told Tapp and Clowes that they regarded sod-that-for-a-lark types as "pariahs." As Rick Parry said, English fans pride themselves on their loyalty.

Yet when Tapp studied how these spectators behaved, he found a peculiar lack of loyalty. To start with the most basic fact: the club's average crowd during the four-year period of study slipped from about 24,000 to just 16,000.

The average across the period was about 21,000, which broke down as follows:

- About 8,000 season-ticket holders
- Another 8,000 places typically filled from a group of 15,000 or so regular attendees
- 5,000 spectators who came from "a 'revolving door' of perhaps 20,000 'casual fans'"

Tapp came up with three labels for the different groups: "fanatics," "committed casuals," and "carefree casuals."

The "fanatics," or Hornbys, were mostly season-ticket holders. Tapp said some of these people were veritable "'soccer extremists' who had commitment to the sport and the club that is arguably unparalleled in other business or leisure sectors." There was the man who, when asked by Tapp's team what he would save if there were a fire in his house, replied, "Oh my [match] programs and tapes. No question. And my wife and kids of course." Many of the fanatics came from the local area and had supported the club since childhood.

But even some of the fanatics were less fanatical than they claimed to be. Tapp found that each season, on average, 1,000 of the 8,000 season-ticket holders did not renew their seats and were replaced by new people. "Even at the fanatic end, the loyalty bucket had significant leaks," he remarked.

The team was playing badly. In one season, a mere 2 percent of fans proclaimed themselves "very satisfied" with performances. However, it was not the bad soccer that was driving them away. When Tapp's team asked people why they were letting their season tickets lapse, the lapsers usually talked about their lives away from the stadium. Fans were much more likely to give up their season tickets if they had children under age five, or if they described their lives as "complicated."

So it wasn't that the lapsers felt less loyal to the team than the people who kept going year in, year out. They were simply at different stages in life. Some regular fans admitted that at one point in life "they had simply lost interest, often in their late teens and early 20s." Others had been "triggered" by a son or daughter to return to the stadium. Older people, whose lives were presumably more stable, were the most likely to renew their season tickets. Tapp surmises that they "have simply settled into some form of auto-repurchase." In other words, showing up to the stadium year in, year out is not a good marker of loyalty. Rather, it is a good marker of age.

At the far end of the scale from the "fanatics" were the "carefree casuals." Few of the carefree casuals claimed to be "loyal supporters." They were "soccer fans" rather than "club fans," they preferred to see a good game rather than a victory for their team, and they treated soccer as just one of several possible activities on a Saturday. Tapp noted, "Being club supporters is not part of their self-image."

Many of the "carefree casuals" sometimes went to watch other teams. Tapp reckons that it is probable that some regulars at Derby County, for instance, also occasionally show up at Derby's rival Nottingham Forest, even if this flies in the face of everything we are always told about English soccer fans.

Tapp adds that these people are mostly not "brand switchers," who switch from supporting one club to supporting another. Very few people love Derby one year, Forest the next, and Carlisle the year after. Rather, these adulterous spectators are engaging in what marketing experts call "repertoire buying": they purchase different brands at different times. In normal consumer markets in almost every country, "repertoire buyers" are thought to outnumber both "brand-loyal" and "price buyers." In soccer, too, repertoire buyers seem to be fairly common. Tapp says, "Repertoire fans took a lot of pleasure from a multiplicity of aspects of the game itself, while single club fanatics were less interested in soccer, more devoted to the club as an entity."

Tapp's middle group of spectators at the Midlands club was made up of "committed casuals." These people didn't go to every match, but they did tend to describe themselves as "loyal supporters." They rarely watched other clubs and were more interested than the "carefree casuals" in seeing their team win. However, they too treated soccer as just one option for their Saturday. Tapp said they "perhaps have their soccer support in perspective with the rest of their lives."

In short, through close-up study very rare in English soccer, he had gotten past the cliché of "We'll support you evermore." Instead he found the same thing that we did: there are some Hornbys in British soccer, but even among the self-proclaimed "loyal supporters" of an inglorious club they are outnumbered by casual fans who can take it or leave it. Tapp ends by cautioning sports marketers that for all the rhetoric of undying love pervading English soccer, fans' "loyalty cannot be relied upon." He urges marketers to "look under the surface of supporter loyalty," where they will find "loyalty patterns quite similar to, say, supermarket goods sectors."

HORNBYS, CLIENTS, SPECTATORS, AND OTHERS

It turns out that few British soccer fans are either Hornbys or BIRGing glory hunters. Rather, most have a shifting relationship with the club or clubs they support. Of the 50 percent of spectators who do not show up for the same fixture from one season to the next, the largest group may well continue to be monogamous fans of that club. They just don't watch every game, or can't afford to go anymore, or are busy raising children, or have moved to another part of the country, or simply care less than they used to. The object of their love might not have changed, but the intensity has. Many of them may once have been Hornbys who fell for a team as eight-year-olds when their fathers took them to their first game. However, by the time they are twenty-eight or eighty-eight they are no longer the same fans. For many people, fandom is not a static condition but a process.

Other lapsed fans will have lost interest altogether. Others still might be shifting their allegiances to another club or clubs, because they have either moved to a new town, started to follow the team their kids support, or simply fallen for better soccer elsewhere. Rachman, for example, explains in his *Prospect* essay that he stopped supporting Chelsea "because they were a terrible team, followed by violent cretins."

Instead he made a two-and-a-half-mile journey within West London and became a QPR fan. In the rhetoric of English soccer, the choice facing the supporter is often presented as stark: either he sticks with his local team, or he becomes a BIRGing glory hunter. However, reality is more nuanced. England is so densely stuffed with professional soccer clubs—forty-three within ninety miles of Manchester, as we saw—that many people can find a new local side without going to the trouble of moving house.

Then there is a dirty secret of English soccer: many fans support more than one team. If you live in Plymouth, say, you might support Plymouth Argyle, Chelsea, and Barcelona, and have a fondness for a half-dozen other clubs, even though if Plymouth ever makes the FA Cup final, you will travel to Wembley decked out as a "lifelong Plymouth fan." Hornby himself, in *Fever Pitch,* supports Cambridge United as well as Arsenal. In fact, whereas the usual analogy for soccer fandom is idealized monogamous marriage, a better one might be music fandom. People are fans of the Beatles, or the Cure, or the Pixies, but they generally like more than one band at the same time, and are capable of moving on when their heroes fade.

As so often, it was Arsène Wenger who put this best. In 2009 he gave Arsenal's website an untraditional account of how he thought fandom worked:

> Soccer has different types of people coming to the game. You have the client, who is the guy who pays one time to go to a big game and wants to be entertained. Then you have the spectator, who is the guy who comes to watch soccer. These two categories are between 40 and 60 [years old]. Then you have two other categories. The first is the supporter of the club. He supports his club and goes to as many games as he can. Then you have the fan. The fan is a guy between 15 and 25 years old who gives all his money to his club.

Obviously Wenger's four categories are not exact. Here and there they even conflict with those of Tapp and Clowes, who found that many fans *lose* interest between fifteen and twenty-five. But Wenger agrees with the other observers that there are several different categories of spectator, of varying emotional intensity, and that people move between these categories depending largely on their time in life.

Ties in soccer fandom are much looser than the rhetoric of "We'll support you evermore" suggests. In that regard, they resemble ties of real existing marriage in Britain today. People still get married promising "till death do us part," but in 2011 there were 117,558 divorces in England and Wales, nearly five times as many as in 1960, even though the number of marriages has plummeted. Over half of all adults in England and Wales are not presently married. A lifelong monogamous marriage has become almost as rare as a lifelong monogamous love of a soccer club.

THE INAUTHENTIC NATION

Against all evidence, the stereotype persists that the typical British soccer fan is a full-on Hornby. No wonder it does, because the tiny percentage of fans who are Hornbys dominate the national conversation about fandom. Of course they do: they are the people who are most motivated to join the conversation. For them, following soccer is not just a hobby but an identity. Also, they make up a disproportionately large share of the soccer economy—"the most valuable customers," Tapp calls them—and so clubs and media listen to them more than to the sod-that-for-a-lark punters. And the Hornbys have a compelling story to tell. Most of the best stories are about love, and these are people who proclaim their love in public every week.

Yet there is a deeper reason the Hornby account of fandom has been so easily accepted in Britain. That is because it tells a story of roots, of belonging—a lifelong love of the club your father or grandfather supported before you—in a country that is unusually rootless. In transient Britain, the story of the rooted Fan is especially seductive.

Britain was the first country on earth where peasants left their native villages to go to work in rootless industrial cities. It was among the first countries where the churches began to empty; a tie that helps root people all over the world has long been extraordinarily weak among native Britons.

Even after the Industrial Revolution, the British never settled down much. The average Briton now changes his residence about once every seven years, more often than all other Europeans except the Nordics and the Dutch, according to a Eurobarometer survey for the European Commission in 2005. Many Britons emigrate. About 5.5 million of them now live outside Britain, as do an additional 50 million–odd people with British ancestry. Probably only India and China have produced diasporas that are as large and as widely spread, says the British government.

It is hard for people this transitory to build up deep ties of any kind, even to soccer clubs. Admittedly, Tapp and Clowes found that many of the "fanatical" supporters of the club they studied had spent their lives in the local town. But it was the club's "casual" fans, who "had often moved to the area as adults," who were more typical of British migratory patterns. For instance, Tapp and Clowes identified one group whom they called "professional wanderers": "people (mainly managers/professionals) who have held jobs in a number of different places who tended to strike up (weakly held) allegiances with local teams, which they retain when they next move." Like most Britons, the professional wanderers were too rootless to become Hornbyesque Fans. None of the casual fans interviewed by Tapp and Clowes "felt a close part of the local community, in contrast to the fanatics."

And Britons have suffered yet another uprooting: as well as leaving their place of birth, many of them have left their class of birth, too. This upheaval began on a large scale in the 1960s. As the economy grew, and more Britons stayed on at school and went to university, a mostly working-class nation turned into a mostly middle-class one. For many people this was a traumatic change. Their fathers had been factory workers, and now they were managers/professionals, with the different set of experiences and attitudes that entails. They lost touch with their roots. Naturally, many of them began to worry about their authenticity deficits.

In the 1990s, British soccer went upscale. The price of tickets jumped. In the food stands outside the stadiums, the proverbial middle-class quiches replaced the proverbial working-class pies. All these changes prompted endless laments for a lost cloth-capped proletarian culture from people who themselves somewhere along the way had ceased to be cloth-capped proletarians. They yearned to be authentic.

All this makes the true Fan a particularly appealing character to Britons. He is the British version of a blood-and-soil myth. Unlike so many actual Britons, the Fan has roots. Generations may pass, and blue collars turn to white, but he still supports his "local" team in what is supposed to be the "workingman's game." Lots of Britons who aren't Hornbyesque Fans would like to be. The Fan is more than just a compelling character. He is a British national fantasy.

14

A FAN'S SUICIDE NOTES

Do People Jump Off Buildings When Their Teams Lose?

It is one of the eternal stories that are told about soccer: when Brazil gets knocked out of a World Cup, Brazilians jump off apartment blocks. It can happen even when Brazil wins. One writer at the World Cup in Sweden in 1958 claims to have seen a Brazilian fan kill himself out of "sheer joy" after his team's victory in the final. Janet Lever tells that story in *Soccer Madness,* her eye-opening study of Brazilian soccer culture published way back in 1983, when nobody (and certainly not female American social scientists) wrote books about soccer. Lever continues:

> Of course, Brazilians are not the only fans to kill themselves for their teams. In the 1966 World Cup a West German fatally shot himself when his television set broke down during the final game between his country and England. Nor have Americans escaped some bizarre ends. An often cited case is the Denver man who wrote a suicide note—"I have been a Broncos fan since the Broncos were first organized and I can't stand their fumbling anymore"—and then shot himself.

Even worse was the suicide of Amelia Bolaños. In June 1969 she was an eighteen-year-old El Salvadorean watching the Honduras–El Salvador game at home on TV. When Honduras scored the winner in the last minute, wrote the great Polish reporter Ryszard Kapuscinski, Bolaños "got up and ran to the desk which contained her father's pistol in a drawer. She then shot herself in the heart." Her funeral was televised. El Salvador's president and ministers, and the country's soccer team walked behind the flag-draped coffin. Within a month, Bolaños's death would help prompt the "Soccer War" between El Salvador and Honduras.

Then there was the Bangladeshi woman who reportedly hanged herself after Cameroon lost to England in the World Cup of 1990. "The elimination of Cameroon also means the end of my life," said her suicide note. In fact, if *The Hindu* newspaper in India is right, Bangladeshis have a terrible proclivity for soccer suicides. After Diego Maradona was thrown out of the World Cup of 1994 for using ephedrine, "about a hundred fans in Bangladesh committed suicide," said an article in *The Hindu* in 2006. (It would be fascinating to know the newspaper's source.)

By now the notion that soccer prompts suicide has become a truism. It is often cited to show the grip of the game over its devotees, and as one reason (along with heart attacks on sofas during televised matches) the average World Cup causes more deaths than goals.

We found that there is indeed an intimate connection between suicide and soccer. However, the connection is the opposite of what is commonly believed. It's not the case that fans jump off buildings when their teams lose. Working with a crack team of Greek epidemiologists, we have found evidence that rather than prompting suicide, soccer stops thousands of people from killing themselves. The game seems to be a lifesaver.

| |

Measured suicide rates rose by 60 percent in the forty-five years to 2011, estimates the World Health Organization. Nearly a million people a year now kill themselves, according to the WHO. That is more than twice as many as died in war worldwide in the average year from 1955 through 2002, and nearly twice the number that die of breast cancer each year. To use Germany as an example: in 2005, 10,260 Germans officially died by suicide, more than were killed by traffic accidents, illegal drugs, HIV, and murder and other violence put together. For Germans under age forty, suicide was the second-most common cause of death. And the reported figures for suicides were understatements, said the University Hamburg-Eppendorf, which runs a therapy center for people at risk of suicide: "There may be a significant share of unrecognized suicides among the death types labeled 'traffic accidents,' 'drugs,' and 'causes of death unknown.'"

The suicide risk varies depending on who in the world you are. If you are an elderly, alcoholic, clinically depressed, divorced Lithuanian man, be very afraid, but suicide rates are relatively low in Latin America, leaving aside for the moment the issue of World Cups. Globally, women attempt suicide more often than men do, but most "successful" suicides are males. In the US, for instance, nearly 80 percent of the 38,364 people who were reported as having killed themselves in 2010 were male. For reasons that nobody quite understands, suicide peaks in spring when daylight hours are longest. In the Northern Hemisphere, that means May and June.

The question of why people commit suicide has preoccupied sociologists since sociology began. In 1897 Émile Durkheim, descendant of a long line of French rabbis, published his study *Suicide*. It wasn't just the first serious sociological study of suicide. It was one of the first serious sociological studies of almost anything. Drawing on copious statistics, Durkheim showed that when people lost their connection to wider society because of a sudden change—divorce, the death of a partner, a financial crisis—they sometimes killed themselves. He concluded that this particular form of suicide "results from man's activities lacking regulation and his consequent sufferings."

A few decades later, sociologists began to wonder whether man's sufferings might possibly include the results of sports matches. The numbers of suicides this caused might be significant: after all, most suicides are men, and sports give meaning to many men's lives. Frank Trovato, a sociology professor at the University of Alberta in Canada, was among the first to investigate the suicide-sports nexus. He found that when the Montreal Canadiens ice hockey team—once described as the national team of French Canada—got knocked out of the playoffs early between 1951 and 1992, Quebecois males aged fifteen to thirty-four became more likely to kill themselves. Robert Fernquist, a sociologist at the University of Central Missouri, went further. He studied thirty American metropolitan areas with professional sports teams from 1971 to 1990 and showed that fewer suicides occurred in cities whose teams made the playoffs more often. Routinely reaching the playoffs could reduce suicides by about twenty each year in a metropolitan area the size of Boston or Atlanta, said Fernquist. These saved lives were the converse of the mythical Brazilians throwing themselves off apartment blocks.

Later, Fernquist investigated another link between sports and suicide: he looked at the suicide rate in American cities after a local sports team moved to another town. It turned out that some of the fans abandoned by their team killed themselves. This happened in New York in 1957 when the Brooklyn Dodgers and New York Giants baseball teams left, in Cleveland in 1995–1996 when the Browns football team moved to Baltimore, and in Houston in 1997–1998 when the Oilers football team departed. In each case the suicide rate was 10 percent to 14 percent higher in the two months around the team's departure than in the same months of the previous year. Each move probably helped prompt a handful of suicides. Fernquist wrote, "The sudden change brought about due to the geographic relocations of pro sports teams does appear to, at least for a short time, make highly identified fans drastically change the way they view the normative order in society." Clearly none of these people killed themselves just because they lost their team. Rather, they were very troubled individuals for whom this sporting disappointment was too much to bear.

Perhaps the most famous recent case of a man who found he could not live without sports was the Gonzo author Hunter S. Thompson. He shot himself in February 2005, four days after writing a note in black marker with the title, "Football Season Is Over":

> No More Games. No More Bombs. No More Walking.
> No More Fun. No More Swimming. 67. That is 17 years past 50.
> 17 more than I needed or wanted. Boring . . .

Thompson, an occasional sportswriter, loved football. One night during the presidential campaign of 1968, he took a limousine journey through New Hampshire with his least favorite person, the Republican candidate Richard Nixon, and they talked football nonstop in the backseat. "It was a very weird trip," Thompson wrote later, "probably one of the weirdest things I've ever done, and especially weird because both Nixon and I enjoyed it." The reminiscence, in *Fear and Loathing on the Campaign Trail '72,* segues into an ominous musing on suicide, as a Nixon aide snatches away the cigarette Thompson is smoking over the fuel tank of the candidate's plane. Thompson tells the aide, "You people are lucky I'm a sane, responsible journalist; otherwise I might have hurled my flaming Zippo into the fuel tank."

"Not you," the aide replies. "Egomaniacs don't do that kind of thing. You wouldn't do anything you couldn't live to write about, would you?"

"You're probably right," says Thompson. As it later turned out, he was wrong. His ashes were fired from a cannon in Aspen, Colorado.

So much for suicides and North American sports. We know much less about the connection between suicides and European soccer. In one of the very few European studies done so far, Mark Steels, a psychiatrist at the University Hospital in Nottingham, asked whether Nottingham Forest's worst defeats prompted local suicides. He looked at admissions for deliberate self-poisoning to his hospital's accident and emergency department on two bad days for Forest: after the team's defeats in the FA Cup final of 1991 and the FA Cup quarterfinal of 1992. He found that both games were followed by an increase in self-poisonings. After the cup final, the rise was statistically significant, meaning that it was unlikely to have happened by chance. Steels concluded that "a sudden disappointment experienced through an entire community may prove one stress too many for some vulnerable members of this community."

| |

All this is fascinating but inconclusive. For starters, the sample sizes of all these studies are pretty small. How many people are admitted to a Nottingham hospital for self-poisoning after a soccer match? (Answer: ten in the twelve hours after the 1991 cup final, nine after the 1992 quarterfinal.) How many people kill themselves in Cleveland in any given month? The other problem is that almost all these researchers pursued what you might call the Brazilian apartment-building hypothesis: that when people suffer a sporting disappointment, they kill themselves. Mostly these are studies of the dogs that barked: people who did commit suicide.

But what if the relationship between suicide and sports is deeper than that? If sports give meaning to fans' lives, if they make them feel part of a larger family of fans of their team, if fans really do eat and sleep soccer like in a Coca-Cola ad, then perhaps sports might stop some of these fans from killing themselves. We wanted to find out whether there were dogs that didn't bark: people who didn't commit suicide because sports kept them going.

It so happens that we have a case study. Frederick Exley was a fan of the New York Giants football team, whose life alternated between incarcerations in mental hospitals and equally unhappy periods spent in the bosom of his family. In 1968 Exley published what he called "a fictional memoir," *A Fan's Notes,* one of the best books ever written about sports. Nick Hornby gave *Fever Pitch* the subtitle "A Fan's Life" in part as a tribute to Exley.

The Exley depicted in *A Fan's Notes* is a classic suicide risk. He is an alcoholic loner separated from his wife. He has disastrous relationships with women, alienates his friends, and spends months at a time lying in bed or on a sofa at his mother's or aunt's house. For a while his only friend is his dog, Christie III, whom he dresses in a mini blue sweatshirt like his own and teaches to stand up like a man. "Like most Americans," Exley writes, "I had led a numbingly chaste and uncommitted existence in which one forms neither sympathies nor antipathies of any enduring consequence."

Only one thing in life provides him with any community: the New York Giants. While living in New York City he stands on the terrace during every home game with a group of Brooklyn men: "an Italian bread-truck driver, an Irish patrolman, a fat garage mechanic, two or three burly longshoremen, and some others whose occupations I forget. . . . And they liked me."

When the Giants are not playing, Exley spends much of his time drinking alone. But when a game is on, he watches—depending on the stage of his life—with his Brooklyn group, or with other people in bars, or with his stepfather at home. Exley is the stepfather's eternal houseguest from hell, but "things were never better between us than on autumn Sunday afternoons": "After a time, hardly noticeable at first, he caught something of my enthusiasm for the beauty and permanent character of staying with someone through victory and defeat and came round to the Giants." Fittingly, the stepfather dies just before a Giants game: "Seated on the edge of the davenport watching the starting line-ups being introduced, he closed his eyes, slid silently to the floor, and died painlessly of a coronary occlusion."

Inevitably, at one point in the memoir, Exley contemplates suicide. He has convinced himself he has lung cancer. Determined to avoid the suffering his father went through, he decides to kill himself instead. Drinking with strangers in bars, he gets into the habit of working "the conversation round to suicide" and soliciting their views on how best to do it. The strangers are happy to oblige: "Such was the clinical and speculative enthusiasm for the subject—'Now, if I was gonna knock myself off . . .'—that I came to see suicide occupying a greater piece of the American consciousness than I had theretofore imagined."

Only one thing keeps Exley going. The Giants are "a life-giving, an exalting force." He is "unable to conceive what [his] life would have been without football to cushion the knocks." The real-life Frederick Exley lived to the age of sixty-three, dying in 1992 after suffering a stroke alone in his apartment. He might never have gotten that old without the Giants.

There may be a great many Exleys around. The viewing figures we saw earlier in this book suggest that sport is the most important communal activity in many people's lives. Nearly a third of Americans watch the Super Bowl. However, European soccer is even more popular. In the Netherlands, possibly the European country that follows its national team most eagerly, three-quarters of the population watch Holland's biggest soccer games. In many European countries, World Cups may now be the greatest shared events of any kind. To cap it all, World Cups mostly take place in June, the peak month for suicides in the Northern Hemisphere. How many Exleys have been saved from jumping off apartment buildings by international soccer tournaments, the world's biggest sporting events?

This is not just a rhetorical question. A study of soccer tournaments and suicide would bring together both an incomparably compelling communal event and a sample the size of several countries. So we set about finding the data.

We needed suicide statistics per month over several years for as many European countries as possible. These figures do not seem to be published anywhere. Luckily, we found out that the Greek epidemiologists Eleni Petridou and Fotis Papadopoulos had laboriously gotten ahold of these data by writing to the statistical offices of several countries. A statistician who works with Petridou and Papadopoulos, Nick Dessypris, went through the numbers for us. He found that in almost every country for which he had numbers, fewer people kill themselves while the national team is playing in a World Cup or a European Championship. Dessypris said the declines were "statistically significant"—unlikely to be due to chance.

Let's take Germany, the biggest country in our study and one that always qualifies for big tournaments. Petridou and Papadopoulos had obtained monthly suicide data for Germany from 1991 through 1997. A horrifying total of 90,000 people in Germany officially killed themselves in this period. The peak months for suicides were March through June.

But when Germany was playing in a soccer tournament—as it did in the Junes of 1992, 1994, and 1996—fewer people died. In the average June with soccer, there were 787 male and 329 female suicides in Germany. However, a lot more people killed themselves in the Junes of 1991, 1993, 1995, and 1997, when Germany was not playing soccer. In those soccer-free Junes, there was an average of 817 male and 343 female suicides, or 30 more dead men and 14 more dead women than in the average June with a big tournament. For both German men and women, the June with the fewest suicides in our seven-year sample was 1996, the month that Germany won Euro '96.

We found the same trend for ten of the twelve countries we studied. In Junes when the country was playing in a soccer tournament, there were fewer suicides. These declines are particularly remarkable given how much alcohol is consumed during soccer tournaments, because drinking would normally be expected to help prompt suicides. Only in the Netherlands and Switzerland did soccer tournaments not seem to save lives; these two countries saw very slight increases in the suicide rate during tournaments. In the other countries, the lifesaving effect of soccer was sometimes spectacular. Our data for Norway, for instance, run from 1988 through 1995. The soccer-mad country played in only one tournament

FIGURE 14.1. Lives saved from suicide during World Cup or European Championship compared to average June

	Male lives saved	*Female lives saved*
Austria	9	-3
Czech Republic	14	6
Denmark	4	4
France	59	8
Germany	30	14
Greece	0	5
Ireland	2	1
Netherlands	-5	0
Norway[a]	[19 lives saved spread across both genders]	
Spain	4	1
Sweden	4	15
Switzerland	-1	-2

[a]The data for Norway were not broken down by gender.

in that period, the World Cup of 1994. The average for the seven Junes when Norway was not playing soccer was 55 suicides. But in June 1994 there were only 36 Norwegian suicides, by far the lowest figure for all eight Junes in our data set. Or take Denmark, for which we have suicide tallies from 1973 through 1996, the longest period for any country. In June 1992 the Danes won the European Championship. That month there were 54 male suicides, the fewest for any June since 1978, and 28 female suicides, the joint lowest (with 1991) since the data set began.

We have tried to make some very rough estimates of how many lives these tournaments saved in each country. "Lives saved" represents the decline in deaths during the average June when a country's national team is playing in a World Cup or European Championship compared to the average June when the team isn't playing. Figure 14.1 shows the tally.

The figures are negative for the Netherlands and Switzerland because more people killed themselves when their teams were playing than when there was no soccer.

The next question is what happens after a team is knocked out. Do all the people who had been saved from suicide by soccer then fall into a void and jump off apartment buildings? If so, you would expect a rise in suicides in the period after the tournament.

FIGURE 14.2. Lives saved by gender in "soccer" years

	Male lives saved	*Female lives saved*
Austria	46	15
Czech Republic	55	12
Denmark	37	47
France	95	82
Germany	61	39
Greece	9	13
Ireland	19	-10
Netherlands	-10	-1
Norway	[92 lives saved spread across both genders]	
Spain	2	-3
Sweden	44	16
Switzerland	20	2

However, we found that in ten of our twelve countries, suicides declined for the entire year when the national team played in a big tournament. Only in the Netherlands did suicides rise in the year when the team played; in Spain the difference was negligible. But in the other ten countries, even after the team got knocked out and the euphoria ended, there was no compensating rise in suicide. To the contrary: it seems that the uniting effect of the tournament lasted for a while afterward, continuing to depress the suicide rate. For each of these ten countries, more lives were saved on average over the entire year than in June alone. Figure 14.2 contains our very rough estimates for lives saved over the entire year when the national team plays in a tournament ("lives saved" represents the decline in deaths during a "soccer" year compared to the average year).

Very roughly, the typical soccer tournament in this period appears to have helped save several hundred Europeans from suicide.

We couldn't find any monthly suicide data for any of the British nations. However, the only two previous studies on this topic that we know of in Britain suggest that the lifesaving effect works there, too.

"Parasuicide" is a suicidal gesture in which the aim is not death but rather self-harm, or a cry for help. One example of parasuicide is taking an insufficient overdose. George Masterton, a psychiatrist in Edinburgh, and his co-author J. A. Strachan studied Scottish parasuicides during and immediately after the World Cups of 1974, 1978, 1982, and 1986. Each time, Scotland had qualified for the tournament. Each time, Masterton and Strachan found a fall in parasuicide for both genders during the tournament that "has been sustained for at least eight weeks after the last game." The Scottish case is a pretty strong piece of evidence against the apartment-building theory of soccer suicides, because if there was ever an excuse for soccer fans to try to kill themselves, it was Scotland's performance at the World Cup of 1978. (The team's fantasist manager, Ally McLeod, had boasted beforehand that the Scots would leave with a "medal of some sort.")

Later Masterton and Anthony J. Mander studied the numbers of people who came to the Royal Edinburgh Hospital with psychiatric emergencies during and after the World Cups of 1978, 1982, and 1986. The researchers found "reductions in all illness categories during and afterwards (with the exception of alcoholism during)." The decline in emergencies applied to both genders, and was more marked after each World Cup than during it. For instance, there was a 56 percent fall in admissions of male neurotics in the weeks after a tournament.

The authors then tried to explain what was going on here:

> There are few outlets which permit a wide and acceptable expression of Scottish nationhood—sport is perhaps the most powerful, and [soccer] is the national game. . . . We would speculate that such a common interest and endeavour, fused with a surge of nationalism, might enhance social cohesion in the manner proposed by Durkheim to explain the decreased suicide rates that accompany times of war.

Social cohesion is the key phrase here. This is the benefit that almost all fans—potential suicides and the rest of us—get from fandom. Winning or losing is not the point. You can get social cohesion even from losing. Very often, a nation will bond over a defeat in a big soccer game. People sob in public, perform postmortems in the office the next morning, hunt for scapegoats together. For Italians, for instance, defeat to North Korea in 1966 was a shared national moment almost as memorable as victory in Berlin in 2006. It is not the case that losing matches makes significant numbers of people so unhappy they jump off apartment buildings. In the US, fans of longtime losers like the Chicago Cubs and the Boston Red Sox baseball teams (Boston only became frequent winners again from 2004) have not killed themselves more than other people, says Thomas Joiner, author of *Why People Die by Suicide,* whose own father died by suicide.

Joiner's article "On Buckeyes, Gators, Super Bowl Sunday, and the Miracle on Ice" makes a strong case that it's not the winning that counts but the taking part—the shared experience. It is true that he found fewer suicides in Columbus, Ohio, and Gainesville, Florida, in the years when the local college football teams did well. But Joiner argues that this is because fans of winning teams "pull together" more: they wear the team shirt more often, watch games together in bars, talk about the team, and so on, much as happens in a European country while the national team is playing in a World Cup. The "pulling together" saves people from suicide, not the winning. Proof of this is that Joiner found fewer suicides in the US on Super Bowl Sundays than on other Sundays at that time of year, even though few of the Americans who watch the Super Bowl are passionate supporters of either team. What they get from the day's parties is a sense of belonging.

That is the lifesaver. In Europe today, there may be nothing that brings a society together like a World Cup with your team in it. For once, almost everyone in the country is watching the same TV programs and talking about them at work the next day, just as Europeans used to do thirty years ago before they got cable TV. Part of the point of watching a World Cup is that almost everyone else is watching, too. Isolated people—the types at most risk of suicide—are suddenly welcomed into the national conversation. They are given social cohesion. All this helps explain why big soccer tournaments seem to save so many female lives in Europe, even though relatively few women either commit suicide or (before about 2000 at least) watch soccer. The "pulling together" during a big soccer tournament is so universal that it drags many women along in a way that club soccer does not. It may also be that during tournaments, some troubled women benefit from a brief vacation from male partners who are distracted by soccer.

Other than sports, only war and catastrophe can create this sort of national unity. Most strikingly, in the week after John F. Kennedy's murder in 1963—a time of American sadness but also of "pulling together"—not one suicide was reported in twenty-nine cities studied. Likewise, in the US in the days after the September 11, 2001, attacks, another phase of national "pulling together," the number of calls to the 1–800-SUICIDE hotline halved to about three hundred a day, "an all-time low," writes Joiner. And in Britain in 1997, suicides declined after Princess Diana died.

Joiner speculates that "pulling together" through sports may particularly suit "individuals who have poor interpersonal skills (often characteristic of severely depressed or suicidal persons)." You don't have to be charming to be a fan among fans.

In 1956 Frederick Exley was drunk, unemployed, and loveless in Chicago. He writes, "Though I had completely disregarded football my first year in that happy city, during the autumn of 1956, after losing my job, I once again found that it was the only thing that gave me comfort." At some point or other in life, we have all known how that feels.

15

HAPPINESS

Why Hosting a World Cup Is Good for You

You don't often see people consciously building a white elephant, but that's what was happening in Brasilia in 2012. Smack in downtown, on the main avenue of Brazil's tropical capital, workers were finishing off a stadium for 70,000 people. The Estadio Nacional was one of twelve stadiums built for the World Cup in 2014. And it was doomed to become redundant even before the tournament ended. Brasilia's tinpot clubs seldom draw 1,000 spectators. Nor will the Rolling Stones regularly be flying into this city in the middle of nowhere to fill the Nacional. Brasilia might as well tear down the stadium after the last World Cup game, and save itself a fortune in maintenance costs. Other host cities like Manaus, Cuiabá, and Natal could do likewise.

It's this kind of waste that brought Brazilians onto the streets in June 2013, demonstrating against their country's hosting of the World Cup and the Rio Olympics of 2016. "We have world-class stadiums—now we need a country to go around them," read one protestor's banner. "A teacher is worth more than Neymar," said another. Worldwide, from Atlanta to the International Olympic Committee's headquarters in Lausanne, Switzerland, people are reaching the same conclusion: hosting sports events doesn't make you rich.

Whenever a country prepares to host a World Cup or an Olympics, its politicians prophesy an "economic bonanza." They invoke hordes of shopaholic visitors, the free advertising of host cities to the world's TV viewers, and the long-term benefits of all the roads and stadiums that will get built. No wonder that nowadays almost every government seems to want to host these events. The bidding to stage the World Cups of 2018 and 2022 was the most cutthroat ever. If only the bidding countries could grasp the real reason for wanting to be a host: hosting doesn't make you rich, but it does make you happier. Brazil will benefit from 2014, but not in money.

II

The 1989 movie *Field of Dreams* is a sentimental redemption story starring Kevin Costner as an Iowa farmer. Growing up the son of a baseball nut, the farmer had dreamed of being a baseball star. As an adult, he hears a voice telling him to build a baseball diamond on his cornfield. "If you build it, he will come" is the film's catchphrase. The moral: building stadiums where they do not currently exist is uplifting and good for you. This originally American idea later spread to soccer around the world.

There is in the US a small industry of "consultants" who exist to provide an economic rationale for "If you build it, he will come." In almost any city in the US at almost any time, someone is scheming to build a spanking new sports stadium. The big prize for most American cities is to host a major league team, ideally an NFL franchise, but if that can't be had, then baseball, basketball, or, if nothing else is going, soccer or even ice hockey. Hosting an American sports franchise has a lot in common with hosting a World Cup. Both the franchise and the World Cup are mobile beasts. Their owners are generally willing to move to whichever city or country offers them the best deal. In the US, owners of sports teams usually demand that the host city's taxpayers pony up for a stadium, with lucrative parking lots thrown in. All this is then handed over to the franchise owner, who also gets to keep the money he makes from selling tickets. About seventy new major league stadiums and arenas were built in the US in the twenty years before the financial crisis of 2008. The total cost: $20 billion, about half of which came from the public. In New Orleans, for instance, the taxpayer paid for the Superdome but not for better levees.

In one typical case in 1989, seventy investors, including one George W. Bush, son of the then American president, paid $83 million for the Texas Rangers baseball club. The Bush group wanted a bigger stadium. Strangely for a phalanx of right-wing millionaires, it decided that local taxpayers should finance it. If that didn't happen, the new owners threatened to move the Rangers elsewhere. The people of the local town of Arlington duly voted to increase the local sales tax by half a percent, raising the $191 million needed for the ballpark.

The president's son George W. became the Rangers' managing director. Mostly this just meant being the official face of the club. He would sit in the stands during games handing out baseball cards with pictures of himself. When he ran for governor of Texas in 1994, he constantly cited his experience in baseball. There wasn't much else on his CV. He was duly elected, and decorated his Austin office with 250 signed baseballs.

In 1998 the Bush group sold the Rangers to Tom Hicks (the man who later became co-owner of Liverpool FC) for $250 million. Most of the value was in the stadium that the taxpayers had built. Bush personally netted $14.9 million. He admitted, "When it is all said and done, I will have made more money than I ever dreamed I would make." Meanwhile, he was already beginning to parlay his governorship into a bigger political prize.

So the trick for American club owners is to persuade the taxpayer to cough up for stadiums. This is where economists come in handy. Economists like to say that people respond to incentives. Well, economists certainly respond to incentives. Anyone hoping to persuade taxpayers to pay for a stadium in the US commissioned an economist to write an "economic impact" study. By a strange coincidence, these studies always showed that the stadium would make taxpayers rich. (One book describing this racket is aptly called *Field of Schemes.*)

The argument typically went as follows: Building the stadium would create jobs first for construction workers, and later for people who worked in it. Fans would flock in from all around ("If you build it, he will come"), and they would spend money. New businesses would spring up to serve them. As the area around the stadium became populated, more people would want to live there, and even more businesses (and jobs) would spring up. "The building of publicly funded stadiums has become a substitute for anything resembling an urban policy," notes Dave Zirin in his *People's History of Sports in the United States.*

The "economic impact" study then typically clothed this model with some big numbers. If you put your mind to it, you could think up a total in benefits that ran into the billions, whatever currency you happened to be working in. Best of all, no one would ever be able to prove that number wrong. Suppose you promise that a stadium will bring a city economic benefits of $2 billion over ten years. If the city's income (hard to measure in the first place) rises by only $1 billion over the decade, then, of course, it was something completely different (the world economy, say) that restricted the income. You could prove the original estimates wrong only if you could estimate how much economic growth there would have been had the stadium never been built—but this "counterfactual" figure is unknowable, precisely because it is a counterfactual. The same economists soon branched out into writing studies that justified ever more extravagant spending on the Olympics.

It would have seemed rude to derail this industry with anything so inconvenient as the truth. But then along came Rob Baade. The quiet, courteous academic seemed an unlikely figure to be taking on the stadium lobby. After all, he is a former top-class athlete himself: at college, Baade captained the Wisconsin basketball team. When the white coach seemed antagonistic to the majority of black players, Baade found himself championing players against coach in what he describes as one of the most difficult years of his life.

Afterward he wanted to do graduate work in public finance, a branch of economics that usually involves many equations and few words. But he also wanted to coach basketball and to apply something of what he had learned while on the Wisconsin team. A colleague told him about a job at Lake Forest College, an idyllic little place just outside Chicago. To the dismay of some of his purist professors, he went to Lake Forest on a temporary appointment and ended up coaching there for eighteen years, while also rising to full professor of economics. He was a good coach, too: the year before he arrived, the team had not won a single game, but within four years they were winning 85 percent of their games.

When you start out as an academic you try to write papers that will grab your colleagues' attention. Baade used his own background to enter the economics of sports, then still almost virgin terrain. At a seminar in New York he presented a paper titled "The Sports Tax." Journalists from the *New York Times* and the *Wall Street Journal* happened to be in the audience, and they zeroed in on what had been almost a throwaway line in his talk: public investment in stadiums does not provide a good return for taxpayers. As a coach himself, Baade might have been expected to join the stadium boosters. Had he done so, he could have earned himself good money in consulting. Instead he went into opposition.

The Heartland Institute, a conservative think tank, asked him to write up his thoughts. There are few issues in American political life where the Right joins with an intellectual liberal like Baade, but the paper he published in 1987 laid out the problem clearly: "Contrary to the claims of city officials, this study has found that sports and stadiums frequently had no significant positive impact on a city's economy and, in a regional context, may actually contribute to a reduction in a sports-minded city's share of regional income."

Baade had asked the awkward questions that stadium boosters always ignored. For instance, where would all the construction workers for the new stadium come from? Wouldn't they have jobs already, and therefore wouldn't a shortage arise somewhere else? Worse still, as competition for their skills intensified, wouldn't costs rise?

Once you start thinking of people as having alternatives rather than just standing around waiting for the stadium to arrive, the economics begin to look less appealing. For every dollar going in, there is probably a dollar going out somewhere else. In particular, if a city has to balance its budget, then spending more on stadiums must mean spending less on hospitals and schools. These lost jobs have to be counted against the stadium's benefits. And if the city doesn't balance its budget, isn't it storing up future burdens for taxpayers, who will have to forgo something, someday?

That is bad enough, but what if the stadium doesn't produce the promised benefits? After all, most stadiums are used for only a few hours a week, and barely at all in the off-season. Even allowing for the occasional rock concert (and there is a limit to how many times Elton John can play in your town), most of the time the neighborhood around the stadium will be deserted. Nobody wants to live in a place like that. The neighborhoods around the old Yankee Stadium or Shea Stadium hardly became desirable, for instance.

Nor did Baade believe that a stadium would draw in much spending from outside the city. Most out-of-town fans would buy a hot dog and beer, watch the game, and leave—hardly an economic bonanza. A mall, or a cineplex, or even a hospital would generate more local spending.

Around the end of the 1980s other economists, too, began asking these awkward questions. However, Baade went one better. To show that the boosters' numbers didn't add up, he generated some numbers of his own. Perhaps he couldn't measure the counterfactual, but he could get close by comparing economic growth in cities that had major league teams with those that didn't. After all, he reasoned, if the boosters were right, then over time cities with stadiums must do better than cities without stadiums.

Baade examined data such as income per head and the numbers of new businesses and jobs created in various cities. The more he looked, the less difference he found between the economic profiles of cities with and without stadiums. All this spending was evidently producing no benefit.

Gradually people took notice. Other economists started to replicate Baade's findings, and found new ways to test the proposition that stadiums create wealth. "Antistadium movements" began in many American cities. (In the TV comedy series *Portlandia,* hipsters in Portland campaign against the mere theoretical possibility of their town's ever trying to bid for the Olympics.)

In the mid-1990s Baade was asked to testify before Congress. On the day of his testimony, Congress was also holding hearings on the Clinton Whitewater affair and on military intervention in Bosnia, but when the stadium hearings started, the other chambers emptied. One of the people in the room was Paul Tagliabue, NFL commissioner and someone all the congressmen wanted to be seen with. Powerful people like Tagliabue were getting quite irritated by Baade's awkward facts.

Academic freedom is a cherished value of American universities, but, as Baade was starting to realize, so is making money. He recalls an old guy coming up to him after one meeting and saying, "You might be right, professor, but if I were you I would watch my back. You're getting in the way of a whole lotta commercial projects." A university seldom likes seeing its employees upset local politicians and businesspeople. Lake Forest College always supported Baade, but at times it would have been convenient had he thought differently.

He kept on telling the truth regardless. Among economists, often not the sportiest of types, he developed a special credibility as a former athlete. This sometimes came in handy, such as when a questioner in a public debate asked, "No disrespect, professor, but what does an economist like you know about athletics?"

Eventually Baade descended on soccer. He and a colleague, Victor Matheson, conducted a study of the impact of hosting the World Cup of 1994 in the US. They looked for evidence of faster economic growth in the host cities, and as usual they found nothing. Yet by now, the old bogus American arguments for hosting sports had spread to other countries.

The raising and dashing of hopes of an economic bonanza became as integral a part of a modern soccer tournament as the raising and dashing of hopes that England would win it. A few months after England hosted Euro '96, for instance, a report by a body called Tourism Research & Marketing said that fewer than 100,000 overseas fans had visited England for the tournament, against a forecast—admittedly plucked out of thin air by the English Football Association—of 250,000. Nor had the visitors spent much. Euro '96 generated about $155 million in direct income for Britain. This was peanuts compared to the $20 billion spent by all overseas visitors to the country in 1996. Meanwhile, a study by Liverpool University and the city council found that the 30,000 visitors to Liverpool during Euro '96 spent only $1.56 million between them. How many jobs had that created? Thirty, all of them temporary.

A few years later Japanese and Korean government officials were predicting that the World Cup of 2002 could boost their economies by a staggering $26 billion and $9 billion, respectively. Of course, after the event there was little sign of any such boost, and indeed some evidence that tourists had stayed away for fear of soccer hooligans. Big sports tournaments attract some visitors, and deter many others. Greek tourism officials estimated in late 2004 that there'd been a 10 percent *fall* in tourist arrivals during that year's Athens Olympics, as vacationers choosing summer destinations steered clear of the frenzy. Nor did the twenty-two stadiums built for the Athens Games generate an economic bonanza. In 2010 an analysis by the *Wall Street Journal* found that twenty-one were unoccupied.

Finally, the weight of this research was starting to stack up. It was becoming obvious that even if you build it, he won't necessarily come. The boosters' claims of economic benefits were growing muted. The estimates produced for the World Cup in Germany in 2006 were altogether more sober. Even a study sponsored by the German soccer federation suggested a mere $2 billion in new benefits. (Similarly in London, estimates of the likely economic benefits from the 2012 Olympics were kept studiously vague.)

Perhaps the best estimate we have of how much visitors to soccer tournaments actually spend was done at the German World Cup. This was the biggest media event in history, a month-long party (except for the boring soccer), yet even here the hosts didn't make much money.

A team of economists, led by Holger Preuss from the University of Mainz, decided to work out how much "new" money visitors to the World Cup actually spent. In the old days, when boosters estimated economic bonanzas, they simply multiplied the number of seats in stadiums by some imaginary spending number (counting meals, hotels, and transportation as well as tickets) to produce an enormous hypothetical sum.

The problem with this method, as serious economists pointed out, is that not every visitor to an event really injects extra spending into the economy. Preuss's team surveyed a large sample of visitors to the World Cup and found that only about one-fifth were foreigners who had traveled to Germany specifically for the soccer. More than half the "visitors" were in fact Germans. For the most part these Germans would have been in Germany anyway, and had there been no World Cup they presumably would have spent their money on other forms of entertainment (such as going to movies or restaurants). If they spent money at the World Cup, they spent less elsewhere in the German economy, which largely offset any economic benefit from the soccer. Of course, some Germans who might otherwise have been spending their money on Spanish vacations stayed home for the soccer. However, their spending was probably offset by other Germans who went abroad precisely to avoid the madness of the World Cup.

The remaining foreign visitors to the World Cup—about a quarter of all visitors—were either "time switchers," who would have come to Germany anyway at some point and simply timed their visit to coincide with the World Cup, or foreigners, who would have been in Germany during the World Cup anyway and just decided to go along and see what all the fuss was about. Preuss's team called this last category "casuals."

"Time switchers" and "casuals" would have added little to spending, because even without the World Cup they would have spent their money in Germany. Preuss's team asked respondents detailed questions about their spending plans. They concluded that the World Cup generated spending by visitors of €2.8 billion. That was negligible beside the Paris Hiltonesque €1 trillion–plus spent annually by consumers in Germany. It was also much less than the German state spent preparing for the tournament. Remarkably, more than a third of that visitor income came from people who never got inside a stadium but merely watched the games on big screens in public places. In short, even the World Cup was barely a hiccup in the German economy.

Almost all research shows the same thing: hosting sports tournaments doesn't increase the number of tourists, or of full-time jobs, or total economic growth. Added to all this are the host's costs. If the economic benefits of putting on these tournaments are muted, the expenses seldom are. Economists Brad Humphreys and Szymon Prokopowicz made some rough estimates of the costs to Poland of hosting just half of Euro 2012. Poland needed to lay on a lot more than just new stadiums, airports, and hotels for fans. UEFA requires, for its own officials and guests, the use of one entire five-star hotel within a forty-five-minute drive of every stadium. The teams need an additional sixteen hotels, most of them five-star. The referees have to be in five-star hotels near the stadiums. The doctors who perform the doping controls need five-stars "in the countryside." Much of the cost of these hotels came courtesy of the Polish government. Poland also had to put up surveillance cameras all over its stadiums and towns.

In all, Humphreys and Prokopowicz estimated that the country would have to spend about $10 billion on Euro 2012. With hindsight, this looks like a serious underestimate. True, some of the infrastructure that Poland bought still has its uses after the tournament. However, much of it doesn't, because the things you need for a soccer tournament—a massive new stadium, roads to that stadium, an airport in a sleepy town—are never quite the same as the things you need for daily life.

Almost all the research points in one direction: hosting doesn't create an economic bonanza. And yet South Africa went into its World Cup in 2010 promising its citizens an economic bonanza. In a sense, the country had to. When about a third of your population lives on less than $2 a day, the government can hardly say it's blowing billions on a month of fun. It has to argue that the soccer will benefit the poor. You then end up with people like Irvin Khoza, who chaired the tournament's local organizing committee, saying things like, "The 2010 World Cup will change the face of the country. It may prove a pivotal point in our development as a young democracy."

The South African ruling class put this message across so energetically that when the country was named host in May 2004, crowds celebrating in the township of Soweto shouted, "The money is coming!" Half the people you met in South Africa in the years before the tournament had a scheme for 2010: buying apartments just to rent them out during the tournament, selling sausage and maize pudding outside stadiums, corralling peasant women to weave beaded flags in the colors of all the participating teams. Much of South African conversation was about such schemes, and in newspaper profiles, when a celebrity described what he was working on, he would often add, "The key thing is to be ready for 2010." The year had become a magic number.

As 2010 approached, the tournament's expected costs inevitably soared. South Africa had initially promised a cheap World Cup. All the stadiums put together, it had said in 2004, would cost only about $170 million. But with FIFA demanding perfection, and every local powerbroker in South Africa wanting his own A-1 stadium, the bill for stadiums ended up about ten times that. This embarrassing overrun may be why copies of South Africa's original bid book were "disappeared."

Some of the South African organizers ended their journey in 2010 feeling rather chastened. We witnessed this one chilly winter's Saturday during the World Cup, in a chic convention center in Johannesburg's business district of Sandton. A few dozen visiting Brazilian officials had taken their seats to listen to South African officials explain what it had really been like to stage the tournament—to hear, in the words of one South African speaker, about "some of our cuts and bruises."

The Brazilian guests were mostly cheery, as befits officials on a "study visit" to a World Cup. But they heard some chilling things. Perhaps the most chilling came from a lady we won't name, to keep her out of trouble. She was a senior official for Gauteng, the province that includes Johannesburg.

She told the Brazilians how in 2009, she had reviewed the projected economic boost that the World Cup would give South Africa. She looked—and found almost nothing. "It wasn't going to be giving us the benefits that we had told the country the World Cup was going to give us," she said. True, the tournament would improve Johannesburg's creaky transport links a bit, but "it wasn't as much as we had thought."

And so, over a year before kickoff, Gauteng quietly discarded hopes of economic boost. Instead it recast the World Cup as an exercise in branding—"almost a 30-day advertisement for Gauteng." That, the lady admitted, was all the tournament had proven to be. "There are a lot of mistakes we made that you hopefully won't make," she told the Brazilians.

After her talk, we buttonholed her to ask why the promised economic boost had never happened. "If you look at all the research about mega-events," she replied, "all the findings are that the economic returns are highly inflated by people hoping to profit from the events."

That's right. For instance, the expected hordes of foreign visitors never reached South Africa. In 2009 the management consultancy Grant Thornton—producer of a stream of upbeat economic forecasts about the World Cup—was predicting 483,000 foreign visitors for the tournament. (Earlier forecasts had been even sunnier.) A retrospective study based on official South African statistics, co-authored by Stefan with Thomas Peeters of the University of Antwerp and Victor Matheson from the College of the Holy Cross, estimates that the number of additional visitors in June and July 2010 was only 220,000, less than half Grant Thornton's prediction. Given that tourist arrivals from countries outside of Africa average about 2 million per year, this represented a boost to tourism, but not a big one. Nor did the economy as a whole see much benefit.

John Saker, chief operating officer of KPMG Africa, said: "The big boost didn't happen."

Predictably, most of the stadiums that South Africa built for the tournament are now white elephants. The country never had any need for them. The larger hosting cities—Cape Town, Johannesburg, Durban, and Pretoria—have for decades possessed large, very decent rugby grounds that can serve the modest needs of local soccer, too. Johannesburg also had the original Soccer City, a stadium rightly touted as the best in Africa when South Africa was bidding for the World Cup.

Very few domestic games outside the Johannesburg region draw more than about 10,000 spectators. Provincial towns like Nelspruit, Polokwane, and Port Elizabeth now have World Cup stadiums, but they do not have clubs in the country's Premier Soccer League. (If you are wondering how Port Elizabeth became a host city, it just happens to be the hometown of Danny Jordaan, the World Cup's chief executive.) In October 2010 the French company SAIL Stadefrance said it was pulling out of its thirty-year lease to operate Cape Town's Green Point Stadium, even before the lease came into effect. The company admitted it had underestimated the cost of running the venue. Quite likely, in the next few years Cape Town will find better uses for that prime piece of land overlooking the Atlantic Ocean than a redundant soccer stadium.

BRAZIL 2014: THE HYPE NEVER CEASES

You would have thought that people would learn from the shame of the South African World Cup; from the way FIFA forced a developing country to build unnecessary stadiums fancy enough for sponsors, while a few miles away people lived in corrugated-iron shacks. In 2009 a senior European soccer official mused to us about putting pressure on FIFA to let Brazil host a cheaper World Cup. It could be done, this man said, if a few powerful soccer federations—Germany, France, the US, England, and some others—argued that Brazil needn't build the most expensive stadiums on earth, just some good solid ones that wouldn't turn into white elephants the day the circus left town.

No such luck, however. One morning in Johannesburg during the World Cup of 2010, one of us, Simon, had breakfast with the Brazilian sports minister, Orlando Silva Jr. The minister was a charming man, wearing the sort of casual clothes we wish our own ministers in Britain would try. And he was really looking forward to hosting the World Cup. "I guess that the cup has served as a stimulus for development and infrastructure here in South Africa," he said, "and we will follow the same path in Brazil." He said his country had deliberately chosen "less developed regions" to host matches, just to give them the chance to develop. Brazil was building airports, ports and stadiums all over. There'd be jobs galore. In short, the World Cup was just what Brazil's economy needed.

Regrettably Silva is no longer in office, having resigned in 2011 over a corruption scandal. However, Brazil 2014 is already looking like a rerun of South Africa 2010. There is the ever-rising cost of stadiums: from an initial estimate of under $1 billion, most of which would be paid by private businesses, to over $3.5 billion (almost entirely funded by the Brazilian taxpayer) by late 2013. And let's just say the estimated cost (or "investment," as officials like to call it) was unlikely to fall. The construction companies knew the stadiums had to be ready by June 2014. This meant they could charge almost whatever they liked to build them; the government would just have to pay.

No wonder the construction of stadiums kept hitting delays. That allowed the construction companies to tell the government at the last minute, "Oops, this is costing more than we thought. Give us more cash or we won't finish on time and you will look stupid in front of the world."

The Brazilian World Cup is a wonderful thing if you happen to own a construction business; not so wonderful if you pay taxes in Brazil, or if you were hoping the government would do something about all the terrible Brazilian roads that don't lead to soccer stadiums.

We confidently predict that in July 2014, when the last of the party animals has tumbled out of a cupboard and flown home, it will turn out that nobody made much more from the tournament than they would have in the regular tourist season.

Having said all that, the Brazilian World Cup will probably have a more worthwhile legacy than the South African one did. For a start, if Brazil has its wits about it, it will piggyback the preparations for the World Cup with the Rio Olympics of 2016. South Africa built infrastructure for one party. Brazil, at least, should be building for two.

More important, Brazil has a greater need than South Africa did for the main legacy of a World Cup: soccer stadiums. Brazil has nearly 200 million inhabitants, almost four times as many as South Africa. It has a much larger soccer-going public: no club in South Africa has an average attendance of over 20,000, whereas several in Brazil do.

And Brazil lacks decent stadiums. When it was named host in 2007, it didn't have a single one good enough for a World Cup. Its soccer fans were watching—or not watching—in the tumbledown stadiums of a poorer era.

A wealthier Brazil can afford better grounds. During the recent boom years, this became more of a middle-class country. It now has more inhabitants able to pay to watch soccer in comfort. The World Cup will make that happen. The government's aim, said Silva at our breakfast, "is to raise the comfort level of our stadiums without excluding the workers." Once the comfort level rises in the shiny new stadiums, more middle-class Brazilians and their families should start coming to league matches. This is what happened in England after the country raised the comfort level of its stadiums in the early 1990s. True, England then was a much richer country than Brazil is today. But Brazil today is richer than its current, run-down stadiums. Admittedly six of the host cities for 2014 don't even have teams in the national championship, but at least the other six stadiums (including a marvelous new Maracanã in Rio) should come in handy after 2014. That's a better ratio than South Africa managed.

If well-off Brazilians start buying expensive tickets to games after 2014, that would make Brazilian clubs richer. An official at Chelsea told us he saw Brazil in the future as "a marketplace of threat for the talent that you have here [in England]." Already, as the country gets richer, Brazilian clubs can afford to keep more of their better players at home. Brazil has ceded its traditional position of soccer's biggest exporter of players to neighboring Argentina. Post-2014, Brazil could have a very good league. After all, the Brazilian economy is bigger than England's, and the country produces some decent soccer players.

If our rosy predictions for Brazilian soccer come true, then that won't make Brazil as a whole richer. Rather, the Brazilian World Cup is best understood as a series of financial transfers: from women to men (who will have more fun), from Brazilian taxpayers to FIFA and the world's soccer fans, and from taxpayers to Brazilian soccer clubs and construction companies. Possibly Brazilian society desires these transfers. Still, we have to be clear that this is what's going on: a transfer of wealth from Brazil as a whole to various interest groups inside and outside the country. This is not an economic bonanza. Brazil is sacrificing a little bit of its future to host the World Cup.

Ah, say the boosters, but the biggest economic benefits from these events are intangible. Think of all the billions of people seeing the host country on TV every night. Saker of KPMG Africa promised that South Africa would benefit from "word of mouth and goodwill for years to come" after 2010. Similarly, Silva told us that the 2014 World Cup would promote Brazil's image in the world. Well, maybe. First of all, as the American sports economist Andrew Zimbalist says, "Brazil is hardly a secret as an international tourist destination." Rio is already the most visited city in the Southern Hemisphere, he notes. Furthermore, there's the risk that the World Cup could *damage* Brazil's brand. That has happened to several Olympic hosts: Munich in 1972, Montreal in 1976, and Atlanta in 1996. The 2014 World Cup might persuade people that Brazil is not a crime-ridden country with terrible traffic; alternatively, it might persuade them that Brazil is precisely that.

It's rare for a truth long known to economists to sink in with the general public, but that is happening on this issue. People everywhere are cottoning onto the truth that building stadiums doesn't bring wealth. In referendums in Europe in 2013, the citizens of Munich voted against bidding for a winter Olympics, and the Viennese against bidding for a summer Games. In the US, the economic crisis seems to have made taxpayers more skeptical of stadium boondoggles. In 2013 the Atlanta Braves and Minnesota Vikings, in cahoots with local politicians, avoided letting locals vote on funding their planned new stadiums—because they suspected people would vote against. When Insider Advantage–Fox 5 polled 1,698 registered voters in Cobb County, Georgia, in November 2013, 56 percent opposed spending local tax dollars on the Braves stadium. Yet later that month, Cobb County commissioners voted for it.

Other international sporting bodies don't want to anger taxpayers the way FIFA has in Brazil. That's partly why the IOC gave the 2020

Olympics to Tokyo: the megacity could better afford to stage the Games than its poorer rivals Istanbul and Madrid. In soccer, UEFA went one step further: it didn't choose a host at all for Euro 2020. The burden would have been too great, explained UEFA's general secretary Gianni Infantino, especially in hard economic times. Instead thirteen countries will share the hosting.

FIFA, too, must have learned from its Brazilian experience. It now knows that to ask a democratic country to fund white elephants is to ask for protests. Much easier to give the World Cup to dictatorships like Russia or Qatar, where protestors are discouraged. Alternatively, you could choose a host country that doesn't need to build world-class stadiums because it already has dozens. Step forward the USA for 2026.

HAPPINESS IS A WORLD CUP

Most people now agree with Rob Baade: hosting a sports tournament doesn't make a place rich. The question then is why countries still bother. Why did so many countries go to such embarrassing lengths to stage the World Cups of 2018 and 2022? The answer has nothing to do with desire for profit. To the contrary: Qatar, which won the bidding for 2022, has so much money that it can afford to waste pots of it on a month of fun. However, the frantic bidding by respectable democracies, such as Australia, the US, England, and Spain, does reveal something about the new politics of happiness slowly emerging in the rich world.

In recent years, social scientists have learned a lot about happiness. Their best source in Europe is the Eurobarometer research program, which is funded by the European Commission. Each year it asks about 1,000 citizens from each European country how happy they are. To quote the exact question: "On the whole, are you very satisfied, fairly satisfied, not very satisfied, or not at all satisfied with the life you lead?"

The survey has been conducted for over forty years. By now some insights have accumulated. Perhaps the most interesting is that having money in itself doesn't make you happy. "There is a paradox at the heart of our lives" is how Richard Layard opens his book *Happiness: Lessons from a New Science,* one of a flood of recent works on the subject. "Most people want more income and strive for it. Yet as Western societies have got richer, their people have become no happier." Layard says that in the US, Britain, and Japan, people have gotten no happier in the past fifty years even as average incomes have more than doubled.

It seems that we humans adapt quickly to our environment. The things we once thought of as luxuries soon become necessities (although, by the same token, our sense of well-being would quickly adapt to losing half our income). What we care about is not our absolute wealth but our rung on the ladder. Ruut Veenhoven, a leading researcher of happiness, says, "When we have overtaken the Joneses, our reference drifts upward to the Smiths, and we feel unhappy again."

Only in countries where income per capita is below about $15,000—countries such as Brazil, the Philippines, and India—has increased wealth brought some happiness. Layard writes, "The reason is clear—extra income is really valuable when it lifts people away from sheer physical poverty." But that very rarely happens in Europe anymore.

Some other truths emerge from the European data. Scandinavians are very happy; eastern Europeans are not. The Irish both north and south of the border are surprisingly happy. Age, sex, and social status matter, too. In western Europe at least, the average person's happiness tends to decline with age until he or she is twenty-six, and then starts to rise again. Women seem to be happier than men, which might help account for their much lower rates of suicide. The more educated people are, the happier they tend to be. Married people are generally happier than unmarried ones. What happens around you in society also matters: when unemployment or inflation rises, people tend to grow unhappier. Spending time with friends and family makes people happy.

And, we discovered, so does hosting soccer tournaments. Staging a World Cup won't make you rich, but it does tend to cheer you up.

The day before the World Cup final of 2006, one of the authors, Simon, visited the street where he used to live in Berlin. Fifteen years before, the Hohenfriedbergstrasse had been a dull-brown place with toilets on the stairwells and potentially fatal ancient coal ovens in every apartment. Nobody ever spoke to anyone else. This time he had to check the street sign to make sure it was the same place. Flags were flying from every house—German flags made in China, but also flags of many other nations—and children were playing everywhere even though they had supposedly gone extinct in Germany. The World Cup seemed to have made a usually gloomy nation happy.

This is typical. Georgios Kavetsos and Stefan Szymanski (with a lot of help from Robert McCulloch, guru of happiness research) took the European Commission's happiness data for twelve western European countries from 1974 to 2004 and checked whether it correlated at all with sports tournaments. The obvious first question was whether people became happier when their national team did well. It turned out that they didn't: there was no visible correlation. Then Kavetsos and Stefan looked at hosting and happiness, and here they found a link. After a country hosts a soccer tournament, its inhabitants report increased happiness.

What Kavetsos and Stefan did was to replicate existing studies of happiness using all the measures researchers usually consider (income, age, marital status, and so on), and then see whether living in a host country made a difference as well. Their data on happiness covered eight separate hosts of tournaments: Italy and France for the World Cups of 1990 and 1998 and for the European championships Italy (1980), France (1984), West Germany (1988), England (1996), and Belgium and the Netherlands (2000). In all but one of these eight host countries, there was a significant uptick in self-reported happiness just after the tournament. The only exception was the UK, where happiness fell slightly just after Euro '96, but then we all know that the UK is not England.

The London Olympics do seem to have boosted British happiness. The UK's Office for National Statistics registered a small rise in self-reported "life satisfaction" from 2011–2012 to 2012–2013, despite the economic crisis. Of the 165,000 British adults polled, 77 percent rated their life satisfaction at seven or more out of ten—up a touch from 75.9 percent in 2011–2012. The ONS commented that the Olympics and the Queen's Diamond Jubilee may have "influenced people's assessment of their . . . well-being."

The mass of evidence is persuasive. However, given that so many other factors influence happiness, we wanted to test whether this effect could be measured even after allowing for the other factors. To do this, several large databases had to be welded together, and in the process the data from some years were lost. For instance, it turns out that the income of respondents was not surveyed in every single year. That left us with data for five hosts: Italia '90, and the Euros of 1984, 1988, and 2000, the last of which had two hosts. Admittedly, this is a small sample, but in all five host countries, happiness rose after the tournament, even allowing for all the other effects that influence happiness. The inhabitants reported a higher level of happiness the year after the tournament than they had the year before, and they reported more happiness in the autumn surveys (that is, held after the tournament) than in the spring surveys (held before the tournament). Interestingly, this is just what the late British soccer writer Arthur Hopcraft observed when England hosted the World Cup in 1966. He wrote two years later:

> The competition released in our country a communal exuberance which I think astonished ourselves more than our visitors. It gave us a chance to spruce up a lot, to lighten the leaden character of the grounds where the matches were played, to throw off much of our inhibition of behavior, particularly in the provinces, so that we became a gay, almost reckless people in our own streets, which is commonly only how we conduct ourselves when we put on our raffia hats in other countries' holiday resorts. Except in the celebrations that greeted the end of the Second World War, I have never seen England look as unashamedly delighted by life as it did during the World Cup.

We found much the same thing in the nations we studied. The jump in happiness was quite large. Citizens of wealthy countries like the Netherlands or France would need to make hundreds of euros more a month to experience a similar leap. One way to express this is that the average person gains twice as much happiness from hosting a soccer tournament as from having higher education. The effect can also be likened to an unexpected increase in income that takes someone from the bottom half of the income distribution to the middle of the top half. It's not quite winning the lottery, but very satisfying nonetheless. If you calculate this for an entire nation, then the leap in happiness from hosting can easily be worth a few billion euros.

In general in the host countries, older men gained the most extra happiness, presumably because many of them were sitting in front of their television sets with little else to do. Lesser-educated people gained more happiness than better-educated ones. Of all the subgroups we studied, only one (a significant one) did not get any happier: women.

The gain in happiness lasts at least a couple of months, given that the tournaments are played in midsummer and the survey is carried out in the autumn. For World Cups, the gain was quite persistent: even two and four years after the tournament, every subgroup we looked at was still happier than before the tournament. European championships, though, lifted happiness only briefly. We found no impact on happiness in the host country a year after the Euro.

But if people gain a lot of happiness after hosting a tournament, they lose a little happiness before it. The ritual fuss over whether the stadiums will be ready, whether hooligans or terrorists will invade their country, and whether their team will be made to look ridiculous appears to cause stress. Six years and four years before hosting a tournament, many of the subgroups we studied showed a decline in happiness.

| |

It turns out that hosting doesn't make you rich, but it does make you happy. This begs a question. If countries want to host soccer tournaments (and American cities want to host major league teams) as part of their pursuit of happiness, why don't they just say so? Why bother clothing their arguments in bogus economics?

The answer is that politicians have still barely discovered the language of happiness. They talk mostly about money. Anything that serves only to make people happy gets derided with the contemptuous phrase "feel-good factor," as if politics should be above such trivialities. Most politicians have simply assumed that the real business of government is to make people richer. For one thing, measuring income is easier than measuring happiness. And so, when politicians argue for hosting tournaments, they typically use the language of money. It is almost the only vocabulary they have. John Kay, writing in the *Financial Times* in 2013 about the costs of the London Olympics, remarked: "A curious puritanism requires politicians to pretend activities intended to make us feel good about ourselves are justified by their contribution to 'the economy.' The Olympiad was a good party, which cost the British population about £200 per head."

But it is becoming clear that in rich countries, more money doesn't make people happier. Robert F. Kennedy was one of the first to see this, remarking in March 1968, three months before he was murdered, that the gross domestic product "measures everything . . . except that which makes life worthwhile." For a few years before the economic crisis hit in 2008, European politicians did begin talking less about money and more about happiness. In Britain in 2006, for instance, the Conservative leader David Cameron tried to introduce the acronym "GWB"—"general well-being"—to counter the decades-old "GDP" for "gross domestic product." He said, "Improving our society's sense of well-being is, I believe, the central political challenge of our times. . . . Politics in Britain has too often sounded as though it was just about economic growth." Instead Cameron wanted politics "to recognize the value of relationships with family, friends and the world around us."

It seems that soccer tournaments create those relationships: people gathered together in pubs and living rooms, a whole country suddenly caring about the same event. A World Cup is the sort of common project that otherwise barely exists in modern societies. We've seen that the mere fact of following a team in the World Cup deters some very isolated people from committing suicide. If playing in a tournament creates social cohesion, hosting one creates even more. The inhabitants of the host country—and certainly the men—come to feel more connected to everyone else around them. Moreover, hosting can boost the nation's self-esteem, and so makes people feel better about themselves.

In the end, the best reason for hosting a World Cup is that it's fun. Brazil's President Dilma Rousseff ought to have been honest and said, "It'll cost us money, we'll have less left over for schools and roads and poor people, but we all love soccer and it should be a fun month, so it's worth it." Then Brazilians could have a clearheaded debate about the true pros and cons of hosting. It's reasonable enough to want to throw the world's biggest party. But you don't throw a party to make money. You do it because it makes you happy.

Hosting makes even politicians happy. Most of their work is frustrating. You try to get money to build, say, roads, but other politicians stop you. Even when you get the money, it's hard to build the roads, because people pop up to object. It's the same with housing or foreign policy or recycling: being a politician is an endless, tedious struggle with your enemies.

But it isn't when you want to host a sports tournament. Suddenly everyone gets on board. While London was bidding for the Olympics, the rower Steve Redgrave pulled an Olympic gold medal out of his pocket during a meeting at the House of Commons, and MPs of all parties began drooling over him. Even going to war doesn't create that sort of unanimous sentiment anymore.

The end of ideology—the disappearance of nationalism, socialism, religion, communism, and fascism from western Europe—means that in good times many politicians have little better to do than to plug sports events using specious arguments. Ken Livingstone wrote when he was mayor of London, "Crucially, the Olympics will also bring much-needed new facilities: an Olympic-size swimming pool in a city that has just two Olympic pools to Berlin's 19, and a warm-up track that would be turned over to community use."

Plainly, arguments like these are just excuses. If you want to regenerate a poor neighborhood, regenerate it. Build nice houses and a train line. If you want an Olympic pool and a warm-up track, build them. You could build pools and tracks all across London, and it would still be cheaper than hosting the Olympics. The only good reason to host an Olympics is that it makes people happy. The politicians behind London's bid did not say so, but they did sense that the voters would reward them for winning the Games. The 8 million Londoners, in particular, have the highest incomes in the European Union, and so would need to receive a fortune in tax rebates to buy the happiness the Games seem to have brought them.

Puritans might rightly argue that even a rich country like Britain has better things on which to spend money. However, the likely gain in happiness from the Olympics does mean the politicians are canny to give the people bread and circuses. In wealthy countries like Britain, the math of hosting and happiness probably stacks up.

But it's much less likely that Brazil will get its money's worth in happiness from hosting the World Cup. This is still very much a sub-$15,000 country, where putting more money in people's pockets would make them happier. And like South Africa, it's among the most economically unequal countries on earth. Both countries have a first-world sector of the economy with the money and skills to host a World Cup—but also a third-world sector that desperately needs the fruits of the money and skills. Millions of Brazilians are still stuck in life-diminishing poverty. Some of them have been pushed out of their slums to make way for the World Cup. Like South Africans, they should ask how many homes with running water could have been built for the cost of their new stadiums.

We already know the World Cup won't make Brazilians richer. It's also probably not the most efficient way to make them happier.

PART III
Countries

Rich and Poor, Tom Thumb, Guus Ghiddink, England, Spain, Saddam, and the Champions of the Future

16

WHY ENGLAND LOSES AND OTHERS WIN

BEATEN BY A DISHWASHER

Here is what we wrote in the first edition of *Soccernomics,* which appeared nine months before the World Cup of 2010 kicked off:

When the England team flies to South Africa for the World Cup, an ancient ritual will start to unfold. Perfected over England's fourteen previous failures to win the competition away from home, it follows this pattern:

PHASE 1: PRETOURNAMENT—CERTAINTY THAT ENGLAND WILL WIN THE WORLD CUP

Alf Ramsey, the only English manager to win the trophy, predicted the victory of 1966. However, his prescience becomes less impressive when you realize that almost every England manager thinks he will win the trophy, including Ramsey in the two campaigns he didn't. When his team was knocked out in 1970 he was stunned and said, "We must now look ahead to the next World Cup in Munich where our chances of winning I would say are very good indeed." England didn't qualify for that one.

Glenn Hoddle, England's manager in 1998, revealed only after his team had been knocked out "my innermost thought, which was that England would win the World Cup." Another manager who went home early, Ron Greenwood, confessed, "I honestly thought we could have won the World Cup in 1982." A month before the World Cup of 2006, Sven Goran Eriksson said, "I think we will win it."

The deluded manager is never alone. As the England player Johnny Haynes remarked after elimination in 1958, "Everyone in England thinks we have a God-given right to win the World Cup." This belief in the face of all evidence was a hangover from empire: England is soccer's mother country and should therefore be the best today. The sociologist Stephen Wagg notes, "In reality, England is a country like many others and the England soccer team is a soccer team like many others." This truth is only slowly sinking in.

PHASE 2: DURING THE TOURNAMENT—ENGLAND MEETS A FORMER WARTIME ENEMY

In five of its last seven World Cups, England was knocked out by either Germany or Argentina. The matches fit seamlessly into the British tabloid view of history, except for the outcome. As Alan Ball summed up the mood in England's dressing room after the defeat to West Germany in 1970, "It was disbelief."

Even Joe Gaetjens, who scored the winning goal for the US against England in 1950, turns out to have been of German-Haitian origin, not Belgian-Haitian as is always said. And in any case, the US is another former wartime enemy.

PHASE 3: THE ENGLISH CONCLUDE THAT THE GAME TURNED ON ONE FREAKISH PIECE OF BAD LUCK THAT COULD HAPPEN ONLY TO THEM

Gaetjens, the accounting student and dishwasher in a Manhattan restaurant who didn't even have an American passport, scored his goal by accident. "Gaetjens went for the ball, but at the last moment, decided to duck," England's captain Billy Wright wrote later. "The ball bounced on the top of his head and slipped past the bewildered Williams."

In 1970 England's goalkeeper Gordon Banks got an upset stomach before the quarterfinal against West Germany. He was okay on the morning of the game and was picked to play, but a little later was discovered on the toilet with everything "coming out both ends." His understudy, Peter Bonetti, let in three soft German goals.

There was more bad luck in 1973, when England failed to qualify for the next year's World Cup because Poland's "clown" of a goalkeeper, Jan Tomaszewski, unaccountably had a brilliant night at Wembley. "The simple truth is that on a normal day we would have beaten Poland 6–0," England's midfielder Martin Peters says in Niall Edworthy's book on England managers, *The Second Most Important Job in the Country*. Poland went on to reach the semifinals of the '74 World Cup.

In 1990 and 1998 England lost in what everyone knows is the lottery of the penalty shoot-out. In 2002 everyone knew that the obscure, buck-toothed Brazilian kid Ronaldinho must have lucked out with the free kick that sailed into England's net, because he couldn't have been good enough to place it deliberately. In 2006 Wayne Rooney would never have been sent off for stomping on Ricardo Carvalho's genitals if Cristiano Ronaldo hadn't tattled on him. These things just don't happen to other countries.

PHASE 4: MOREOVER, EVERYONE ELSE CHEATED

The Brazilian crowd in 1950 and the Mexican crowd in 1970 deliberately wasted time while England was losing by keeping the ball in the stands. The CIA (some say) drugged Banks. Diego Maradona's "hand of God" single-handedly defeated England in 1986. Diego Simeone playacted in 1998 to get David Beckham sent off, and Cristiano Ronaldo did the same for Rooney in 2006.

Every referee opposes England. Those of his decisions that support this thesis are analyzed darkly. Typically, the referee's nationality is mentioned to blacken him further. Billy Wright, England's captain in 1950, later recalled "Mr Dattilo of Italy, who seemed determined to let nothing so negligible as the laws of the game come between America and victory." The referee who didn't give England a penalty against West Germany in 1970 was, inevitably, an Argentine. The Tunisian referee of 1986 who, like most people watching the game, failed to spot the "hand of God" has become legendary.

PHASE 5: ENGLAND IS KNOCKED OUT WITHOUT GETTING ANYWHERE NEAR LIFTING THE CUP

The only exception was 1990, when the team reached the semifinal. Otherwise, England has always been eliminated when still needing to defeat at least three excellent teams. Since 1970, Bulgaria, Sweden, and Poland have gotten as close to winning a World Cup as England has.

Perhaps England should be relieved that it doesn't finish second. As Jerry Seinfeld once said, who wants to be the greatest loser? The science writer Stefan Klein points out that winning bronze at the Olympics is not so bad, because that is a great achievement by any standards, but winning silver is awful, as you will always be tortured by the thought of what might have been.

England has never been at much risk of that. The team won only five of its eighteen matches at World Cups abroad from 1950 through 1970, and didn't qualify for the next two tournaments in 1974 and 1978, so at least it has been improving since. The general belief in decline from a golden age is mistaken.

PHASE 6: THE DAY AFTER ELIMINATION, NORMAL LIFE RESUMES

The one exception is 1970, when England's elimination may have caused the Labour Party's surprise defeat in the British general election four days later. But otherwise the elimination does not bring on a nationwide hangover. To the contrary, England's eliminations are celebrated, turned into national myths, or songs, or commercials for pizza chains.

PHASE 7: A SCAPEGOAT IS FOUND

The scapegoat is never an outfield player who has "battled" all match. Even if he directly caused the elimination by missing a penalty, he is a "hero."

Beckham was scapegoated for the defeat against Argentina in 1998 only because he got a red card after forty-six minutes. Writer Dave Hill explained that the press was simply pulling out its "two traditional responses to England's sporting failure: heralding a glorious defeat and mercilessly punishing those responsible for it, in this case Posh Spice's unfortunate fiancé."

Beckham wrote in one of his autobiographies that the abuse continued for years: "Every time I think it has disappeared, I know I will meet some idiot who will have a go at me. Sometimes it is at matches, sometimes just driving down the road." He added that he kept "a little book in which I've written down the names of those people who upset me the most. I don't want to name them because I want it to be a surprise when I get them back." One day they will all get upset stomachs.

Often the scapegoat is a management figure: Wright as captain in 1950, Joe Mears as chief selector in 1958, and many managers since. Sometimes it is a keeper, who by virtue of his position just stood around in goal rather than battling like a hero. Bonetti spent the rest of his career enduring chants of "You lost the World Cup." After retiring from soccer, he went into quasi exile as a mailman on a remote Scottish island.

In 2006 Cristiano Ronaldo was anointed scapegoat. Only after a defeat to Brazil is no scapegoat sought, because defeats to Brazil are considered acceptable.

PHASE 8: ENGLAND ENTERS THE NEXT WORLD CUP THINKING IT WILL WIN IT

That's what we wrote in 2009. We are not usually this prescient. If we predicted England's experience in South Africa in 2010 precisely, it's only because over the decades the route map of England's eliminations had become perfectly clear.

In phase one of our sequence, England flew to South Africa expecting to win the World Cup. That expectation wasn't particularly ludicrous: Fabio Capello's team had qualified with more dash than ever before, winning nine out of ten qualifying games.

Phase two was, "During the Tournament England Meets a Former Wartime Enemy." Following the 4–1 thumping by the Germans in Bloemfontein, England has now exited against Germany or Argentina in six of its last eight World Cups.

We called phase three "The English Conclude That the Game Turned on One Freakish Piece of Bad Luck That Could Happen Only to Them."

In 2010 this was of course Frank Lampard's shot that bounced inside the German goal without the referee noticing. As Lampard himself had lamented after England's previous elimination, in 2006, "It seems to be the English way to lose in bizarre circumstances but it wears you down. It gets to the point where you want to tell Lady Luck to f*** off and take her bad sister with her."

Phase four is "Morever, Everyone Else Cheated." FIFA should have been using goal-line technology, and the German keeper should have fessed up that Lampard had scored.

In phase five, "England Is Knocked Out Without Getting Anywhere Near Lifting the Cup." Had the English somehow beaten Germany, instead of losing by three goals, they would have then needed to beat Argentina, Spain, and Holland.

In phase six, normal life resumed the day after elimination. Riots broke out in English cities in the summer of 2011, not the summer of 2010.

In phase seven, the manager Capello was chosen as the nation's scapegoat. The Italian had raised English hopes by making his players look like world-beaters for two years, before finally pulling off the mask in South Africa to reveal them as the usual losers. Furthermore, as a foreigner he made a perfect scapegoat.

The World Cup as ritual has a meaning beyond soccer. The elimination is usually the most-watched British television program of the year. It therefore educates the English in two contradictory narratives about their country: one, that England has a manifest destiny to triumph, and, two, that it never does. The genius of the song "Three Lions," English soccer's unofficial anthem, is that it combines both narratives: "Thirty years of hurt / Never stopped me dreaming."

There is an alternative universe in which Beckham didn't get sent off, Banks's stomach held up, Lampard's goal counted, and so on. In that universe England has won about seven World Cups. Many English people think they would have preferred that. But it would have deprived the nation of a ritual that marks the passing of time much like Christmas or New Year's and celebrates a certain idea of England: a land of unlucky heroes that no longer rules the world, although it should.

Yet with that failure in 2010, something changed. To adapt T. S. Eliot, humankind can only take so much reality. England's umpteenth disappointment seems to have finally convinced the nation's fans and media to shed the fantasy of manifest destiny. When the understated Roy Hodgson replaced Capello as manager in 2012, he seemed intent on reducing expectations from low to zero. "It's difficult to say what would constitute 'success' at Euro 2012," he mused at his first press conference. "I'd like people to cut us a bit of slack." People did. When his team lost the European quarterfinal on penalties to a former wartime enemy, Italy, nobody was very surprised.

Finally, the English have become realistic. Perhaps helped by a general decline in national status, they are beginning to realize they are just another country, without any manifest destiny to triumph.

A PERFECTLY DECENT TEAM

Any mathematician would say it's absurd to expect England to win the World Cup.

England wins just over two-thirds of its matches. To be precise, from 1990 to 2010 (counting from the end of the 1990 World Cup to the end of the 2010 World Cup) England played 224, won 122, tied 57, and lost 45. If we treat a tie as half a win, this translates into a winning percentage of 67.2 percent. If we then break this down into five four-year World Cup cycles England's winning percentage has ranged between 65 and 76, except for the 1998–2002 cycle, when it slumped to 60 percent. In other words, its performance for most of recent history has been very constant.

Yes, these statistics conceal some ghastly mishaps as well as some highs, but the statistics tell us that the difference between anguish and euphoria is a few percentage points.

On the face of it, winning two-thirds of the time—meaning bookies' odds of 1–2 on—is not too shabby in a two-horse race. Of course, some countries do even better. Brazil's winning percentage is nearly 75 percent. But against most teams, England is the deserved favorite. In the 1990–2010 period, England's win percentage was ninth best in the world.

The problem comes when we try to translate this achievement into winning tournaments. England's failure to win anything since the holy year of 1966 is a cause of much embarrassment for British expatriates in bars on the Spanish coast.

It is tricky to calculate the exact probability of England qualifying for a tournament, because it requires an analysis of many permutations of events. However, we can reduce it to a simple problem of multiplicative probability if we adopt the "must-win" concept. For example, England failed to qualify for Euro 2008 by coming in third in its group behind Croatia and Russia. In doing so it won seven matches, lost three, and tied twice (for an average winning percentage of exactly 66.66 percent). It was narrowly beaten by Russia, which won seven, lost two, and tied three times (a winning percentage of 70.83 percent).

Suppose that to guarantee qualification you have to win eight games outright. Then the problem becomes one when you have to win eight out of twelve, where your winning probability in each game is 66 percent. Calculating this probability is a bit more complicated, since it involves combinatorics.

The answer is a probability of qualification of 63 percent. That means that England should qualify for fewer than two-thirds of the tournaments it enters. In fact, from 1970 through 2014 England qualified just over 70 percent of the time: for eight out of eleven World Cups and seven out of ten European championships. Given that the number of qualifying matches has risen over time, England's performance is somewhat better than you might expect.

The sad fact is that England is a good team that does better than most. This means it is not likely to win many tournaments, and it doesn't. When we first published this book, we called the British edition *Why England Lose*. Going into the 2010 World Cup, English people often asked us: "Aren't you worried about your title? What if England win?" We weren't very worried. Later we changed the title anyway, because it turned out (amazingly) that few English people wanted to buy a book called *Why England Lose*.

Until 2010, the English tended to think that England should do better. The team's usual status around the bottom of the world's top ten was not good enough. The national media, in particular, felt almost perpetually let down by the team. England was "known as perennial underachievers on the world stage," according to the tabloid *The Sun*; its history "has been a landscape sculpted from valleys of underachievement," said *The Independent* newspaper; the former England captain Terry Butcher grumbled in the *Sunday Mirror* in 2006 that "historical underachievement has somehow conspired to make England feel even more important."

"Why does England lose?" is perhaps the greatest question in English sports. In trying to answer it, we hear strange echoes from the field of development economics. The central question in that field is, "Why are some countries less productive than others?" The two main reasons England loses would sound familiar to any development economist. So would the most common reason falsely cited for why England loses. Here are those three reasons for England's eliminations—first the false one, then the correct ones.

BRITISH JOBS FOR BRITISH WORKERS? WHY THERE ARE TOO MANY ENGLISHMEN IN THE PREMIER LEAGUE

When pundits gather to explain why England loses, their favorite scapegoat of the last few years is imports: the hundreds of foreigners who play in the Premier League. Here is England's midfielder Steven Gerrard speaking before England lost at home to Croatia and failed to qualify for Euro 2008: "I think there is a risk of too many foreign players coming over, which would affect our national team eventually if it's not already. It is important we keep producing players."

After all, if our boys can barely even get a game in their own league, how can they hope to mature into internationals? After England's defeat to Croatia, FIFA's president, Sepp Blatter, Manchester United's manager, Alex Ferguson, and UEFA's president, Michel Platini, all made versions of Gerrard's argument. In 2013 Greg Dyke, the new chairman of England's Football Association, warned: "In the future it's quite possible we won't have enough players qualified to play for England who are playing regularly at the highest level in this country or elsewhere in the world. As a result, it could well mean England's teams are unable to compete seriously on the world stage."

These men are effectively blaming imports for the English lack of skills. The reasoning is that our own workers don't get a chance because they are being displaced by foreign workers. Exactly the same argument is often made in development economics. Why are some countries not very productive? Partly because their inhabitants don't have enough skills. The best place to learn skills—such as making toothpaste, or teaching math, or playing soccer—is on the job. To learn how to make toothpaste, you have to actually make it, not just take a class to learn how to make it. But if you are always importing toothpaste, you will never learn.

That is why, for more than half a century, many development economists have called for "import substitution." Ban or tax certain imports so that the country can learn to make the stuff itself. Import substitution has worked for a few countries. Japan after the war, for instance, managed to teach itself from scratch how to make all sorts of high-quality cars and electrical gadgets.

The idea of import substitution in the Premier League has an emotional appeal to many English fans. Britons often complain about feeling overrun by immigrants, and few spots in the country are more foreign than a Premier League field on match day. Some clubs have wisely dispensed with Englishmen almost altogether. All told, Englishmen accounted for only 37 percent of the minutes played by individual players in the Premier League in the 2007–2008 season before Croatia's night at Wembley. By the 2012–2013 season, only 32 percent of starters in the league were English. To some degree, English soccer no longer exists.

"It is my philosophy to protect the identity of the clubs and country," Platini has said. "Manchester United against Liverpool should be with players from Manchester and Liverpool, from that region. Robbie Fowler was from Liverpool. He grew up in that city, it was nice, but now you don't have the English players."

Imagine for a moment that Platini somehow managed to suspend EU law and force English soccer clubs to discriminate against players from other EU countries. If that happened, Platini and Gerrard would probably end up disappointed. If inferior English players were handed places in Premier League teams, they would have little incentive to improve. This is a classic problem with import substitution: it protects bad producers.

What then tends to happen is that short-term protection becomes long-term protection.

But, in fact, Platini's entire premise is wrong. If people in soccer understood numbers better, they would grasp that the problem of the England team is not that there are too few Englishmen playing in the Premier League. To the contrary: there are too many. England would do better if the country's best clubs fielded even fewer English players.

You could argue that English players account for "only" 32 percent of starting players in the Premier League. Or you could argue that they account for a massive 32 percent of starting players, more than any other nationality in what is now the world's toughest league. The Dutch, Portuguese and Uruguayans dream of accounting for 32 percent of starters in the Premier League, or indeed in any big league. The English have about sixty-five to seventy players starting regularly in the world's toughest league. That should be enough to make up a decent squad of twenty-two.

In other words, English players get a lot of regular experience in top-level club soccer. Even if we lump together the world's three toughest leagues—the Premier League, Spain's Primera División, and Germany's Bundesliga—then only Germans and Spaniards play more tough club soccer. But certainly English players get far more experience in top-level soccer than, say, Croatians or Russians do.

The experience of competing against the best foreign players every week has probably helped English internationals to improve. Englishmen have had to get better just to stay in their club teams. They now learn about international soccer every week.

Indeed, since the Premier League has become more international, England's performances have improved. The switch from a mostly British league to a mostly foreign one can be dated to 1995, the year of the "Bosman ruling" that allowed European players to play anywhere in Europe. Let's compare England's performances in the era of a British league, from 1968 through 1992, to its performances since 1998. (We have consciously excluded the World Cup of 1966, which was an anomalous event given that England were playing at home.) In that first "British" period through 1992, England reached one World Cup semifinal, in 1990. However, that was an exception. In those years, England reached the quarterfinals of major tournaments only four times in thirteen attempts. By contrast, in the "international" period since 1998, it has reached four quarterfinals in just eight attempts. Moreover, its win percentage at major tournaments jumped from 52 percent in 1968–1992 to 62 percent in the "international" period (counting a tie as worth half a win). The figures suggest that if anything, the international league has been good for the England team.

In fact, you could argue that in recent years, as the Premier League has gotten ever stronger, England's players have been playing too much rather than too little top-class international club soccer. The Premier League is becoming soccer's NBA, the first global league in this sport's history. So the players earn millions of dollars. So the league is all-consuming, particularly if you play for one of the big clubs, as almost all regular English internationals do. The players have to give almost all their energy and concentration in every match. It's a little easier even in the German or Spanish leagues, where smaller teams like Mainz or Osasuna cannot afford to buy brilliant foreigners.

Clearly an athlete can't peak in every match. If you are running in the Olympics, you plan your season so that you will peak only at the Olympics, and not before. If you play soccer for, say, Croatia and for a club in a smaller league (even in Serie A), you can husband your energy so as to peak in big international matches—for instance, when you are playing England at Wembley.

By contrast, English players have to try to peak every week for their clubs. In no other country do players face as many demanding games a season. No clubs in any other country play as many European games as the English do. Daniele Tognaccini, longtime chief athletics coach at AC Milan's "Milan Lab," probably the most sophisticated medical outfit in soccer, explains what happens when a player has to play sixty tough games a year: "The performance is not optimal. The risk of injury is very high. We can say the risk of injury during one game, after one week's training, is 10 percent. If you play after two days, the risk rises by 30 or 40 percent. If you are playing four or five games consecutively without the right recovery, the risk of injury is incredible. The probability of having one lesser performance is very high."

So when English players play internationally, they start tired, hurt, and without enough focus. Often they cannot raise their game. Harry Redknapp said when he was manager of Portsmouth, "I think England games get in the way of club soccer for the players now. Club soccer is so important, the Champions League and everything with it, that England games become a distraction to them." Moreover, players in the intense Premier League are always getting injured, and their clubs don't give them time to recover. That may be why half of England's regulars couldn't play against Croatia, and why Wayne Rooney played two successive World Cups while half-fit. For some of the same reasons, the US often disappoints in basketball world championships.

In short, if England wanted to do better in international matches, it should export English players to more relaxed leagues, like, for example, Croatia's. Indeed, if more young English players spent some learning years abroad, they would probably absorb more international knowledge.

England's former manager Eriksson understood the problem of English exhaustion. When one of the authors of this book asked him why England lost in the quarterfinals in the World Cup of 2002 and in Euro 2004, he said his players were tired after tough seasons. Was that really the only reason? "I would say so," Eriksson replied. "If you're not fit enough . . . In Japan, we never scored one goal the second half."

Ashley Cole, reflecting on the World Cup of 2006, notices the same phenomenon but cannot explain it: "We had to be honest . . . and recognize something was amiss in the second halves. We just didn't know what." However, some of his smarter teammates did seem to know. Here is Lampard looking back on 2006:

> Throughout the tournament we had suffered in the heat. Our second-half performances were invariably below the standard of the first period and at its worst—against Paraguay in Frankfurt—most of us could barely walk, never mind run, in the latter stages of the match.

This echoes Gerrard's account of the previous tournament: "The truth was that England were knackered at Euro 2004. . . . A long, hard season took a terrible toll." In 2010 in South Africa, too, England never scored in the second half. Capello later told the FIFA website why he thought England didn't win summer tournaments: "They're the least fresh of any of the competing national sides, because their league doesn't have a break. It's like when you're driving a car: if you stop halfway to put fuel in then you'll definitely get where you want to go, but if you don't there's always the chance you'll be running on empty before you reach your goal. In my opinion the soccer played in the first half of the English season is much better than in the second half."

It is possible to dismiss all these claims of tiredness as self-serving. But if there has to be a single culprit for England's summer failures, we suspect it's more likely to be fatigue than the foreign influx.

In any case, English fans want to see teams full of foreign players. Platini wonders whether Liverpudlians can identify with a Liverpool team full of foreigners. Well, they seem to manage. Judging by the Premiership's record crowds despite its record ticket prices, fans still identify enough. England can have an excellent league, or it can have an English league, but it can't have both. Given the choice, fans seem to prefer excellence. In that sense, they are typical consumers. If you try to substitute imports, then, at least at first, consumers have to put up with worse products. They generally don't like that.

THE PROBLEM OF EXCLUSION: HOW ENGLISH SOCCER DRIVES OUT THE MIDDLE CLASSES

The Romans built their empire with an army drawn from every part of society. Only when the militia became an elite profession open just to particular families did the empire start to decline. When you limit your talent pool, you limit the development of skills. The bigger the group of people you draw from, the more new ideas that are likely to bubble up. That's why large networks like the City of London and Silicon Valley, which draw talent from around the world, are so creative. So is the Premier League.

The problem of English soccer is what happens before the best English players reach the Premier League. The Englishmen who make it to the top are drawn very largely from one single and shrinking social group:

the traditional working class. The country's middle classes are mostly barred from professional soccer. That holds back the national team.

There are many ways to classify which social class someone was born into, but one good indicator is the profession of that person's father. Joe Boyle, with some help from Dan Kuper, researched for us the jobs of the fathers of England players at the World Cups of 1998, 2002, and 2006. Boyle ignored jobs the fathers might have been handed after their sons' rise to stardom. As much as possible, he tried to establish what the father did while the son was growing up. Using players' autobiographies and newspaper profiles, he came up with the list below. It doesn't include every player (asked, for instance, what Wayne Bridge's dad did for a living, we throw up our hands in despair), but most are here. Another caveat: some of the dads on the list were absent while their boys were growing up. That said, their professions are shown in Figure 16.1 on the following page.

Many of these job descriptions are imprecise. What exactly did Rob Lee's dad do at the shipping company, for instance? Still, it's possible to break down the list of thirty-four players into a few categories. Eighteen players, or more than half the total, were sons of skilled or unskilled manual laborers: Vassell, Terry, Shearer, Seaman, Scholes, Rooney, Merson, McManaman, Ince, Heskey, Gerrard, Fowler, Adams, Batty, Beckham, Campbell, Ferdinand, and Downing. Ashley Cole with his "working-class upbringing" by a single mother is probably best assigned to this category, too. Four players (Jenas, Lampard, Mills, and Owen) had fathers who worked in soccer. Le Saux and Joe Cole were both sons of fruit and vegetable traders. Anderton's dad ran a moving company, which seems to have failed, before becoming a cab driver. Sheringham's father was a policeman. Carragher's and Dyer's dads ran a pub and a social club, respectively. That leaves only five players out of thirty-four—Crouch, James, Lee, Southgate, and Walcott—whose fathers seem to have worked in professions that required them to have had an education beyond the age of sixteen. If we define class by education, then only 15 percent of England players of recent years had "middle-class" origins.

The male population as a whole was much better educated. Of British men between ages thirty-five and fifty-four in 1996—the generation

FIGURE 16.1. **Employment of World Cup fathers**

Player	*Father's job*
Tony Adams	Roofer
Darren Anderton	Ran moving company; later a taxi driver
David Batty	Sanitation worker
David Beckham	Heating engineer
Sol Campbell	Railway worker
Jamie Carragher	Pub landlord
Ashley Cole	None given, but in his autobiography describes "a grounded working-class upbringing in east London"
Joe Cole	Fruit and vegetable trader
Peter Crouch	Creative director at international advertising agency
Stewart Downing	Painter and decorator on oil rigs
Kieron Dyer	Manager of Caribbean social club
Rio Ferdinand	Tailor
Robbie Fowler	Laborer; later worked night shift at railway maintenance depot
Steven Gerrard	Laborer (bricklaying, paving, and so on)
Emile Heskey	Security worker at nightclub
Paul Ince	Railway worker
David James	Artist who runs gallery in Jamaica
Jermaine Jenas	Soccer coach in the United States
Frank Lampard	Soccer player
Rob Lee	"Involved in a shipping company"
Graeme Le Saux	Ran fruit and vegetable stall
Steve McManaman	Printer
Paul Merson	Coal worker
Danny Mills	Coach in Norwich City's youth academy
Michael Owen	Soccer player
Wayne Rooney	Laborer, mainly on building sites; often unemployed
Paul Scholes	Gas-pipe fitter
David Seaman	Garage mechanic; later ran sandwich shop, then worked at steelworks
Alan Shearer	Sheet-metal worker
Teddy Sheringham	Policeman
Gareth Southgate	Worked for IBM
John Terry	Forklift-truck operator
Darius Vassell	Factory worker
Theo Walcott	Royal Air Force administrator; later joined services company working for British Gas

of most of these players' fathers—a little more than half had qualifications above the most basic level, according to the British Household Panel Study.

English soccer's reliance on an overwhelmingly working-class talent pool was only moderately damaging in the past, when most English people were working class. In the late 1980s, 70 percent of Britons still left school at the age of sixteen, often for manual jobs. But by then the growth of the middle class had already begun. In fact, middle-class values began to permeate the country, a process that sociologists call "embourgeoisement." It happened on what used to be the soccer terraces, which because of high ticket prices are now slightly more middle class than even the country at large.

Nowadays, more than 70 percent of Britons stay in school past the age of sixteen. More than 40 percent enter higher education. More and more, Britain is a middle-class nation. Yet because soccer still recruits overwhelmingly from the traditional working classes, it excludes an ever-growing swath of the population. That must be a brake on the England team.

The shrinking of the talent pool is only part of the problem. Until at least the late 1990s British soccer was suffused, without quite knowing it, by British working-class habits. Some of these were damaging, such as the sausages-and-chips diet, or the idea that binge drinking is a hobby. "Maybe in earlier generations the drinking culture carried over from the working-class origins of the players," wrote Alex Ferguson in his 1999 autobiography. "Most of them came from families where many of the men took the view that if they put in a hard shift in a factory or a coalmine they were entitled to relax with a few pints. Some footballers seem determined to cling to that shift-worker's mentality. . . . Also prevalent is the notion that Saturday night is the end of the working week and therefore a good time to get wrecked." Of course, "problem drinking" exists in the British middle classes, too. Equally of course, most working-class people have no issues with alcohol. However, Ferguson is explicitly describing a traditional working-class attitude.

Another problem was that the British working classes tended to regard soccer as something you learned on the job, rather than from educationalists with diplomas. It was the attitude you would expect of an industry in which few people had much formal education. The late Ernie Walker, longtime secretary of the Scottish Football Association, who worked for decades to introduce coaching courses in Scotland, told us that clubs mocked his attempts as "some newfangled thing got up by college boys—as if there was shame in being educated." He recalls that *coaching* and *tactics* became "shame words." "People would say, 'The trouble with soccer today is that there is too much coaching.' That's like saying, 'The trouble with school is that there's too much education.'"

It would be crazy to generalize too much about the working classes. There is a strong working-class tradition of self-education. Large numbers of postwar Britons became the first people in their families to go to college. Nonetheless, the anti-intellectual attitudes that Walker encountered do seem to be widespread in the British game.

These attitudes may help explain why English managers and English players are not known for thinking about soccer. When the Dutchman Johan Cruijff said, "Soccer is a game you play with your head," he wasn't talking about headers.

Over the past fifteen years these traditional working-class attitudes have begun to fade in British soccer. Foreign managers and players have arrived, importing the revolutionary notions that professional athletes should think about their game and look after their bodies. Andy Carroll's drinking now marks him out as an exception in the higher reaches of the English game. But one working-class custom still bars middle-class Britons from professional soccer: what you might call the "antieducational requirement."

Most British soccer players still leave school at sixteen. The belief persists that only thus can they concentrate fully on the game. The argument that many great foreign players—Ruud Gullit, Dennis Bergkamp, Tostao, Socrates, Osvaldo Ardiles, Jorge Valdano, Slaven Bilic, Josep Guardiola, Andres Iniesta, Fernando Redondo, Kaká, and others—stayed in school after sixteen, or even attended college, is ignored. This is probably because many British coaches and players are suspicious of educated people.

It is true that the clubs' new academies are meant to help players keep studying, but in practice this rarely happens. A few years ago one of us visited the academy of an English club. It's an academy of some note: two of its recent graduates first played for their countries while still teenagers. But all the boys we met there, bright or otherwise, were sent to do the same single lowly vocational course in leisure and tourism to fulfill the academy's minimum educational requirements. Together the boys caused such havoc in class that all the other students had dropped out of the course. It's not that soccer players are too busy to study; they rarely train more than a couple of hours a day. Rather, it's that being studious is frowned upon.

English soccer consequently remains unwelcoming to middle-class teenagers. For instance, Stuart Ford, who at seventeen played for England Schools, gave up on becoming a professional because he got tired of listening to rants from uneducated coaches. Being middle class, he always felt like an outsider. He recalled, "I was often goaded about my posh school or my gross misunderstanding of street fashion. That was just from the management." Instead he became a Hollywood lawyer. Later, as a senior executive at a Hollywood studio, he was one of the people behind an unsuccessful bid to buy Liverpool FC.

Or there was the youth trainee at Oldham Athletic, whose teammates hounded him as an intellectual snob after he walked into the club one day carrying a copy of the midmarket newspaper the *Daily Mail.* He told us years later, "Aside from the clubwide piss-taking, I had Deep Heat rubbed into the lining of my slips. I took so much verbal (and physical) abuse that month that I often wonder what would have happened had it been the *Financial Times.*" This man, incidentally, studied for that same vocational course in leisure and tourism with several future Premier League players.

One of the few remotely middle-class Englishmen to have made the national team in recent decades is Graeme Le Saux. He has a middle-class accent, reads the upmarket *Guardian* newspaper, and when he joined Chelsea, looked forward to exploring London's galleries and museums. Naturally, throughout his career in soccer Le Saux was abused by his fellow professionals. So far, so typical. What's curious is the particular slant the abuse took. The heterosexual Le Saux was branded "gay." Liverpool's Robbie Fowler once pretended to offer him his bottom on the field during a game. Le Saux has said that during another match, the great metrosexual David Beckham called him a "poof" (derogatory British slang for gay), though a spokesman for Beckham denied the allegation. Non-Britons may struggle to interpret these subtle cultural markers, but the point to grasp is that in the complicated British class debate, "gay" can be a synonym for "middle class" (and not in a good way).

Some of the more educated foreign players in the Premier League must view these goings-on with dismay. As they have no assigned place in the British class system, they have a touch more freedom to be intellectual. However, Erik Thorstvedt, Tottenham's Norwegian goalkeeper of the 1990s, does recall bread rolls being chucked at his head when he opened a broadsheet newspaper on the team bus.

If the British working classes get little education, that is mainly the fault of the middle-class people who oversee the UK's school system. Nonetheless, the educational divide means that any middle-class person entering British soccer feels instantly out of place.

Many middle-class athletes drift to cricket or rugby instead. Often, this represents a direct loss to soccer. For most people, sporting talent is fairly transferable until they reach their late teens. Many English soccer players, like Gary Neville and Gary Lineker, were gifted cricketers, too. Some well-known rugby players took up rugby only as teenagers, when they realized they weren't going to make it in soccer. And in the past, several paragons represented England in more than one sport. Only a few sports demand very specific qualities that can't be transferred: it's hard to go from being a jockey to being a basketball player, for instance. But English soccer competes with other ball games for talent, and it scares away the educated middle classes.

This is particularly sad because there is growing evidence that sporting talent and academic talent are linked. The best athletes have fast mental reactions, and those reactions, if properly trained, would make for high-caliber intellects.

Interestingly, some people inside English soccer have become aware of the game's class discrimination. Daniel Hargreaves, who works for Everton's academy with the remit to make sure its decisions are evidence-based (the sort of job that didn't exist in English soccer a few years ago), has spotted the club's tendency to scout mainly in working-class neighborhoods. "Traditionally we have core areas where we think we find players," he says. "But there's a growing middle-class, there are more green spaces in the middle-class areas." Has Everton operated an unintentional bias against the middle classes? "I think evidence would suggest that's the case."

But for now, this class bias helps explain why even though the academies of English clubs are the richest in the world, England doesn't produce better players than poor nations. Instead of trying to exclude foreigners from English soccer, it would be smarter to include more middle-class English people. Only when there are England players with educated accents—as happens in Holland, Argentina, and even Brazil (Leonardo, Socrates, and Kaká, for instance)—might the national team maximize its potential.

CLOSED TO INNOVATIONS: ENGLISH SOCCER'S SMALL NETWORK

When the Internet arrived, many pundits predicted the decline of the city. After all, why live in a small apartment in East London when you could set up your laptop in an old farmhouse overlooking a sheep meadow?

The prediction turned out to be wrong. Cities have continued their growth of the past two hundred years, which is why apartments in Brooklyn became so expensive. Meanwhile, the countryside has turned into something of a desert, inhabited by a few farmers and old people and used by the rest of us mostly for hiking. It turns out that people still want to live in dirty, overcrowded, overpriced cities. And the reason they do is the social networks. To be rural is to be isolated. Networks give you contacts.

Someone you meet at a party or at your kids' playground can give you a job or an idea. Just as the brain works by building new connections between huge bundles of neurons, with each connection producing a new thought, so we as individuals need to find ourselves in the center of the bundle to make more connections.

Networks are key to the latest thinking about economic development. Better networks are one reason that some countries are richer than others. As it happens, networks also help explain why some countries have done better at soccer than England. English soccer's biggest problem until very recently was probably geography. The country was too far from the networks of continental western Europe, where the best soccer was played.

Once upon a time, England was at the center of soccer's knowledge network. From the first official soccer international in 1872, until at least the First World War, and perhaps even until England's first home defeat against Hungary in 1953, you could argue that England was the dominant soccer nation. It was the country that exported soccer know-how to the world in the form of managers. The English expatriate manager became such a legendary figure that to this day in Spain and Italy a head coach is known as a "mister."

Many English people clung to the belief in England's supremacy long after it had ceased to be true. The astonishment each time England didn't win the World Cup ended only with the team's abject failures in the 1970s.

The gradual British decline in soccer echoes the decline in Britain's economic status. The country went from supreme economic power under Queen Victoria to having its hand held by the International Monetary Fund in the late 1970s. Admittedly, in soccer as in economics, most observers exaggerated Britain's slide. The country's position in the top ten largest economies was never much in doubt. But in soccer it became clear by 1970 at the latest that dominance had shifted across the Channel to the core of western Europe. For the next forty years, that part of the Continent would be the most fertile network in soccer. And Britain was just outside it.

Western Europe's grip on global soccer probably peaked at the German World Cup of 2006. The region has only about 400 million inhabitants, or 6 percent of the world's population, yet only once in that entire tournament did a western European team lose to a team from another region: Switzerland's insanely dull defeat on penalties to Ukraine, a match that was the nadir of 10,000 years of human civilization.

In 2006 even Brazil couldn't match western Europe. Argentina continued its run of failing to beat a western European team in open play at a World Cup since the final against West Germany in 1986 (though it did win two of the eight subsequent encounters against Europeans on penalties). Big countries outside the region, like Mexico, Japan, the US, and Poland, could not match little western European countries like

Portugal, Holland, or Sweden. If you understood the geographical rule of that World Cup, you could sit in the stands for almost every match before the quarterfinals confident of knowing the outcome.

As we'll discuss in our final chapter, by 2010 the dominance of western Europe was waning slightly. In South Africa, western European countries lost six of their twenty-nine games against teams from other regions. In part, this must have been because the tournament was held outside western Europe. In part, it was because other regions have begun to copy western European methods. Yet even in 2010, first, second, and third place all went to western Europeans.

Western Europe excels at soccer for the same fundamental reason it had the scientific revolution in the sixteenth and seventeenth centuries and was for centuries the world's richest region. The region's secret is what the historian Norman Davies calls its "user-friendly climate." Western Europe is mild and rainy. Because of that, the land is fertile. This allows hundreds of millions of people to inhabit a small space of land. Moreover, as Malise Ruthven, the scholar of Islam, has pointed out, Europe has "a higher ratio of coast to landmass than any other continent or subcontinent, and a coastline some 23,000 miles long—equivalent to the circumference of the globe." No wonder Europeans were the first people to sail the world. Geography has always helped them exchange ideas, inside their continent and beyond. In short, they are networked.

From the World Cup in Germany, you could have flown in two and a half hours to any one of about twenty countries containing roughly 300 million people in total. That is the densest network on earth. There was nothing like that in Japan at the World Cup of 2002: the only foreign capital you can reach from Tokyo within that time is Seoul. South Africa, host in 2010, was even more isolated. And the only foreign capital within two hours flight of Brazil's biggest city, Sao Paulo, is Asunción in Paraguay.

For centuries now, the interconnected peoples of western Europe have exchanged ideas fast. The scientific revolution could happen in western Europe because its scientists were near one another, networking, holding a dialogue in their shared language: Latin. Copernicus, Polish son of a German merchant, wrote that the earth circled the sun. Galileo in Florence read Copernicus and confirmed his findings through a telescope.

The Englishman Francis Bacon described their "scientific method": deductions based on data. England at the time was very much a part of the European network.

A typical product of that network was the lens grinder, a crucial new machine in the development of the microscope in the early 1660s. Robert Hooke in London invented a new grinder, which made lenses so accurate that Hooke could publish a detailed engraving of a louse attached to a human hair. But meanwhile Sir Robert Moray, a Scot in London who knew what Hooke was up to, was sending letters in French about the new grinder to the Dutch scientist Christiaan Huygens. Thanks to Moray, Huygens had previously gotten ahold of details of Hooke's balance-spring watch.

Moray and Huygens "sometimes wrote to each other several times a week," writes the historian Lisa Jardine. Their letters crossed the Channel in days, or about as quickly as mail does now. Meanwhile, the French astronomer Adrien Auzout in Paris was getting copies of some of their letters. So Hooke's breakthroughs were being spread to his European competitors almost instantly.

All this irritated Hooke. But the proximity of many thinkers in western Europe created an intellectual ferment. That is why so many of the great scientific discoveries were made there. These discoveries then helped make the region rich.

Centuries later, soccer spread the same way. In the nineteenth century the game infected western Europe first, because there it had the shortest distances to travel. Later the proximity of so many peoples brought the region two world wars. After 1945, western Europeans decided they could live crammed together only under a sort of single government: the European Union. Borders opened, and the region became the most integrated in the history of the world.

Again the best ideas spread fastest there, just as they had in the scientific revolution. The region's soccer benefited. One of the men who carried tactical ideas around Europe was Arrigo Sacchi. His father was a shoe manufacturer in Ravenna, Italy, and the young Sacchi used to accompany him on business trips. He saw a lot of games in Germany, Switzerland, France, and the Netherlands. "It opened my mind," he later said. As manager of AC Milan in the 1980s, he imported a version of Dutch soccer that revolutionized the Italian game.

Another great European networker was Arsène Wenger. While growing up in a village in the French Alsace, near the German border, he used to watch the legendary German soccer program *Die Sportschau* on Saturday afternoons. He became a fan of Borussia Mönchengladbach, and generally absorbed German soccer. Later Wenger took a French coaching course and came to admire Dutch "total football." The point is that he was taking in influences from all the countries around him. It was easy because they were so close.

Ideas spread even more quickly in European soccer than in other economic sectors, because soccer is the most integrated part of the Continent's economy. Only about 2 percent of all western Europeans live in a different European Union country, because few companies bother hiring bus drivers or office administrators from neighboring countries. In some professions, language barriers stop workers from moving abroad. But many soccer players do find work abroad, largely because television advertises their wares to employers across Europe. And so most of the EU's best players have gathered in the English and Spanish leagues or at Bayern Munich, and meet one another on weekday nights in the Champions League. This competition is the European single market come to life, a dense network of talent. There's always much debate about the superiority of one soccer model over another—the Bundesliga versus the Premier League versus the Spanish league and Italy's Serie A—but the real point is the intensity of competition inside Europe, on the field and in the boardroom. That forces the big clubs constantly to strive for improvements.

The teams in the Champions League can draw talent from anywhere in the world. Nonetheless, an overwhelming majority of their players are western Europeans. With the world's best players and coaches packed together, the world's best soccer is constantly being refined there.

The best soccer today is Champions League soccer, western European soccer. It's a rapid passing game played by athletes. Rarely does anyone dribble, or keep the ball for a second. You pass instantly. It's not the beautiful game—dribbles are prettier—but it works best. All good teams everywhere in the world now play this way. Chris Anderson and David Sally showed in their book *The Numbers Game* how statistically alike the top European leagues are. Whether in the English Premier League, Serie A, the Bundesliga or Spain's premier division, the average team completed similar numbers of passes per game, of similar lengths, and had comparable numbers of shots and corners. In all four leagues, the average game produces somewhere between 2.5 and 3 goals. The differences between these nations "are cosmetic, shallow," the authors conclude. "If it was not for the shirts, you would not be able to tell them apart." All four leagues are producing western European soccer. Even the Brazilians adopted the Champions League style in the 1990s. They still have more skill than the Europeans, but they now try (and often fail) to play at a European pace. Brazil has been losing dominance in soccer even as it gets richer, because it is excluded from the knowledge networks of western Europe. It has struggled to work out that slow dribbling rarely beats fast passing.

Western Europe has discovered the secret of soccer. More precisely, a core group of western European countries has, namely, five of the six nations that in 1957 founded the European Economic Community, ancestor of the European Union. (We'll leave out the sixth founding nation, the hopeless minnow Luxembourg.) Germany, France, Italy, Holland, and even Belgium don't all play in exactly the same style. Holland and Italy, say, are rather different. But they all adhere to the basic tenets of rapid collectivized western European soccer. Here are some results from the period 1968–2006:

- The core five countries won twelve European championships and World Cups between them.
- The countries at the corners of Europe—the Brits, the Iberians, the Balkans, the former Soviet bloc, and Scandinavian nations north of the Baltic Sea—between them won one: Greece's European Championship of 2004, delivered by a German coach.
- Europe's only other trophies in this period went to Denmark and Czechoslovakia. Denmark enjoys an utterly permeable border with the five core countries. Czechoslovakia was the exception, the only eastern European country to win anything in this period.

Countries separated from the core of the EU—either by great distance, by poverty, or by closed borders under dictatorships—often underperform in soccer. In the vast landmass running from Portugal in the southwest to Germany in the northeast, and including Croatia and Bosnia just east of Italy, every country of more than 2 million inhabitants qualified for the World Cup 2014. The nations that didn't make it were on Europe's margins: the Scots, Irish, and Welsh, all the Scandinavians, the Turks, and most of Europe's eastern edge. The countries at great distance—and it can be a distance of the mind rather than geographical distance—are often out of touch with core European soccer. Many countries on the margins have traditionally had dysfunctional indigenous styles of soccer. The Greeks, for instance, dribbled too much. The Brits played mindless kick-and-rush.

Again, this is explained by theories of networks. If you are on the periphery, like the British were until recently in soccer, it's harder to make new connections, because you have to travel farther. Worse, those not on the periphery see you as only a second-best connection. You are the end of the line, not the gateway to a new set of connections. That's why foreign countries stopped hiring English coaches or even English players. As a result, the people on the periphery become more and more isolated and insular. The Ukrainian manager Valeri Lobanovsky was a soccer genius, but during the days of the Soviet Union he was so isolated that when a Dutch journalist came to interview him in the mid-1980s, Lobanovsky pumped him for information about Holland's players. As we'll discuss later in the book, Spain had the same problem under General Franco's dictatorship. "Europe ends at the Pyrenees" was the saying in those days.

Gradually isolation becomes your mind-set: after a while you don't even *want* to adopt foreign ideas anymore. Anyone who has spent time in England—particularly before 1992—has witnessed this attitude. Isolation can lead you into your own blind alleys that nobody else appreciates. For instance, the long refusal of English players to dive may have been an admirable cultural norm, but they might have won more games if they had learned from continental Europeans how to buy the odd penalty.

Happily, the era of British isolationism is now over. This era began on Sunday, September 3, 1939, when the country's borders closed on the outbreak of the Second World War. In soccer, that isolation deepened when English clubs were banned from European competitions after the Heysel disaster of 1985. They lost what modest network they had.

But between 1990 and 1994, British isolation began to break down: English clubs were readmitted to European competitions, new laws enforced free movement of labor and capital within the EU, and Eurostar trains and budget airlines connected Britain to the Continent. London turned into a global city. English became the global language. Nowadays southern England, at least, belongs to core Europe, just as it did during the scientific revolution.

The end of isolationism meant, for a while, the end of English soccer managers managing England or the best English clubs. You wouldn't appoint a Frenchman to manage your baseball team, because the French don't have a history of thinking hard about baseball. And you wouldn't appoint an Englishman to manage your soccer team, because the English don't have a history of thinking hard about soccer. After repeated failures with the traditional British style of kick-and-rush, the English embraced European soccer. England hired a Swedish manager with long experience in Italian soccer, Sven Goran Eriksson.

At this, the conservative *Daily Mail* newspaper lamented, "The mother country of soccer, birthplace of the greatest game, has finally gone from the cradle to the shame." It was a wonderful statement of "English exceptionalism": the belief that England is an exceptional soccer country that should rule the world playing the English way. However, the obvious statistical truth is that England is not exceptional. It is typical of the second-tier soccer countries outside the core of western Europe.

The numbers strongly suggest that England needed foreign knowledge. From 1990 through 2011 England had two foreign managers and seven English managers, including two caretakers (Howard Wilkinson and Peter Taylor). On every measure the foreigners won hands down:

	Games won	*Win percentage (counting tie as half a win)*	*Qualifications for tournaments*
Foreign managers	62%	73%	5/5
English managers	49%	64%	4/6

Eriksson should be remembered as the great qualifier: for the first time since the 1960s, he ensured that England consistently made it to the major tournaments. But foreign managers have also performed slightly better at the final tournaments themselves: Eriksson and Capello's England teams never lost at the group stages, and reached three quarterfinals and one round of sixteen. By contrast, the English managed one semi (at home at Euro '96), one appearance in the last sixteen, and two exits in the first round.

Quite clearly, foreign managers have overachieved with England. This is not merely because Eriksson and Capello had a "golden generation" of players to work with. Many of the same men who played well for the Swede and the Italian performed abysmally for Steve McClaren and Kevin Keegan. It's painful to imagine how well England might have done if the FA had stopped discriminating against foreigners decades earlier. In the same way, British cycling and cricket have recently become world-class by stealing foreign ideas. In tennis Andy Murray in 2013 became the first male Briton to win Wimbledon since 1936 largely because as a teenager he had taken himself off to an academy in Barcelona. (If only some English soccer players had made the same move.)

When it comes to England's soccer coaches, it may sound odd that a foreign passport can make such a difference. After all, you might think that England's players these days have enough foreign experience of their own. They play with and for and against foreigners at their clubs every week. Michael Owen, the first England international to play his entire professional career after the border-opening Bosman ruling of 1995, told us that he had grown up a "European" rather than a purely English footballer. Surely players like him no longer need foreign managers?

Why they do was best demonstrated that miserable night at Wembley against Croatia in 2007. A team of Englishmen managed by an Englishman played like caricatures of Englishmen. Gerrard in particular was a remarkable sight, charging around in the rain at top pace, hitting impossibly ambitious passes, constantly losing the ball. He played like a headless chicken, or like an English footballer circa 1988.

For Liverpool, Gerrard usually plays like a European sophisticate. He has mastered the international, globalized style of top-class modern football. The problem against Croatia was that there wasn't a foreigner on the field or the bench to check him. When things began going badly, he shed that cosmopolitan skin, returned to childhood, and played like an Englishman of old. He and all the other England players had grown up until about the age of twenty playing an only slightly diluted version of English football. Because of that upbringing, national football cultures continue to exist. That's why England still needs a foreign manager to correct its players' flaws.

Other peripheral countries from Greece to the US have followed the English example, and hired foreign coaches from the core of Europe. Importing know-how turned out to be an excellent remedy for the problem of isolation, which makes it even odder that in 2006 England did an about-face and appointed the Englishman McClaren, who had never even worked abroad. The English Football Association didn't realize that England, as a recovering isolationist, still needed foreign help. Rooney, for one, seems to have known better. Here he is in his autobiography, damning the newly appointed McClaren with faint praise: "But he's a good coach, always smiling. I'm glad he's got the job. I think he was the best Englishman available."

By hiring Fabio Capello to succeed McClaren in 2007, England accepted the need for continental European know-how. Capello was like one of the overpaid consultants so common in development economics, flying in on business class to tell the natives what to do. His job was to teach the English some of the virtues of western European soccer.

To cite just one of those virtues: *a game lasts ninety minutes.* Habitually, English players charge out of the gate, run around like lunatics, and exhaust themselves well before the match is over, even if they aren't hung over.

You see this in England's peculiar scoring record in big tournaments. In every World Cup ever played, most goals were scored in the second halves of matches. That is natural: in the second half players tire, teams start chasing goals, and gaps open up on the field. But England, in its last seven big tournaments since 1998, scored twenty-seven of its forty-three goals in the first halves of matches. The team's record in crucial games is even starker: in the matches in which it was eliminated from tournaments, it scored eight of its nine goals before halftime. In other words, England performs like a cheap battery. This is partly because it plays in such an exhausting league, but also because it doesn't seem to have thought about pacing itself.

Italians know exactly how to measure out the ninety minutes. They take quiet periods, when they sit back and make sure nothing happens, because they know that the best chance of scoring is in the closing minutes, when exhausted opponents will leave holes. That's when you need to be sharpest. In the World Cup of 2006, typically, Italy knocked out Australia and Germany with goals in the final three minutes.

England has already bought Italian know-how. In Hodgson, it deliberately chose a coach who had spent most of his career abroad.

Now all it needs to do is include its own middle classes and stop worrying about foreigners in the Premier League, and it will finally stop underachieving and perform as well as it should. But hang on a moment: Who says England underachieves?

SHOULD DO BETTER: IS ENGLAND WORSE THAN IT OUGHT TO BE?

That England underachieves is usually taken for granted in the British media. After all, the team hasn't won anything since 1966, and sometimes doesn't even qualify for tournaments. Clearly that is not good enough for "the mother country of soccer, birthplace of the greatest game."

But does England really underachieve? Or is it just that the English expect too much of their team? To answer this, we first need to work out how well England should do, *given its resources.*

Before we are accused of looking for excuses, let's consider what is and isn't possible. A five-year-old can't win the hundred-meter finals at the Olympics, and neither can a seventy-year-old. You aren't going to have a career in the NBA if you are only five feet tall, and you'll never ride the winner in the Kentucky Derby if you are six foot eight. It is very unlikely that you will have a career in show jumping if your parents earn less than $40,000 per year, you probably won't win a boxing match if you've never had any training as a boxer, and you won't have a shot at being world chess champion unless you can persuade a team of grand masters to act as your seconds. Genetics are beyond our control; training depends partly on our own effort, but partly on the resources that other people give us.

What is true for the individual is also true for the nation. During his tenure an England soccer manager cannot easily (a) increase the size of the population from which he will have to draw the talent, (b) increase the national income so as to ensure a significant increase in the financial resources devoted to developing soccer, or (c) increase the accumulated experience of the national team by very much. (England played nearly eight hundred games from 1872 through 2000, and currently plays around a dozen games per year, so each extra game doesn't add much to the history.)

Yet in any international match, these three factors—the size of the nation's population, the size of the national income, and the country's experience in international soccer—hugely affect the outcome. It's unfair to expect Jamaica, say, to perform as well as much larger, more experienced, and richer Germany. It is fairer to assess how well each country *should* perform given its experience, income, and population and then measure that expected performance against reality. Countries like Jamaica or Luxembourg will never win a World Cup. The only measure of performance that makes any sense for them is one based on how effectively they use their limited resources. The same exercise makes sense for England, too, if only as a check on tabloid hysteria: Does England really underperform given what it has to work with?

In absolute terms England is about tenth in the world. But we want to know how well it does in relative terms—not relative to the expectations of the media but relative to English resources. Might it be that England in fact *overachieves,* given the country's experience, population, and income?

To work this out, we need to know the soccer results for all the national teams in the world. Luckily, we have them. There are a number of databases of international matches, but one of the best was assembled by Russell Gerrard, a mathematics professor at Cass Business School in London. By day Gerrard worries about mathematical ways to represent the management problems of pension funds. For example, one of his recent papers is snappily titled "Mean-Variance Optimization Problems for the Accumulation Phase in a Defined Benefit Plan." It concerns, among other things, Lévy diffusion financial markets, the Hamilton-Jacobi-Bellman equation, and the Feynman-Kac representation. As you might expect, Gerrard has been meticulous in accumulating the soccer data, which took him seven years of his life. His database runs from 1872 through 2001 and includes 22,130 games. We have now updated it to cover all international games up to 2012.

RUSSELL GERRARD'S BRILLIANT SOCCER DATABASE

Later in the book, we will crunch Gerrard's data to discover which is the best soccer country on earth, and which punches most above its weight. But here, let's limit ourselves to a sneak preview of where England stands.

The distant past is of limited relevance. Let's therefore concentrate on recent history, the five World Cup cycles from 1990 through 2010. This was by no means a golden age for England. The country didn't even qualify for the European Championship of 2008 or the World Cup in 1994, and its best moment in these two decades was the lost semifinal at Euro '96. As we've already seen, England played 224 matches in these twenty years. It won 54 percent of them and tied 25 percent, for a "win percentage" of 67 percent (remember that for these purposes we treat a tie as half a win). That is near the middle of the country's historical range.

We want to see how much of a team's success, match by match, can be explained by population, wealth, and experience. However, win percentage is not the best measure of success, because any two wins are not the same. We all know that a 1–5 away win against a certain someone is not the same as a tame 1–0. Put another way, if England plays Luxembourg and wins only 1–0, it's more likely that the Luxembourgian press will be in ecstasy than the British tabloids.

Instead we chose goal difference as our measure, since for any match we expect that the greater the difference between the two teams' populations, wealth, and experience, the greater will be the disparity in scores. (Of course, a positive goal difference tends to be highly correlated with winning.)

We then analyzed Russell's database of matches using the technique of multiple regression. A reminder: multiple regression is the mathematical formula for finding the closest statistical fit between one thing (in this case success of the national team) and any other collection of things (here experience, population, and income per head). For each international match you simply input the population, income per head, and team experience of the two nations at that date, and in seconds you get a readout telling you how sensitive (on average) the team's performance is to each factor. We will also take into account home advantage for each match.

Collecting the data is usually the toughest part. We have assembled figures for the population, soccer experience, and income per capita of 163 countries. We will unveil our findings about the other 162 countries in the next few chapters. Here, we will focus just on England and its supposed underperformance.

We ran our regression and immediately made several discoveries about international soccer. First, home-field advantage alone is worth a lead of about two-thirds of a goal. Obviously that is nonsense if applied to a single game, but think of it this way: playing at home is like having a goal's head start in two out of every three games. Second, having twice as much international experience as your rival is worth just over half a goal a game. In fact, experience turns out to matter much more than the size of your population, which is why the Swedes and Croats do better in soccer than very large but inexperienced China and India. Having twice your opponent's population is worth only about one-tenth of a goal. Having twice the gross domestic product (GDP) per head is worth about as little. In other words, although being large and rich helps a country win soccer matches, being experienced helps a lot more. That is not good news for the US.

It should be added that our estimates are statistically very reliable. Not only is there not much doubt that these factors matter, but there is little doubt about the size of the effects. It is these effects that make the first rounds of World Cups fairly predictable.

However, much still remains unexplained. Experience, population, and income per capita combined explain only just over a quarter of the variation in goal difference. That is good news: if we could predict outcomes perfectly by just these three factors, there would not be much point in watching World Cups at all. Nonetheless, the fact that these three factors explain so much tells us that, up to a point, soccer is rational and predictable.

For now, we are interested only in England. Are its resources so outstanding that it should do better than merely ranking around tenth in the world?

First let's look at experience. England is one of the most experienced countries in soccer. It played 885 internationals between 1872 and the end of the 2010 World Cup. According to our data, only Sweden played more (923). However, England's much vaunted history is not worth much against the other leading soccer nations, because most of them have now accumulated similar amounts of experience. Brazil, Argentina, and even Hungary had all played more than 800 internationals by 2010. When it comes to our second variable, national income, England scores high, too. It is usually one of the richest of the serious soccer countries. Where England falls short is in size. What often seems to go unnoticed is that England's population of 53 million puts it at a major disadvantage to the countries it likes to measure itself against in soccer. Not only is Germany much bigger, with over 80 million inhabitants, but France has 66 million and Italy 60 million. Among the leading European nations, England is ahead only of Spain (47 million). So in soccer terms, England is an experienced, rich, but medium-sized competitor.

Then we ran the numbers. We calculated that England, given its population, income, and experience, "should" score on average 0.19 goals per game more than its opponents. To get a feel for how this works, consider England's performance at the World Cup of 1998. England played Tunisia, Romania, Colombia, and Argentina, all on neutral ground, so there was no home-field effect. Facing Tunisia in its opening game, England had a population five times larger, a GDP per head four times larger, and two times more international experience than its opponent. That combination gave an expected goal difference of one goal in England's favor. In the event, England won 2–0 and so did better than expected.

Against Romania, England had the advantage of twice the population, five times the income per head, and a bit more experience (other countries have been playing soccer for longer than the English sometimes like to think). All this gave England an expected advantage of about half a goal. England's 2–1 defeat meant that it underperformed by one and a half goals.

Next England played Colombia, with a slight advantage in population, four times the income per head, and double the experience. The package was worth an advantage of almost an entire goal (you start to see how the Tom Thumb World Cup might be organized), but again England overperformed, winning 2–0.

Then came Argentina: as everyone in England knows, the English lost on penalties. Should England have done better? Well, it had a slight advantage in population over Argentina, double the income per head, but barely any more experience. Putting all that together, a fair score would have been a tie, which is exactly what happened after 120 minutes. Pity about the penalties, though.

Our model allows us to reexamine every game ever played. The glorious uncertainty of soccer means that there are many deviations from expectations. However, if we average the difference between expectations and results for each country, we get a picture of whether any national team systematically outperforms or underperforms relative to its resources. Our finding: England in the 1990–2010 period outscored its opponents by 0.87 goals per game. That was 0.68 more than we had predicted based on the country's resources. In short, England was not underperforming at all. Contrary to popular opinion, it was overperforming by two-thirds of a goal per game. It might be argued that England isn't winning the all-important games (perhaps because of tiredness in the final stages of major tournaments), but the fact is that losses are rare events. And as we'll show, England's overperformance has been getting even better in recent years.

As an example of this overachievement, let's take England's encounters with Poland. England played the Poles ten times between 1990 and 2010, winning seven and tying three times, with a goal difference of plus twelve. Over the period England's population was about 25 percent larger than Poland's, its income per head about two and a half times greater, and its international experience about 20 percent more. These should have contributed to a positive goal difference of about one half, one, and one half, respectively, or a total of plus two over the ten games. So England's goal difference of plus twelve was ten goals better than we might have expected. That is not too shabby.

Later in the book we will reveal our global table for relative performance from 1990 through 2010: a ranking of the teams that did best relative to their countries' experience, income, and populations. For now, we'll just say that England came in seventeenth out of 163 countries. This in itself is a large leap forward in recent years. When we did the same calculation in earlier editions of this book, covering the period from 1980 to 2001, England came in only sixty-seventh out of 189 countries. It has risen in the last decade from a group of moderate overachievers, including countries such as Russia, Morocco, Ivory Coast and Mozambique, to a level of overachievement comparable with the likes of Honduras, Croatia, South Korea, and Italy. Like England, all these teams scored about 0.6 to 0.8 goals per game more than they "should" have, given their populations, income, and experience.

However, England doesn't benchmark itself against Honduras or Morocco. It's more interesting to see whether England overperforms "more" than the teams it sees as its rivals: the best countries in the world. Here's a ranking of the game's giants, plus England, based on how many goals per game each scored above expectations in the 1990–2010 period:

	Outperformance (in goals per game)
Brazil	1.486
Spain	1.196
Germany	0.978
Czech Republic	0.954
Argentina	0.949
Netherlands	0.906
Portugal	0.863
France	0.797
England	0.681
Italy	0.605

It turns out that England's overachievement—though large compared with almost all other countries on earth—isn't very good when you class them beside the giants of the game. Still, England overachieved more than Italy, even though the Italians won a World Cup in this period and England didn't.

Our conclusion: England does just fine. The team actually performs better than expected, given what it has to start with. All it needs to bring home some trophies is better timing—it must win fewer friendlies and more World Cup semis—and a few million more inhabitants. Consider the England-Germany semifinal at Euro '96. Both countries had similar levels of experience, and by 1996 Germany's lead over Britain in income per capita had slipped to only about 10 percent. However, according to our analysis, England's home advantage (worth just under half a goal in a game between Europeans) was largely wiped out by Germany's much larger population. That made the expected goal difference only 0.49 in favor of the English home team, not far short of the tie that materialized in open play. In the end Gareth Southgate missed his penalty in the shootout, and England lost.

Overall in the 1990–2010 period, England played Germany nine times. England won three, and lost six (once on penalties). Its goal difference over the nine games was minus one. Given Germany's slight lead in GDP per head in these years, but particularly given England's shortage of people, that is almost exactly the goal difference we would have predicted. The "thirty years of hurt" shouldn't be a mystery. England simply should not expect to be world-beaters. As so often, Jamie Carragher in his autobiography gets it right:

> The psychology of our international game is wrong. England ought to be embracing the idea of being the underdog on the world stage. . . . We should be reveling in the image of the plucky outsider trying to unbalance the superpowers of Argentina and Brazil, while matching the French, Germans and Italians.

Still, it is true that over its history, England could have gotten luckier. A better penalty here, a stronger goalkeeper's stomach there, Darren Anderton's shot rolling home in extra time against Germany at Euro '96 instead of hitting the post, and it all could have been different. What we see here is partly the enormous role of luck in history. We tend to think with hindsight that a team that did well in a particular tournament was somehow always going to do well and a team that lost was doomed to do so. The winner's victory comes to seem inevitable. This is a common flaw in the writing of any kind of history.

In fact, though, inevitable victories hardly ever happen in soccer tournaments. Perhaps the only recent case was Brazil at the World Cup of 2002. Just how dominant the country was dawned on a leading European club manager a few months after the final. This manager was trying to sign Brazil's goalkeeper, Marcos. After all, Marcos was a world champion. Marcos visited the club and did some physical tests, in which he didn't perform particularly well. Never mind, thought the manager, the guy won the World Cup. So he offered Marcos a contract. At two o'clock the next morning, the manager was awakened at home by a phone call. It was Marcos's agent.

The agent said, "I'm sorry, but Marcos won't sign for you."

The sleepy manager said, "All right, but why not?"

Then the agent confessed. A couple of years before the World Cup, Marcos had broken his wrist. It had never healed properly. But his old club manager, Luiz Felipe Scolari, became manager of Brazil and put Marcos on the team. Suddenly Marcos was going to a World Cup. Every day at the tournament, the agent explained, Marcos was in pain. He could barely even train. In matches he could barely catch a ball. Every day Marcos told himself, "I really must tell Scolari about my wrist." But he could never quite bring himself to. So he went on, day after day, until he found that he had won the World Cup. Brazil was so superior that it won the World Cup with a crocked goalkeeper.

However, such dominance is very rare. Normally, the differences between teams in the final stages of a World Cup are tiny. The difference between an England team being considered legendary or a failure is two to three games, each generally decided by a single goal, over two years. After all, the difference between making a World Cup and spending the summer on the beach can be just a point. Sometimes it's a point that you lost by hitting the post. Sometimes it's a point garnered by a rival in a match you didn't even play in.

Once you're at the World Cup, the difference between going home ignominiously in the first round and making the semifinals is often a matter of a few inches here or there on a couple of shots. The greatest prize in the sport hinges on a very few moments. Jonathan Wilson puts it well in his *Anatomy of England*: "One moment can shape a game, and one game can shape a tournament, and one tournament can shape a career. Football is not always fair." Wilson points out "one of the major problems of international football: that there is so little of it huge conclusions are drawn from individual games." As Arsène Wenger has noted, European championships are over in three weeks, and any team in a league can be top of the table after three weeks.

In those short tournaments, England have probably been unluckier than most. Over lunch in London in October 2013, the FA's chairman Greg Dyke, who has spent a lot of time asking people in the game why England lose, told us: "There's another argument. The guy who owns Brentford [the small London club that Dyke supports] is Matthew Benham, right? He's very rich. He's made all his money gambling on football. He employs top-quality graduates, maths graduates. All they do is study football around the world. He does everything on statistics. Everything is on probabilities. He says, the single biggest factor why England haven't done well is because they've been unlucky."

Luck is particularly important in World Cups, we interjected.

"And also," said Dyke, "the number of times you're knocked out on penalties."

Of the ten tournaments for which England have qualified since 1990, they have exited six on penalties.

Dyke continued: "He [Benham] says you can alter the chances of winning or losing on penalties, but not by a lot. So if the luck had gone the other way, his argument is that we'd have won one or two of those and we wouldn't be sitting here having this conversation."

Yet there we were, having this conversation.

There is a similar issue with luck in Major League Baseball, notes Michael Lewis in *Moneyball*: "The season ends in a giant crapshoot. The playoffs frustrate rational management because, unlike the long regular season, they suffer from the sample size problem." Lewis means that because there are so few games in the playoffs—because the "sample size" is so small—random factors play an outsize role in determining the winner.

Most soccer fans understand that luck matters, even if they construct a post-fact story about the tournament that makes either victory or humiliation seem fated from the start. But our data point to an even scarier truth than the existence of fluke: namely, there is barely any difference between "brilliant" and "terrible" England teams. It looks suspiciously as if England for most of its modern history—at least before Capello arrived—has been more or less equally good.

This may sound hard to believe. Fans feel strongly about the qualities of managers and players. There are periods of national optimism and national pessimism, associated with the view that the England team is either strong or disgraceful.

But in fact, watching England play resembles watching a coin-tossing competition. If we focus on outright victories, then England on average wins just over 50 percent of its games; the rest it either ties or loses. So just as a coin has half a chance of landing heads up and half tails up, England in the average game has about half a chance of winning and half of not winning.

We assigned a "1" for each win and a "0" for a loss or a tie, and examined the sequence of England's four hundred games from 1972 through 2007. Before we discuss this sequence, let's look at coin tossing. If you tossed a coin four hundred times, you would expect on average to get two hundred heads and two hundred tails. However, there is no reason to think that the outcomes would alternate (heads, tails, heads, tails . . .). Sometimes you will get sequences of a few heads, sometimes a few tails. Crucially, though, there would be no relationship at all between the current coin toss and the last one. If you toss a fair coin there is always a fifty-fifty chance of heads, whatever sequence has occurred up to this point. There is no statistical correlation between current coin tosses and past coin tosses, even if the average of any sequence is always around 50 percent.

Here is our finding: England's win sequence over the four hundred games is indistinguishable from a random series of coin tosses. There is no predictive value in the outcome of England's last game, or indeed in any combination of England's recent games. Whatever happened in one match appears to have no bearing on what will happen in the next one. The only thing you can predict is that over the medium to long term, England will win about half its games outright. We have seen that the outcome of matches can be largely predicted by a country's population, income, and experience. However, this explains only the *average* outcome. In other words, if England were smaller, poorer, or less experienced, it would have a lower percentage of wins, but the sequence of those wins would still be unpredictable.

To make sure that our finding was right, we constructed a few random sequences of 1s and 0s to see if they looked like England's results.

FIGURE 16.2. England win percentage

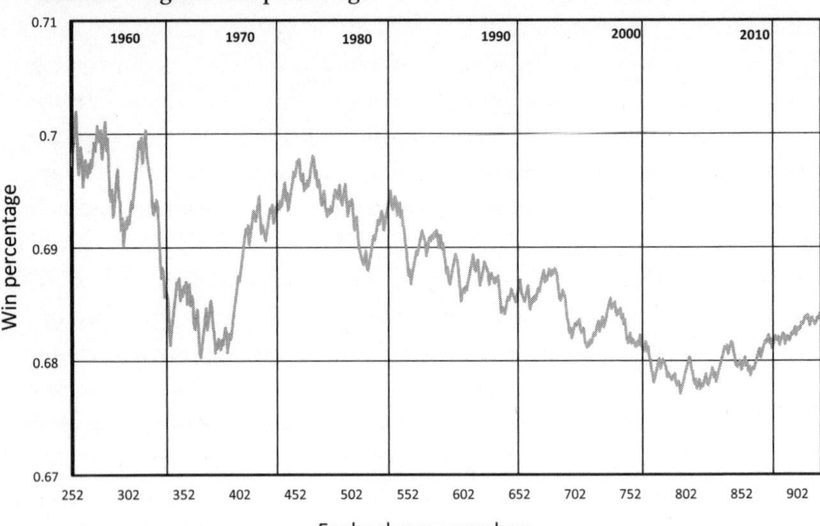

Often we found more apparent correlation in our random sequences than in England's results.

Contrary to all popular opinion, it may be that for most of modern soccer history the strength of the England team has barely ever changed (which would make the entire apparatus of punditry attached to the team instantly redundant). Figure 16.2 shows the win percentage of the England team from 1950 to 2013 (again counting ties as worth half a win). Apart from a few moments in the 1950s it has not risen above 70 percent, and it has never fallen below 67.5 percent. The overall picture is one of steady but extremely slow decline, punctuated by two eras of exceptional performance. One of those eras was the late 1960s, when England was world champion. The other period of clear improvement began in the early 2000s and continues today.

On the whole, though, very little has changed over sixty years. A star player might fade or retire, but in a country of about 50 million people, there is always someone coming up who is near enough his level to make almost no difference. Over the long term, the three key factors that determine a country's performance are very stable. The British economy boomed in the 1990s and is now dropping down the global wealth rankings, but measured over the past century Britain has always been one of the wealthiest nations in the world. Equally, its share of the soccer population changes only glacially. And while the England team gains experience, so do its main rivals. The only key factor that changes is home advantage. Given that playing at home is worth a lead of two-thirds of a goal per game in global soccer, it's little wonder that England won the World Cup in England in 1966.

Otherwise, England's performances in good or bad times are much the same. It's just that fans and the media seek to see patterns where none exist. Nick Taleb, the financial investor who wrote *The Black Swan: The Impact of the Highly Improbable,* famously explained that we are constantly fooled by randomness. In neuroscientific terms, our rational brains are egged on by our emotional brains to find patterns even if there aren't any. In the end, the best explanation for the short-term ups and downs of the England team is randomness.

THE CAPELLO EFFECT

At least, that was true before Capello arrived. It appears that the Italian changed something. Despite the ritual English disappointment in South Africa, it does seem that taking his reign as a whole, England under him was better than it ever had been. That is exactly what you would expect, if he imported the latest continental know-how.

As we've seen, Capello was the nominated scapegoat for the World Cup of 2010. But it is unfair to judge him on just four matches, played at a time when England was suffering its ritual end-of-season fatigue. (Capello's star, the ailing Rooney, had been squeezed like a lemon by Manchester United that spring.) Taking Capello's English years as a whole, from 2008 until his resignation in February 2012, his results stand out.

Most obviously, his winning percentage of 75 (counting ties as half a win) was higher than anyone else's (and 14 percentage points above his immediate predecessor, McClaren). As we've noted earlier, in no other four-year period from 1978 through 2007 did England's winning percentage rise above 68 percent. Capello also won a higher proportion of games outright than any of his predecessors. True, he had the good luck of coaching in the aftermath of the breakups of the Soviet Union and Yugoslavia. There are now far more weak little countries in European soccer, the likes of Slovenia and Kazakhstan, which England generally beats. But the previous five regular England managers enjoyed the same advantage, and none of them has stats to match Capello's.

What's also noticeable is how freely his teams scored. They beat their opponents by an average of 1.48 goals a game, about half a goal better than the typical modern England manager. Scoring was easier for prewar England sides and for Walter Winterbottom's teams in the immediate postwar period, because many international sides in those days were rubbish: in May 1947, for instance, Winterbottom's England won 0–10 away to Portugal, not a result that England has threatened to match since.

Capello was succeeded by Hodgson, who started even better than the Italian did. By the time his England had beaten Poland 2–0 at Wembley in October 2013 to qualify for the Brazilian World Cup, Hodgson's win percentage after twenty-two games was 77 percent—fractionally above Capello's, and the highest in English history.

Admittedly his team then lost two straight exhibition games to dilute his numbers. We are still fairly confident that Hodgson's boys will fly home from Brazil in tears. Ultimate failure is only to be expected, despite England's improvement in recent years. The difference with past World Cups is that English fans now expect failure too. It has taken nearly fifty years of hurt, but the fantasy of manifest destiny has finally been discarded.

17

THE CURSE OF POVERTY

Why Poor Countries Are Poor at Sports

When Didier Drogba was five, his parents put him on a plane in the Ivory Coast and sent him to live with an uncle in France. The six-hour flight, alone with his favorite toy, passed in a blur of tears and tissues.

About a decade later Drogba's father lost his job at a bank in Ivory Coast, and the family moved to a suburb of Paris, where they were reunited with their exiled son. Eight Drogbas ended up living in an apartment of about 110 square feet. "A very large wardrobe, really," Drogba recalled in his autobiography. "Hard. Very hard. Even enough to drive you crazy." The apartment was cold, and his little brothers were so noisy he couldn't concentrate on his schoolwork. "Luckily, my father had allowed me to start playing soccer again."

There is a myth that poor people are somehow best equipped to make it as sportsmen. A cliché often used about them is that sport is their "only escape route from poverty." The poor are supposedly figuratively "hungrier" than the rich. If they are black, like Drogba, they are sometimes thought to have greater genetic gifts than white people. And the evidence that poor people excel at sports seems to be in front of our eyes. England is not the only national soccer team dominated by players from lowly backgrounds. France since the 1990s has generally fielded a majority of nonwhite players, and few Brazilian internationals are sons of corporate lawyers, either. Most of the world's best soccer players started life poor: South Americans like Diego Maradona, who as a toddler almost drowned in a local cesspit, Africans like Samuel Eto'o who appear to support hundreds of people back home, or European immigrants like Zlatan Ibrahimovic or Zinedine Zidane, who grew up in some of the toughest neighborhoods on the Continent. Drogba's childhood was only slightly more Dickensian than most. The origins of American basketball players and football players are mostly lowly, too. The best preparation for sporting greatness seems to be a poor childhood.

Yet it is not. The facts show that the world's poor people and poor countries are worse at sports than rich ones. It is true that poorer immigrants in rich countries often excel at sports, but the reasons for that have nothing to do with skin color or "hunger."

Let's look at poor countries first. The vast majority of countries on earth are even more firmly excluded from sporting success than England is, simply because they are poor. This becomes apparent in a simple exercise to discover which country is the world's best at sports and which country is best for its size.

To find the best countries, we combined the historical results from many major international sporting events: the Summer and Winter Olympics, World Cups in several sports, and the most popular individual sports. For some sports the data go back more than a century, for others, only a couple of decades. For all sports, we took November 2013 as the end point.

Our methodology is not perfect. We started with the men's world cups in biggish sports that have seldom or never been featured at the Olympics. We ranked the top five countries in these sports, based first on the number of world titles they have won, and in case of ties, on finishes in the final four. We gave the best country in each sport five points, the second four, the third three, the fourth two, and the fifth one. There is no need to read the rankings for every sport, but following are the detailed points tallies for those who are interested:

Rugby Union

New Zealand	5
Australia	4
South Africa	3

England	2
France	1

Cricket

Australia	5
India	4
West Indies	3
Pakistan	2
Sri Lanka	1

Baseball was trickier. Historically the US dominates the sport. However, it traditionally sends amateurs or minor leaguers to the world cup. The US ranks only third all-time in the tournament. But we used our judgment to rank it as the world's best country in baseball, producing this ranking:

US	5
Cuba	4
Venezuela	3
Colombia	2
South Korea	1

Basketball is an Olympic event. However, as the world's second most popular team game it deserves additional input in this quest. We therefore added the results of the basketball world cup. Again the US rarely fields its best players, and historically ranks second behind Yugoslavia. But using common sense we placed the US first here, too, producing this ranking:

US	5
Yugoslavia/Serbia & Montenegro	4
USSR/Russia	3
Brazil	2
Argentina	1

Favoring the US in baseball and basketball did not affect the outcome of our quest.

The only women's world cup we counted was soccer. Women's soccer is an Olympic event, too, but far more popular than most other women's team games, and therefore it seemed to merit more input. The rankings for women's soccer:

US	5
Germany	4
Norway	3
Japan	2
Sweden	1

We also assessed popular individual sports that have seldom or never been represented in the Olympics. We rewarded countries for triumphs by their citizens. In tennis we counted men's and women's Grand Slam tournaments—tennis being a rare sport in that it is played widely by women. We used only results from the "Open era" starting in 1968, when tennis became very competitive.

Men's Tennis

US	5
Sweden	4
Australia	3
Spain	2
Switzerland	1

Women's Tennis

US	5
Germany/West Germany	4
Australia	3
Belgium	2
Yugoslavia/Serbia	1

In golf we used the results of the men's majors:

US	5
Britain (including all four home countries)	4

South Africa	3
Australia	2
Spain	1

In cycling we counted victories by citizens of each country in the Tour de France, a more prestigious event than the world championship. We didn't count doped winners like Lance Armstrong who were later stripped of their titles:

France	5
Belgium	4
Spain	3
Italy	2
Luxembourg	1

In auto racing we chose the most prestigious competition, Formula I, thus discriminating against the US, which prefers its own races. Again, we counted world championships by citizenship. The rankings:

Britain	5
Germany	4
Brazil	3
Argentina	2
Finland, Australia, Austria, France	1 each

We did not include the world cups of popular sports like volleyball and ice hockey, because these are Olympic sports, and so we will assess them through their role in the Olympics' all-time medals table. Boxing was too hard to assess, as there are various rival "world championships." We also excluded the athletics world cup. Athletics is copiously represented at the Olympics, and for most of the history of its world cup, the entrants have been entire continents rather than single countries.

Clearly the Summer and Winter Games deserve to carry more weight in our quest than any single world cup. In the Summer Olympics of 2012, medals were awarded in twenty-six sports. Many of these, such as archery or kayaking, are played by very few people. Still, because of the event's profusion of sports and its prestige, we gave the Summer Games ten times the weighting of world cups in single sports. So we gave the top country in the all-time medals table 50 points rather than 5 points for a single world cup. Because the whole planet competes in the Olympics—unlike, say, in baseball or cricket—we rewarded the top ten rather than five countries in the all-time medals table. The ranking:

US	50 points
USSR/Russia	40
Germany	30
Italy	20
Britain	10
France	8
East Germany (GDR)	6
Sweden	4
China	2
Norway	1

We gave the Winter Olympics three times the weighting of a world cup. Because few countries play winter sports, we rewarded only the top five in the all-time medals table:

USSR/Russia	15 points
Norway	12
US	9
Germany (including West Germany)	6
Austria	3

Finally, the soccer world cup. Soccer is an Olympic sport, but it is also the planet's most popular game. We gave its world cup six times the weighting of world cups in other sports, and rewarded the top ten countries in the all-time points table. The ranking:

Brazil	30 points
Germany	24
Italy	18

Argentina	12
England	6
Spain	5
France	4
Netherlands	3
Uruguay	2
Sweden	1

We then totaled up all the points. Here are our top twenty-three sporting countries on earth:

US	89
Germany (including West Germany)	72
USSR/Russia	58
Italy	40
Brazil	35
Britain	27
France	19
Australia	18
Norway	16
Argentina	15
Spain	11
Sweden	10
East Germany, Belgium, South Africa	6
Yugoslavia/Serbia & Montenegro, New Zealand	5
Austria, India, Cuba	4
Netherlands, West Indies, Venezuela	3

The winner, the US, deserves particular praise given that we omitted two of its favorite sports, football and NASCAR, because nobody else plays them. Germany, in second place, would have gotten closer to the American total if we had credited the united country with East Germany's Olympic medals (and forgotten all the male growth hormones that went into winning them). The USSR/Russia in third place can be slightly less pleased with itself, because it won most of its points when it was still a multinational empire. Britain was fourth when we first calculated this table in 2006, but has since dropped to sixth, despite the London Olympics.

Australia in eighth place did brilliantly given that we ignored its prowess at its very own version of football, "Aussie Rules." Brazil was the best developing country by a very long way, and not just thanks to soccer. It has also diversified successfully into basketball and Formula I auto racing. India (1.2 billion inhabitants, 5 points for cricket) and China (1.3 billion, 2 points for the summer Olympics) were the biggest flops per capita. The Arab world combined got zero points.

But which country is world champion per capita? To find out, we worked out how many points each country scored per million inhabitants (using their population figures for 2013). That produced this top ten of overachievers:

Norway	3.19
Luxembourg	1.88
New Zealand	1.14
Sweden	1.05
United Germany (excluding the GDR's Olympic Medals)	0.88
Australia	0.79
Italy	0.66
Uruguay	0.59
West Indies (or the nations that together supply almost all West Indian cricketers, namely, Jamaica, Trinidad and Tobago, Guyana, Barbados, and Antigua)	0.58
Belgium	0.54

Heia Norge. The country that we very nearly crowned as the most soccer mad in Europe now turns out to be the best per capita at sport. Norway's lead is so large that it would most probably have won our sporting Tom Thumb trophy even with a different scoring system—even, say, if we had halved its points for being the best Winter Olympics nation. This is a country where at a state kindergarten in suburban Oslo in midafternoon, among the throng of mothers picking up their toddlers, someone pointed out to us an anonymous mom who happened to be an Olympic gold medalist in cross-country skiing. Norway won more points in our competition than all of Africa or Asia (excluding Oceania) put together. We could even have omitted the Winter Olympics—almost a Norwegian fiefdom—and the country still would have finished sixth in our efficiency table.

But the main thing the top of our rankings demonstrates is the importance of wealth. Our efficiency table for sports bears a curious resemblance to another global ranking: the United Nations' human development index. This measures life expectancy, literacy, education, and living standards to rank the countries of the world according to their well-being. We found that a nation's well-being is highly correlated with its success in sports. No prizes for guessing which country topped the UN's rankings for human development in 2012: *Heia Norge,* again.

New Zealand and Australia, third and sixth in our sporting rankings, were sixth and second for human development in 2012. Sweden, fourth in the world for sports, was joint seventh for human development. Germany was fifth in sport, fifth in human development. The only poorer nations that sneaked into our sporting top ten were Uruguay and the West Indian nations. However, even these poor cousins were all classified by the UN as "very highly" or "highly" developed countries except Guyana, whose development was "medium." Generally the most developed countries also tend to be best at sports.

The case of Norway shows why. It's Norwegian government policy that every farmer, every fisherman, no matter where he lives in the country, has the right to play sports. And Norway will spend what it takes to achieve that. Just as supermarkets have sprouted all over Britain, there are all-weather sports grounds everywhere in Norway. Even in the unlikeliest corners of the country there's generally one around the corner from your house. Usually the locker rooms are warm, and the coaches have acquired some sort of diploma. A kid can play and train on a proper team for under $150 a year, really not much for most Norwegians. Almost everyone in the country plays something. Knut Helland, a professor at Bergen University who has written a book on Norwegian sports and media, notes that Norway has the biggest ski race in the world with about 13,000 participants. "I'm taking part in it myself," he adds. When the European Commission studied time use in European countries in 2004, it found that the Norwegians spent the most time playing sports: on average, a whopping thirteen minutes a day. People all over the world might want to play sports, but to make that possible requires money and organization that poor countries don't have. Money buys sporting trophies.

After we published the first edition of *Soccernomics,* Christopher Anderson, a political scientist at Cornell University, and later co-author of *The Numbers Game,* riposted that we placed undue weight on wealth. In his paper "Do Democracies Win More?" Anderson analyzed all soccer World Cups from 1950 through 2006. The key to winning wasn't so much wealth, he argued, as democracy.

That may well be true. Wealth and democracy tend to correlate very closely. Almost all rich countries (leaving aside a few oil states in the Middle East) are democracies. That makes it tricky to separate the effects of wealth from the effects of democracy. Anderson might well be right that democracy contributes more to winning soccer games (note also that in making our case, we were looking at many sports rather than just soccer). Perhaps the average quality of schooling in different countries—if you could measure it perfectly—would be an even better predictor of success in soccer. After all, schooling is a pretty good gauge of how well a country channels resources to all its people. If you're good at providing schools for everyone, as most democracies are, then you are probably also good at providing good soccer fields and coaches for everyone. It's impossible to say whether Norway is good at sports because it's rich, or because it's a democracy, or because it's highly educated. Rather, being rich and democratic and well-educated and good at sports are all part of the same thing.

However you measure it, poor countries are generally poorer at sports. It's no coincidence that China won nothing at sports before its economy took off and that it topped the medals table at the Beijing Olympics afterward. Most African countries barely even try to compete in any sports other than soccer and a few running events. And the best place to find out why the world's poor do worse than the world's rich is South Africa, where some very poor and very rich neighborhoods are almost side by side, separated only by a highway or a golf course.

South Africa is the one African country to score any points at all in our sporting table. Yet it owes almost all those points to an ethnic group that makes up less than 10 percent of the country's inhabitants: white people.

Only about 4.6 million of the 51 million South Africans are white. Nonetheless, whites accounted for fourteen of the fifteen players in the

Springbok rugby team that won the world cup in 1995, thirteen of the fifteen who won it in 2007, as well as all five South African golfers who have won majors, and most of the country's best cricketers. If we treated white South Africa as a separate country, then its six sporting points would have put it in third place in the world in our sporting efficiency table. That is entirely predictable. South African whites were nurtured under apartheid on almost all the resources of the country.

The national teams of South African whites remain world-class in their respective sports. Nonwhite South Africa's national team does less well. At the time of writing, in January 2014, the Bafana Bafana soccer team, sometimes known at home as the "Banana Banana," is sixty-second in FIFA's rankings, far behind Panama and the Cape Verde Islands. Even that represents quite a big rise in recent years. The Bafana just missed qualifying for the African Nations Cup of 2012, having failed to figure out that the team needed to beat rather than tie Sierra Leone in the last qualifying game. (The scenes of the Bafana wasting time in the final minutes to preserve the tie would have been hilarious were they not a terrible reflection on the state of math teaching in South Africa.)

Here are five vignettes to explain why black South Africa and other poor nations fail at sport:

YOU ARE WHAT YOU EAT: JOHANNESBURG

Steven Pienaar, Everton's South African midfielder, has the frame of a prepubescent boy. There's hardly a European soccer player as reedy as he is. But in South African soccer his body type is common. Frank Eulberg, a German who spent about five minutes as assistant coach of the Kaizer Chiefs, South Africa's best team, says that when he arrived at the club, sixteen of the players were shorter than five foot nine. "I sometimes thought, 'Frank, you're in the land of the dwarves.'"

Most likely, Pienaar is reedy because he grew up malnourished and without much access to doctors. He was born in a poor Coloured township in 1982, the height of apartheid, when almost all money and health care went to whites. Growing tall is not just a matter of what you eat. When children become ill, their growth is interrupted, and because poor children tend to get ill more often than rich ones, they usually end up shorter.

Most of the players who represented South Africa in 2010 were born in nonwhite townships in the 1980s. And so the ghost of apartheid bugged the Bafana at their own World Cup. One reason South Africans are so bad at soccer is that most of them didn't get enough good food. There are big strong black South Africans like Lucas Radebe and Aaron Mokoena, but not very many of them.

Apartheid, based on the bogus ideology that races are different, ended up creating white, black, "Coloured," and Indian South Africans who really were like separate peoples. The whites on average tower over the blacks. No wonder the cricket and rugby teams are so much better than the Bafana. "Well, they have their moments," laughs Demitri Constantinou.

This descendant of Greek immigrants, an exercise scientist at Wits University in Johannesburg, directs FIFA's first medical center of excellence in Africa. When we met, he was running a project with the South African Football Association to help develop young soccer players. Constantinou's team tested the health of all the players selected for SAFA's program. In a Woolworths tearoom in one of Johannesburg's posh northern suburbs, among white ladies having afternoon tea, he says, "The biggest issue was nutrition." Is malnutrition one reason African teams perform poorly at World Cups? "I think yes. And I think it has been overlooked as a possible cause."

Hardly any players in the latter stages of the World Cup of 2006 were shorter than about five foot eight, Constantinou notes. "There is a minimum height." If a large proportion of your male population was below that height, you were picking your team from a reduced pool. Conversely, though he didn't say it, one reason that Norway and Sweden (two of the three tallest countries in the world) excel at sports is that almost all their male inhabitants are tall enough. They are picking their teams from a full pool.

A BEAST INTO A TOOTHPICK: CAPE TOWN

George Dearnaley is a big, ruddy white man who looks like a rugby player, but in fact he was once the Bafana's promising young center forward. Dearnaley never got beyond promising, because when he was in his early twenties his knee went. He didn't mind much. He spoke a bit of Zulu and had studied literature and journalism at college in Toledo, Ohio, and so he joined the soccer magazine *Kick Off*. He became its publisher as well as the author of an excellent column.

Over an English breakfast in a Cape Town greasy spoon near the *Kick Off* offices, Dearnaley reflected on the Amazulu team in Durban where his career peaked. Seven of his teammates from the Amazulu side of 1992 were now dead, out of a squad of about twenty-four. Dearnaley said, "One guy died when his house exploded, so that was probably a taxi war or something. But the rest must have been AIDS. One player, a Durban newspaper said he was bewitched. A six-foot-four beast of a man, who was suddenly whittled down to a toothpick."

Constantinou says it's quite possible that a fifth of the Bafana's potential pool of players for 2010 carried the HIV virus. Not many people now remember Emmanuel "Scara" Ngobese, once a great South African "dribbling wizard," who died at age twenty-eight in a Johannesburg hospital on May 11, 2010, a month before the World Cup kicked off. His cause of death was given as "tuberculosis." Scara won the league with the Kaizer Chiefs in 2005, and played once for the Bafana. How many South Africans who could have played in 2010 were dead instead?

THE DARK SIDE OF THE MOON: SANDTON, JUST OUTSIDE JOHANNESBURG

It was quite a step for Danny Jordaan to organize a World Cup, because until he was thirty-eight he had never even seen one. The chief executive officer of the FIFA World Cup 2010 grew up a million miles from the world's best soccer. Being in South Africa under apartheid was not quite like being on the moon, or being in North Korea, but it was almost as isolated. South Africa was the last industrialized country to get television, in 1976, because the white government was afraid of the device. Even after that hardly any blacks had TV sets, and FIFA did not allow its World Cup to be broadcast in the apartheid state. So the first time Jordaan saw a World Cup on television was in 1990.

The country's isolation continued even after that. As far as most South Africans were concerned, international soccer might still as well have been happening on Mars. Jordaan told us, "South Africans played on their own. We thought we were so smart. That's why when we played our first competitive match against Zimbabwe [in 1992], every South African knew we were going to hammer Zimbabwe. But Zimbabwe had this little player called Peter Ndlovu. Nobody knew Peter Ndlovu. By halftime it was 3–0 for them. That was the first entry into international soccer. That really shook this country."

As late as 1998, when South Africa entered its first World Cup, large swaths of the population assumed that the Bafana would win it. After all, everyone knew that their native style of "piano and shoeshine"—essentially, doing tricks on the ball while standing around—was just like Brazilian soccer but better. The Bafana did not win the World Cup.

Black South Africa was isolated twice over: first by sanctions, then by poverty. However, isolation—a distance from the networks of the world's best soccer—is the fate of most poor countries. Their citizens can't easily travel to Italy or Germany and see how soccer is played there, let alone talk to the best coaches. Some can't even see foreign soccer on television, because they don't have a television. And only a couple of the very best players in these countries ever make it to the best leagues in the world.

One reason poor countries do badly in sports—and one reason they are poor—is that they tend to be less "networked," less connected to other countries, than rich ones. It is hard for them just to find out the latest best practice on how to play a sport.

Playing for national teams in Africa hardly lifts the isolation. Most poor, isolated African countries compete only against other poor, isolated African countries. At best, they might encounter the world's best once every four years at a World Cup. No wonder they have little idea of what top-class soccer is like.

"THE ORGANIZERS. IT'S THE BIGGEST PROBLEM": LONDON

For mysterious reasons, in 2006 someone decided that the Bafana should play their annual charity match, the Nelson Mandela Challenge, not in the magnificent 78,000-seat FNB Stadium just outside Johannesburg, but more than 5,000 miles away at Brentford's Griffin Park in West London.

On a gray November London afternoon the day before the game, the Bafana were in their gray-colored three-star hotel on the outskirts of Heathrow Airport. In the lobby were flight crews, traveling salesmen, and cheery men in green-and-yellow tracksuits hanging with their entourage: the Bafana Bafana. Their opponents, the Egyptians, who were also staying in the hotel, had congregated in the bar. Apparently Egypt was furious. It had been promised a five-star hotel, and a match fee that had yet to materialize.

Pitso Mosimane, the Bafana's caretaker manager—a big, bald, bullet-headed man—was also hanging around the lobby. Mosimane complained that African coaches never got jobs in Europe. He gestured toward the bar: "The coach of Egypt, who won the African Cup of Nations. Don't you think he could at least coach a team in the English first division?" Then Mosimane went off for a prematch practice at Griffin Park.

Minutes later he was back at the table. "That was quick," someone remarked. "No, we didn't train!" Mosimane said. Nobody had bothered telling Brentford the Bafana were coming, and so the field wasn't ready for them. Now they would have to play the African champions without having trained on the field. "And I'm carrying players who play for Blackburn Rovers and Borussia Dortmund, and you know? We're laughing about it." Mosimane jerked a thumb toward four men in suits drinking at the next table: "The organizers. It is the biggest problem. This wouldn't happen with any other national team."

He was wrong. Organizational mishaps are always happening to national teams from poor countries. On most sub-Saharan African national teams that make it to a World Cup, players and officials have a ritual dispute over pay about a week before the tournament. In 2002 Cameroon's dispute got out of hand, whereupon the squad made a brief airplane odyssey through Ethiopia, India, and Thailand before finally landing in Japan four days late. Jet-lagged and confused, the Indomitable Lions were knocked out in the first round. In 2006, Togo's players spent much of their brief stay at the country's first World Cup threatening to go on strike because of their pay dispute. They worried that after the tournament was over, Togo's federation might never get around to paying them. Eventually FIFA sidestepped the federation, paid the players' bonuses directly, and told them to play or else, but it is little wonder that the team lost three matches out of three.

To win at sports, you need to find, develop, and nurture talent. Doing that requires money, know-how, and some kind of administrative infrastructure. Few African countries have enough of any.

"COLOURED" BEATS "BLACK": THE CAPE FLATS

If you stand on Table Mountain at night and look down at Cape Town, you will see a city of lights. Next to the lights are the railway tracks. And on the far side of the tracks are "black spots": Coloured townships without lights. These are the rainy, murderous Cape Flats where most of South Africa's best soccer players grew up.

Benni McCarthy—South Africa's record goal scorer—comes from the Cape Flats. So does the man just behind him in the scoring charts, Shaun Bartlett. So does Benni's old friend Quinton Fortune, for years a loyal reserve at Manchester United.

The key point is that according to the racial classifications of apartheid, still tacitly used by most South Africans today, none of these players is "black." They are "Coloured": a group of generally lighter-skinned people, mostly derived from the lighter African tribes of the Cape, though some descend from Asian slaves and mixed white-black liaisons. Less than 10 percent of South Africans are Coloured, while about three-quarters are black. However, Coloureds often make up as much as half of the Bafana team. Pienaar, for instance, is from a Coloured township outside Johannesburg. This density of Coloured talent is a legacy of apartheid.

Under apartheid, the Coloureds were slightly better off than the blacks. They had more to eat and more opportunities to organize themselves. In the Coloured Cape Flats, for instance, there were amateur soccer clubs with proper coaches like you might find in Europe. Not so in black townships, where a boys' team would typically bc run by a local gangster or the shebeen owner, who seldom bothered much with training.

To the irritation of many South African blacks, the Bafana have been a largely Coloured team for much of their history since 1992. The blacks are simply too poor to compete within their own country, let alone with

Europeans. Even in the simplest game, the poor are excluded by malnutrition, disease, and disorganization. Poor people in poor countries do worse at sports.

That leaves one thing unexplained: Why is it that so many of the best European soccer players—Zidane, Drogba (officially an Ivorian but raised in France), Ibrahimovic, Rooney, Cristiano Ronaldo—come from the poorest neighborhoods in Europe?

It cannot be that boys from the ghetto have an unquenchable hunger to succeed. If that were so, they would do better at school and in jobs outside soccer. There must be something about their childhoods that makes them particularly well suited to soccer. That reason is practice.

Malcolm Gladwell, in his book *Outliers: The Story of Success,* popularized the "10,000-hour rule." This is a notion from psychology, which says that to achieve expertise in any field you need at least 10,000 hours of practice. "In study after study, of composers, basketball players, fiction writers, ice-skaters, concert pianists, chess players, master criminals," says neurologist Daniel Levitin in *Outliers,* "this number comes up again and again. Ten thousand hours is equivalent to roughly three hours a day, or 20 hours a week, of practice over 10 years. . . . No one has yet found a case in which true world-class expertise was accomplished in less time."

The 10,000-hour rule has since been questioned by academics in various fields. It may indeed not apply in very physical sports like running or jumping, where somebody with the perfect genes can become world-class without much training. However, in a highly skill-based sport like soccer, Gladwell's essential point is correct: practice makes perfect.

In soccer, it is the poorest European boys who are most likely to get the most practice. They tend to live in small apartments, which forces them to spend time outdoors. There they meet a ready supply of local boys equally eager to get out of their apartments and play soccer. Their parents are less likely than middle-class parents to force them to waste precious time doing homework. And they have less money for other leisure pursuits. A constant in soccer players' ghosted autobiographies is the monomaniacal childhood spent playing nonstop soccer and, in a classic story, sleeping with a ball. Here, for instance, is Nourdin Boukhari, a

Dutch-Moroccan soccer player who grew up in an immigrant neighborhood of Rotterdam, recalling his childhood for a Dutch magazine:

> I grew up in a family of eight children. . . . There was no chance of pocket money. . . . I lived more on the street than at home. . . . And look at Robin van Persie, Mounir El Hamdaoui and Said Boutahar. And I'm forgetting Youssef El-Akchaoui. [Like the other players Boukhari mentions, El-Akchaoui became a professional soccer player.] Those boys and I played on the street in Rotterdam together. We never forget where we came from and that we used to have nothing except for one thing: the ball. . . .
>
> What we have in common is that we were on the street every minute playing soccer, day and night. We were always busy, games, juggling, shooting at the crossbar. The ball was everything for me, for us. We'd meet on squares.

By the time these boys were fifteen, they were much better players than suburban kids. The importance of practice also explains why blacks raised in American ghettos are overrepresented in basketball and football.

But it would be misleading to say these European soccer players grew up "poor." By global standards, they were rich. Even in Cristiano Ronaldo's Madeira, Rooney's Croxteth, or Zidane's La Castellane, children generally got enough to eat and decent medical care. It is true that Cristiano Ronaldo grew up in a house so small that they kept the washing machine on the roof, but in black South Africa, that washing machine would have marked the family as rich. Besides the 10,000-hour rule, there is another rule that explains sporting success: the $15,000 rule. That's the minimum average income per person that a country needs to win anything. There is only one way around this: be Brazil.

18

TOM THUMB

The Best Little Soccer Country on Earth

In 1970, when Brazil won its third World Cup, it got to keep the Jules Rimet trophy. The little statuette of Nike, then still known chiefly as the Greek goddess of victory, ended up in a glass case in the Brazilian federation's offices in Rio de Janeiro. One night in 1983 the trophy was stolen. It has never been seen since.

However, the point is that everyone agrees that Brazil deserves the Jules Rimet. The fivefold world champion is undoubtedly the best country in soccer history. Our question here is a different one: Which country is best after taking into account its population, experience, and income per capita? If Brazil is the absolute world champion, who is the relative one, the biggest overperformer? That overachieving country deserves its own version of the Jules Rimet trophy—call it the Tom Thumb. And which countries are the worst underachievers relative to their resources? Along the way we will have to consider several impressive candidates and make some judgment calls before coming up with our winner and loser.

First of all, if we are dealing with statistics, we have to construct our arguments on the basis of large numbers of games played. There have only been nineteen World Cups through 2010, and most of these involved hardly any countries from outside Europe and Latin America. So crunching the numbers from World Cups might at best tell us something about the pecking order among the long-established large soccer nations.

But when the difference between, say, Argentina's two victories and England's one comes down to as little as Maradona's "hand of God" goal, or the difference between Italy's four and France's one to a comment by Marco Materazzi about Zidane's parentage, then the statistician needs to look elsewhere. Happily, since national teams play a lot of games, we have plenty of data. As in Chapter 16, we will rely on Russell Gerrard's remarkable database of games, which we have updated to 2012.

The number of international matches has soared over time. Between the foundation of FIFA in 1904 and the First World War the number rose quickly to 50 per year. After 1918 growth resumed. By the eve of the Second World War, there were more than 100 international matches a year. But this was still a world dominated by colonial powers, and only with the independence movement after the war did international competition mushroom. In 1947 there were 107 international matches; by 1957 there were 203; by 1967, 308. Few new countries were founded in the next two decades, but the number of international matches continued to rise thanks to the jet plane, which made travel less of a pain and more financially worthwhile. In 1977 there were 368 international matches; in 1987 there were 393. At that point the world seemed to have reached some sort of stable equilibrium.

But then the Soviet Union broke up into fifteen separate states, and Yugoslavia collapsed. The new countries flocked into FIFA. At the same time the commercial development of soccer meant that cash-hungry national associations were eager to play lucrative friendlies. In 1997 there were 850 international games, more than double the figure of a decade before. Since then growth has slowed but not stopped altogether, reaching a figure of 923 in 2007.

If we concentrate on just the twenty-year cycle from the end of the 1990 World Cup to the end of the 2010 World Cup—the post–cold war era—a list of the most successful teams features the usual suspects. Let's rank the top ten countries by the percentage of games won, or, given that around one-third of matches are ties, by the "win percentage" statistic calculated by valuing a tie as worth half a win.

The top few teams are much as you would expect. Spain—as we'll discuss in the next chapter—has been the world's leading soccer nation for a surprisingly long time. And even in a twenty-year period when Brazil

FIGURE 18.1. **The top ten national teams by win percentage, 1990–2010**

	P	*Won*	*Tied*	*wpc*	*GD*
Spain	195	0.656	0.215	0.764	1.272
Brazil	296	0.615	0.240	0.735	1.311
France	213	0.577	0.277	0.716	0.939
Germany	226	0.606	0.199	0.706	1.040
Argentina	236	0.576	0.246	0.699	0.839
Netherlands	192	0.552	0.281	0.693	1.010
Italy	200	0.525	0.310	0.680	0.690
England	193	0.528	0.295	0.676	0.865
Portugal	185	0.535	0.276	0.673	0.903
Czech Republic	156	0.571	0.199	0.670	0.904

tried to reinvent its national style of soccer, its win percentage was almost 75 percent. That equates to bookmakers' odds of 3 to 1, or about as close as you can get to a sure thing in a two-horse race.

If we look at Brazil's performance over time, some interesting insights emerge. Here are the team's results by decade:

FIGURE 18.2. **Brazil: The disaster of 1950 as the start of something beautiful**

Decade	*P*	*W*	*T*	*L*	*F*	*A*	*Wpc*
1910s	15	6	4	5	28	24	0.533
1920s	24	10	4	10	35	34	0.500
1930s	22	14	1	7	60	49	0.659
1940s	43	23	7	13	127	68	0.616
1950s	96	62	18	16	229	100	0.740
1960s	115	78	16	21	275	134	0.748
1970s	101	65	27	9	188	62	0.777
1980s	117	73	28	16	222	83	0.744
1990s	166	108	38	20	366	137	0.765
2000s	157	96	36	25	323	118	0.726

•Key to the chart: P= Matches played, W = Matches won, T = Matches tied, L = Matches lost, F = Goals for, A = Goals against, Wpc = Winning percentage (victories as a percentage of all matches, counting ties as worth half a victory)

Viewed in the light of history, it's little wonder that Brazil lost at home to Uruguay in the World Cup final of 1950. The Brazilians simply weren't that good then. Their hubris at that tournament had no historical basis. It's only in the 1950s that Brazil turned into soccer's superpower. Indeed, in the fifty years since then the team's performance has been strikingly consistent: Brazil's winning percentage (counting ties as worth half a win) hovered between 73 percent and 78 percent in each of the past six decades. If you had to pick a particular golden age, it would probably be 1964 to 1985, but our main finding is great stability of performance, even in the supposedly fallow twenty years after 1970. World Cups, as we have seen, usually turn on a couple of crucial matches, which in turn are usually decided by one goal each. The pundits then investigate these crucial matches for meaning, when in fact the best explanation of the outcome of such a tiny sample of games might be chance. The broader story of Brazil in the past fifty years is consistent excellence. Still, if Brazil is going to remain at the top, it will probably need to plug into the western European knowledge networks. In recent World Cups Brazil has sometimes looked ponderous against the best European teams. It ought to consider the revolutionary step of hiring a western European manager. If Brazil can combine the world's best players with the world's most advanced tactics, the result could be scary.

There's just one other finding of note. Brazil performs better in World Cup years. It wins about 5 percent more often in years with a World Cup, and the difference is statistically significant. That sounds counterintuitive: after all, the team would tend to face tougher competition in those years. However, the sordid truth is that most of the time, Brazilian internationals coast a little. They don't raise their game for qualifiers against Bolivia or Nike-inspired friendlies against Asian countries. In these off years, weary stars sometimes cry off claiming injury, and agents sometimes finagle places in the team for players who need a foreign transfer. But in a World Cup year, when everyone is playing for his place, Brazil is at its best.

You might think that 1990 to 2010 was a time of decline for Argentina. After all, in these years it never even reached the World Cup semifinals, whereas in 1986 and 1990 it had won a World Cup final and then lost another only on a dubious penalty. Yet in fact the 1980s—the decade

FIGURE 18.3 **Argentina's results: Where is the Maradona effect?**

Decade	*Played*	*Won*	*Drawn*	*Lost*	*Winning %*	*Winning % (counting draw as half a win)*
1902–1910	20	12	4	4	0.60	0.70
1911–1920	64	30	12	22	0.47	0.56
1921–1930	77	40	20	17	0.52	0.65
1931–1940	44	29	6	9	0.66	0.73
1941–1950	50	37	8	5	0.74	0.82
1951–1960	79	51	12	16	0.65	0.72
1961–1970	81	33	24	24	0.41	0.56
1971–1980	114	60	30	24	0.53	0.66
1981–1990	95	33	35	27	0.35	0.53
1991–2000	130	74	35	21	0.57	0.70
2001–2010	127	77	26	24	0.61	0.71

of Diego Maradona's greatness—was match for match the worst decade in Argentina's soccer history. The country's winning percentage slumped to a miserable 53 percent.

But for his "hand of God" in 1986, Maradona might have gone down in history as a brilliant underperformer, much like his contemporary Zico. Argentina's uneven performances during Maradona's era, as well as his rather sporadic club career, underline a difference between him and his little successor: Maradona never provided weekly brilliance the way Lionel Messi has. On the other hand, genius may in part be the ability to perform when it matters most.

In any case, Argentina's relative failure in his era probably wasn't Maradona's fault. The team's results seem to track the country's economic fortunes: in the 1980s, both declined.

Until well after the Second World War, Argentina was one of the richest countries on earth. Indeed, in the 1940s it exported beef to a starving Europe. No wonder that decade was also its best in soccer. But later Argentina became, in the words of Maradona's former teammate Jorge "El Filósofo" Valdano, "the world's first undeveloping country." The 1980s were the "lost decade": average income shrank from $7,500 per head in 1980 to $5,700 in 1990.

The past twenty years have been a roller coaster for the Argentine economy, but ultimately a great success in that income per head has risen to nearly $16,000 in 2010. That represents almost a trebling of real income since 1990. Admittedly there was a terrible recession around 2001, when the banking system collapsed, and Argentina devalued its peso and defaulted on its debts. Yet for much of the time since then, the economy has grown at close to 10 percent a year. Some economists are predicting a new Armageddon, but it hasn't come yet.

It's notable that as the economy has bounced back, so has the soccer team (though admittedly not in the knockout stages of World Cups). Argentina's winning percentage has shot back up to 70 percent in the twenty years since 1990, a level it had previously reached only in the good old 1950s. Returning to that standard was quite an achievement. Since the 1950s soccer has become a global sport, and many new countries have joined the race for supremacy. The international game today is more competitive than ever. Argentina's comeback deserves a compliment.

The Czech Republic and Portugal also warrant particular praise for making our top ten of most successful soccer teams. Each country has only 10 million inhabitants, compared to the 47 million–82 million of the large European nations and Brazil's 178 million. Some readers may also be surprised to find England in the top ten, given England's false reputation as "notorious underachievers."

Pace Brazil and Argentina, one thing our top ten tells us is that Europeans have dominated international soccer. The continent provides eight of the ten best countries. We have seen that this is partly thanks to Europe's unmatched knowledge networks. Those networks rest on tradition: European nations are generally older, and have played international soccer longer, than the rest of the world. It may also help that until very recently, control of global soccer largely remained in Europe. FIFA makes the rules of the game from a posh suburb of Zurich, and although western Europe has only 6 percent of the world's population, it has hosted ten out of nineteen World Cups. (A mark of how power in global soccer is shifting is that the region might now have to wait decades before hosting another.)

But tradition does not in itself secure dominance. If it did, then British companies would still dominate industries like textiles, shipbuilding, and car making. Dominance is transitory unless producers have the resources to stay ahead of the competition. The key resource in soccer is talent. Generally speaking, the more populous countries are more likely to have the largest supply of talented people. We have also seen that rich countries are best at finding, training, and developing talent. In short, it takes experience, population, and wealth to make a successful soccer nation.

The easy bit is recognizing this. The hard work is assembling the data to answer our question: Which countries do best relative to their resources of experience, population, and wealth?

Thankfully, Russell's data can help us with the issue of experience. He has recorded every single international game in history. With his list, we can measure the cumulative number of games a country had played up to any given date. We have seen that the most experienced soccer countries had played more than seven hundred international matches through 2000. Pedants might dispute some of the exact numbers—identifying international games is often a judgment call if we go back more than fifty years, when arrangements could be quite informal—but even if our figures were off by 5 percent, it wouldn't significantly affect the statistical analysis.

We also have data on each country's income. The measure typically used is gross domestic product. GDP is the total value of all goods and services bought and sold within an economy. (It includes imports and exports but excludes income from assets owned overseas and profits repatriated to foreign countries.) The best sources for GDP figures are the Penn World Tables, produced by the Center for International Comparisons at the University of Pennsylvania. The center has estimates of GDP for 167 countries between 1950 and 2011. To measure the economic resources available to each person, it divides GDP by population. Admittedly, there are all sorts of finicky issues involved in making comparisons across countries and across time, not to mention worries about measurement error and statistical reliability. Nonetheless, these data are the best we've got.

Now we run the multiple regressions we described in Chapter 16. Our aim is to find the connection between goal difference per game and our three key inputs—population, wealth, and experience—while also allowing for home advantage.

After all these pyrotechnics, we can make another ranking. But this time we can compensate all the world's national teams for that trio of factors beyond their control: experience, population, and income per head.

FIGURE 18.4. The top ten overachieving national teams in the world, allowing for population, wealth, and experience, all games, 1990–2010

	Played	*Won*	*Tied*	*wpc*	*GD*	*Out-performance*
Brazil	296	0.615	0.240	0.735	1.311	1.486
Spain	195	0.656	0.215	0.764	1.272	1.196
Iran	225	0.516	0.280	0.656	0.969	1.019
Germany	226	0.606	0.199	0.706	1.040	0.978
Iraq	157	0.414	0.287	0.557	0.573	0.962
Czech Republic	156	0.571	0.199	0.670	0.904	0.954
Argentina	236	0.576	0.246	0.699	0.839	0.949
Netherlands	192	0.552	0.281	0.693	1.010	0.906
Portugal	185	0.535	0.276	0.673	0.903	0.863
Mexico	362	0.486	0.243	0.608	0.721	0.839

The final column of the table is the one to notice. It shows what you might call each country's "outperformance," the gap between the goal difference it "should" have achieved against opponents given its national resources and experience and what it actually did achieve (listed in the penultimate column). Brazil, the most overachieving country in soccer according to this table, scores nearly 1.5 goals per game more than you would expect judging by its resources. All our top ten scored on average about a goal per game more than their resources would predict. Of our original "absolute" top ten, Brazil, Spain, Germany, Argentina, the Czechs, the Dutch, and the Portuguese all survive in this "relative" top ten. It turns out that these countries aren't merely very good in absolute terms. They are also overachieving relative to their resources. As for Mexico, we suspect its presence in the top ten is only because it spends so much of its time playing Caribbean islands, tiny central American countries, and Canada. Viewed from Mexico City, even the US is a soccer superpower. The Mexicans would win a lot fewer games (and would sink in our rankings) if they were moved into the South American confederation.

There are only two big surprises in our top ten of relative overachievers: Iran and Iraq. (If George W. Bush is reading this: at least be thankful that North Korea isn't there.) For a start: kudos to the Iranians. The international sanctions don't seem to have had much impact on their soccer. They qualified for the World Cup of 2014, and if they now start to open to the world, they could get even better.

But the stunner, for us, is Iraq. The years from 1990 to 2010—two Gulf Wars, massacres, sanctions, Saddam, near–civil war—were not happy ones for Iraqis. Nonetheless, over twenty years it scored nearly a goal a game more than you would expect given its resources.

It did so even while under the thumb of Saddam's family, which loved sports. Each April Baghdad celebrated Saddam's birthday by hosting the "Saddam Olympics." You may not have caught these on ESPN, but as late as 2002, with Baghdad's Russian-Iraqi Friendship Society as sponsor, Iraq attracted athletes from seventy-two countries. And not many people know that Baghdad was also bidding to host the real Olympics in 2012 before events intervened.

Saddam left control of the soccer team to his bestial son Uday. A playboy and pervert, who walked with a limp after an assassination attempt, Uday motivated his players by threatening to amputate their legs if they lost. One former international reported being beaten on the soles of his feet, dragged on his bare back through gravel, and then dipped in raw sewage so that his wounds would be infected. Some players spent time in Abu Ghraib prison. After Kuwait came to Baghdad in 1981 and won, one of the ruling family's helpers beat up the referee, who was then "driven hurriedly to the airport and put bleeding on a plane out of the country," writes Declan Hill in his book on global match fixing, *The Fix*.

Stories like these from Iraqi defectors prompted FIFA to send a committee to Iraq to investigate. The Iraqis produced players and coaches who swore blind that it was all lies. FIFA believed them, and so the Lions of Mesopotamia were allowed to keep on collecting prizes.

Only when American troops entered Baghdad in 2003 did they find the prison Uday maintained in the basement of Iraq's Olympic headquarters. It featured "a rack and a medieval torture device used to rip open a man's anus," writes James Montague in his *When Friday Comes: Football in the War Zone*.

But despite everything, under Saddam the Lions of Mesopotamia were the strongest team in the world's largest continent. Though they had to play on neutral ground for much of Saddam's reign due to the war with Iran, they qualified for the World Cup of 1986 and for three Olympics. As Iraqi supporters used to chant (often while firing bullets into the air), "Here we are Sunni—yah! Here we are Shiite—yah! Bring us happiness, sons of Iraq!" Even Kurds supported the Lions. Montague calls the team "arguably the last symbol of national unity left in Iraq." Only from the 1990s, as Saddam's regime became even more isolated and brutal, did Iraqi soccer decline. Its win percentage from 1980 to 2001 was still a magnificent 67 percent; in the turmoil from 2002 through 2012, it dipped to a merely impressive 55 percent.

All this may be a case of people immersing themselves in soccer because it was their only form of public expression. Huthyfa Zahra, an Iraqi artist who now produces soccer-themed "pop art" from the safety of nearby Abu Dhabi, says, "Even during the wars, in the nineties, there were bombs above us, and we were playing in the streets. Because we didn't have anything to do."

Why were the Lions so good under Saddam? Zahra is surprised to hear that they were. "We are much better now," he replies, "because the players play without fear now. If you don't feel comfortable, you can't play." He points out that since the fall of Saddam and Uday, Iraq's Lions have finished fourth in the Athens Olympics and won the Asian Cup of 2007. Iraqis may now finally be getting the chance to devote most of their energies to soccer. The American writer Nir Rosen reported in 2010:

> On my trips to Iraq in years past, I made a habit of scanning the walls of Baghdad neighbourhoods for bits of sectarian graffiti, spray-painted slogans that were pro-Mahdi Army, pro-Saddam, anti-Shiite or pro-insurgency. This time, however, there were almost none to be found; the exhortations to sectarian struggle had been replaced with the enthusiasms of youthful football fans: now the walls say "Long Live Barcelona."

Still, the presence of both Iran and Iraq in the top five of our "overachievers" table does illustrate the problem of comparing national teams from different continents. It is hard to imagine that either country would have done all that well against the other teams in the top ten. In fact, they have hardly ever played against the global big boys (neither Saddam's nor Mahmoud Ahmadinejad's boys got many invitations to exhibition games at Wembley). Mostly, Iran and Iraq beat Middle Eastern and Asian countries.

FIGURE 18.5. Top ten European teams by win percentage, games between European countries, 1990–2010

	Played	*Won*	*Tied*	*wpc*	*Goal difference*
Spain	151	0.623	0.232	0.738	1.298
France	157	0.592	0.274	0.729	0.955
Italy	166	0.542	0.295	0.690	0.729
Germany	159	0.585	0.208	0.689	0.925
Croatia	134	0.552	0.269	0.687	0.657
Netherlands	146	0.534	0.274	0.671	1.014
Czech Republic	135	0.570	0.193	0.667	0.911
Portugal	156	0.519	0.282	0.660	0.827
England	140	0.507	0.300	0.657	0.864
Romania	161	0.503	0.248	0.627	0.634

Furthermore, GDP statistics for poorer countries outside Europe (especially countries in the midst of war or sanctions) are notoriously unreliable. In general, there is more "noise" in all the data for countries outside Europe, meaning that we struggle to pick up the influence of the factors we are interested in. It's like listening to a radio with poor reception: the meaning of the words is hard to make out.

It therefore makes more sense to focus on Europe alone. Europe is a more homogeneous place than the world as a whole, meaning that differences, especially in income and experience, tend to be smaller. Second, the data are better: Europeans have been collecting them for longer, and they have a relatively long history of transparent record keeping (though there are some very suspicious European statistics). Last, most of the world's dominant teams are grouped together in Europe, playing against pretty much the same set of opponents. It all adds up to a fairly accurate picture of how well each European team performs.

Let's first rank the best European teams on their absolute performance, without taking into account their population, experience, or GDP. Taking only those games played between European teams (that is, eliminating games where at least one team comes from outside Europe), Figure 18.5 presents the "absolute" top ten ranked by win percentage.

Bunched at the top are the four European superpowers of modern times: Spain, France, Italy, and Germany. Very impressively, the Croats are only the tiniest notch behind them. For the most part, a knowledgeable fan would have been able to predict the European top ten (with the possible exception of Romania).

However, things become more interesting after we correct for population, experience, and GDP. Now a new picture emerges. We find that in Europe, home-field advantage boosts a team by a little under half a goal per game, compared with two-thirds of a goal in global soccer. Experience also counts for less in Europe than in the world in general, though it remains the most important of our key variables in winning soccer matches. Having twice the experience of your opponent gives you an advantage of about 30 percent of a goal per game. By contrast, population and GDP count for more in European soccer than they do in global soccer. Having twice the population as the other team is worth a quarter of a goal per game in Europe. Having twice the opponent's income per capita is worth about one goal every six games. So the factors in order of importance are (1) playing at home, (2) experience, (3) population, and (4) GDP.

Figure 18.6, the European efficiency table (the first of its kind, as far as we know), may be the most telling we have, so we rank every team for which we have data.

Again, the most important number is in the last column: each country's "relative goal difference." It turns out that all the leading European nations—Spain, France, Germany, Italy, and England—overachieve relative to their already considerable resources. These are large, well-connected countries, all of them richer than the European average. They should do well, but they are doing even better than expected. Against European opponents, each scores at least half a goal per game more than its resources would predict.

In eastern Europe, Croatia, Romania, and Serbia/Montenegro are overachievers. It's no coincidence that these are among the best-connected eastern European countries. Prague before communism was an unmistakably central European city, with many ties to Germany and Italy. Very soon after the fall of communism the Czechs had reforged networks with their western neighbors. Croatia and Serbia spent the communist era in the most open communist country, Yugoslavia, which among other things sent many soccer players to western clubs. And Rumania was an outlier in the Soviet bloc, always resistant to the USSR's control. After the fall of

FIGURE 18.6. **Overachievers: Ranking of European national teams, correcting for population, wealth, and experience, all games between two European opponents, 1990–2010**

	Played	*Won*	*Tied*	*wpc*	*GD*	*Out-performance*
Spain	151	0.623	0.232	0.738	1.298	1.185
Czech Republic	135	0.570	0.193	0.667	0.911	1.010
Netherlands	146	0.534	0.274	0.671	1.014	0.957
Portugal	156	0.519	0.282	0.660	0.827	0.888
Croatia	134	0.552	0.269	0.687	0.657	0.840
Romania	161	0.503	0.248	0.627	0.634	0.769
France	157	0.592	0.274	0.729	0.955	0.745
Serbia and Montenegro	61	0.361	0.328	0.525	0.426	0.687
England	140	0.507	0.300	0.657	0.864	0.668
Sweden	170	0.494	0.265	0.626	0.671	0.622
Germany	159	0.585	0.208	0.689	0.925	0.615
Italy	166	0.542	0.295	0.690	0.729	0.504
Denmark	162	0.469	0.259	0.599	0.451	0.439
Bulgaria	136	0.419	0.250	0.544	0.257	0.439
Republic of Ireland	119	0.420	0.353	0.597	0.412	0.346
Norway	155	0.458	0.290	0.603	0.568	0.341
Greece	169	0.491	0.231	0.607	0.325	0.257
Poland	178	0.421	0.253	0.548	0.157	0.156
Ukraine	127	0.386	0.307	0.539	0.071	0.151
Switzerland	132	0.409	0.273	0.545	0.242	0.098
Turkey	157	0.369	0.287	0.513	0.025	-0.006
Israel	137	0.358	0.277	0.496	0.073	-0.017
Bosnia-Herzegovina	80	0.350	0.175	0.438	-0.238	-0.037
Slovakia	126	0.333	0.262	0.464	-0.143	-0.043
Russia	133	0.459	0.286	0.602	0.586	-0.066
Montenegro	20	0.250	0.400	0.450	-0.250	-0.130
Belgium	121	0.355	0.264	0.488	-0.058	-0.139
Finland	146	0.301	0.281	0.442	-0.144	-0.163
Hungary	159	0.327	0.220	0.437	-0.189	-0.202

(Continues)

FIGURE 18.6. Overachievers *(continued)*

	Played	*Won*	*Tied*	*wpc*	*GD*	*Out-performance*
Slovenia	124	0.306	0.258	0.435	-0.258	-0.211
Belarus	112	0.268	0.232	0.384	-0.393	-0.218
Latvia	151	0.272	0.205	0.374	-0.444	-0.247
Georgia	128	0.242	0.203	0.344	-0.570	-0.290
Albania	124	0.242	0.250	0.367	-0.565	-0.351
Lithuania	147	0.286	0.190	0.381	-0.524	-0.360
Austria	114	0.316	0.237	0.434	-0.263	-0.399
Iceland	111	0.261	0.216	0.369	-0.523	-0.558
Moldova	119	0.218	0.227	0.332	-0.882	-0.569
Armenia	93	0.140	0.215	0.247	-1.172	-0.895
Cyprus	133	0.271	0.165	0.353	-0.947	-1.061
Estonia	165	0.139	0.242	0.261	-1.309	-1.212
Azerbaijan	107	0.112	0.234	0.229	-1.542	-1.252
Kazakhstan	52	0.058	0.212	0.163	-1.462	-1.306
Malta	146	0.096	0.151	0.171	-1.829	-1.921
Luxembourg	110	0.045	0.127	0.109	-2.164	-2.715

the Ceaucescu communist regime, the country's Latin-derived language helped it network with Italy, Spain, and France.

Now that we've reviewed all the evidence, who gets the Tom Thumb trophy—the poor, small, inexperienced man's Jules Rimet—for the relatively best team on earth? Which country does best allowing for experience, population, and income? Well, one day we'd like to see this played out on grass. Let's have a World Cup in which teams start with a handicap, settled by a panel of econometricians chaired by Professor Gerrard. But until that great day comes, all we have is our model. Clearly the Croats, Czechs, Iranians, and Portuguese have done wonders with their modest resources. However, the country that stands out most given what it has to work with is Iraq, even taking into account its easy Asian schedule. If the country ever achieves normality, then watch out, world.

Only one great question remains: which is the relatively worst team on earth? Figure 18.7 shows the worst underperformers relative to their population, income, and soccer experience.

FIGURE 18.7. **Worst underperformers, 1990–2010, entire world (of 116 teams with more than 100 games played)**

		Played	*Won*	*Tied*	*wpc*	*Under-performance*
116	Luxembourg	120	0.050	0.142	0.121	-2.371
115	Malta	158	0.114	0.152	0.190	-1.921
114	Estonia	195	0.169	0.246	0.292	-1.158
113	Cyprus	140	0.271	0.179	0.361	-1.141
112	Armenia	106	0.160	0.217	0.269	-1.076
111	Azerbaijan	132	0.167	0.235	0.284	-1.042
110	Sri Lanka	102	0.235	0.235	0.353	-0.881
109	Venezuela	192	0.240	0.234	0.357	-0.867
108	Swaziland	112	0.205	0.295	0.353	-0.830
107	Benin	109	0.220	0.220	0.330	-0.811

Luxembourg is the shocker. The country of just over half a million people ought to be bad at soccer, but in fact it's much, much worse than it should be. That seems surprising. It's sandwiched amid some of the best soccer nations on earth. If you judge by the map, Luxembourg is smack in the middle of the western European knowledge network. But networks are never simply geographical. Nobody in soccer wanted to network with Luxembourg because the country was too small to support a decent league or to produce many good players. Top-class foreign coaches and players were never spotted at the Jeunesse Esch stadium passing on their know-how. Admittedly, the nation's dry spell of fifteen years without a win ended with Paul Koch's legendary last-minute penalty save against Malta in 1995, but even after that the Luxembourgeois hardly hit the heights. In 2001 Joel Wolff, secretary-general of the country's FA, confessed to us in a world exclusive interview, "Let's say that we have arrived at a relative nadir." Whenever managers recited the verity, "There are no more minnows in international soccer," they were forgetting Luxembourg.

Happily, the country has improved a touch in recent years. There was the legendary 2–1 triumph over mighty Albania at home in 2011, and the 3–2 slaying of Northern Ireland in 2013. Still, looking at our period of study, we give Luxembourg the *Soccernomics* award for the relatively worst soccer team on earth.

19

MADE IN AMSTERDAM

The Rise of Spain and the Triumph of European Knowledge Networks

On the chilly Johannesburg evening of July 11, 2010, we proponents of Soccernomics genuinely thought we might be within five minutes of deciding the World Cup final. In extra time at Soccer City, Holland and Spain were still tied 0–0. Simon, sitting in the media stand, was barely watching the game anymore. Instead he was rereading on his laptop the PDF file that we had sent the Dutch camp that morning. The file's author was Ignacio Palacios-Huerta, the economics professor featured earlier in this book, who in 2008 had given Chelsea an analysis of Manchester United's penalty-takers for the Champions League final.

This time Ignacio, working day and night, had provided Holland with an analysis of the Spanish penalty-takers. (True, Ignacio has a Spanish passport, but as a Basque he was perfectly happy to see Spain lose.) With a penalty shoot-out looming in Johannesburg, the PDF suddenly made compelling reading. For instance, Ignacio had predicted that Xavi and Andres Iniesta, as right-footed players who didn't usually take penalties, would probably hit their kicks to the right of the Dutch keeper Maarten Stekelenburg. And Fernando Torres almost always kicked low. Against him, Stekelenburg would need to dive to the ground fast. "It's a report we can use perfectly," the Dutch goalkeeping coach Ruud Hesp had e-mailed us that morning. Now it looked as if we might be about to help the Dutch win the World Cup. Alternatively, if our advice was wrong, we might be about to help them lose it.

Just then, down on the field, Cesc Fabregas found Iniesta unmarked as if in some childhood training session on the sunny fields of Barcelona's academy, the Masía. Iniesta fired home. Simon closed the PDF and began writing his match report.

For all our best efforts, Spain's win was about as inevitable as victories in World Cups get. The country once derided as eternal losers had not merely become world champion; it was also the best team in the world. (Many world champions are not.) In fact, Spain had probably been best in the world for nearly a decade before 2010. Then, in 2012, it completed an unprecedented triple of European title, world title, European title. This Spain was arguably the best national team ever. Crucially, the country owed its triumphs in large part to its location in interconnected western Europe. The rise of Spain is the perfect example of our network theory: why the countries of western Europe still rule soccer.

II

Spain hadn't always been so connected. General Francisco Franco, Spain's fascist ruler from 1936 until his death in 1975, had isolated the country from the rest of Europe. Jimmy Burns, the Anglo-Spanish writer born in Madrid in 1953, recalls in his *When Beckham Went to Spain*:

> Spain was virtually a closed economy. I spent part of my childhood between England and Spain, smuggling things from London to Madrid, never the other way round—clothes, gramophone records, books and magazines. While England seemed to be very much part of the world, Spain even to my young eyes struck me as something of a world of its own, where kids of my age all seemed to be taught by either priests or nuns.

The cosmopolitan Real Madrid of Burns's childhood, studded with imported stars such as Alfredo di Stefano (from Argentina), Ferenc Puskás (Hungary), and Raymond Kopa (France), was very much the exception in Franco's Spain. Few foreigners wanted to join lesser clubs in this poor country, and those who tried to come were often blocked. For most of the 1960s Spain officially let in only foreign players of Spanish descent. In fact many Latin American players invented Spanish ancestors to get in—one Argentine claimed his father had come from "Celta," which isn't a town at all but the name of the club in Vigo—but even these imports didn't transform Spanish soccer. There weren't many of them, and they mostly weren't very good. Nor did Spanish players of the Franco era go abroad to learn new tricks.

Spain's isolation in those years was usually reflected in the national team's results. Though the country won the European Championship at home in 1964, in the period before western Europe made its great leap in soccer know-how, for the next forty years the Spaniards did almost nothing in international tournaments.

What saved Spain's soccer was the country's opening to Europe and the world. Spanish isolation began to break down in the last years of Franco's life. In 1973, just after Spain reopened its borders to foreign soccer players, FC Barcelona imported the great Dutchman Johan Cruijff. It is possible to draw a direct line between Cruijff's arrival in Barcelona and Spain's victory in Johannesburg thirty-seven years later.

Signing Cruijff had not been easy. Franco's regime often obstructed Spanish companies from making foreign payments, and Barcelona ended up having to register the player as a piece of agricultural machinery. In another mark of the isolationist climate of the time, an elderly Barça director lamented to the club's secretary Armand Carabén, "A Dutchman in the Nou Camp! What's the world coming to? This is pure madness. A man from the land of butter comes to the land of olive oil. Does nobody understand that even if he plays nicely, his stomach will be a mess within four days?"

But Cruijff was more than just stomach and legs. Possibly more than any other great player, he was brain, too. He was a philosopher of soccer, and the most important thing about soccer, for Cruijff, was the pass. He could (and often did) spend hours talking about the pass. You never passed into a teammate's feet, he lectured, but always a meter in front of him, to keep the pace in the game. While the first man was passing to the second man, the third man already had to be in motion ready to receive the second man's pass. Cruijff talked people silly about the pass.

In the early 1970s he and Barcelona's Dutch manager, Rinus Michels, introduced Spaniards to a form of Dutch "total football." The two men had arrived at just the right time. Besides opening to the world, Spain was then beginning its long economic rise.

Cruijff played his last game for Barcelona in 1978, but Spain would hear from him again. Much later, he would bring his ideas on soccer back to Catalonia. They would provide the underpinnings first of the great Barça sides, and eventually of the Spanish world champions of 2010.

Cruijff had planned to retire as a player after leaving Barcelona. However, he lost his money in a series of ill-advised ventures, most notably a pig farm, and had to start playing again. After a spell in the North American Soccer League with the Washington Diplomats and the Los Angeles Aztecs, he finished playing at Ajax in 1984. He stayed in Amsterdam, and a year later became manager of the club that he had first entered in the early 1950s as a toddler from down the road. As manager he went to the fields where Ajax's boys' teams played, fields that had practically been his backyard, and said that everything had to change. Years before Cruijff transformed Barcelona's academy, he transformed Ajax's.

Everything he did there was the sum of a lifetime's thinking about soccer. Cruijff once said that before he was thirty, he had done everything on instinct; but after thirty, he began to understand why he did it. No longer would Ajax's youth teams aim to win matches, the club's new manager told a surprised set of volunteers. From now on, the only purpose of the youth teams would be to turn talented boys into adult stars. That meant, above all, creating two-footed players who were masters of positional play and the pass. The boys in Ajax's academy would spend much of their time playing passing games, especially Cruijff's favorite, six against three. Cruijff's longtime assistant Tonny Bruins Slot recalled in the Dutch magazine *Voetbal International* in 2011, "Making triangles, getting a numerical advantage in midfield, speed of action in a small space, putting pressure on an opponent: everything was in there."

For Ajax's boys' teams, even matches became practical classes. Sometimes kids were put in older age groups, where they could no longer get by on natural brilliance or speed and had to develop guile, too. Often the coaches deliberately played boys out of position. "That began with

[Dennis] Bergkamp," said Bruins Slot. "He was a wonderful attacker anyway and the right-back in the under-18s just wasn't good enough. So we put Dennis in that position for a while. He managed it with his fingers in his nose [a Dutch phrase meaning "without any trouble"]. Also, Dennis could now put himself inside the mind of a defender, which would be useful to him as a striker. That was a success, so we began to do it more often."

Cruijff was always looking for lessons from other disciplines. An opera singer, Lo Bello, was brought in to teach Ajax's players how to breathe. In winter, when pitches were frozen, the boys attended lectures: a great female Ping-Pong player taught them how to deal with stress; a groundsman told them how to look after their gear; and a onetime promising youngster who had never made it explained where he had gone wrong.

Cruijff ran a red thread through the entire club, from the youngest boys' eleven to the first team. Every Ajax team in every age group played the same 4–3–3 formation as the great Holland and Ajax teams of the 1970s. (Cruijff said that only with 4–3–3 could every zone on the field be occupied.) When the opposition's left-back had the ball, Ajax's players from the under-eights to the first team knew exactly which positions they had to occupy to press him. When the outside-right from the under-eighteens made his professional debut, he felt entirely at home. That's one reason Cruijff happily threw kids into big European games: the seventeen-year-old Bergkamp turned a Swedish fullback and part-time policeman inside out one night, and returned to school in Amsterdam the next day.

And partly, it was simply that Cruijff was a born teacher. One of us, Simon, experienced it himself. When Simon interviewed the great man in his Barcelona mansion in 2000, Cruijff rose from his sofa and taught him how to kick with his left foot. "Look"—he demonstrated—"whether you kick with your right or left, the point is that you are standing on one leg. And if you stand on one leg, you fall over. So you need to adjust your balance, and the only way to do that is with your hand, your arm." And he kicked an imaginary ball with his left foot, flinging out his right arm. Simon's left foot improved instantly.

Cruijff left Ajax in 1988 after yet another argument, and stayed away until 2011, when he returned to the club as a director and spiritual godfather. However, Ajax's youth academy has always stuck to the Cruijffian model. It works. Over the past twenty years, homegrown Ajax players (including foreigners who joined the club as teenagers) have included Bergkamp, Edwin van der Sar, Frank and Ronald de Boer, Edgar Davids, Clarence Seedorf, Patrick Kluivert, Nwankwo Kanu, Zlatan Ibrahimovic, Maxwell, Steven Pienaar, Cristian Chivu, Rafael van der Vaart, Wesley Sneijder, Nigel de Jong, Jan Vertonghen, and most recently the Dane Christian Eriksen, who joined Tottenham in 2013.

In 1995 a largely homegrown Ajax team had beaten Milan in the Champions League final, with eighteen-year-old Kluivert scoring the winner. A few months later Simon visited Amsterdam to find out how the world could copy Ajax's model. After all, soccer progresses largely through international copying. Co Adriaanse, then the head of Ajax's youth academy, sat in the metal container that was his office and scoffed, "It's not a recipe for pancakes! Other clubs don't have a club style. They don't start with kids at eight years old. They don't have the quality. And there's no continuity."

Indeed, not even Arsène Wenger at Arsenal has managed to replicate Ajax's recipe. Something is lacking. In Wenger's years in London since 1996, Arsenal's youth teams have produced very few future stars: Ashley Cole (already nearly sixteen when Wenger inherited the club), Fabregas (sixteen when Wenger nabbed him from Barcelona), Gaël Clichy (nearly eighteen when he came to London from France), and most recently Jack Wilshere.

Only one club has learned Ajax's recipe: Barcelona. No wonder, because Cruijff carried the recipe across in person. It's the perfect case study of intra-European knowledge transfer. When the Dutchman moved from Amsterdam to the Nou Camp as head coach in 1988, he did something that few Barça coaches had ever done before: he went to the fields where Barcelona's youth teams played. There he saw a skinny kid in central midfield hitting perfect passes. "Take that boy off at halftime," he told the boy's coach. "Why?" asked the coach. "Because I'm putting him in the first team," said Cruijff. The skinny kid, whose name was Pep Guardiola, spent a decade in Barcelona's first team. From 2008 through 2012, Guardiola managed the Spanish, European, and world champions. He once said, "Johan Cruijff taught me the most. I worked six years with him and learned a terrific amount." Guardiola was only the latest in a line of Cruijffians in the Nou Camp. Guardiola's predecessor, Frank Rijkaard, was an Amsterdammer and an Ajax man. Rijkaard got the Barcelona job on Cruijff's recommendation despite having just been relegated from the Dutch Premier division with Sparta Rotterdam. Louis van Gaal, Barcelona's coach from 1997 through 2000, was also an Amsterdammer and Ajax man, though he absolutely did not get the job on Cruijff's recommendation. Van Gaal had played for Ajax in the early seventies, at the same time as Cruijff, but only in the second team. Van Gaal appears to have harbored a jealousy of Cruijff ever since. Though the personal feud between the two men has amused Dutch fans for years, both of them think almost exactly the same way about soccer. When Van Gaal came to Barcelona, he cemented the club's veneration of the pass. He advanced the careers of great passing kids like Xavi and Iniesta. Van Gaal and later Rijkaard didn't always win on the field, but they continued the transfer of Dutch know-how to Catalonia that Cruijff had begun in 1973.

When Guardiola became Barcelona's head coach, he restored and updated Cruijffism. How this works was explained to us in 2009 by Albert Capellas, then coordinator of Barça's youth academy. We met Capellas over beers in a Swiss hotel bar. A couple of weeks later, he was giving us a tour of the Masía, or farmhouse, the unlikely headquarters of Barça's academy until the little brick building with the sundial on the front was finally closed in 2011.

The day we visited the Masía, in October 2009, you could simply walk in off the street. There were no guards. Inside you got a coffee and a friendly welcome at the bar. It felt like the house of a large Catholic family. A deliveryman stopped by and carried an enormous ham into the kitchen. There was a room with foosball and billiards tables, but when we visited they were covered, because the boys in the Masía had to study for school. The doors to the garden were open, to let the sun flood in. In the garden stood a sculpture of a female body, which must have provoked the odd stray thought among the Masía's all-male residents.

From the upstairs windows of the Masía, you could look out onto the Nou Camp. You could almost touch it here. The boys of the Masía actually slept in the stadium; the little farmhouse had gotten too small to house them.

But that morning, nine months before the World Cup in South Africa kicked off, the Masía still felt as cozy as the canteen at the old, now destroyed little Ajax stadium, De Meer. Both places resembled neighborhood cafés, where men gathered for fellowship and coffee. Part of Ajax and Barcelona's secret is that they are local clubs, run by largely the same bunch of local men for decades. These locals are interested in the talented kids of today, because in ten years' time, when the kids are in the first team, the locals expect still to be around.

When the staff sat down to explain how the Masía worked, you felt as if you were being transported back to Amsterdam in 1985. For a start, said Capellas, Barça's youth teams all played the same 4–3–3 as the first team. When the opposition's left-back had the ball, Barça's players, from the under-eights to the first team, knew exactly which positions they had to occupy to press him. When the outside-right from the under-eighteens made his professional debut, he felt entirely at home. That was one reason Barcelona happily threw kids into big games: Iniesta, Xavi, and Messi were all playing regularly in the world's biggest stadium while still in their teens.

There were a lot of things the Masía didn't worry about. Until players reached their mid-teens, said Capellas, "we don't think about competition, or not so much." Boys' matches were treated as practical classes. The Masía didn't care about size, either. Nobody minded that Messi and Iniesta were short. Capellas said, "If he's small or if he's tall, for us that is not important. We don't test for physical capacities. We are always thinking about the technical and tactical capacities of each player." The players barely ever did fitness training without the ball. Even speed was of limited relevance. Guardiola, a slow runner, had moved the ball fastest.

Nor did the boys train much. Ninety minutes a day was enough, Capellas told us. Schoolwork took up much more of their time, because like Ajax, Barcelona knew that most of its players would never turn pro. This was not a ruthless corporation. "We treat our fifty boys like our family," said Pep Boade, Barça's grizzled old chief scout, and this didn't appear to be cant. Many youth academies are ruled by militaristic brutes, but Barça's coaches sounded like traditional Catholic mothers. When a boy was cut from the Masía, sometimes his rival would cry from guilt at having been better. Capellas said, "Messi and Iniesta don't live here anymore, but this is their home, they come by to eat, if they have a problem they come to talk to us, as they would to a mother or father. For us they are not stars. It's Leo, it's Bojan, it's Andres. Andres is humble. We say, 'You are a good man, you are an incredible person, don't lose your values.'"

In one regard, though, the Masía was hyperprofessional. What mattered to Barça, as to Ajax, was passing. Both academies fetishized the pass. Soccer, to Cruijff, was about making passing "triangles" on the field. If a player could do that, Cruijff picked him. That remains Barça's principle. Capellas recited the mantra, "Always the players must find triangles." Training, then, is a deep study of passing.

To pass, or to stop the other team from passing, you also need to know exactly where to be. The average player has the ball for only 53.4 seconds every game (according to Chris Carling, the English performance analyst at Lille in France) so any player's main job is to occupy the right positions for the other eighty-nine minutes and 6.6 seconds. The boys in the Masía spend a lot of time playing four against four, with two touches of the ball allowed, and with three "joker" players who join whichever team has the ball. You win this game by being in the right position: soccer as a sort of chess, rather than soccer as physical combat. In the sun of the Masía, just as at Ajax's youth complex De Toekomst ("The Future"), where the chill wind sweeps in off the highway, some great future players spent the mornings of their youth making Cruijffian triangles.

Our tour of the Masía ended in the dining room, where in late morning you could already smell a tasty lunch. "Home cooking," Capellas noted. On the plain whitewashed walls were pictures of Masía teams past. Capellas and Boade found the picture from 1988, with an absurdly skinny young Guardiola. Two other boys in the photo later became his assistant coaches at Barça. One of them, Tito Vilanova, would succeed him as head coach in 2012 before resigning a year later because of throat cancer.

Guardiola was another part of the Masía's secret. The academy produced the boys; he sent them on in the stadium next door. Capellas said, "When we play Real Madrid's youth teams, we are equal. Don't think Real doesn't have good youth players." Yet Real's boys rarely make the first team, because Madrid keeps buying stars. By contrast, Guardiola, like Cruijff, was a man of the club who knew exactly what was cooking in the Masía, even in the second-string youth teams.

"You have to have someone up there who says, 'Go in,'" said Capellas. That was easy when the kid was as good as Messi or Iniesta. But Guardiola had done the same with Pedro, not an obvious star, and he had stuck in the first team. In the sun outside the Masía, Capellas used his foot to draw a circle on the ground: Guardiola went from the Masía to the first team and then recruited from the Masía again. The circle was round, said Capellas.

Barça has been lucky, the club's then chief executive Joan Oliver admitted to us in 2009: "Yeah, good fortune exists always in the world, in every kind of industry. It's not possible always to guarantee that we will have a Messi or an Iniesta or a Xavi from the academy. Perhaps you could not get the best player of the world from your academy, but we get six, seven first-team players." That is not to mention Masía exports such as Jose Reina (Napoli) and Mikel Arteta (Arsenal).

FROM THE MASÍA TO JOHANNESBURG

In short, once Spain's isolation had been lifted in the last years of Franco, Barcelona began building a style based on knowledge transfer from Amsterdam. Eventually Spain adopted this made-in-Amsterdam game. At Euro 2008, the World Cup in South Africa and again at Euro 2012, the Spaniards often looked as if they were still making their triangles at morning practice at the Masía. They passed the ball up and down like little men filling in a crossword puzzle at top speed. Whenever they went 1–0 up, they simply made sure the opponent never got the ball again. The World Cup final was the forty-fourth straight game in which Spain had won after scoring first. Everyone knew exactly how the men in red played, yet it was impossible to beat them because they had become Cruijffian masters of the pass.

Spain became a great soccer nation because it joined European knowledge networks. This might sound like too neat a theory—the sort of thing you get when you let academics loose on something as mysterious and intuitive as soccer. Luckily, though, the facts seem to match our theory. Let's look at Spain's results, decade by decade:

We'll take the 1920s as an illustration of what Figure 19.1 shows. Spain won twenty-three of its thirty-two matches in the decade, or 72

FIGURE 19.1. The rise of Spain

Decade	*Played*	*Won*	*Tied*	*Lost*	*Winning %*	*Winning % (counting a tie as half a win)*
1920s	32	23	4	5	0.72	0.78
1930s	25	13	5	7	0.52	0.62
1940s	19	8	6	5	0.42	0.58
1950s	44	20	13	11	0.45	0.60
1960s	60	28	13	19	0.47	0.58
1970s	59	29	18	12	0.49	0.64
1980s	103	49	28	26	0.48	0.61
1990s	98	57	26	15	0.58	0.71
2000s	128	91	25	12	0.71	0.81

percent. It also tied four games. If we count a tie as worth half a win, then Spain's total winning percentage for the decade was 78 percent. The figure in the last column for each decade is the most telling one. It provides the best measure of Spain's success decade by decade.

The table demonstrates how closely Spain's soccer success tracks the country's integration with Europe. In the 1920s, before the civil war of the 1930s, Spain performed very well. But then isolation descended under Franco. From the 1930s through the 1980s, Spain's winning percentage hovered around a disappointing 60 percent. The team was winning about half its games, and drawing another quarter. That European Championship of 1964 was an anomaly. The broader story was that a poor, shut-off Spain was struggling to access the world's best soccer know-how. In these sorry decades Di Stefano, the Argentinian–turned Colombian–turned Spanish international, summed up Spain's soccer history in a phrase: "We played like never before, and lost like always."

But in 1986 Spain joined the European Union—a sort of formal entry into European networks. Soon afterward, the Spanish national team improved sharply. We have seen that a country's success at soccer correlates with its wealth. And Spain from the 1980s was growing richer fast. In the 1960s and 1970s its income per capita had been stuck at about 60 percent of the average of the core fifteen member nations of the EU. In the 1980s and 1990s Spain began to catch up. The Barcelona Olympics of 1992 nicely captured the rise: the Games showcased a "new Spain," and a young Spanish soccer team guided by twenty-one-year-old Pep Guardiola won gold.

Yet during this period the Spaniards continued to be mocked in international soccer as "notorious underperformers." Like England, they just couldn't match the big nations in big tournaments. However, the criticism was wrong. Even in these "bad" decades, Spain was already overachieving given its modest resources of people and wealth. It was simply not big or rich or connected enough to expect to match the leading nations in soccer.

Let's take the relatively recent period 1980 to 2001. For Spain this was a fallow period: failure in a World Cup hosted at home, and no performance of note save an appearance in the final of Euro 1984, which is remembered chiefly for goalkeeper Luis Arconada's fumbling of Michel Platini's free kick.

In absolute terms Spain's winning percentage (counting ties as half a win) of about 66 percent in that period ranked it somewhere near the bottom of the global top ten, around the same level as England. But we want to measure Spain's relative performance: how it achieved relative to its resources.

First let's look at experience. By 2001 Spain had played 461 internationals in its history. That itself is a marker of isolation. We've seen that according to Russell Gerrard's data, Sweden by 2001 was the most experienced country in international soccer, with 802 internationals. England, Argentina, Hungary, Brazil, and Germany (including West but not East Germany) had all played over 700 each. Spain—cut off for so many years—lagged.

When it comes to our second variable, wealth, Spain still fell short of most of its rivals. In the 1980s and 1990s it was significantly behind Germany, France, England, and even Italy.

And Spain was small. When people complain that the country underperforms, they usually mean it does worse than the giants of international soccer. Well, no wonder, given that Spain is much smaller than they are. Not only did Brazil in 1990 dwarf Spain's then population of 39 million people, but so did Germany, France, Italy, and even that other "notorious underachiever," England.

We calculated that Spain, given its population, income, and experience in the 1980–2001 period, "should" have scored on average 0.3 goals per game more than its opponents. But Spain did much better than that: it outscored opponents by nearly 0.9 goals, averaging nearly 0.6 goals more than expected. Of the teams that played at least one hundred games in this period, Spain was the eighth-best overperformer in the world. The country was an overachiever long before it began winning prizes. Until very recently, it just wasn't quite big or rich or experienced or lucky enough to win anything.

Consider, for instance, its record against Italy in those years. Over that period Spain's population, income per head, and international experience was on average about 30 percent inferior to Italy's. Given that, we would have expected Spain's goal difference to be about minus two over its four games against Italy. Instead Spain overachieved, notching a win, two ties, and a defeat with a goal difference of zero.

In short: Spain's bad times were not bad at all. It always was overachieving. But in the past twenty years or so, even taking into account the recent economic crisis, Spain's resources have improved. Since Spain joined the EU, the country's average income has risen to about three-quarters of the core EU's average. Its population has grown to 47 million. Spain has also become fully networked in Europe. Its best soccer players now experience the Champions League every season. A richer, more populous, more experienced, and more networked Spain became first a serious contender, and finally (thanks to its continued overachievement) the best team on earth.

Wealth, size, and integration have translated into goals. In the 1990s Spain's win percentage (still treating ties as worth half a win) shot up to over 70 percent. In the 2000s it was over 80 percent, with Spain losing just 12 percent of its games. From 2000 through 2009 the country won 71 percent of its matches outright, a long-term performance about as good as any other national team's since international soccer took off in the 1930s. Brazil never managed it. Even the all-conquering Italy of the 1930s won just 70 percent of its games that decade. Spain had become a great team long before it won titles. Here is Wayne Rooney in his autobiography describing a Spain-England exhibition game in 2004, a time when the Spaniards were still considered eternal losers:

> Spain had been taking the mickey, passing the ball back and forth, and showboating which upset me. When that happens, you have to try and break up your opponents' passing game by getting stuck into them, tackling hard and quickly. Perhaps I overdid it because I was so frustrated, but we couldn't get a kick of the ball. Not nice.

Of course the emergence from isolation cannot by itself explain Spain's success. Intangibles matter too—the sudden emergence of several great individuals, such as Xavi and David Villa. Spain was the only team at the 2010 World Cup with as strong a personnel as the best club teams. No other country in the tournament fielded eleven players who were starters at big clubs. Spain was massively overperforming its size and wealth, but that overperformance was possible only because of the end of isolation. Nor, clearly, has the financial crash of 2008 hurt Spain's national team. Despite the recession, the collapse of property values, and unemployment of over 20 percent, Spain has remained networked with the rest of Europe.

It was wonderfully appropriate that the Spaniards sealed their rise in a World Cup final against their mentor country. This was the Cruijff versus Cruijff final. Probably for the first time, both teams in soccer's biggest game were, in their origins, the product of one man. It was a triumph of intra-European knowledge transfer. That night in Johannesburg, the old Amsterdammer living in Barcelona must have felt like the proud father of twins—albeit that the Dutch twin behaved like a fratricidal delinquent.

Seven of the fourteen Spaniards who played in the match had spent time in the Cruijffian Masía; seven of the fourteen Dutchmen had come from Ajax's Cruijffian academy. One of those seven Dutchmen, Eljero Elia, had never even made it into Ajax's first team. Khalid Boulahrouz and André Ooijer, who sat on the Dutch bench that night, were also rejects of the Ajax academy. When even your dropouts are staffing the second-best national squad on earth, you are doing pretty well. Not as well as the Spaniards, though. Had Spain been able to field just one other product of the Masía—and when the Argentine Messi was a boy the Spaniards had begged him to play for their national youth teams—FIFA could have dispensed with the 2010 World Cup altogether and simply handed Spain the trophy at a quick ceremony in Zurich.

The Holland-Spain final was best understood as "Jungian mirroring," summed up David Winner, author of *Brilliant Orange: The Neurotic Genius of Dutch Soccer*: "Holland's path to the world title is blocked by the more authentic version of their better selves. It is now Spain who play Dutch soccer." That is how Cruijff saw it, too. "I thought my country would never dare to play like this and would never give up its own way of playing," he said after the game. He continued:

> Even without great players like in the past, a team has its own style. I had the wrong end of the stick. . . . They didn't want the ball. And unfortunately, and it's hard to say so, they played dirty. So bad that they really should quickly have been down to nine men. Then they made two such mean tackles that I felt the pain myself. This nasty, vulgar, hard, closed game that wasn't watchable and was barely soccer anymore—yes, with that they could trouble Spain. They played anti-soccer.

But perhaps Holland had to, because the Spaniards were now better at soccer. The Dutch had taught the Spaniards how to play, just as in the Dutch-Spanish Eighty Years' War (1568 to 1648) the Dutch had sold the Spaniards arms. In Johannesburg, Holland paid for it.

20

CORE TO PERIPHERY

The Future Map of Global Soccer

On a snowy night in Amsterdam, a dozen or so Dutch soccer writers and ex-players have gathered in an apartment in the dinky city center. Guus Hiddink walks in and grabs someone's shoulders from behind by way of greeting. Growing up with five brothers gave him a knack for male bonding. (Hiddink appears to find women more exotic, and his cohabitation with his then mistress in Seoul shocked Koreans.)

The evening starts with a soccer quiz, at which the future manager of Chelsea, Russia, and Turkey performs indifferently. Then there is food and soccer talk until the early morning. Though Hiddink is the senior figure at the table, he never tries to dominate. He likes telling stories—about his former player Romario, or his old roommate at the San Jose Earthquakes, George Best—but when others interrupt he is just as happy to lean back in his chair and listen. He is a solid, soothing, jowly presence. "You can feel he's at ease," Boudewijn Zenden, one of his former players, told us, "so if he's at ease, the others are at ease. He creates this environment where you feel safe."

Hiddink—a great success as a coach until 2008, less so in his declining years—has a special place in the latest stage of soccer's history. In the twenty-first century, he became one of the world's main exporters of soccer know-how from western Europe to the margins of the earth. We saw in Chapter 16 that from about 1970 to 2000, the six founding members of the European Economic Community dominated soccer thinking and won almost all the game's prizes. These countries perfected what you might call the continental European style: a fast, physical, collectivist soccer.

But then these countries began exporting their expertise. Hiddink and other Dutch, German, French, and Italian expat managers established themselves in Hiltons and westerners' compounds around the planet. In the past few years they have helped several new soccer countries—Russia, Australia, and South Korea, to name a few—catch up with the managers' own native countries. It's because of men like these that England will not be the best soccer country of the future. Hiddink's native Holland appears even more thoroughly doomed. On the new map of soccer, which Hiddink helped to draw, his own country will shrink to a dot. Soccer know-how is being globalized fast.

FROM THE BACK CORNER TO THE WORLD

Born in 1946, Hiddink grew up close to what was just becoming the epicenter of global soccer knowledge. He is the son of a village schoolteacher and Resistance hero from a small town in the Achterhoek, or "Back Corner," about five miles from the German border. The Back Corner is wooded and quiet, one of the few empty bits of the Netherlands, and on visits home from stints in Seoul or Moscow, Hiddink enjoys tooling along its back roads on his Harley-Davidson Fat Boy. "Pom-pom-pom-pom-pom." He puffs out his cheeks to mimic the motor's roar.

He grew up milking cows, plowing behind two horses, and dreaming of becoming a farmer. But Dutch farms were already shedding labor, and he became a soccer coach instead. At nineteen he took an assistant's job at the Back Corner's semiprofessional club, De Graafschap, where his father had played before him. He then made an unusual career move: from coach to player. The head coach, seeing that his young assistant could kick a ball, stuck him in the team, and thus began a sixteen-year playing career.

The handsome, round-faced, wavy-haired playmaker was too lazy and slow for the top, yet he was present at a golden age. The Dutch 1970s shaped Hiddink. Holland, playing what foreigners called "total football," a new kind of game in which players constantly swapped positions and thought for themselves, reached two World Cup finals. Dutch clubs won four European Cups. Off the field, Dutch players of Hiddink's generation answered foreign journalists' questions with sophisticated discourses in several languages. For a keen observer like Hiddink, the players' constant squabbles provided object lessons in how to keep stars just about functioning within a collective.

Dutch soccer's renown at the time helped even a second-rate player like Hiddink find work abroad, with the Washington Diplomats and the San Jose Earthquakes. "I was Best's roommate," says Hiddink, enjoying the quirky American word, and he mimics himself fielding the phone calls from Best's groupies: "George is not here. George is sleeping."

It was the start of a world tour whose recent destinations have included South Korea, Australia, a suite in a five-star hotel in Moscow (where, according to the president of the Russian FA, he spent a fortune ordering cappuccinos from room service), and Istanbul. Hiddink got the Koreans playing the best soccer in their history at the World Cup of 2002, the Australians playing their best ever in 2006, and the Russians at Euro 2008.

True, he then failed to take the Russians to the World Cup of 2010, and the Turks to Euro 2012. There are signs that after passing sixty he lost some of his drive. Moreover, once almost all countries began trying to acquire western European know-how, he lost some of his first-mover advantage. Nonetheless, Hiddink and other expat western European coaches like him are helping to shift power in soccer from their own region to the rest of the world. It's no coincidence that this is happening just as economic power is shifting in the same direction.

1889–2002: OFF THE PLANE WITH A LEATHER SOCCER BALL

Soccer seems to have a quality that enables it eventually to conquer every known society. The first exporters of the game were Victorian British sailors, businessmen, missionaries, and colonial officers. In 1889, to cite a typical story, twenty-one-year-old Englishman Frederick Rea disembarked on the island of South Uist off the west coast of Scotland to work as a headmaster. A couple of years later two of his brothers visited, carrying with them a leather soccer ball. Within two decades the game had conquered South Uist. Shinty, a stick sport that had been played there for 1,400 years, "was wiped like chalk from the face of the island," wrote Roger Hutchinson in the British soccer journal *Perfect Pitch* in 1998, "supplanted, like a thousand of its distant relatives from Buenos Aires to Smolensk, by a game almost as young and innocent as Frederick Rea himself." Today soccer is the dominant sport on South Uist. It conquered because of its magic.

Victorian Britons spread the game to continental Europe, Latin America, and bits of Africa. However, for a century Asia and North America remained almost immune. Contrary to myth, soccer took a long time to become a global game. What people called the "World Cup" should until the 1980s have been called "the Euro–Latin American Duopoly." Though most people on the planet lived in Asia, the continent's only representative at the World Cup of 1978 was Iran. Even in 1990 the British Isles had more teams at the World Cup (three) than all of Asia combined (two). Many Asian countries still barely knew about soccer. When that year's World Cup final was shown on Japanese television, there was a surprising studio guest: baseball player Sadaharu Oh. "Mr. Oh," he was asked during the match, "what is the difference between sliding in baseball and in soccer?" In Australia, too, soccer then was still marginal. Johnny Warren, an Australian international and later TV commentator on the game, called his memoirs *Sheilas, Wogs, and Poofters,* because according to Australian myth in the years before Hiddink landed there, women, immigrants, and homosexuals were the three core elements of the national soccer public.

But by 1990 the so-called third wave of globalization was under way. Increased world trade, cable television, and finally the Internet brought soccer to new territories. Roberto Fontanarrosa, the late Argentine cartoonist, novelist, and soccer nut, said, "If TV were only an invention to broadcast soccer, it would be justified."

Suddenly the Chinese, Japanese, Americans, and even many urban Indians could see soccer's magic. They saw it even more clearly than the people of Uist had a century before. Soccer by now had the prestige of being the world's biggest sport, and everyone wanted a piece of its fans' passion. Soccer is often mocked for its low scores, but precisely because goals are so scarce, the release of joy is greater than in other sports. When the former goalkeeper Osama bin Laden visited London in 1994, he watched four Arsenal matches, bought souvenirs for his sons in the club shop, and remarked that he had never seen as much passion as among soccer supporters.

Just then soccer was capturing the last holdouts. On May 15, 1993, Japan's J-League kicked off. The next year China acquired a national professional league, and in 1996 the US and India followed. A therapist we met in San Francisco nicely described the game's impact on new converts. When she'd first seen a World Cup on TV, her reaction was: "Why didn't anybody ever tell me about this?" She hadn't stopped watching soccer since. She stands for millions of Americans (and Indians, Chinese, inhabitants of South Uist, and so on).

From the 1990s the new marginal countries began to hire European coaches who could quickly teach them the latest in soccer. By the turn of the millennium, Hiddink was an obvious candidate for export. He had won the European Cup with PSV Eindhoven, had managed clubs in Turkey and Spain, and had taken Holland to the World Cup semifinal in 1998. After he passed fifty, he felt his ambition begin to wane. Never a workaholic to start with, the boy from the Back Corner had by now proven himself. He had met with triumph and disaster and treated those two impostors just the same. He had gone from villager to cosmopolitan. He had fallen in love with golf. Soccer was becoming just a hobby.

He took a break and in 2001 popped up in his first missionary posting, as manager of South Korea. As part of the globalization of soccer, the country was due to cohost the 2002 World Cup with Japan. South Korea had played in several World Cups before but had never won a single match, and in 1998 had lost 5–0 to Hiddink's Holland.

When Hiddink landed in Seoul, history was beginning to work in his favor. Like many emerging nations, the South Koreans were getting bigger. Thanks to increased wealth, the average height of a South Korean man had risen from five foot four in the 1930s to about five foot eight by 2002. That meant a bigger pool of men with the physique required to play international soccer. In an interview during a Korean training camp in the Back Corner, a year before the World Cup, Hiddink told us he'd caught Koreans using their smallness as an excuse in soccer. He added, "But I won't allow that. I won't let them say beforehand, 'They're a bit bigger and broader; we're small and sad.' And gradually I notice that some of our players are big, too, and know how to look after themselves." The "height effect" was also quietly lifting many other emerging soccer countries, from China to Turkey.

But the Koreans had other problems. The Dutch psychological quirk had been squabbling. The Korean disease, as Hiddink soon discovered, was hierarchy. In Korean soccer, the older the player, the higher his status. A thirty-one-year-old veteran international was so respected he could coast. At meals, the group of older players would sit down at the table first, and the youngest last.

Whereas Dutch players talked too much, Koreans were practically mute. "Slavishness is a big word," Hiddink said that day in the Back Corner, "but they do have something like: if the commander says it, we'll follow it blindly. They are used to thinking, 'I'm a soldier. I'll do what's asked of me.' And you have to go a step further if you want to make a team really mature. You need people who can and will take the team in their hands." Hiddink wanted autonomous, thinking "Dutch," players: a center half who at a certain point in the game sees he should push into midfield, a striker who drops back a few yards. He was teaching the Koreans the Dutch variant of the continental European style.

Hiddink said of his players, "Commitment is not their problem. Almost too much. But if your commitment is too high, you often lose the strategic overview."

Hiddink had started out in Korea by kicking a couple of the older players out of his squad. He made a young man captain. He asked his players to make their own decisions on the field. "That makes them a bit freer, easier," he said. Shortly before the World Cup, he brought back the jilted older players, who by then were pretty motivated.

However, the educational process in Korea was always two-way. During his eighteen months in the country, Hiddink learned a few things himself. Already during his stints in Turkey and Spain he had begun freeing himself from the national superiority complex that pervades Dutch soccer: the belief that the Dutch way is the only way. In Holland, soccer is a thinking person's game. When the Dutch talk about it, the concepts to which they always return are *techniek* and *tactiek*. *Passie*, or passion, was a quality they associated with soccer players from unsophisticated countries, such as England. In Korea, Hiddink learned that it was actually pretty important. Even when speaking Dutch he tends to describe this quality with the English word *commitment,* perhaps because there is no obvious Dutch equivalent.

He had also learned what every successful missionary knows: respect the native way of life, or at least pretend to, because otherwise the natives won't listen to you. That afternoon in the Back Corner he said, "I don't go to work on the culture of the country. I just leave it; I respect it. I only do something about the conditions that they need to perform on the pitch. And of course there are a couple of things off the field that do influence that."

At the 2002 World Cup the Koreans played with a fervor rarely seen in soccer. Helped by bizarre refereeing decisions, the country from soccer's periphery reached the semifinal.

Korea had craved global recognition, and Hiddink achieved it. Korean cities planned statues in his honor, and a caricature of his face appeared on Korean stamps. Hiddink's autobiography appeared in a Korean print run of a half million, despite having to compete with an estimated sixteen Hiddink biographies. In the Back Corner, Korean tour buses made pilgrimages to the Hiddink ancestral home. Soon after the World Cup, the man himself dropped by to visit his octogenarian parents. "Well, it wasn't bad," admitted his father. "Coffee?"

2002–2004: THE PERIPHERY TAKES OVER INTERNATIONAL SOCCER

During that World Cup of 2002, other peripheral soccer countries were emerging, too. Japan reached the second round, the US got to the quarters, and Korea was conquered in the match for third place by Turkey, which hadn't even played in a World Cup since 1954.

We said in Chapter 16 that a country's success in soccer correlates strongly with three variables: its population, its income per capita, and its experience in soccer. For Turkey as for many other emerging countries, all three variables were improving fast.

From 1980 through 2001, Turkey was the second-worst underperformer in European soccer. It scored a full goal per game fewer than it should have given its vast population, decent experience in international soccer, and admittedly low incomes.

But just as that period was ending, the Turks were improving. It is no coincidence that the country went from being a pathetic soccer team to an occasional contender in Europe at the same time as it grew from a midsize European state into the continent's third–most populous nation. Turkey had 19 million inhabitants in 1945, double that by 1973, and over 80 million by 2013. In Europe, only Russia and Germany have more. While Turkey's population grows, most European countries are losing people. Add several million Turks in the diaspora, and the relative youth of most Turks, and the country starts to rival even Germany in its soccer potential. And Turkey is just one of many developing countries whose population is fast outstripping that of rich countries.

At the same time, Turkey's economy was booming, and it was using some of the new money to import soccer knowledge. In Chapter 16, we had measured a country's soccer experience by how many matches its national team had played. However, there is a shortcut to gaining experience: import it. This process began for Turkey in June 1984, when West Germany got knocked out of the European championship. The Germans sacked their coach, Jupp Derwall. That year he joined Galatasaray and began to import the continental European style of soccer into Turkey.

Derwall and other German coaches (as well as the Englishman Gordon Milne at Besiktas) got Turkish players actually working. They also introduced the novel idea of training on grass. Turkish television began showing foreign matches, which introduced some Turkish viewers to the concept of the pass.

Before Derwall's arrival, the average Turkish player had been a tiny, selfish dribbler. Derwall shipped German-born Turks into Galatasaray. The German Turks were bigger than Turkish Turks thanks to a better diet, and they trained like Germans. Admittedly, soon after arrival in Istanbul they were exposed to the sultanesque harem lifestyle of many Turkish players and their game deteriorated, but it was a start. Diaspora Turks—mostly from Germany—have continued to give Turkey a fast track to European soccer know-how. No other national team in Europe includes as many players who grew up in other European countries.

In 1996 Turkey qualified for its first major tournament since 1954. Though it didn't score a goal or register a point at Euro '96, it was judged to have done quite well. It has since reached two semis and a quarterfinal at major tournaments.

Despite a fallow period after 2008, globalization has improved Turkish soccer. Turks came to the realization that every marginal country needs: there is only one way to play good soccer—combine Italian defending with German work ethic and Dutch passing into the European style. ("Industrial soccer," some Turks sulkily call it.) In soccer, national styles don't work. You have to have all the different elements. You cannot win international matches playing traditional Turkish soccer. You need to play continental European soccer.

Both Hiddink's and Turkey's experiences point to an important truth: in soccer, "culture" doesn't matter much. Perhaps, as the former French president Giscard d'Estaing said when he drafted the European Union's failed constitution, Turkey had "a different culture, a different approach, a different way of life," but it didn't stop the Turks getting better at soccer. Cultures are not eternal and unalterable. When they have an incentive to change—like the prospect of winning more soccer matches, or perhaps the prospect of getting richer—they can change.

Turkey was only one of many countries brave enough to jettison its traditional soccer culture. Most countries on the fringes of Europe had dysfunctional indigenous playing styles. The ones on the southern fringe—Greece, Turkey, Portugal—favored pointless dribbling, while the British and Scandinavians played kick-and-rush. Gradually they came to accept that these styles didn't work.

Nobody did better out of abandoning their roots and adopting continental European soccer than Turkey's friends across the water, the Greeks. The Greek national team had traditionally played terrible soccer in front of a couple thousand spectators. During foreign trips, its camp followers—friends, journalists, and miscellaneous—would hang around the team hotel drinking espressos with players until the early morning. When Greece somehow made it to the World Cup of 1994, it ended up regretting it. At the team's training sessions outside Boston, an outfield player would stand in the goal while the others blasted shots into the bushes. They spent most of the tournament traveling the East Coast of the US to receptions with Greek Americans, though they did find time to be thrashed in three matches. In 2002, Greece gave up on the Greek style and imported a vast chunk of experience in the person of an aging German manager, Otto Rehhagel.

The Rhinelander was the prototypical postwar West German collectivist. He had grown up a healthy drive across the border from Hiddink, amid the ruins of postwar western Germany. An apprentice housepainter and bone-hard defender, Rehhagel was brought up on the "German virtues" of hard work and discipline. As a coach in Germany for decades, he aimed to sign only collectivist European-type players whose personality had been vetted by his wife over dinner in the Rehhagel home. Everywhere he tried to build an organization. Sacked as manager of Arminia Bielefeld, he sighed, "At least thanks to me there is now a toilet at the training ground." On later visits to Bielefeld with other clubs, he always inquired about his toilet.

Rehhagel quickly rooted out Greece's cult of the soloist, introduced core European soccer, and took the team to Euro 2004 in Portugal. There he went around saying things like, "Now that I am coaching Greece, I want to make one philosophical statement. Please write it down: man needs nothing more than other people." Banal as this sounded, it must have resonated in postwar West Germany. Certainly the Greek players, who pre-Rehhagel never seemed to have heard of collective spirit, had begun preaching the notion in many languages. "We was very good organized," said Zisis Vryzas after Greece beat France in the quarterfinals. Angelos Charisteas, the reserve at Werder Bremen who would become the highest scorer of Euro 2004, eulogized, "We have a German coach, he has a German mentality, and we play like a German team." In fact, Greece had made the same journey as Turkey: from midget dribblers to boring European soccer thanks to German coaching.

Rehhagel himself called it "learning from European soccer." At the time becoming "European"—code for becoming organized—was the aspiration of many marginal European countries, in soccer and outside. Just as these countries were joining the European Union, they were absorbing

European soccer. The final of Euro 2004 pitted Greece against another recently marginal country. The Greeks beat the Portuguese 1–0 thanks to another header from Charisteas, who soon afterward would be a reserve again at Ajax. It turned out that with merely half-decent players, a good continental European coach, and time to prepare, almost any marginal country could do well.

2005–2006: EVEN AUSTRALIA

In this new climate, the best continental European coaches could pick their posts. Hiddink received many offers to take teams to the World Cup of 2006, but he chose the most marginal country of all: Australia.

In 1974, while Hiddink was still absorbing total soccer in the Back Corner, Australia had qualified for its first World Cup as Asia's sole representatives. The Socceroos of the day were part-timers, and some had to give up their jobs to go to Germany. The German press was particularly interested in the milkman-cum-defender Manfred Schaefer, who had been born in Hitler's Reich in 1943 and came to Australia as a child refugee after the war. At one point in the tournament West Germany's striker Gerd Müller asked him if he really was an amateur. Well, Schaefer proudly replied, he had earned $4,600 by qualifying for the World Cup. "That's what I earn a week," said Müller.

The Australians achieved one tie in three matches at the World Cup. "However," writes Matthew Hall in his excellent book about Australian soccer, *The Away Game,* "their thongs, super-tight Aussie Rules–style shorts and marsupial mascots endeared them to the German public."

In the next thirty years, soccer sank so low in Australia that the country's soccer federation was sometimes reduced to filming its own matches and giving them to TV channels for free. Australian club soccer was punctuated by weird vendettas between Balkan ethnic groups. Only in 1997, during the new wave of globalization, were the Socceroos of 1974 publicly honored in their own country.

Then, in 2005, Hiddink landed with a mission to teach European soccer. First he gathered the Australian team in a training camp in his native Back Corner. His first impression: "What a bunch of vagabonds. Everyone came in wearing a cap, or flip-flops. One had on long trousers, another shorts, and another Bermuda shorts. I said, 'What is this?' 'Well, that's how we live.' 'Hello, but you probably play like that, too.'"

Hiddink spent Australia's first training session in the Back Corner watching his new charges fly into each other like kamikaze pilots. "You don't have to chase these guys up," he remarked. After a half hour he stopped the game. When the players' cries of "Come on, Emmo!" "Hold the ball, Johnno!" "Let's go!" and the streams of "Fucking" had finally faded, Hiddink asked them to shout only when a teammate was in trouble and needed coaching. That would improve everyone's vision of play, he said. The game resumed in near silence. It was Australia's first baby step toward continental European soccer.

Just as he had with the Koreans, Hiddink was turning the Australians into Dutch soccer players. That meant giving them the intellectual discipline needed for the World Cup. The Australian way was to train hard, play hard, but then relax with late-night beers in the hotel bar. Hiddink wanted the players thinking on their own about their jobs. Working hard wasn't enough. Since the Australians already had "commitment" and *passie*, Hiddink was teaching them to think like Dutchmen. The Socceroos tended to run to wherever the ball was. Hiddink forbade them from entering certain zones. In European soccer, doing the right things is always better than doing a lot of things.

He had noticed that at the Confederations Cup of 2005, shortly before he took over, where the Socceroos had lost all their three games and conceded ten goals, all four Australian defenders would often stay back to mark a single forward. That left them short elsewhere on the field. No semiprofessional Dutch team would be so naive.

Hiddink was surprised that the Australians were so willing to listen to him. They understood that they had a chance to learn the European style from the man himself. Hiddink had always excelled in dealing with difficult characters: Romario, Edgar Davids, or the Korean Ahn Jung-Hwan. He knew just how to touch them. But the Australians, he admitted, were "zero difficult."

Except perhaps Mark Viduka, Australia's best but not its most committed player. Hiddink recalled later, "He came in with, 'Oh, I'd like to go to a World Cup, but it's going to be difficult. We've never made it, and I'm not fit.'" Hiddink sent the Socceroos' physiotherapist to work with

Viduka at his club, Middlesbrough. This didn't merely get the player fit. It made him feel wanted. Hiddink also made Viduka his captain, to make sure he would be inside the tent pissing out rather than outside pissing in.

It was striking how quickly the Socceroos learned European soccer. Once again, "culture" seemed to be no obstacle. In November 2005, only a couple of months after Hiddink had started part-time work with them (he was also coaching PSV at the other end of the globe), they beat Uruguay in a playoff to qualify for the World Cup. Suddenly the *Melbourne Herald Sun* found itself wondering whether the sport of "Aussie Rules" football could remain dominant in Australia's southern states. Already more Australian children played soccer than Aussie Rules and both rugby codes combined.

The newspaper's worries appeared justified when a few months later, just before the World Cup of 2006, an Australia-Greece soccer friendly drew 95,000 people to the Melbourne Cricket Ground. In no city in Europe or Latin America could such a game have drawn such a crowd. Australia had also just become approximately the last country on earth to acquire a national professional soccer league.

And then Hiddink led the Socceroos to the second round of the World Cup of 2006. Great crowds of Australians set their alarm clocks to watch at unearthly hours. Soon after the Socceroos got back from Germany, Australia launched its own (disastrous) bid to stage a World Cup. What had happened on Uist more than a century before is now threatening to happen in Oz. A century from now, Aussie Rules might exist only at subsidized folklore festivals.

2006–2009: HIDDINK TO GHIDDINK IN A MOSCOW HOTEL SUITE

After Australia, Hiddink could have had almost any job in soccer. In an ideal world, he would have liked to manage England. Of all the world's marginal soccer countries, England had the most potential because it was rich and fairly large and had recently rejoined the network of core countries.

Hiddink also relished the specific challenges of managing England. He had the psychological expertise to inspire tired multimillionaires. He loved dealing with difficult characters; Wayne Rooney would be a cinch for him. And he would have improved the thinking of a team that had everything but intellect. As a lover of the bohemian life, he would have been happy in London, and his girlfriend would have been an hour from her beloved Amsterdam. But Hiddink couldn't bear the thought of British tabloids crawling over his family, and so he decided to spread his continental European know-how to Russia instead.

Like England, Russia had always been removed from the best western European soccer know-how. The country didn't have much of a tradition. The excellent Soviet side of the 1980s had been largely Ukrainian. But now, after communism, Russia's door to the West had opened slightly. There was potential here.

Admittedly, the country's population was collapsing rather than growing, as Russian men drank themselves to death. However, when Hiddink took the job, the Russian economy was moving the right way. In the decade from 1998, Russian income per capita nearly doubled. The country's new oil money bought Hiddink's brain. (Oil in general has become one of the dominant financial forces in modern soccer.)

As in Korea, Hiddink's job was to force his players to be free. Traditionally, Russian soccer players had the "I only work here" demeanor of *Homo sovieticus.* They feared their coaches as much as they feared the mafiosi who stole their jeeps. They shoved safe sideways passes into each other's feet, because that way nobody could ever shout at them. There was *zaorganizovannost,* overorganization.

Ghiddink, as the Russians call him, joked with his players, relaxed them. As a "punishment" in training, a player might have a ball kicked at his backside, while the rest of the squad stood around laughing. The times helped: this generation of Russian players could barely remember the USSR. Armed with iPhones and SUVs, they had left the periphery and joined the global mainstream.

As he had in Korea, Hiddink practically ordered his players to think for themselves, to give riskier passes, to move into new positions without his telling them to. Marc Bennetts, author of *Soccer Dynamo: Modern Russia and the People's Game,* said, "It's as if he's beaten the Marxism-Leninism out of them." At Euro 2008, Russia's hammering of Ghiddink's native Holland was the ultimate triumph of a marginal country over a core one. It also provided the almost unprecedented sight of Russian soccer players having fun. They swapped positions and dribbled, knowing that if they lost the ball no one would scream at them. After the game, their best player, Andrei Arshavin, muttered something about "a wise Dutch coach" and cried.

Russia lost in the semis of Euro 2008 to another former marginal country, Spain. By then, after twenty-two years in the European Union, Spain was so networked that it didn't even need a foreign coach to win the Euro.

Spain, Russia, and Turkey, another semifinalist at Euro 2008, were all beneficiaries of the spread of soccer know-how to marginal countries. When all countries have about the same soccer information, and converging incomes, the countries with the most inhabitants usually win. Three of the four semifinalists at Euro 2008 (Russia, Germany, and Turkey) had the largest populations in Europe.

The rise of the periphery is now upsetting soccer's traditional order. We've noted that western European teams lost six matches to nations from other regions in South Africa in 2010, compared with only one (on penalties) in Germany in 2006. The old ruling countries now have to keep learning tactically to stay on top. The English haven't. The Spaniards, Germans, and Dutch have. They constantly exchange knowledge with each other.

But in the long term, even that might not be enough to save small core countries like Holland, Denmark, or the Czech Republic. Their populations and economies are almost static, and they have exported their soccer knowledge. What made them unique between 1970 and 2000 was their networks. Now that the networks have expanded to include much of the world, they are probably doomed.

2014–?: THE PERIPHERY WINS THE WORLD CUP

Until the late 1990s the cliché in soccer was that an African country would "soon" win the World Cup. Everyone said it, from Pelé to the 1950s England manager Walter Winterbottom. But it turned out not to be true, mostly because although African populations were growing, their incomes remained too low to import much good soccer experience.

FIGURE 20.1. US team's results by decade, 1947–2010

Period	*Games*	*W*	*T*	*L*	*Goals for*	*Goals against*	*Win percentage*	*Goals scored per game*	*Goals conceded per game*
Prewar	26	9	2	15	54	83	0.385	2.1	3.2
1947–1960	40	11	3	26	72	160	0.313	1.8	4.0
1961–1970	22	6	4	12	32	49	0.364	1.5	2.2
1971–1980	81	22	19	40	81	161	0.389	1.0	2.0
1981–1990	88	32	22	34	103	101	0.489	1.2	1.1
1991–2000	202	83	52	67	271	210	0.540	1.3	1.0
2001–2010	168	96	25	47	282	169	0.646	1.7	1.0

A better tip for future World Cups might be Iraq. If the country remains halfway stable, it's likely to do even better than it did in its years of madness. However, the best bets for the future are probably Japan, the US, or China: the three largest economies on earth, which can afford good European coaches, where potential soccer players have enough to eat and don't get terrible diseases.

Just look at how far the US has come in the last sixty years. The team's results, decade by decade, are shown in Figure 20.1.

The nadir for "Team USA" was the postwar period up to 1960. This coincided with the peak of American dominance as a superpower and the American dream. It might sound odd that the world's mightiest country was such a mouse at soccer, but in fact for most of these years the US felt little need to measure itself against other countries. It had its own games. Prewar, an American team staffed largely with recent immigrants had played fairly often against Europeans and South Americans. After the war the number of games slumped.

But we can see that from the 1970s, the US grew more interested in soccer. The North American Soccer League took off, the national team began playing more often, especially against Europeans, and results improved. Things continued to get better in the 1980s (when the US started playing more against South Americans) and then again in the 1990s when the country returned to World Cups. It's not that the US started scoring more goals; rather, it gradually learned to concede fewer.

Defense is always more mechanical than offense, so it appears that in these decades the US was learning from the rest of the world, and from foreign coaches like Bora Milutinovic. The country's soccer was emerging from isolation. Yet when we calculated the world's worst underachieving nations for the period 1980–2001, the US still made our bottom ten on earth. Given the country's fabulous wealth and enormous population, it "should" have scored nearly three-quarters of a goal more per game than it did. Its win percentage in those 21 years (counting ties as half a win) was just 52 percent.

In the twenty-first century, though, the US's win percentage has jumped to 65 percent, double what it was before 1960. Admittedly that statistic flatters the country. Lately the Americans have been playing fewer internationals against teams from the strongest continents, Europe and South America. In the decade through 2010, for the first time since the 1970s, the US played the majority of its games against North and Central American teams. That is not the way to learn best practice. The US has been slowly erasing its historical underperformance, but to keep improving it needs to keep meeting the world's leading countries instead of Jamaica.

We think the Americans, Chinese, and Japanese will keep improving. Already there are omens of success. Both the US and Japan reached the last sixteen of the South African World Cup and were unlucky not to go further. The US has the most young soccer players of any country, and Major League Soccer is expanding fast; Japan plans to host the World Cup again by 2050 and win it; China topped the medals table at the Beijing Olympics. These countries are starting to dominate female soccer: in the women's World Cup final of 2011, Japan beat the US. In the Olympic final the next year, the US beat Japan. In the women's game, where no country has much experience, big, rich nations win.

In men's soccer too, the US, Japan, and China are fast closing the experience gap. They have overtaken the Africans en route to the top. In the new world, distance no longer separates a country from the best soccer. Only poverty does.

AFTERWORD

The Best of Times

"Absolutely crazy," commented Jürgen Klinsmann, coach of the US national team, after Real Madrid paid Spurs $132 million for Gareth Bale in 2013. "I think that all those huge transfers—I don't know if you can justify that stuff anymore. It's kind of out of control," Klinsmann told the BBC.

He was expressing a broadly felt disquiet: that soccer's transfer fees, debts, wages, ticket prices, spoiled players, and general hype have gotten out of hand. Many people have argued that the "soccer bubble" is bound to burst, just as the American housing bubble did after 2006. Jim Spence, writing about English soccer's ticket prices on the BBC website in 2011, contributed some other metaphors: "If football's elastic snaps, the game will be caught with its trousers down very soon, charging these kinds of prices. . . . Football has to be careful not to cut its own throat and see that lifeblood drain away to leave a lifeless corpse."

We disagree. We don't think there is a soccer bubble. We do think the game has never had it so good, but we also think it will have it even better in years to come as soccer continues to conquer the world. Like it or not, expect leading players to become even more "overpaid" and the game even more overhyped in the future.

Not long ago, there was very little money in soccer. By the 1970s, most western Europeans had acquired TV sets (except in Spain, where in 1970 only 28 percent of households had one). However, they hardly ever used those TVs for watching soccer. Europe's state broadcasters of the day barely screened the game. In most countries it wasn't possible to watch regular league competition, week in, week out, in the way that American viewers could watch baseball or gridiron football. European sponsors weren't very interested in soccer, and so almost the only people putting money into the sport were the ones showing up at the weekend at their local club's run-down stadium. In 1974, the total income of all of European professional soccer was probably a bit over $200 million. That made it a slightly bigger business than American Major League Baseball ($153 million) or the National Football League ($172 million), but it was a little amoeba compared to Hollywood. In 1974, total box-office receipts for the movie industry in the US alone were $1.9 billion.

But then something changed. Over the last thirty years, sports have been the fastest growing segment of the entertainment business, and soccer has been the fastest growing sport.

This is mostly thanks to TV. When rights to live broadcasts of the English Football League were first sold, in 1983, they fetched just £2.5 million a year (then about $4 million). However, in the early 1990s the multi-channel era reached Europe. TV moguls like Rupert Murdoch and Silvio Berlusconi used some of the new channels to show soccer. It rapidly became clear that even the most popular soap operas—which for decades had glued entire nations to the sofa—couldn't get a fraction of the audience commandeered by the biggest soccer games. Moreover, the soaps' scriptwriters couldn't write fast enough to generate enough material to fill the schedules.

Soccer clubs became de facto producers of TV content. That changed the game. When you're on television every week, you have to smarten yourself up. Run-down stadiums full of misbehaving fans no longer cut it. It's no coincidence that the refurbishing of English stadiums and the first sale of the rights to satellite TV happened almost simultaneously in the early 1990s. In the new TV era, with smarter stadiums, soccer hooliganism has declined across most of western Europe. Since 2002, the buildup to the World Cup has no longer been overshadowed by angst about thugs.

On the field, too, the violence has been taken out of the game. In the past, being a creative player was a hard life. The tackles that George Best had to endure on Manchester United's right wing in the 1960s almost resembled the sackings of quarterbacks in the NFL. In 1966 Pelé limped out of the World Cup; in 1983 Diego Maradona had his time at Barcelona ruined by an assault by Andoni Goikoetxea ("The Butcher of Bilbao"); and in 1992 Marco van Basten's career was effectively ended by injuries at the age of twenty-eight. But in the TV era, the authorities began to crack down on thuggish defending. Before the World Cup of 1998, FIFA actually made the tackle from behind a sending-off offense. These curbs have freed creative players. In our day, Lionel Messi, Cristiano Ronaldo, and Zlatan Ibrahimovic have been able to thrill fans week in, week out for years, almost unsullied by injuries or fear.

With a better spectacle on offer, and stadiums more comfortable, no wonder clubs in the best leagues began charging more for tickets. No wonder, too, that in the 2000s viewers beyond Europe began switching onto European games. A club like Manchester United started life as a club in Manchester. It soon became a club in England, later a club in Europe, and today it is a global club.

Soccer is now, by a large and constantly growing margin, the planet's favorite game. There was a landmark moment in 2009, when the Champions League final overtook the Super Bowl as the world's most watched sporting event: 109 million viewers versus 106 million, according to the Futures Sport + Entertainment consultancy. Even in the Canadian prairie town of Edmonton, crowds took over downtown to celebrate Barcelona's victory over Manchester United. Perhaps even more significantly, in 2013 the soccer video game FIFA 12 sold 13.5 million copies worldwide; Madden NFL 13, the most popular video game for gridiron, sold a mere 5.6 million. The market for these games is kids, and today's kids vote with their Playstations. Soccer—notably European soccer—is inheriting the globe. That's why movie stars nowadays want to hang out with soccer players, rather than vice versa.

Not even the economic crisis has stunted the game's rise. Even after 2008, European clubs kept growing their revenues by 5 percent a year, against the tide of almost every other business. By 2012, European soccer had become a much bigger industry than any of its American competitors:

Sector	*Annual revenues in billions of dollars*
European soccer	24.6
US movie theaters	10.8
National Football League	8.8
US Major League Baseball	7.5

It's in the context of soccer's current revenues that we must see its current debt. In 2013 European clubs owed a cumulative €7.7 billion (about $10 billion), according to UEFA. That's a lot more than they owed a decade ago—but now they have a lot more money to pay it with.

The soccer economy is not a bubble, because its higher spending is funded by higher revenues. Madrid could afford to pay a world-record fee for Bale because from 1997 to 2013 its revenues had jumped sixfold to $792 million. With all that money in the game, of course players are earning enormous salaries and becoming spoiled. These are the problems of success.

It's perfectly reasonable to make a moral critique of the new soccer. You can say: "I remember the time when my local team consisted of local boys earning the same sort of wages as most people in our town. I don't like the moneyed soccer of today." That's fair enough. You can still find the old local soccer if you drop down a division or two, but perhaps you still want to go to Arsenal or Manchester United and find everything more or less as it was in 1974, and you can't. It's reasonable to resent that. After all, most of us like soccer because it connects us with our childhood. But it's illogical to jump from a moral preference ("I dislike the new soccer") to an economic prediction ("This is a bubble that's going to burst"). You might loathe today's big soccer, but the fact is that it's probably only going to get bigger.

Back in the 1960s, the English soccer agent Ken Stanley told his client George Best: "Think about what football will be like when it's truly a world game. Think of the size of America. Think of every boy in Africa having a team shirt and a ball at his feet. Think about China and Japan and the rest of the Far East. There are billions of people out there, George. The game is still growing. They'll be watching you on television in Peking and Calcutta before long."

For all the global growth we've seen in the last decade, Stanley's prophesy is only just starting to come true. The English Premier League, in particular, is working very hard at tapping new markets. Kevin Alavy, the managing director of the Futures Sport + Entertainment consultancy whom we met earlier in the book, says that often the Premier League enters a new territory by offering itself on free-to-air TV. That's what it did in eastern Europe, across the former Soviet Union, and more recently in Indonesia. Until a few years ago, hardly any of the 247 million Indonesians knew soccer. But given the chance to watch top-class English games on TV for free, many began watching. In recent years, says Alavy, "typically Indonesia has been the number one market by TV audiences for the Premier League." Once Indonesians were hooked, the Premier League gave them a new TV rights deal that offered them far less free soccer.

Using these methods, says Alavy, "Football now touches all countries without exception. That is different to twenty years ago." However, he adds, soccer still has great scope for global growth. The game has only just begun to penetrate the world's four most populous countries, China, India, the US, and Indonesia, which between them account for about 45 percent of humanity.

In China and India, says Alavy, fewer than 10 percent of the population "really, really cares about football." The Premier League currently earns only about 3 cents in TV rights per Chinese person, compared with about $56 per Singaporean, according to the business website Sportingintelligence.com. That's room for growth. Then there are the large economies of Japan, Canada, and Australia, where soccer is also growing fast. One measure of the unrealized potential is that the Premier League still earns more from TV rights inside England (about $4.8 billion total from 2013 through 2016) than in the rest of the world put together (about $4 billion).

Those proportions won't stay that way for long. And all of European soccer will keep tapping away at those new overseas markets. One prediction: in the next few years, the Champions League will grow its global TV audiences by admitting the champions of countries such as the US, China, and Japan. These teams will replace the Polish or Dutch champions, or the Italian number three. The problem of travel will be solved by making the non-European teams play their three European games back to back. And their home audiences will switch on in the millions.

Pessimists warn that people might well watch more soccer, but stop paying for it. After all, consumers now illegally download much of their music for free, so why not Arsenal-Chelsea? Already, with a bit of Internet savvy, you can watch plenty of games online. However, the consultancy PwC, in its report "Outlook for the Global Sports Market to 2014," is reassuring. It says: "Research and indeed the experience of pay-TV broadcasters with exclusive sports content confirm that people are prepared to pay for additional value."

Better, for the first time ever, viewers no longer need a TV to watch soccer. Increasingly, they can choose their platform: cell phones, tablets, Xboxes. That means they can watch on the subway, in Starbucks, or during the lunch break at the office. Already, most young viewers watch games with a "second screen" up, so that they can chat with fellow fans on Twitter or Facebook. Within a couple of decades, technology should make the viewing experience even more fun: if you want, you will have holograms of players running around your living room.

In thirty years' time, when European stadiums are packed with Asian fans paying $500 for their tickets, we may well look back and say, "Can you imagine that in 2013 you could get into a Premier League game for $100 and have money left over for a pie?" Or perhaps by then everyone will be watching Major League Soccer instead.

ACKNOWLEDGMENTS

Dozens of people helped make this book possible. We would like to thank Peter Allden, Dave Berri, Victor Bichara, Issa Martinez, Joe Boyle, Edward Chisholm, Dennis Coates, Bastien Drut, Rod Fort, Bernd Frick, Julien Bracco Gartner, Brian Goff, Sunil Gulati, Jahn Hakes, Pauline Harris, Brad Humphreys, Paul Husbands, Kristján Jónsson, Kai Konrad, Dan Kuper, Markus Kurscheidt, Mike Leeds, Ben Lyttleton, Wolfgang Maennig, Roger Noll, Andrew Oswald, Holger Preuss, Skip Sauer, Philip Soar, Henk Spaan, and Lia Na'ama ten Brink.

We got ideas and information from Kevin Alavy, Rob Baade, Rob Bateman, Vendeline von Bredow, Carl Bromley, Tunde Buraimo, Pamela Druckerman, Gavin Fleig, Mike Forde, Rod Fort, Russell Gerrard, Matti Goksoyr, Norbert Hofmann, Adam Kuper, Hannah Kuper, Kaz Mochlinski, Jean-Pierre Meersseman, James Nicholson, Ignacio Palacios-Huerta, Ian Preston, Antoinette Renouf, Placido Rodriguez, Mark Rosentraub, Andreas Selliaas, Simon Wilson, Axel Torres Xirau and Paul in 't Hout; from Benjamin Cohen, Jonathan Hill, Mark O'Keefe, and Alex Phillips at UEFA; and from David O'Connor and Andrew Walsh at Sport+Markt.

The following were fantastic collaborators: Kevin Alavy, Wladimir Andreff, Giles Atkinson, Tunde Buraimo, Luigi Buzzacchi, Filippo dell'Osso, David Forrest, Pedro Garcia-del-Barrio, Steve Hall, David Harbord, Takeo Hirata, Tom Hoehn, Georgios Kavetsos, Stefan Késenne, Tim Kuypers, Umberto Lago, Stephanie Leach, Neil Longley, Susana Mourato, Susanne Parlasca, Thomas Peeters, Ian Preston, Steve

Ross, Rob Simmons, Ron Smith, Tommaso Valletti, Jason Winfree, and Andy Zimbalist.

Gordon Wise and Kate Cooper were hardworking and imaginative agents, Carl Bromley thought from the start that this book should appear in the United States, and he, Sandra Beris, Antoinette Smith, and Annette Wenda helped make the American edition much better than it could have been without them.

We also want to thank all the interviewees quoted in the text.

NOTE FROM THE AUTHORS

CHAPTER 2

1. Our view of transfers was recently challenged in the book *Pay as You Play,* written by three Liverpool fans, Paul Tomkins, Graeme Riley, and Gary Fulcher. The book is a treasure trove of interesting financial facts, with the added benefit that the authors are donating all their royalties to the children's charity Postpals.

Pay as You Play uses data on transfer fees put together by Riley, by day a senior accountant at Adecco, by night an accomplished soccer statto. He collected figures for transfer fees paid by Premier League clubs since 1992–1993 from newspapers and any other sources he could find. It's a true labor of love.

The authors' approach to transfers is very reasonable. As they point out, adding up the total transfer fees paid for all the players in a squad over many years is misleading because of inflation in transfer fees—the average spend per player has roughly doubled in a decade. The authors therefore convert past transfer fees into the "current transfer fee purchase price" (CTPP), using average transfer fees as an index. For example, Thierry Henry cost Arsenal an estimated £10.5 million in 1999, which converts to a CTPP of £24.6 million. By giving every transferred player a value, they can compare a team's spending on transfers to performance in the league.

When Tomkins then published a blog by Zach Slaton headlined "*Soccernomics* Was Wrong: Transfer Expenditures Matter," naturally we sat up and took notice.

Slaton argued that transfer fees were just as good a predictor of league position as is wage spending. One of us (Stefan) contacted Slaton and the authors to find out a bit more about what was going on. Riley kindly showed us the data he had used to calculate his index.

It then became clear where the differences lay. The *Pay as You Play* index refers only to transfer fees paid. But when we said that spending on transfers bears little relation to where a club finishes, we were referring to net transfer spending—transfer fees paid minus transfer fees received. (We have clarified that point in this edition.) The net figure is the crucial one, because hardly any clubs can just keep buying players without occasionally selling some to stop their spending from going too far out of whack. The only free-spending exceptions in English soccer are Manchester City since 2008, and Chelsea since 2003. Once you look at net spending, it's clear that very few clubs run successful transfer policies: their net spending barely predicts where they finish in the league. If managers and clubs were valuing players accurately, you'd expect to see a significant correlation between net spending and performance, at least over time.

The reliability of the *Pay as You Play* data is also doubtful. Data on wages is pretty accurate: it's drawn from each club's audited financial accounts, which are publicly available in England. But transfer fees quoted

Player	Pay for Play (£)	Transfermarkt.co.uk (£)
Mannone V	350000	440000
Almunia M	500000	0
Silvestre M	750000	836000
Song A	1000000	3520000
Eboue E	1540000	1936000
Fabianski L	2000000	3828000
Vela C	2000000	2640000
Fabregas F	2250000	2816000
van Persie R	3000000	3960000
Denilson	3400000	4400000
Diaby V	3500000	2640000
Gallas W	5000000	0
Ramsey A	5000000	5632000
Sagna B	6000000	7920000
Adebayor M	7000000	8800000
Walcott T	12000000	9240000
Nasri S	12800000	14080000
Arshavin A	15000000	14520000

in the media are less trustworthy. Take the following comparison of transfer fees paid for members of Arsenal's 2008–2009 squad from *Pay as You Play* data and from another reputable source, transfermarkt.co.uk:

There are clearly some big differences here. No wonder, as transfer fees are almost never officially disclosed, only leaked to the media by the club or the player's agent, generally with a spin. Nonetheless, and given these caveats, the *Pay as You Play* index does quite well at explaining the variation in team performance in the Premier League for the years covered.

That's hardly surprising. A club that spends a big transfer fee buying a player will almost always also spend a big sum on his wages. So in this sense, in the very short term, gross transfer fees can be almost as good an explanation of success as wages. However, real success in the transfer market means buying cheap and selling dear. For that you need to know a club's net spending, which shows very little correlation with team performance. The transfer market remains far from efficient.

SELECT BIBLIOGRAPHY

BOOKS

Anderson, Chris, and David Sally. *The Numbers Game: Why Everything You Know About Football Is Wrong.* London: Viking, 2013.

Andreff, Wladimir, and Stefan Szymanski, eds. *Handbook on the Economics of Sport.* Cheltenham: Edward Elgar, 2006.

Andrews, David L. *Manchester United: A Thematic Study.* London: Routledge, 2004.

Ball, Phil. *Morbo: The Story of Spanish Football.* London: WSC Books, 2001.

Bellos, Alex. *Futebol: The Brazilian Way of Life.* London: Bloomsbury, 2002.

Bennetts, Marc. *Football Dynamo: Modern Russia and the People's Game.* London: Virgin Books, 2008.

Biermann, Christoph. *Die Fußball-Matrix: Auf der Suche nach dem perfekten Spiel.* Cologne: Kiepenheuer & Witsch, 2009.

Bose, Mihir. *The Spirit of the Game: How Sport Made the Modern World.* London: Constable & Robinson, 2011.

Burns, Jimmy. *Hand of God: The Life of Diego Maradona.* London: Bloomsbury, 1996.

———. *When Beckham Went to Spain: Power, Stardom, and Real Madrid.* London: Penguin, 2004.

Carragher, Jamie. *Carra: My Autobiography.* London: Corgi Books, 2009.

Cole, Ashley. *My Defence: Winning, Losing, Scandals, and the Drama of Germany 2006.* London: Headline, 2006.

Dobson, Stephen, and John Goddard. *The Economics of Football.* Cambridge: Cambridge University Press, 2001.

Drogba, Didier. *"C'était pas gagné . . . "* Issy-les-Moulineaux: Éditions Prolongations, 2008.

Epstein, David. *The Sports Gene: What Makes the Perfect Athlete.* London: Yellow Jersey Press, 2013.

Exley, Frederick. *A Fan's Notes.* London: Yellow Jersey Press, 1999.

Ferguson, Alex. *Managing My Life: My Autobiography.* London: Hodder and Stoughton, 2000.

———. *My Autobiography.* London: Hodder and Stoughton, 2013.

FIFA TMS Global Transfer Market 2012. Zurich: Fifa TMS, 2013.

Foot, John. *Calcio: A History of Italian Football.* London: Fourth Estate, 2006.

Gerrard, Steven. *Gerrard: My Autobiography.* London: Bantam Books, 2007.

Ginsborg, Paul. *A History of Contemporary Italy.* London: Penguin, 1990.

Gladwell, Malcolm. *Outliers: The Story of Success.* London: Allen Lane, 2008.

Gopnik, Adam. *Paris to the Moon.* New York: Random House, 2000.

Hall, Matthew. *The Away Game.* Sydney: HarperSports, 2000.

Hamilton, Aidan. *An Entirely Different Game: The British Influence on Brazilian Football.* Edinburgh: Mainstream Publishing, 1998.

Hamilton, Duncan. *Immortal: The Approved Biography of George Best.* London: Century, 2013.

Hill, Declan. *The Fix: Soccer and Organized Crime.* Toronto: McLelland and Stewart, 2008.

Holt, Richard, and Tony Mason. *Sport in Britain, 1945–2000.* London: Wiley-Blackwell, 2000.

Hopcraft, Arthur. *The Football Man: People and Passions in Soccer.* London: Aurum Press, 2006.

Hornby, Nick. *Fever Pitch.* London: Indigo, 1996.

Kapuściński, Ryszard. *The Soccer War.* New York: Vintage International, 1992.

Kok, Auke. *1974: Wij waren de besten.* Amsterdam: Thomas Rap, 2004.

Kolfschooten, Frank van. *De bal is niet rond.* Amsterdam and Antwerp: L. J. Veen, 1998.

Lampard, Frank. *Totally Frank.* London: HarperSport, 2006.

Lever, Janet. *Soccer Madness.* Chicago: University of Chicago Press, 1983.

Lewis, Michael. *Moneyball.* New York: W. W. Norton, 2004.

Mandela, Nelson. *The Long Walk to Freedom.* London: Abacus, 1995.

Montague, James. *When Friday Comes: Football in the War Zone.* Edinburgh: Mainstream Publishing, 2008.

Mora y Araujo, Marcela, and Simon Kuper, eds. *Perfect Pitch 3: Men and Women.* London: Headline Book, 1998.

Nieuwenhof, Frans van de. *Hiddink, Dit is mijn wereld.* Eindhoven: De Boekenmakers, 2006.

Norridge, Julian. *Can We Have Our Balls Back, Please? How the British Invented Sport and Then Almost Forgot How to Play It.* London: Penguin, 2008.

Oliver and Ohlbaum Associates and Fletcher Research. *Net Profits: How to Make Money Out of Football.* London: Fletcher Research, 1997.

Orakwue, Stella. *Pitch Invaders: The Modern Black Football Revolution.* London: Victor Gollancz, 1998.

Peace, David. *The Damned United.* London: Faber and Faber, 2006.

Rooney, Wayne. *My Story So Far.* London: HarperSport, 2006.

Silver, Nate. *The Signal and the Noise: Why So Many Predictions Fail—But Some Don't.* London: Penguin Press, 2012.

Simons, Rowan. *Bamboo Goalposts: One Man's Quest to Teach the People's Republic of China to Love Football.* London: Macmillan, 2008.

Szymanski, Stefan. *Playbooks and Checkbooks: An Introduction to the Economics of Modern Sports.* Princeton, NJ: Princeton University Press, 2009.

Szymanski, Stefan, and Tim Kuypers. *Winners and Losers: The Business Strategy of Football.* London: Penguin Group, 1999.

Szymanski, Stefan, and Andrew Zimbalist. *National Pastime: How Americans Play Baseball and the Rest of the World Plays Soccer.* Washington, DC: Brookings Institution Press, 2005.

Taylor, Peter. *With Clough by Taylor.* London: Sidgwick and Jackson, 1980.

Tomkins, Paul, Graeme Riley, and Gary Fulcher. *Pay as You Play: The True Price of Success in the Premier League Era.* Wigston: GPRF Publishing, 2010.

Turnbull, John, Thom Satterlee, and Alon Raab, eds. *The Global Game: Writers on Soccer.* Lincoln: University of Nebraska Press, 2008.

Varley, Nick. *Parklife: A Search for the Heart of Football.* London: Penguin, 1999.

Vergouw, Gyuri. *De Strafschop: Zoektocht naar de ultieme penalty.* Antwerp: Uitgeverij Funsultancy, 2000.

When Saturday Comes. Power Corruption and Pies: A Decade of the Best Football Writing from "When Saturday Comes." London: Two Heads Publishing, 1997.

White, Jim. *Manchester United: The Biography.* London: Sphere, 2008.

Wilson, Jonathan. *Inverting the Pyramid: A History of Football Tactics.* London: Orion, 2008.

———. *The Anatomy of England: A History in Ten Matches.* London: Orion, 2010.

Wortmann, Sönke. *Deutschland. Ein Sommermärchen: Das WM-Tagebuch.* Cologne: Kiepenheuer & Witsch, 2006.

Zirin, Dave. *A People's History of Sports in the United States.* New York: New Press, 2008.

ARTICLES AND RESEARCH PAPERS

Anderson, Christopher. "Do Democracies Win More? The Effects of Wealth and Democracy on Success in the FIFA World Cup." Paper presented at the annual meeting of the Midwest Political Science Association, Chicago, 2011.

Baade, R. "Professional Sports as Catalysts for Metropolitan Economic Development." *Journal of Urban Affairs* 18, no. 1 (1996): 1–17.

Berlin, Peter. "Playing by the Numbers." *Financial Times,* February 1, 1992.

Feenstra, Robert, Robert Inklaar, and Marcel P. Timmer. "The Next Generation of the Penn World Table." Available for download at www.ggdc.net/pwt. 2013.

Gabaix, Xavier. "Zipf's Law for Cities: An Explanation." *Quarterly Journal of Economics* (MIT Press) 114, no. 3 (August 1999): 739–767.

Hicks, Joe, and Grahame Allen. A Century of Change: Trends in UK Statistics Since 1900. House of Commons Library Research Paper 99/111. London: House of Commons Library, December 1999.

Hirshleifer, J. "The Paradox of Power." *Economics and Politics* 3 (1991): 177–200.

Kavetsos, Georgios, and Stefan Szymanski. "National Well-Being and International Sports Events." *Journal of Economic Psychology* 31, no. 3 (April 2010): 158–171.

McGrath, Ben. "The Sporting Scene: The Professor of Baseball." *New Yorker*, July 7, 2003.

Palacios-Huerta, Ignacio. "Professionals Play Minimax." *Review of Economic Studies* 70, no. 2 (2003): 395–415.

Peeters, Thomas, and Stefan Szymanski. "Financial Fair Play in European Football." *Economic Policy* (forthcoming 2014).

Peeters, Thomas, Victor Matheson, and Stefan Szymanski. "Tourism and the 2010 World Cup: lessons for developing countries." *Journal of African Economies* (forthcoming 2014).

Szymanski, Stefan. "Income Inequality, Competitive Balance, and the Attractiveness of Team Sports: Some Evidence and a Natural Experiment from English Soccer." *Economic Journal* 111 (2001): F69–F84.

———. "A Market Test for Discrimination in the English Professional Soccer Leagues." *Journal of Political Economy* 108, no. 3 (2000): 590–603.

Tapp, A. "The Loyalty of Football Fans—We'll Support You Evermore?" *Journal of Database Marketing and Customer Strategy Management* 11, no. 3 (April 1, 2004).

Tapp, A., and J. Clowes. "From 'Carefree Casuals' to 'Professional Wanderers': Segmentation Possibilities for Football Supporters." *European Journal of Marketing* 36, no. 11 (2002).

Taylor, Matthew. "Global Players? Football, Migration and Globalization, c. 1930–2000." *Historical Social Research* 31, no. 1 (2006): 7–30.

MAGAZINES

Hard Gras (Netherlands)
Johan (Netherlands, now defunct)
So Foot (France)
Voetbal International (Netherlands)

INDEX

ABOUT THE AUTHORS

Simon Kuper is the award-winning author of *Soccer Against the Enemy*; *Ajax, the Dutch, the War: The Strange Tale of Soccer During Europe's Darkest Hour*, and, with Stefan Szymanski, the national best-seller *Soccernomics*. He writes a weekly sports column in the *Financial Times*, and has previously written soccer columns for the *Times* and the *Observer*. In December 2007, he won the annual Manuel Vazquez Montalban prize for sportswriting, awarded by the Colegio de Periodistas de Catalunya and FC Barcelona's foundation. He lives in Paris, France.

Stefan Szymanski is the Stephen J. Galetti Collegiate Professor of Sport Management at the University of Michigan's School of Kinesiology. Tim Harford has called him "one of the world's leading sports economists." With Simon Kuper, he has been co-author on all previous editions of *Soccernomics*. He lives in Ann Arbor, Michigan.

The Nation Institute

The Nation.

Founded in 2000, **Nation Books** has become a leading voice in American independent publishing. The inspiration for the imprint came from the *Nation* magazine, the oldest independent and continuously published weekly magazine of politics and culture in the United States.

The imprint's mission is to produce authoritative books that break new ground and shed light on current social and political issues. We publish established authors who are leaders in their area of expertise, and endeavor to cultivate a new generation of emerging and talented writers. With each of our books we aim to positively affect cultural and political discourse.

Nation Books is a project of The Nation Institute, a nonprofit media center established to extend the reach of democratic ideals and strengthen the independent press. The Nation Institute is home to a dynamic range of programs: our award-winning Investigative Fund, which supports ground-breaking investigative journalism; the widely read and syndicated website TomDispatch; our internship program in conjunction with the *Nation* magazine; and Journalism Fellowships that fund up to 20 high-profile reporters every year.

For more information on Nation Books, the *Nation* magazine, and The Nation Institute, please visit:

www.nationbooks.org
www.nationinstitute.org
www.thenation.com
www.facebook.com/nationbooks.ny
Twitter: @nationbooks